Modernising Public Procurement

The New Directive

François Lichère, Roberto Caranta
and Steen Treumer (eds.)

Modernising Public Procurement

The New Directive

DJØF Publishing
2014

François Lichère, Roberto Caranta and Steen Treumer (eds.)
Modernising Public Procurement. The New Directive

1. edition

Cover: Bo Helsted
Print: Ecograf, Højbjerg

Printed in Denmark 2014
ISBN 978-87-574-3385-2

Sold and distributed in Scandinavia by:
DJØF Publishing
Copenhagen, Denmark
Email: forlag@djoef.dk
www.djoef-forlag.dk

Sold and distributed in North America by:
International Specialized Book Services (ISBS)
Portland, USA
Email: orders@isbs.com
www.isbs.com

Sold in all other countries by:
The Oxford Publicity Partnership Ltd
Towcester, UK
Email: djof@oppuk.co.uk
www.oppuk.co.uk

Distributed in all other countries by:
Marston Book Services
Abingdon, Oxon, UK
Email: trade.orders@marston.co.uk
www.marston.co.uk

Foreword

Foreword by the Editors of the European Procurement Law Series

The sixth volume in the Series has not the usual format made of country reports and comparative analysis. The approval of the new public contracts directives including the Public Procurement Directive 2014/24/EU was just too relevant an opportunity to be missed. In the same go, Directive 2014/23/EU on concession contracts and 2014/25/EU on utilities procurement have also been approved, often reproducing the main novelties found in the Public Procurement Directive.

The primary objective of the revision of the EU public procurement regime has been simplification and so-called flexibilisation. The intention was to give the regime an overhaul and to make significant changes of existing obligations and to introduce important new requirements. This book focuses on the essence of these changes, starting from the same definition of public procurement contract to end with changes to concluded contracts. In between, many very important aspects of the reform are analysed, such as the new rules on in house and public-public partnerships, on qualification, on the new and more flexible award procedures, including those aimed at fostering innovation. The new procedural rules allow an unprecedented wide scope for negotiation and dialogue which presents both risks and opportunities. Specific attention is also paid to the new emphasis on strategic procurement, including to the benefit of SMEs, and to the renewed efforts to exploit e-procurement and aggregated purchasing.

The book provides answers to the questions whether the objectives of the reform have been attained in the main areas covered by it? Did the European legislator succeed in making the rules simpler and more flexible and has the reform led to more than just a fine-tuning of the EU public procurement regime?

The answers to these questions are obviously of utmost importance for the evolution of EU public procurement law. The different contributions provide an in-depth analysis of most of the new provisions in Directive 2014/24/EU and so we think the book will be very valuable to academics and practitioners called to apply the new provisions. It is submitted that in some cases these provisions have immediate relevance, since some of them to a large extent are codifying the case law (such as for instance with Article 12 on in-house providing and on horizontal cooperation/"public public partnerships" and Article 72 on contract changes and the duty to retendering). Guidance in understanding how these provisions relate with the case law is therefore necessary and we hope welcome.

The value added of having contributors from many jurisdictions is not lost in this new book, since it brings together different sensibilities to the central topics of the reform (just one instance: the merits of widening the discretion of contracting authorities) while at the same time making the results of the analysis immediately accessible to practitioners having more experience in domestic than in EU law.

The next volume will follow again our usual format, with even more emphasis on comparative analysis. It will focus on qualification.

We would finally like to thank François Lichère for hosting us in Aix-en-Provence to discuss the modernisation of EU public procurement law and for co-editing the present volume, and Annalisa Aschieri and Romain Micalef for preparing the tables and the index. More thanks are due to our most helpful publisher, Jeppe Markers, who has now taken the lead in helping us producing the books of the Series.

Roberto Caranta – Steen Treumer

University of Turin – University of Copenhagen

Contents

Evolution of the EU Public Procurement Regime: The New Public Procurement Directive

Steen Treumer

1. Introduction

The primary objective of the revision of the EU public procurement regime including the new Public Procurement Directive[1] has been simplification and so-called flexibilisation of the regime.[2] The intention has been to give the regime an overhaul and to make significant changes of existing obligations and to introduce important new requirements. This book focuses on the essence of these changes. It is considered whether the objectives have been reached in the main areas covered by the reform: Did the European legislator succeed in making the rules simpler and more flexible and has the reform led to more than just a fine-tuning of the EU public procurement regime? The answer to these questions is of utmost importance for the evolution of EU public procurement law.

The analysis in this chapter starts with an assessment in sections 2 and 3 of whether the legislator generally realised the objectives of simplification and flexibilisation and thereby managed to significantly develop the EU public procurement regime. Subsequently follows a brief account of the correlation between the new Directive and the case law of the Court of Justice of the European Union (hereafter the Court of Justice) in section 4. It is important to be aware that the new Public Procurement Directive not only codifies the case

1. Directive 2014/24/EU of 26 February 2014.
2. See COM(2011)896 final, 2011/0438 (COD). Proposed procurement directive. Explanatory Memorandum section 1.

law as there is at least one important example of "overruling" of the case law of the Court of Justice. The reader should also be aware that the Court of Justice in a few instances recently has developed the state of law even further than what follows from the newly adopted Directive. Then follows an analysis in section 5 of some of the shortcomings and their likely consequences: The unfortunate tendency to regulate in the Preamble instead of in the substantive provisions and deliberately unclear provisions inserted in order to reach a compromise. Finally, this chapter ends with concluding remarks in section 6.

2. Simplification?

It was predicted that simplification was a highly unlikely outcome of the legislative process leading to the new Public Procurement Directive.[3] This part of the reform is therefore not surprisingly the easiest part to assess. The European legislator did essentially not succeed in simplifying the regime.[4] The complexity and volume of the regulation have increased once again and the new Public Procurement Directive remains a lawyer's paradise.

The number of Recitals has increased to 138 that take up numerous pages in the Official Journal of the European Union. To make things even worse the European Legislator has consistently inserted statements in the Recitals that ought to have been a part of the substantive provisions because they contain obligations, consider concepts or other issues of essence for the interpretation of the new public procurement regime. This tendency, its background and likely consequences are considered in further detail in section 5 of this chapter.

Then there are various novelties that add to the degree of complexity as for instance the new regulation intended to promote the competitiveness of SMEs and namely the division into lots, the limitation of participation re-

3. See S. Treumer, "Flexible Procedures or Ban on Negotiations? Will More Negotiation Limit the Access to the Procurement Market?" 135 (at p. 147) in G.S. Ølykke, C.R. Hansen and C.D. Tvarnø (eds.), EU Public Procurement – Modernisation, Growth and Innovation, Jurist – og Økonomforbundets Forlag 2012.
4. See also S. Arrowsmith, "Special Issue- The New EU procurement Directives: Part I; Editors Note", Public Procurement Law Review 2014 p. 81 that emphasise that the European legislator introduces many significant changes and many new requirements thereby again greatly complicating the system, despite the stated aim of simplification.

quirements and direct payments to subcontractors.[5] The degree of complexity is further increased when it comes to the so-called sustainable procurement that in the 2004 reform only was labelled as secondary considerations.[6]

However, the objective of simplification was absolutely unrealistic to achieve unless the approach of the legislator had been completely changed. The background for this is that a regulation of a field tends to reflect its level of complexity. In a situation where the legislator has to balance fundamental and conflicting interests this will typically call for a complex solution with a substantial number of provisions outlining numerous main rules and most likely a plethora of exceptions. This is not per se to be considered a problem as long as the regulation creates legal certainty and balances the involved interest in a reasonable manner. So a better objective would be to ensure legal certainty while at the same time doing justice to the involved interests at stake.

As an alternative the European legislator could instead have chosen to limit itself to outlining the essential concepts, procurement principles and their main consequences thereby leaving the Member States a wide discretion as to how these principles should be interpreted at national level.[7] The obvious disadvantage of this approach would be that it would lead to significant variations in the level of protection in the Member States. A homogeneous understanding of the consequences of the principles of equal treatment and of transparency would be very remote if this approach was followed and such a state of law would be highly unlikely to increase cross-border bidding. However, it would probably be possible to create systems at national level that were just as efficient as the current for the competition between tenderers established in a given Member State as the increased margin of discretion would make it easier for the national legislator to take into account the different challenges at national level. It is for instance relevant to adapt a system to the level of corruption and to the level of professionalism and education of those that are in charge of public procurement.

5. See M. Trybus, "The Promotion of Small and Medium Sized Enterprises in Public Procurement: A Strategic Objective of the New Public Sector Directive?" in the current publication.
6. See D.C. Dragos and B. Neamtu, "Sustainable Public Procurement in the EU: Experiences and Prospects" in the current publication.
7. Cf. S. Arrowsmith, "Modernising the European Union's public procurement regime: A blueprint for real simplicity and flexibility", Public Procurement Law Review 2012 p. 71.

3. Flexibilisation

The current regime takes the considerations of equal treatment and of transparency extremely far and can be characterized as a system based on a fundamental distrust to the contracting entities covered by the rules. The system does not give much credit to the many contracting entities that actually have the best intentions of getting value for money and that have an in-depth knowledge of the rules. The current rules are so rigid that they to a very large extent rule out a pragmatic and flexible approach. In other words there appears to be a clear need of increased flexibility.

The essential news is that the new Public Procurement Directive in many respects clearly ensures a much more flexible approach. Some of the most important changes of the public procurement regime ensure increased access to negotiations and dialogue before, during and after the tender procedure as will be further outlined below in section 3.1. A range of additional topics is considered in section 3.2.

3.1. Negotiations and dialogue before, during and after the tender procedure

One of the most heavily criticized features of the EU public procurement regime has been "the ban on negotiation". It is necessary briefly to outline the current state of law and the notion of the concept. The EU Public Procurement Directives establish certain procedures which must be followed when a contracting entity wants to conclude a contract covered by the rules. It follows from the Public Sector Directive that contracting authorities as a main rule must apply the open procedure and the restricted procedure. The most important common feature between the open and restricted procedure is that negotiation between the contracting entity and the economic operators about changes of the future contracts is excluded as a main rule. This feature is normally referred to as the ban on negotiations. It should be added that there is a limited access to dialogue for the purpose of clarifying or supplementing the content of the tenders or the requirements of the contracting entity.[8]

The new Public Procurement Directive does not remove the ban on negotiation or soften up its consequences when a contracting authority applies the

8. See section 6 of the chapters on the state of law in selected Member States in M. Comba & S. Treumer (eds.), Award of Contracts in EU Procurements, DJØF Publishing 2013. The case law of the Court of Justice on the issue is extremely limited. See judgment of 29 March 2012 in C-599/10, SAG ELV Slovensko and Others [2012] E.C.R. I-10873.

open procedure or the restricted procedure. The increased flexibility is instead ensured through the introduction of the new procedure "innovation partnership" and more importantly by a truly remarkable widening of the scope of the flexible tender procedures, the negotiated procedure and competitive dialogue.[9] It is apparent that contracting authorities after the implementation of the new Public Procurement Directive frequently will have access to the flexible tender procedures contrary to the current state of law. This entails a fundamental change in approach with far-reaching implications. The most important consequence is that it to a higher degree will be possible to obtain an economically more efficient outcome than under the current regime. However, the increased flexibility will surely also make it easier for contracting authorities to discriminate some tenderers and/or favor others. Another obvious disadvantage closely linked to the first mentioned is that increased flexibility to some extent will scare off potential tenderers as they might fear that contracting authorities will take advantage of the increased lack of transparency by discrimination of tenderers.

Contracting authorities are also not free to negotiate with potential tenderers prior to the start of the procedure or free to agree on changes with its contractual partner after the conclusion of the contract.

The typical problem linked to dialogue prior to the start of the tender procedure relates to the so-called technical dialogue between the contracting authority and one or more of the tenderers. Such a dialogue can lead to a violation of the principle of equal treatment, and a tenderer that has been involved in technical dialogue may, or in some cases, shall be excluded as a consequence. This follows from the fact that the technical dialogue might have given these firms a clear advantage in the competition for the public contract as they can have obtained additional information concerning the contract in question and an advantage in time compared to the competitors. The technical dialogue also implies an apparent risk of distortion of competition as the firm can seek to influence/affect the elaboration of the tender specification and arrangement of the tender procedures to its own advantage.

The Public Sector Directive explicitly lists a number of reasons for exclusion of tenderers and due to the practical relevance and fundamental importance of the issue in public procurement practice it could have been expected that technical dialogue was considered in the substantive provisions of

9. See P. Telles and L.R.A. Butler, "Public Procurement Award Procedures in Directive 2014/24/EU" in the current publication. See also J. Davey, "Procedures Involving Negotiation in the New Public Procurement Directive: Key Reforms to the Grounds for Use and the Procedural Rules", Public Procurement Law Review 2014 p. 103.

the Directive. However, this is not the case. Instead the European legislator dealt with the issue in the Recitals to the Preamble to the Directive that even is misleading on two very important points.[10]

The provisions in the new Public Procurement Directive now consider the implications of technical dialogue. Article 57 lists conflict of interest in the meaning of Article 24 on the list of reasons that can lead to exclusion of tenderers. Article 24 also covers the conflict of interest due to technical dialogue. Also on this point the new Directive increases flexibility as it follows from Articles 57 and 24 that exclusion of the tenderer should be a measure of last resort.[11]

Negotiations and dialogue after the tender procedure between the contracting authority and its contractual partner – the winning tenderer – is a subject-matter that only has been considered to a very limited extent in theory and practice until it was addressed in a landmark case from the Court of Justice in 2008.[12] The background for this is not that the issue lacks importance but the EU Public Procurement Directives have so far been focused on the actions of the contracting authority until the conclusion of the contract. The access to change the concluded contract has therefore frequently been overlooked and also denied. Nevertheless, the state of law is now clear as it is certain that substantial changes of concluded contracts can lead to a duty to retender the contract if the contracting authority wants to contract ex house.

The European legislator has chosen to regulate the issue in a rather detailed manner in Article 72 of the new Public Procurement Directive. Article 72 ensures that contracting authorities can adopt a flexible approach to a broad range of contract changes. Article 72(1)(d) on corporate restructuring operations and insolvency is a noteworthy example of this with a very flexible approach to changes after insolvency. Article 72(1)(a) also allows diligent contract authorities a broad margin for changes through careful drafting of the contract terms. The regulation of changes caused by unforeseen circumstances is relatively flexible and clearly allow more scope for changes that the cur-

10. See S. Treumer, "Flexible Procedures or Ban on Negotiations? Will More Negotiation Limit the Access to the Procurement Market?" 135 (on p. 149) in G.S. Ølykke, C.R. Hansen and C.D. Tvarnø (eds.), EU Public Procurement – Modernisation, Growth and Innovation, Jurist – og Økonomforbundets Forlag 2012.
11. See in further detail A. Sanchez Graells, "Exclusion, Qualitative Selection and Short-listing in the New Public Sector Procurement Directive 2014/24" in the current publication.
12. See C-454/06, Pressetext Nachrichtenagentur GmbH v Republik Österreich (Bund) APA-OTS Originaltext-Service GmbH and APA Austria Presse Agentur registierte Genossenschaft mit beschränkter Haftung [2008] E.C.R. I-4401.

rent regime. The provision on small-scale-modifications in Article 72(2) is also important and flexible in its approach.[13]

3.2. Other examples of provisions ensuring a flexible approach

The following examples have been selected because they have caused academic discussion and have been considered in public procurement case law in the Member States.

One of the most relevant issues concerns the reaction towards an applicant or tenderer that has not complied with the requirements for the documentation to be submitted in order for the contracting authority to exclude or select the potential tenderers. Article 51 in the Public Sector Directive briefly regulates the issue and supports a restrictive approach to such shortcomings. It appears to follow from this provision that it is not possible for a contracting authority to ask for subsequent submission of documentation in case this was originally not forwarded to the authority. The provision in Article 56(3) of the new Public Procurement Directive now ensures that contracting authorities can request the economic operators to submit documents that are missing provided that such requests are made in full compliance with the principles of equal treatment and transparency.[14] It should be noted that the issue has recently been considered by the Court of Justice in C-336/12, Manova as will be commented upon in further detail in section 4.[15]

Separation of selection and award criteria and in particular the possibility of considering experience and CV's in the award phase is another highly relevant theme because of recent case law from the Court of Justice and because of its relevance for the outcome of the competition for the contract. The case law of the Court of Justice could be interpreted as ruling out the use of award criteria relating to CV's and experience in the award phase.[16] The restrictive approach pursued by the Court of Justice has been criticized in legal litera-

13. See S. Treumer, "Regulation of Contract Changes in the New Public Procurement Directive" in the current publication.
14. See A. Sanchez Graells, "Exclusion, Qualitative Selection and Short-listing in the New Public Sector Procurement Directive 2014/24" in the current publication.
15. C-336/12, Ministeriet for Forskning, Innovation og Videregående Uddannelser v Manova A/S, judgment of 10 October 2013 (not yet reported).
16. See in particular C-532/06, Lianakis and Others [2008] E.C.R. I-251 and the Special Issue of the Public Procurement Law Review from 2009, pp. 103-164 (edited by S. Treumer) with seven articles on the application and implications of the judgment in Lianakis on the separation of selection and award criteria.

ture.[17] Contracting authorities frequently consider experience and CV's of key personal of crucial importance for the award of the contract. It is also notable that the approach of national courts and review boards prior to and also after the Lianakis ruling typically has been based on acceptance of the use of such criteria and evidence also in the award stage under certain conditions. The European Commission has traditionally not supported this flexible approach at national level. Instead the Commission until recently insisted on a restrictive approach to the issue. It was therefore remarkable that the Commission's draft proposal for a new Procurement Directive[18] was based on a flexible approach allowing contracting authorities to take into consideration "the organization, qualification and experience of the staff assigned to performing the contract in question" as award criteria under certain conditions.[19] Article 67(2)(b) now establishes that the contracting authority in the award phase can consider the organisation, qualification and experience of staff assigned to performing the contract, where the quality of the staff assigned can have a significant impact on the level of performance of the contract.

Another issue of importance concerns the consequences of a conviction by final judgment for corruption or fraud, and also money laundering or participation in a criminal organisation. It follows from Article 45(1) that such an economic operator must be excluded. In addition, it follows from Article 45(2) that any economic operator may be excluded if it has been convicted by a judgment which has the force of res judicata of any offence concerning its professional conduct or has been found guilty of grave professional misconduct. The argument of so-called self-cleaning has been raised to avoid exclusion in legal literature and in the practice of some Member States.[20] The rationale behind this argument has been that an economic operator could regain the possibility of participating in competitions for public contracts by demon-

17. See S. Treumer, "The Distinction between Selection and Award Criteria in EC Public Procurement Law: A Rule without Exception", Public Procurement Law Review 2009 p. 103 and P. Lee, "Implications of the Lianakis decision" p. 82 in G. Piga and S. Treumer (eds.), The Applied Law and Economics of Public Procurement, Routledge 2013. P. Lee was very blunt in his criticism and submitted that the Court of Justice in its recent case law on the issue "has made a fundamental mistake" and an error "that is causing great difficulty right across Member States".
18. Proposal for a Directive on public procurement COM(2011) 896 final.
19. See Article 66(2)(b) of the Draft.
20. See S. Arrowsmith, H-J. Priess and P. Friton, "Self-cleaning as a Defence to Exclusions for Misconduct: An Emerging Concept in EC Public Procurement Law?", Public Procurement Law Review 2009 p. 257. The issue has for instance been at stake in Germany with regard to the company Siemens.

strating that it has taken effective measures to ensure that wrongful acts will not occur in the future. The state of law on this issue has been uncertain but the European legislator has now explicitly stated self-cleaning is indeed possible and specified the conditions. The relevant provision is Article 57(6) of the new Public Procurement Directive.[21]

4. Relationship between the new Public Procurement Directive and the case law of the Court of Justice

An introduction on the new Public Procurement Directive would not be complete without an account of the relationship between the Directive and the case law of the Court of Justice. This is a consequence of the role of the Court in European integration as an important lawmaker whose activity supplements the ordinary legislative process.[22] Until the late 90s the Court of Justice had only addressed relatively few cases in the field of public procurement. The cases mainly dealt with issues that were relatively simple such as late or incorrect implementation, illegal use of the negotiated and accelerated procedures and the definition of a contracting authority covered by the public procurement rules. This changed and the number of procurement cases has increased considerably and several of the cases have clarified fundamental aspects of EU public procurement law. Thus, the case law of the Court of Justice has been the inspiration of some of the most fundamental and important novelties in the new Public Procurement Directive.

An important example of this is the explicit regulation of the so-called extended in-house rule and of horizontal cooperation/"public public partnerships" (a contract concluded between two or more contracting entities under certain conditions) in Article 12 of the Directive.[23] The Court of Justice had prior to the regulation in the new Public Procurement Directive repeatedly considered the implications of its own ruling on in-house providing from

21. See A. Sanchez Graells, "Exclusion, Qualitative Selection and Short-listing in the New Public Sector Procurement Directive 2014/24" in the current publication.
22. Cf. S. Treumer, "Recent Trends in the Case Law from the European Court of Justice" p. 17 in R. Nielsen and S. Treumer (eds.), The New EU Pubic Procurement Directives, DJØF Publishing 2005.
23. See M. Burgi, "Contracting authorities, in-house services and public authorities cooperation" and G. Racca, "Joint Procurement Challenges in the Future Implementation of the New Directives" in the current publication. See also Vol. 1 of the European Procurement Law Series: M. Comba and S. Treumer (eds.), The In-House Providing in European Law, DJØF Publishing 2010.

1999.[24] The acceptance of horizontal cooperation in the case law of the Court of Justice is just a few years old and has therefore until date only been considered in a few cases.[25] The European Commission's initial proposal went far beyond the state of law outlined by the Court of Justice and additional criteria and new indefinite legal terms were included. Moreover, it was debatable whether the initially proposed rules were in compliance with EU primary law. Substantial changes made during the legislative proceedings are an improvement in this respect, but it is still uncertain whether the new rules will be workable.[26]

The fundamental definition of public procurement contracts is regulated in Article 2 of Public Sector Directive and has been the subject of several cases before the Court of Justice. The European legislator has intended to clarify the concept and the implications of the case law by introducing a new definition in Article 1(2) of the new Public Procurement Directive. However, it is hard to reconcile some parts of the definition with some cases from the Court of Justice and in particular a recent case.[27]

Another example relates to the consequences of changes of the concluded public contract. As previously mentioned this was a subject-matter that has only been considered to a very limited extent until it was addressed in a landmark judgment in the pressetext-case from 2008.[28] The European legislator has chosen to regulate the issue in a rather detailed manner in Article 72 of the new Public Procurement Directive.[29] However, with regard to this issue the European legislator has developed the state of law on this issue beyond what could be deduced from the case laws of the Court of Justice at least on some points.

It was for example definitely not clear whether transfer of contracts to a third party after insolvency would be an option and it has been assumed in the

24. See C-107/98, Teckal [1999] E.C.R. I-121.
25. See C-480/06, Commission v Germany [2009] E.C.R. I-4747.
26. See for a detailed analysis Martin Burgi, "Contracting authorities, in-house services and public authorities cooperation" in the current publication.
27. See Case C-306/08 Commission v Spain [2011] ECR I-4541 and the analysis in section 2 of R. Caranta, "Mapping the Margins of EU Public Contracts Law: Covered, Mixed, Excluded and Special Contracts" in the current publication.
28. See C-454/06, pressetext Nachrichtenagentur GmbH v Republik Österreich (Bund) APA-OTS Originaltext-Service GmbH and APA Austria Presse Agentur registierte Genossenschaft mit beschränkter Haftung [2008] E.C.R. I-4401.
29. See S. Treumer, "Regulation of Contract Changes in the New Public Procurement Directive" in the current publication.

case law of some Member States that this was not possible.[30] Such a possibility could even be perceived as conflicting with the ruling in the pressetext-case as the Court in this case stipulated that "as a rule, the substitution of a new contractual partner for the one to which the contracting authority had initially awarded the contract must be regarded as constituting a change to one of the essential terms of the public contract in question".[31] Nevertheless, the European legislator has now clarified that a transfer after insolvency without retendering is possible under certain conditions as outlined in Article 72(1)(d)(ii) of the new Public Procurement Directive. This can actually be considered as a "codification" of the administrative practice of the European Commission instead.[32] The Commission does not have a settled practice but its civil servants have accepted a sale in several cases where emphasis has been put on the fact that bankruptcy is an extraordinary event that follows from circumstances that can be objectively established and where a change of the contractual partner is natural in the context. It has in all cases – that the undersigned have knowledge of – been a condition that the terms of the contract in principle was unchanged and that renegotiation of the terms of the contract in reality did not take place. Furthermore, it was a condition that a real assessment of the qualifications of the potential buyer took place and that this third party had the necessary qualifications. Finally, there was also an assessment of whether the circumstances indicated circumvention either when the original contract was concluded or at the time of the subsequent sale of the contract.

However, the European legislator has not only developed the state of law further than the Court of Justice on some issues. The new provision on award criteria in Article 67(2)(b) that allows consideration of organisation, qualification and experience of staff assigned to performing the contract, where the quality of the staff assigned can have a significant impact on the level of performance of the contract is in reality an "overruling" of the case law of the Court of Justice.[33] The new provision is better aligned with the general trend

30. See S. Treumer, "Transfer of Contracts Covered by the EU Public Procurement Rules After Insolvency", Public Procurement Law Review 2014 p. 21.
31. See para 40 of the judgment.
32. See S. Treumer, "Transfer of Contracts Covered by the EU Public Procurement Rules After Insolvency", Public Procurement Law Review 2014 p. 21.
33. See further on the issue section 3.1. above. See also R. Caranta, "Award criteria under EU law (old and new)" p. 21(at p. 37) in M. Comba and S. Treumer (eds.), Award of Contracts in EU Procurements, DJØF Publising 2013 where Caranta points out that "A long line of cases stretching from Beentjes to Lianakis has thus been shelved for good". Cf. P. Bordalo Faustino, "Award Criteria in the New EU Directive on Public

in the case law from national courts and review boards[34] and the need of consideration of these issues in many procedures in particular concerning services contracts and public works.

Finally, it should be remembered that the case law of the Court of Justice is very dynamic so it is even possible to find a recent example of an important new provision where the case law of the Court already has developed the state of law a few steps further than outlined in the new Public Procurement Directive. This is the case with regard to the reaction towards an applicant or tenderer that has not complied with the requirements for the documentation to be submitted in order for the contracting authority to exclude or select the potential tenderers. Article 56(3) allows subsequent submission of documentation in case this was originally not forwarded to the authority provided that such requests are made in full compliance with the principles of equal treatment and transparency. It follows from the ruling in C-336/12, Manova that this presupposes that the request relates to particulars or information, such as a published balance sheet, which can be objectively shown to pre-date the deadline for applying to take part in the tendering procedure concerned. In addition, the Court of Justice specified that this is ruled out if the contract documents required provision of the missing particulars or information, on pain of exclusion. The background for this is that it falls to the contracting authority to comply strictly with the criteria which it has itself laid down.

5. Important Shortcomings of the New Public Procurement Directive

The European legislator has in the adoption of the new Public Procurement Directive frequently confused substantive provisions and Recitals in the Preamble of the Directive. Furthermore, it appears frequently to have used the legal technique "constructive ambiguity" in order to strike compromises. These tendencies and their consequences will be addressed below in sections 5.1 and 5.2.

Procurement", Public Procurement Law Review 2014 p. 124 that at p. 129 writes that it is now undoubtedly a part of the permissible award criteria.

34. See in particular C-532/06, Lianakis and Others [2008] E.C.R. I-251 and the Special Issue of the Public Procurement Law Review from 2009, pp 103-164 (edited by S. Treumer) with seven articles on the application and implications of the judgment in Lianakis on the separation of selection and award criteria.

5.1. Confusion of substantive provisions and Recitals

The European Legislator has frequently inserted statements in the Recitals that ought to have been a part of the substantive provisions because they contain obligations, concepts or very clear cut elements of relevance for the interpretation of substantive provisions in the new Public Procurement Directive. So in other words several considerations in the Recitals are provisions in disguise. As an example, the European legislator has specified in Recital 94 that contracting authorities that makes use of the possibility in Article 67(2)(b)[35] should ensure, by appropriate contractual means, that such staff can only be replaced with the consent of the contracting authority which verifies that the replacement staff affords an equivalent level of quality. Recital 94 outlines an obligation that ought to have been part of the substantive provisions as originally suggested by the European Commission.[36]

A second example concerns one of the exceptions to the duty to retender outlined in Article 72(1)(c) on unforeseen circumstances. The condition or notion of "unforeseen circumstances" has only rarely been put to the test in the case law of the Court of Justice. National case law interpreting this condition also seems to be limited. It would therefore have been relevant to outline the content of the notion in the substantive provisions of the Public Procurement Directive. Instead the legislator chose to elaborate extensively on the subject-matter in Recital 109 of the new Public Procurement Directive. The need of clarification was evident. The placement in the Recitals was quite the contrary.

A third example relates to the duration of framework agreements.[37] As for the duration of the framework agreement itself, the new Public Procurement Directive maintains the duration of 4 years in principle. As far as the duration of the subsequent contract is concerned, the substantive provisions of the Directive remain silent. However, Recital 62 clarifies that "the duration of the individual contracts based on a framework agreement does not need to coincide with the duration of that framework agreement, but might, as appropriate, be shorter or longer." This is in accordance with the interpretation of the

35. The possibility of considering the organisation, qualification and experience of staff assigned to performing the contract in the award phase mentioned earlier in this chapter.
36. The regulation of the issue was moved from the material provisions to the considerations. Compare with Article 66(2)(b) of the Commission's Draft proposal from December 2011.
37. See F. Lichère and S. Richetto, "Framework Agreements, Dynamic Purchasing Systems and Public E-Procurement" in the current publication.

European Commission on the issue. However, again the issue ought to have been considered in the substantive provisions of the new Public Procurement Directive for the sake of legal certainty.

The manifest tendency to implicit regulation through the Recitals has allegedly been promoted by certain stakeholders in the legislative process. This approach seemed to have been considered as a tool that ensured that the substantive provisions did not become too long and thereby that the legislator lived up to the promised simplification. This is definitely a misunderstanding. It only makes the new Public Procurement Directive more difficult to apply and makes the state of law even more blurred. Firstly, the practitioner has to seek and find the "hidden regulation" in the Recitals. Once this is identified the next challenge arises: How are you supposed to handle for instance obligations or other substantial elements contained in the Recitals? According the case law of the Court of Justice, to a Recital may cast light on the interpretation to be given to a legal rule but it cannot in itself constitute a legal rule, cf. Case C-215/88, Casa Fleischhandels-Gmbh.[38] The controversial approach of the European legislator will equally pose problems for the Member States in the transposition of the new Public Procurement Directive and for courts and complaints boards in the years to come.

5.2. "Constructive ambiguity" including inconsistency between substantive provisions of the Directive and Recitals

In a number of instances legislation is adopted with an intended lack of clarity. The phenomenon is frequently referred to as "constructive ambiguity" and appears to be applied rather frequently in negotiations leading to EU legislation.[39] The background for this phenomenon is that stakeholders in the legislative process have disagreed about the regulation of the issue in question. Nevertheless, they did agree to regulate the issue and settled on an unclear provision/regulation in order to strike a compromise. The French Supreme Court – Conseil d'Etat – has phrased this elegantly with a remark along the following lines: Where the lawyer's seek precision, diplomats practice the not-spoken and do not avoid the ambiguous.[40]

38. C-215/88, Casa Fleischhandels-Gmbh v Bundesanstalt [1989] E.C.R. I-2789. See para 31. The concrete case concerned a Regulation and not a Directive.
39. See S. Treumer, "Konstruktiv uklarhed" – om tilsigtet uklar EU-lovgivning og dens negative konskvenser" p. 347 in Jens Hartig Danielsen (ed.), Max Sørensen 100 år, Jurist- og Økonomforbundets Forlag 2013.
40. See Conseil d'Etat, Rapport Public 1992, Etudes no. 44 where it is stated "Là òu les jurists cherchent la precision, les diplomats pratiquent le non-dit et ne fuient pas

The use of constructive ambiguity ensures that the issue is regulated in spite of disagreement and the unclear legal sources can often lead to different interpretations. The latter is crucial as the legal source therefore can legitimize the upholding of a questionable national practice or regulation of the issue. It can also be interpreted as an implicit acceptance hereof from the European legislator. Furthermore, the outcome can also be presented as a diplomatic victory even though the reality is that the issue remains unsettled.

In some instances the unclear wording will be part of a substantive provision. A variant that is also frequently seen is that the legislator deliberately avoids to regulate the issue in the substantive provisions of the Directive or that you include considerations in a preamble that are very difficult to combine with the regulation in the substantive provisions of the Directive. It is possible to identify a broad range of issues where the European legislator in the adoption of the new Public Procurement Directive presumably has settled disagreement by application of constructive ambiguity.

The possible disclosure of the scoring method in the award phase is a good illustration. It is a well-known "secret" that the choice of scoring method (not the criteria, sub-criteria or their weighting but for instance a mathematical matrix according to which you distribute points for the various elements that are part of the evaluation of the bid) often can be decisive for the outcome of a given tender procedure. So if there is no duty to disclosure the scoring method in advance it might be possible for the contracting authority to steer the award with the result that it avoids some tenderers or can chose a favoured tenderer. It could have been expected that the issue was considered in the substantive provisions of the new Public Procurement Directive. This is particularly so because recent case law from the Court of Justice appears to indicate that a contracting authority is under an obligation to announce the scoring method to the tenderers prior to submission of bids.[41] The issue is not addressed in the substantive provisions. Instead there is a rather blurred statement on the issue in Recital 90 according to which "contracting authorities should be obliged to create the necessary transparency to enable all ten-

l'ambiguité". See also N. Fenger, Forvaltning & Fællesskab – Om EU-rettens betydning for den almindelige forvaltningsret: Konfrontation og frugtbar sameksistens, Jurist- og Økonomforbundets Forlag 2004 p. 439 that quotes the report from CE.

41. See in particular C-532/06, Lianakis and Others [2008] E.C.R. I-251 where it is stated that according to the case-law, the ensuing obligation of transparency, requires that potential tenderers should be aware of all the elements [italics by the author]to be taken into account by the contracting authority in identifying the economically most advantageous offer, and their relative importance, when they prepare their tenders.

derers to be reasonably informed of the criteria and arrangements [italics by the author] which will be applied in the contract award decision".

The lack of consideration of the issue is not based on lack of relevance and it is now up to the national legislator to consider the issue. It can be added that contracting authorities in a broad range of countries already have imposed an obligation to announce the scoring method in advance.[42] That is not the case in Denmark which was one of the countries in charge of the negotiations leading to the new Public Procurement Directive.[43] It will therefore be interesting to follow the approach to the issue in the forthcoming implementation of the new Public Procurement Directive.

Another example relates to the ground for the use of the flexible tender procedure outlined in Article 26(4) of the new Public Procurement Directive. It is not entirely clear from the wording of the substantive provision how flexible the new provision is intended to be. However, if you scrutinize the wording of the Recitals you get the impression that the grounds should be interpreted in an extremely flexible manner. Could it be that for instance the European Commission wanted a more limited access to the flexible tender procedure than a given range of Member States and the disagreement was settled by the use of constructive ambiguity? That is likely. We have seen the consequences of such an approach previously with regard to the grounds for use of competitive dialogue in the Public Sector Directive. That lack of clarity led to an unfortunate uncertainty with regard to the scope of the procedure and to a very hesitant application of the procedure in a broad range of Member States.[44]

An excellent example of complete disregard of a subject-matter that most likely is a consequence of constructive ambiguity relates to Article 72. The Draft of the European Commission included an important provision in Article 72(7)(b) that has now been deleted. The provision was based on a remarkable restrictive approach to changes with the aim of remedying a breach of contract. The Draft ruled out changes aiming at remedying deficiencies in the

42. See P. Bordalo Faustino, "Evaluation models in public procurement: A comparative law perspective" p. 339 (at p. 353) in M. Comba & S. Treumer (eds.), Award of Contracts in EU Procurements, DJØF Publishing 2013.
43. The Danish Complaints Board for Public Procurement has consistently held that there is not such an obligation under EU procurement law. See S. Treumer, "Award of contracts covered by the EU Public Procurement rules in Denmark" p. 39 in M. Comba & S. Treumer (eds.), Award of Contracts in EU Procurements, DJØF Publishing 2013.
44. See the extensive and comparative analysis in S. Arrowsmith and S. Treumer (eds.), Competitive Dialogue in EU Procurement, Cambridge University Press 2012.

performance of the contractor, which can be remedied through the enforcement of the contractual obligations. This would have been far-reaching as it would cut off the use of some of the tools available under contract law. The Draft was criticized by the undersigned that questioned whether the Draft was in accordance with the current state of law and predicted that the Draft was likely to be challenged in the negotiations on this point.[45] What remains is fundamental legal uncertainty on an important issue that repeatedly occurs in public procurement practice.

The legal uncertainty caused by the use of constructive ambiguity increases the transaction costs for contracting authorities and tenderers alike. It should also be noted that there is a considerable risk that the unclear legal sources remain unaltered after future revisions of the EU public procurement Directives. The negative implications of the use of constructive ambiguity tend to be overlooked. However, they are significant and one of the reasons why EU public procurement law remains a lawyers paradise also after the adoption and implementation of the new Public Procurement Directive.

6. Concluding remarks

The European legislator did not succeed in simplifying the EU public procurement regime that remains a lawyer's paradise. This was not a big surprise as the objective of simplification was absolutely unrealistic to achieve unless the approach of the legislator had been completely changed. The legislator has been much more successful in ensuring that a flexible approach will be possible for the contracting entities in the future. One of the most important changes of the public procurement regime is increased access to negotiations and dialogue before, during and after the tender procedure.

The case law of the Court of Justice has been the inspiration of some of the most fundamental and important novelties in the new Public Procurement Directive. Important examples are the regulation in Article 12 on in-house providing and on horizontal cooperation/"public public partnerships" and Article 72 on contract changes and the duty to retendering.

Nevertheless, the European legislator has frequently regulated issues in the Preamble instead of in the substantive provisions. The legislator appears also frequently to have used "constructive ambiguity" in order to reach a com-

45. See section 3 of S. Treumer, "Regulation of contract changes leading to a duty to retender the contract: The European Commission's proposals of December 2011", Public Procurement Law Review 2012 p. 153.

promise. Both tendencies increase legal uncertainty and will have far reaching implications in public procurement practice in the years to come.

Bibliography

(Chapters in the current publication are not listed here but in the footnotes)

S. Arrowsmith, H-J. Priess and P. Friton, "Self-cleaning as a Defence to Exclusions for Misconduct: An Emerging Concept in EC Public Procurement Law?", Public Procurement Law Review 2009 p. 257.

S. Arrowsmith and S. Treumer (eds.), Competitive Dialogue in EU Procurement, Cambridge University Press 2012.

S. Arrowsmith, "Modernising the European Union's public procurement regime: A blueprint for real simplicity and flexibility", Public Procurement Law Review 2012 p. 71.

S. Arrowsmith, "Special Issue- The New EU procurement Directives: Part I; Editors Note", Public Procurement Law Review 2014 p. 81.

P. Bordalo Faustino, "Evaluation models in public procurement: A comparative law perspective" p. 339 in M. Comba & S. Treumer (eds.), Award of Contracts in EU Procurements, DJØF Publishing 2013.

P. Bordalo Faustino, "Award Criteria in the New EU Directive on Public Procurement", Public Procurement Law Review 2014 p. 124.

R. Caranta, "Award criteria under EU law (old and new)" p. 21 in M. Comba and S. Treumer (eds.), Award of Contracts in EU Procurements, DJØF Publising 2013.

M. Comba and S. Treumer (eds.), The In-House Providing in European Law, DJØF Publishing 2010.

N. Fenger, Forvaltning & Fællesskab – Om EU-rettens betydning for den almindelige forvaltningsret: Konfrontation og frugtbar sameksistens, Jurist- og Økonomforbundets Forlag 2004.

J. Davey, "Procedures Involving Negotiation in the New Public Procurement Directive: Key Reforms to the Grounds for Use and the Procedural Rules", Public Procurement Law Review 2014 p. 103.

P. Lee, "Implications of the Lianakis decision" p. 82 in G. Piga and S. Treumer (eds.), The Applied Law and Economics of Public Procurement, Routledge 2013.

U. Neergaard, Catherine Jacqueson & G.S. Ølykke, Public Procurement Law: Limitations, Opportunities and Paradoxes, The XXVI FIDE Congress in Copenhagen, 2014, Congres Publications Vol. 3.

S. Treumer, "Recent Trends in the Case Law from the European Court of Justice" p. 17 in R. Nielsen and S. Treumer (eds.), The New EU Pubic Procurement Directives, DJØF Publishing 2005.

S. Treumer, "The Distinction between Selection and Award Criteria in EC Public Procurement Law: A Rule without Exception", Public Procurement Law Review 2009 p. 103.

S. Treumer, "Regulation of contract changes leading to a duty to retender the contract: The European Commission's proposals of December 2011", Public Procurement Law Review 2012 p. 153.

S. Treumer, "Flexible Procedures or Ban on Negotiations? Will More Negotiation Limit the Acces to the Procurement Market?" 135 (on p. 147) in G.S. Ølykke, C.R. Hansen and C.D. Tvarnø (eds.), EU Public Procurement – Modernisation, Growth and Innovation, Jurist – og Økonomforbundets Forlag 2012.

S. Treumer, "Award of contracts covered by the EU Public Procurement rules in Denmark" p. 39 in M. Comba & S. Treumer (eds.), Award of Contracts in EU Procurements, DJØF Publishing 2013.

S. Treumer, "Konstruktiv uklarhed" – om tilsigtet uklar EU-lovgivning og dens negative konskvenser" p. 347 in Jens Hartig Danielsen (ed.), Max Sørensen 100 år, Jurist- og Økonomforbundets Forlag 2013.

S. Treumer, "Transfer of Contracts Covered by the EU Public Procurement Rules After Insolvency", Public Procurement Law Review 2014 p. 21.

G.S. Ølykke, C.R. Hansen and C.D. Tvarnø (eds.), EU Public Procurement – Modernisation, Growth and Innovation, Jurist – og Økonomforbundets Forlag 2012.

Variations in the scope of the new EU public procurement Directives of 2014: Efficiency in public spending and a major role of the approximation of laws

Mario E. Comba

1. Introduction

With the final approval of the new Directives on public procurement, the debate has spread on all legal problems entailed by the new regulation, with particular attention to the modifications introduced in comparison to the provisions of the 2004 Directives, which is in fact the driving idea of this book. In this context, also the question of the legal basis – or, more broadly, the scope – of the new Directives has to be addressed because, even if perhaps this issue can be perceived as not having an immediate practical impact, it is however of great importance in the general interpretation of the Directives and can thus have interesting consequences on many new (and old) rules contained in the Directives.

In this chapter it will be argued that the variations of the scope of the public procurement Directives can be perceived and appreciated only through an analysis over the long period, and that is why all public procurement Directives are covered here, from the first set of 1969 to the last ones of 2014. In particular, the Directives of 2014 introduce for the first time in their recitals efficiency in public spending and, at the same time, reinforce the importance of the approximation of laws as a legal basis.

In paragraphs 2 and 3 it will be demonstrated that the evolution of such modifications can be traced through the history of the public procurement Directives, where of course a greater attention is accorded to the Directives of

2004 and in particular to the new Directives of 2014. Paragraph 4 describes the debate about one of the two modifications, that is efficiency in public spending, while the other does not seem to have raised many comments so far. In paragraph 5 the consequences of the above described evolutions in the scope of public procurement Directives will be discussed. In particular, it will be argued that the two modifications in the scope of public procurement introduced or reaffirmed in Directives of 2014 can have great consequences in the interpretation and application of Directives of implementing national legislation.

2. Treaty foundations of the public procurement Directives

It is well known that public procurement does not feature as such in any version of the European Treaties (from the Treaty of Rome of 1957 to the Lisbon Treaty of 2009) but are subject to detailed secondary legislation, starting in the 1970s and fully implemented only in the 1990s.[1] The absence of detailed regulation about public procurement is justified by several reasons,[2] among which the fact that the importance of public procurement for building the Internal Market was not so clear at the beginning. However if this is true for the original Treaties and perhaps until the Treaty of Maastricht (1992), the acquired relevance accorded to public procurement in the 1990s would have perhaps justified the insertion of a specific provision in the subsequent modification of the Treaties as happened for other policies. For example, the Economic and Social Cohesion Policy was first inserted in the Single European Act, entered into force in 1987, while completely absent in the 1957 Treaties. More likely, the choice not to "constitutionalise" public procurement regulation can be justified with the need to not overload the Treaties with highly specialised rules. This happens with other international trade agreements which do not include public procurement but address it in separate documents, most notably, the WTO regulates public procurement with the separate GPA.[3] In addition, since the legal basis for the secondary regulation of public procurement was already well rooted in the Treaties, the necessity to introduce a specific policy in the Treaties was probably not too strongly felt. Furthermore, the differences of legal systems of the Member States suggested

1. M. Trybus, Public contracts in European Union Internal Market Law: Foundations and Requirements, in Noguellou-Stelkens (eds), Droit compare des contrats publics, Bruylant, Bruxelles, 2010, p. 81.
2. Four reasons for that choice are listed and analyzed by Trybus, fn 1., p. 83 – 84.
3. Trybus, fn 1, p. 83 – 84

the use of flexible legal tools, namely Directives, to introduce a set of rules allowing a margin of discretion for their transposition.[4]

2.1. From the 1970s to the 1990s

Under this perspective, an accurate examination of the legal basis of the public procurement Directives can be useful to understand the Treaty foundation of such regulation. It is in fact only through an analysis over the long period that the variations of the scope of the public procurement Directives can be perceived and appreciated, in connection with the influence of decisions from the European Court of Justice. On its turn, the analysis of the evolving scope of Directives on public procurements is an essential tool to interpret the provisions of the Directives because one can argue, for example, that the same provision can have different meanings according to the new scopes declared by more recent Directives as opposed to previous ones.

As for works contracts, Council Directive of 26 July 1971, concerning the coordination of procedures for the award of public works contracts, clearly states that "the simultaneous attainment of freedom of establishment and freedom to provide services in respect of public works contracts awarded in Member States on behalf of the State or regional or local authorities or other legal persons governed by public law entails not only the abolition of restrictions but also the co-ordination of national procedures for the award of public works contracts": hence the double legitimation of the public procurement Directives, stemming both from the abolition of restrictions (in the name of freedom of establishment and freedom to provide services) and from the coordination of national procedures. The legal basis referred to in the cited Directive consists therefore of articles 57 (2), 66 and 100 of the Treaty establishing the Economic European Community (EEC). Art. 57(2) EEC, in the framework of the right of establishment, empowered the Council to enact Directives "regarding the co-ordination of legislative and administrative provisions of Member States concerning the engagement in and exercise of non-wage-earning activities" and art. 66 extended such a competence in the field of the free movement of services. Art. 100 EEC empowered the Council to enact Directives "for the approximation of such legislative and administrative provisions of the Member States as have a direct incidence of the establishment and functioning of the Common Market". Council Directive 89/440/EEC, amending Council Directive 71/305/EEC, maintains the same legal basis, citing articles 57(2), 66 and 100 of EEC.

4. C.H. Bovis, EU Procurement Law, Elgar, Cheltenham, 2012, p. 8 – 11.

The first Directive regulating the public procurement of goods was Directive of the Commission 70/32 EEC of 17 December 1969 ("on provision of goods to the State, to local authorities and to other official bodies") which extended the rules of Directive of the Commission of 7 november 1966, forbidding quantitative restriction in the Intra-Community trade to Member States and public bodies. The main idea was that the then existing regime of public procurement, based on the protection of national industries, was to be considered as a non-tariff barrier to intra-Community trade and was hence to be eliminated. The following Council Directive 77/62/EEC of 21 December 1976, coordinating procedures for the award of public supply contracts only refers in the introduction to art. 100 EEC even if art. 30 is mentioned in the following recitals and thus seemingly reduces the importance to the right of establishment and of free movement of goods.[5] The same reference can be found in Council Directive 88/295/EEC of 22 March 1988, amending Directive 77/62/EEC. The reason for this difference between the legal basis of the Work Directive (art. 57(2), 66 and 100 of EEC) and the Supplies Directive (only art. 100 EEC) is not easy to understand because it is not explained by the recitals of these Directives.

The rising importance of public procurement for the realisation of the Internal Market began to be fully appreciated by the end of the 1980s[6] and particularly with the research funded by the Commission on the "The cost of non-Europe",[7] vol. 5, part A of which deals specifically with public procurement: "The cost of non-Europe in public sector procurement". The main issue of the document is the comparison between intra-Community trade in the private and public sectors: while the first had risen substantially since the incep-

5. It seems noteworthy to underline the different location where the reference to the Treaty is made: if in the very first paragraph of the Directive, where the formula "Having regard to the Treaty establishing the European Economic Community and in particular art. ___ thereof" is proclaimed, or in the recitals containing the extensive motivation of the Directive. If the authors of the Directive choose to differentiate the location where the pertaining articles of the Treaty were mentioned, that cannot mean but a different value of the citation and hence a different importance of the primary rule mentioned in the construction of the legal basis of the Directive. If art. 30 of the Treaty is not mentioned in the very first paragraph, but only in the following recitals, while art. 100 is mentioned at first, that means that the two articles have a different importance and art. 100 is more relevant than art. 30.
6. "From the mid-1980s, the regulation of public procurements in the European Union became a priority", Bovis, cit. fn. 4, p. 14.
7. W.S. Atkins Management Consultants in association with Eurequip SA-Roland Berger & Partner-Eurequip Italia, The cost of non-Europe, Bruxelles, 1988.

tion of the EEC in 1957, the latter had remained very low: public entities only (or almost only) buy from their national industries.[8] The consequence was that certain national industries where the public sector was a major – if not dominant – purchaser, such as for example telecommunications, gas distribution, power generation and distribution, railways, airports, intra-Community competition is not encouraged with the consequence of the European industries being less competitive in world markets. Finally, this led to greater expenditures for national governments, which could be reduced by removing barriers to trade in public purchasing. Point 2.3 of the Report explicitly mentions "Savings in Public Expenditure", stating that, according to the findings of the Commission, potential savings in annual public expenditure could vary from 9 to 19 billions Ecu,[9] plus additional advantages, such as benefits for private sector purchasers of similar goods and an important impact on the rate of innovation.

Apart from the almost touching optimistic perspective on the future effects expected from the regulation of public procurement, what is striking when reading the Report is the importance that was given to the savings on public expenditure as one of the reasons (perhaps the main reason) for justifying the effort to implement more pervasive legislation on public procurement. The scope of regulating public procurement appears not to be the completion of the Internal Market as such, as it appears in the recitals of the Directives, but instead the reduction of public spending. In other words, it seems that while the legal reasons and consequently the legal basis for public procurement regulation through the EU are those mentioned in the recitals of Directive, i.e. the abolition of restrictions in the name of freedom of establishment and freedom to provide services and the coordination of national procedures, the economic reason is the reduction of public spending of national governments.

The set of Directives on public procurement enacted after the Report on the cost of non-Europe begins with a first Directive on public service contracts: Council Directive 92/50 EEC of 18 June 1992 relating to the coordination of procedures for the award of public service contracts. The introduction of the Directive only mentions articles 57(2) and 66 EEC, but not article 100 on approximation of legislations, with a scheme symmetrically opposite to

8. In fact, according to Bovis, "The main reason for regulating public sector and utilities procurement is to bring their respective markets parallel to the operation of private markets", cit. fn. 4, p. 11.
9. The ECU (European currency unit) was used as a currency uniti in Europe until the introduction of the Euro. The rate exchenge ECU-Euro was 1:1, so that 1 ECU is equivalent to 1 Euro.

the first Directive on public procurement of goods, which mentioned art. 100 but not articles 57 (a) and 66 EEC. The first recitals of these Directives are full of references to the completion of the Internal Market and to the fostering of competition, without even mentioning the savings of public expenditures.

Council Directive 93/36/EC of 14 June 1993, coordinating procedures for the award of public supply contracts keeps the same setting as the previous Directive of 1977 as far as its legal basis is concerned: only art. 100 of the EC Treaty (EC) is mentioned (approximation of legislation) and no reference to the articles on freedom of movement is made. In the following recitals the attainment of the freedom of movement of goods is – obviously – mentioned, but with the specification that it entails "not only the abolition of restrictions but also the coordination of national procedures for the award of public supply contracts".

Finally, Council Directive 93/37/EC of 14 June 1993, concerning the coordination of procedures for the award of public works contracts, keeps faith to the legal basis of the first Directive on public works of 1971, mentioning in the declaration of its legal basis both the abolition of restrictions – art. 57(2) and 66 – and the approximation of legislations – art. 100 EC. And in the following recitals the same formula as in the other Directives of the 1990s can be found: "the simultaneous attainment of freedom of establishment and freedom to provide services in respect to public works contracts (…) entails not only the abolition of restrictions but also the coordination of national procedures for the award of public works contracts". Again, there is no mention of savings in public expenditures.

2.2. The 2004 Directives: introducing for the first time "secondary considerations" in the text of the Directive, among the aims of public procurement

During the ten years between the enactment of the 1993 Directives and the 2004 Directive on public procurement, Directive 2004/18/EC of the European Parliament and of the Council of 31 march 2004, on the coordination of procedures for the award of public works contracts, public supply contracts and public service contracts, the European Court of Justice (ECJ) introduced at least two major innovations which can be related to the issues discussed in this chapter.

The first was the possibility for Member States to pursue their own policies through the regulation of public procurement, even if within the strict limits set by the ECJ.[10] Although this idea was already explored prior to 2004 by legal doctrine and by decisions of the Court, as well as in EC official documents, it is only in the 2004 Directives that it is explicitly incorporated in the legislation, while previously it was neither mentioned in the introduction nor in the recitals of Directives. In fact Directive 2004/18/EC states in recital 1 that the Directive is based on ECJ case-law, in particular case-law on award criteria which "clarifies the possibilities for the contracting authorities to meet the needs of the public concerned, including in the environmental and/or social area, provided that such criteria are linked to the subject-matter of the contract, do not confer an unrestricted freedom of choice on the contracting authority, are expressly mentioned and comply with the fundamental principles mentioned in recital 2". At the same time reference to the Treaty principle of freedom of establishment and freedom to provide services is made in recital 2. This is still quite a shy reference to the so called "secondary" or "horizontal" policies, especially if compared to what is now stated in Directive 2014/24/EU as discussed in the chapters of Dragos, Trybus, and Butler in this book, but nevertheless it is the first time that a Directive on public procurement diverges from the double legitimation scheme stemming both from the abolition of trade restrictions in the name of freedom of establishment and freedom to provide services and goods and from the coordination of national procedures. While green and social policies are allowed, still no mention is made to savings in public spending as another autonomous objective.

However, in recital 5 a reference to best value for money appears: after having introduced green considerations in public procurement, the recital provides that the Directive clarifies how the contracting authorities may contribute to the protection of the environment whilst ensuring the possibility of obtaining best value for money. It seems here that best value for money appears only as a limit for contracting authorities in the introduction of green considerations and is not, therefore, an objective per se of public procurement

10. Among others, see Case C-225/98, Commission v. France (Nord Pas de Calais"), 2000, ECR I-7445; Case C-513-99, Concordia Bus Finlans v. Helsingin Kaupunki (Concordia Bus Finland), 2000, ECR I-7213; Case C-448/01, EVN AG v. Austria (EVN-WIenstrom), 2003 ECR I-14527. See also: S. Arrowsmith – P. Kunzlik (eds), Social and Environmental Policies in EC Procurement Law, Cambridge University Press, 2009; R. Caranta – M. Trybus (eds), Green and Social Procurements in Europe, Copenhagen, Djoef Publishing, 2010.

from an EU law perspective.[11] Best value for money appears again in recital 46, where the award criteria are described, but just to say that in the most economically advantageous tender the contracting authority chooses which one offers best value for money.

It appears to be the typical case that where the same Directive is based on different legal bases reasons, that one is principal and the others incidental. The ECJ has recognized and classified such cases stating that it is obvious that every piece of legislation is always intended to follow not only one objective, but can be used also for some secondary objectives, and in fact when a measure "pursues two aims or (that) it has two components and if one of those aims or components is identifiable as the main one, whereas the other is merely incidental, the measure must be founded on a single legal basis, namely, that required by the main or predominant aim or component".[12]

Another relevant principle set by ECJ case-law in that period was the application of Treaty principles also to under the threshold public procurements.[13] In the Vestergaard case,[14] the Court concluded that "Notwithstanding the fact that a pubic works contract does not exceed the threshold laid down in Directive 93/37 and does not thus fall within its scope, article 30 of the Treaty precludes a contracting authority from including in the contract documents for that contract a clause requiring the use in carrying out the contract of a product of a specified make, without adding the words 'or equivalent'".[15] The result is that, according to recital 2 of Directive 2004/18/EC, the Treaty principles of the free movement of goods, of freedom of establishment and to provide services are applicable in the award of all public contracts concluded in the Member States, but only contracts above a certain value require a Community coordination of national procedures. One can deduct that the Treaty technique of approximation of legislation is peculiar of public procurements above the threshold, while other Treaty principles are common to

11. See Arrowsmith – Kunzlik, cit. fn. 9, p. 34 – 35 and fn. 57, where it is maintained that recital 5 is not conclusive since it only indicate that the Directives seeks to integrate environmental protection and best value for money, buti t does not indicate that achieving best value for money is one of the Directive objectives.
12. Judgment of 19 July 2012, Parliament / Council (C-130/10) ECLI:EU:C:2012:472.
13. R. Caranta, The Borders of EU Public Procurement Law, in D. Dragos – R. Caranta (eds), Outside the EU Procurement Directives – Inside the Treaty?, Copenhagen, Djoef Publishing, 2012, p. 25 – 60. See also Trybus, cit. fn. 1, p. 97 – 118.
14. Case C-59/00, 2001, Vestergaard ECR I-9505
15. The principle was the reaffirmed in important cases held after the enactment of the 2004 Directive: see among other Case C-6/05, Medipac-Katzntzidis, 2007, ECR I-4557; Joined cases C-147/06 and C-148/06, SECAP, 2008, ECR I-3565.

above and below the threshold contracts. In reality, the first paragraph of the Directive, in declaring its legal basis, mentions art. 47(2), 55 and 95 EC[16] and thus both the classical legitimations for public procurement regulation are formally relevant. But the framework of the Directive seems to shed more light on the need of coordinating national procedures for awarding contracts above the threshold, which is the objective of the Directive.

The 2004 Directive is therefore characterised, as to the legal basis, by two main new features in comparison to the Directives of 1992 and 1993. First, it admits new objectives other than the classical double legitimation stemming from the abolition of non-tariff barriers and the approximation of laws. That new element breaches a well consolidated tradition in the description of the legal basis of the public procurement Directives, dating back from the first Directives of the 1970s discussed above, and opens the way for the developments that will be examined in the following paragraph about the 2014 Directives. The latter, perhaps less evident and less easily detectable, consists of the growing importance accorded to the principle of approximation of legislations against the principle of abolition of non-tariff barriers, which raises some interesting questions both of a practical[17] and a dogmatic[18] nature.

16. Since Directive 2004/18/EC consolidates the rules for public works, services and supplies, the declaration of a common legal basis, consisting both in principles of the internal market and of approximation of legislatures, rides out the problem, noticed in par. 1.1, of the different treatment of these principles in work contracts Directives (where they were both mentioned), in service Directives (where only internal market principles were mentioned) and in supply Directives (where only approximation was mentioned).
17. If approximation of legislatures is the main legal basis of public procurement Directive, then member States are not allowed, when implementing Directives into national legislation, to introduce requirements or rules which are not provided in the Directive, even if in order to enact a more strict regime of competition. The scope being that of uniformity, any divergence from the model provided by the Directive is contrary to the scope of the Directive. In more general terms, the EU Commission criticizes the phenomenon of the so called "gold plating", see COM (2010()543 final; see also M. Comba – S. Richetto, Horizontal Cross-Fertilization and Cryptotypes in EU Administrative Law, in Review of European Administrative Law, vol 5 (2012), pag. 153 – 165.
18. The reference is to the European Economic Constitution, as described in M. Poiares Maduro, We The Court. The European Court of Justice and the European Economic Constitution, Hart, Oxford, 1998, pages 103 – 149. According to Poiares Maduro, the European Treaties can give rise to three different models of Economic Constitution: the centralised one (p. 110 – 126), based on the assumption that after the negative integration, positive integration must follow; the competitive one (p. 126 – 143), foster-

3. The 2014 Directives: efficiency of public spending as a driving force in the preparation of the new Directives on public procurement

The set of new Directives enacted in 2014 is the result of a long procedure of consultation and negotiation that commenced with the green books of 2012. The set consists of Directive 2014/24/EU of the European parliament and of the Council of 26 February 2014, on public procurement and repealing Directive 2004/18/EC and by two other Directives: Directive 2014/25/EU on utilities procurement and Directive 2014/23/EU on public concessions. In this chapter only the public procurement Directive will be examined, since it is the object of this book. In particular, the appearance of a new objective for public procurement, never explicitly mentioned in previous Directives (even if always 'unconsciously' present), will be explored and proved: reference is made here to the efficiency of or savings in public spending.

To support the Impact Study[19] which accompanied the Proposal for the new Directive, the EU Commission ordered a series of external studies, which were used as a basis, together with other documents, for the preparation of the Evaluation Report published on 24 June 2011. Out of the seven external studies, two consisted in a cost-benefit analysis of procurement procedures and the others were about cross-border procurement, strategic use of public procurement, utilities procurement, SME access to public procurement and electronic procurement. This can be seen as a first hint of how important the efficiency of public spending was, for the Commission, when drafting of the new Directives.

ing competition among member states and thus preferring economic integration to political integration and the decentralized one (p. 143 – 149), implying State regulation subject to the negative rule of non discrimination. Those three models coexists in the EU Treaties and compete with each other, shaping the European Economic constitution through their continuous interplay. In the field of public procurements, if approximation of legislations has to prevail, the centralized model would be preferred, because approximation is focused on positive integration through the application of the principle of uniformity of legislation.

19. Commission Staff Working Paper – Impact Assessment, Accompanying the document "Proposal for a Directive of the European Parliament and of the Council on Public Procurement and the Proposal for a Directive of the European Parliament and of the Council on Public Procurement by entities operating in the water, energy, transport and postal sectors", Bruxelles, 20SEC(2011) 1585 final december 2011, SEC(2011) 1585 final.

In fact the Impact Study, when examining the policy context (par. 2), states that, even if the first Directives of the 1970s were only aimed at transparency, regularity, fairness to ensure openness and non-discrimination, through further developments further aims were added. This resulted in legislation intended to: (i) promote efficient EU wide and trans-border competition for contracts, (ii) *deliver best value for money* and (iii) aid the fight against corruption. Consequently, when the Impact Study explains the objectives of the policy (par. 3), the first consideration is that the objectives of existing public procurement policies are still relevant. "Indeed, given the current strained public finances, they may be even more relevant since they seek to ensure that public procurement policy fulfils its potential and delivers value for money to society".[20] The three general objectives identified by the Impact Study are then corresponding to the three polices mentioned before and, in particular, the second general objective: "deliver the best value for money whilst achieving the best possible procurement outcomes for society (hence, ultimately, making the best use of taxpayer's money"),[21] while the first has to do with cross-border competition and the third with the fight against corruption. In the list of Specific Objectives (point. 3.2), the first place is occupied by "Improve the cost-efficiency of EU public procurement rules and procedures".

In the following part of the Impact Study, single options of amendment are analytically considered in relation to the operational objectives stemming from the Specific Objectives mentioned before, in order to present a series of proposals for the modification of the present Directives.

Given this background, it is not surprising that the "Explanatory Memorandum" prepared by the Commission to accompany the Proposal published on 20th December 2011 pinpoints as the first objective of the Proposal the achievement of Horizon 2020, which implies the "most efficient use of public funds". In addition, two complementary objectives are identified, the first being "Increase the efficiency of public spending to ensure the best possible procurement outcomes in terms of value for money (…)" and the second the strategic use of public procurement.

When examining the legal elements of the Proposal (point 3), the Explanatory Memorandum, after declaring the usual legal basis, consisting in what are now after the Treaty of Lisbon articles 53 (1), 62 and 114 TFEU, tackles the subsidiarity statement and affirms that "European-wide procurement pro-

20. Impact assessment, cit. fn 5, p. 30.
21. Impact assessment, cit. fn 5, p. 30.

cedures provide transparency and objectivity in public procurement resulting in considerable savings and improved procurements outcomes that benefit Member States' authorities and, ultimately, the European taxpayer". And since this objective cannot be sufficiently achieved through the action of the individual Member States, which will inevitably create divergent requirements and regulations, the Proposal complies with the subsidiarity principle.

The Memorandum explains in point 2 that the Proposal was based, in addition to the Green Paper, also on a comprehensive evaluation of the impact and effectiveness of EU public procurement legislation. The studies assessed mainly the "cost and effectiveness of procurement procedures", in addition to issues of cross-border procurement, SME access to the public procurement market and the strategic use of public procurement.

Looking to the text of the Proposal itself, it is interesting to mention that recital 2 of the Commission proposition explicitly declares that public procurement "plays a key role in the Europe 2020 strategy (…) while ensuring the most efficient use of public funds" and for that purpose the existing procurement Directives have to be revised and modernised "in order to increase the efficiency of public spending (…)". The amendments proposed by the European Parliament IMCO[22] were even more explicit. They introduced in recital 1, in the listing of principles deriving from the free movement of goods, together with equal treatment, non-discrimination and mutual recognition, also the principle of "efficient management of public funds". Moreover, they added in recital 2, after the already mentioned objective to increase the efficiency of public spending, also that to "ensure value for money". Even if these amendments were not accepted in the Compromise text, they testify a clear-cut position of the IMCO Committee of the European Parliament in favour of recognizing the function of public procurement as a tool to increase of the efficiency of public spending. However, the text of the final compromise still contains the reference to efficiency in public spending already present in the Commission Proposal of 2011.

The text of recital 2, with the reference to the "the most efficient use of public spending" and the "efficient management of public funds" remains unchanged in the actual text of the Directive, as finally approved by the European Parliament and the Council on the 26 February 2014 and published on 28 March 2014. Best value for money is cited in recital 47, where it is said that research and innovation contribute to achieving best value for public

22. See the compared texts of the Commission proposal, EP IMCO amendments, Council General approach and Compromise Proposal, in Council of the European Union, Interistitutional file 2011/0438 (COD).

money and in recital 91, which replies the text of recital 5 in Directive 2004/18 about green considerations.

This quite impressive series of references to the efficiency of public spending in the preparatory documents of the new Directives and in the text of the Directive itself may induce to believe that it is not possible any more to ignore the problem by saying that this is only a question of inaccurate wording or obiter dicta statements. The Commission explicitly declares many times that the original objectives of the procurement Directives, as first enacted in the 1970s, are now to be matched with (if not substituted by) further aims, like strategic procurement, the fight against corruption and the pursue of efficiency in public spending.[23] This means that a general genetic modification of the procurement Directives has occurred, which was already perceived for strategic procurement and, perhaps, for the fight against corruption, but seems to be for the first time strongly enhanced in the new Directives for efficiency in public spending, probably also in consideration of currently strained public finances. Surprisingly enough, it seems that commentators simply do not mention it, or dismiss it with some set phrases, perhaps due to the systematic and specific difficulties entailed by this modification, which will be dealt with in the following paragraph.

4. The debate about efficiency in public spending as an objective of public procurement

It is not surprising that the objective of the EU Directives on public procurement was accurately analysed when the issue of secondary (or horizontal) consideration arose in the public debate, particularly in relation to the 2004 Directive which, as mentioned in par. 1.2, which explicitly mentioned in its recitals objectives different from those directly connected to the internal market for the first time. In fact, only when it became necessary to differentiate secondary (or horizontal) objectives, the need to define the primary objective of the public procurement Directives arose, in order to define it as opposed to the secondary. One of the most accurate studies on the subject by Arrowsmith and Kunzlik[24] states that the only legal objective for the public procurement

23. To be true, these considerations are applicable to the Classical Directive, while for Utilities Directive it is perhaps still central the issue of opening the Member states market to European companies. See Europe economics, Taking Stock of utilities procurement, A Report of DG Internal Market, London, 11 February 2011.
24. Arrowsmith – Kunzlik, cit. fn. 9, p. 30 – 37.

Directives is the development of the internal market, through three main means: the prohibition of discrimination, the requirement of transparency in order to prevent discrimination and finally the removal of restrictions on the access to the market. If one looks closer, the main objective is the prohibition of discrimination, since the other two can be considered as instrumental to the first: transparency and the elimination of trade barriers are in fact aimed at the elimination of discrimination on a national basis and consequently to the fostering of cross-border trade, which remains the first and foremost objective of public procurement, ever since the first Directives of the 1970s.

In this framework, there is no room for pursuing efficiency in public spending, which, according to Arrowsmith and Kunzlik,[25] is not and cannot be an autonomous objective of EU Directives on public procurement. It remains, however, to explain the presence of so many references in official European documents to the connection between public procurement and value for money. As we have seen in paragraph 1, even if not in the text of Directives, the idea that public procurement was strictly linked to value for money is mentioned at least since the report "The cost of non-Europe" of 1988 and then in an increasing number of following official documents.

A possible explanation of this potential contradiction is that value for money is a consequence of public procurement, not an objective: "better value for money is certainly one of the benefits intended to follow from the internal market and, in particular, from the procurement Directives (…) On the other hand, the EC procurement rules are not directed at achieving value for money per se in a way that is separate from internal market objectives, as some of the statements above might imply".[26] And again: "saving public money expenditures and improving the quality of services simply do not in and of themselves contribute to the creation of an internal market".[27]

Nor, according to Arrowsmith and Kunzlik, can it be said that pursuing value for money is a substitute for the operation of the market, because the Treaty is only concerned with obstacles to cross border trade, not with efficient behaviour of contracting authorities.

In effect, what can be said is, elaborating from this position, that the Treaty only assumes the point of view of economic operators wanting to sell their products, services or works in other Member States and therefore does not care about possible positive consequences of an increase in cross-border trade like the saving of public money. On the other hand, value for money is what

25. Arrowsmith – Kunzlich, cit. fn. 9, p. 30 – 27.
26. Arrowsmith – Kunzlich, cit. fn. 9, p. 32 – 33.
27. Arrowsmith – Kunzlich, cit. fn. 9, p. 33.

can be seen from the point of view of Member States – which is not that of the Treaty – but is however that of the Masters of the Treaty. In other words, what happens in reality is the same thing, but it is seen as removing trade barriers and discrimination from the point of view of economic operators – which is the point of view of the Treaty – while it is seen as value for money from the point of view of the contracting authorities of the Member States. It can also happen that the two points of view do not coincide, i.e. in the case in which a contracting authority is compliant with procurement rules for purchasing a good which is however completely useless: competition is respected, but not value for money.[28] Or the opposite case in which the contracting authority decides to automatically eliminate an abnormally low offer under the threshold, which may be considered contrary to fair competition, even if consistent with efficiency needs of the contracting authority.[29] But it can be said that these are exceptional cases, since as a general rule the two aspects of eliminating discrimination and saving public money coincide.

This theory of competition and efficiency in public spending as being "two sides of the same coin" or, if we prefer, as being the result of two different points of view in analysing the same phenomenon could be criticized if one thinks that competition is fostered at an European level, while best value for money is an objective for national governments. If competition yields the result of foreign companies being awarded public contracts, that could in theory harm the national economy – and thus, consequently, conflict with the pursuit of efficiency in public spending. But in practice, direct cross-border awards in EU public procurement was assessed in 2007-2009 as low as 1,6% of overall EU procurement, while indirect cross-border participation through subsidiaries for the same period is only 11,4%. If the value of public procurement contracts is taken into account, direct cross-border participation is assessed at 3,5% and indirect cross-border participation through affiliates at 13,4%.[30] The consequence of these figures is that the EU rules on competition in public procurement do in reality foster only or mostly competition

28. ECJ, Judgment of 1 June 2006, P&O European Ferries (Vizcaya) / Commission (C-442/03 P and C-471/03 P, ECR 2006 p. I-4845) ECLI:EU:C:2006:356 (even if in this case the conflict was between Public procurement and State aid, it comes out that the purchase of tickets for maritime transportation was useless for the contracting authority and thus the public money was badly spent)
29. ECJ, Joined cases C-147/06 and C-148/06 Secap and Santorso (2008) ECR I-3565.
30. EU Commission, "Final Report on Cross-border procurement above EU thresholds", march 2011, p. 104. See also "Green Paper on the modernisation of EU public procurement policy: Towards a more efficient European Procurement Market" COM(2011) 15 final, fn 9, pag. 4.

among national economic operators, for the award of public contracts, which strengthen national economies to reduce the costs of procurement without helping foreign companies.

Coming back to Arrowsmith and Kunzlik, the series of references to efficiency of public spending in the preparatory documents of the new Directives and in the text of the Directive itself are explained, as a simple "confusion"[31] of the two different points of view and not as the introduction of a new legal basis for public procurement, in conflict with the Treaty. However, the theory of "confusion", which was perhaps plausible in relation to the Directives of 2004, where no mention of value for money was included in the text (but only in different documents of the Commission) is more critical today, because the Directives of 2014 explicitly mention the most effective use of public funds in recital 2. In fact, an early comment to the Commission's Green Paper of 2011 was very critical with the introduction of any reference to efficiency of public spending, stating that it was in conflict with the Treaty both because it is not an internal market competence but a Member State responsibility and because it was contrary to the principle of subsidiarity.[32]

In effect, the pursuit of efficiency in public spending is a competence of the Member States, whose legislation, under different legal schemes and with different tools, regulates public procurement under that perspective. Differently from the EU Treaties, which tackle the issue from the point of view of economic operators, Member States see it from the point of view of the contracting authorities and therefore are concerned not so much with competition but with value for money. Each individual Member State has of course a different approach to the problem, depending on its legal tradition and historical developments: from the United Kingdom, where value for money is the most important objective, to Spain, whose Sustainable Economic Act of 2011 imposes the predominance of sustainability over value for money considerations.[33] In any case, it is self-evident that no national legislation can be aimed

31. It is the word used by Arrowsmith – Kunzlik, cit. fn. 9, p. 32.
32. R. Boyle, EU procurement green paper on the modernisation of EU public procurement policy: a personal response, in P.P.L.R. 2011, 5, NA171-184, p. NA 173 – NA 174.
33. The analysis of some member States' legislation in relation to the scope of public procurement can be found in the national reports published in R. Caranta – M. Trybus, (eds.) The Law of Green and Social Procurement in Europe, Copehnagen, Djoef, 2010. In particular, see the comparative report by M. Comba, Green and Social Considerations in Public Procurement Contracts: A Comparative Approach, in Caranta-Trybus, cit., p. 299 – 319.

at fostering cross-border public procurement, unless of being forced to do so in the implementation of the European Directives.

Another possible explanation for the reference to the most effective use of public funds in the EU Directives on public procurement can be found in Chris Bovis' Handbook on EU Public Procurement Law, according to which "the regulation of public procurement exposes an economic and a legal approach to the integration of public markets in the European Union".[34] This is an approach not so different from the previous one, in as much as it follows the theory of the "double point of view", even if here the divide between the two different points of view is not an institutional one (European Union against Member States), but has to do with a different subject specialization (economic against legal). There is a legal scope for Directives, which is the enactment of the Treaty principles of competition in the internal market, and an economic approach, more sensible to practical effects deriving from the abolition of trade barriers, which entails important consequences on the structure of European industry as well as on prices.[35]

The relevant ECJ case law does not analyse carefully the issue of the purpose of the public procurement Directives,[36] limiting itself to repeat a formula which refers to the elimination of trade barriers and fostering competition. In a recent case, the Court stated that: "In accordance with the case-law of the Court, the principal objective of the EU rules in the field of public procurement is the opening-up to undistorted competition in all the Member States with regard to the execution of works, the supply of products or the provision of services; that entails an obligation on all contracting authorities to apply the relevant rules of EU law where the conditions for such application are sat-

34. Cristopher H. Bovis, Eu public procurement law, cit. fn. 4, page 5.
35. Another explanation which is perhaps more pragmatic lies with the idea that the reference to better value for money in the new Directive has to do with "marketing" considerations: in order to counter the increasing disfavor of the imposition of public procurement procedures, the Commission tries to "sell" the new Directives with the argument that public procurement entails value for money and not only internal market objectives, which is probably less "sexy". A subtler version of this explanation is the following, for which I am grateful to Prof. Martin Trybus who suggested it to me during the EPLS meeting in Munich (July 2014). The insertion of the value for money motivation in the recitals of the Directive was made in consideration of those Member States which use the technique of cut and paste for the implementation of Directives: having the value for money motivation already incorporated in the Directive, those Member States do not have to make the effort to insert it in their national legislation implementing the Directive, but can take the Directive as it is and transform it to a piece of internal legislation.
36. Arrowsmith – Kunzlik, cit. fn. 9, page 34.

isfied".[37] However, the Court does not address the issue of the qualification of best value for money in relation to the legal basis of the Directive. Best value for money is cited in ECJ decisions about public procurement. not in relation to its legal basis, but only when award criteria are concerned,[38] and this citation "merely reflects the fact that selection of the best tender is in fact the objective of procedures in national law".[39]

5. Concluding remarks

Examining the evolving self-declared objectives of the public procurement Directives from the first ones enacted in the 1970s to the more recent ones of 2014, one cannot fail to notice that, whilst until the 1992-93 Directives, the legal basis had always been referred to the double standard of elimination of trade barriers and approximation of national legislation, in the 2004 Directives green and social considerations appear. But it is with the 2014 Directives that the most relevant innovation is introduced because, along with the strengthening of green, social and innovative considerations, also efficiency of public spending is listed in the first recitals of the Directive as one of the objectives of public procurement. However, efficiency of public spending is substantially different from the classical "secondary" or "strategic" objectives (like environment, full employment, innovation), since it is not part of a Eu-

37. ECJ, Judgment of 8 May 2014, Datenlotsen Informationssysteme (C-15/13) ECLI:EU:C:2014:303, par. 22.
38. See for exemple ECJ, Judgment of 10 May 2012, Commission / Netherlands (C-368/10) ECLI:EU:C:2012:284, par. 83 and 86; Judgment of 21 July 2011, Evropaïki Dynamiki / EMSA (C-252/10 P, ECR 2011 p. I-107*, Summ.pub.) ECLI:EU:C: 2011:512, par. 29 and 30. But see the opinion of the Advocate general Jacobs in case C-174/03, par. 58, where it seems that best value for money is a consequence of the elimination of trade barriers: "In addition, the purpose of the Community rules governing procurement in the utilities sectors is to address the circumstances which led entities operating in those sectors to award contracts on a national basis. According to the preambles to the past, present and future Directives regulating procurement in the utilities sectors, there are two main interrelated causes for discriminatory procurement, namely, the closed nature of the markets in which the relevant entities operate and the various ways in which national authorities can influence the behaviour of those entities. (24) It is assumed that where entities operate under undistorted competitive conditions, market forces will by themselves ensure that the best value for money is sought in every contract, and that there is therefore no need to subject their procurement to detailed award procedures".
39. Arrowsmith – Kunzlich, cit. fn. 9, p. 34 – 35.

ropean policy, but pertains exclusively to Member State competence. At the same time, the 2004 Directives reinforce the importance of approximation of legislations as legal basis, inducing to think it has become the primary legal basis, as opposed to freedom of establishment and free movement of goods and services.

These two innovations need an accurate analysis in order to verify their consistency and possible legal consequences on the structure of the Directives and on interpretation of individual provisions.

As for efficiency for public spending, the first problem is if the EU has competence in this field, considering articles 2 ff of the Lisbon Treaty (TEU) and considering the subsidiarity principle. All the other new objectives of the Directive (green, social, innovative, corruption) can be connected to specific EU policies. Efficiency in public spending cannot, because it rests exclusively with the competence of Member States.

Traditionally, efficiency in public spending is a matter of national public administrations: every Member State (excepting UK, perhaps) had national legislation enacted prior to the start of the EU setting rules for public contracts in order for public administrations to act efficiently. The EU legislation of public procurement was added to this pre-existing national legislation creating a double standard because it was perceived as protecting foreign companies and not national public administrations.

According to the doctrine analysed in this paper, one has to conclude that efficiency in public spending cannot be an objective of the Directive and that the citations of that scope in the recitals of the 2014 Directives are only the result of "confusion".[40] The consequence is that all the rules contained in the Directive which seem to be grounded solely on efficiency in public spending have to be carefully examined and their effects verified in the light of the legitimate objectives of the Directive. Just to give an example, arts. 37 and 38 of Directive 2014/24/EU, allowing provisions on centralised purchasing and occasional joint procurement, should be strictly interpreted and verified against their effect on cross-border procurement (as it is in fact warned by recital 53) because the fact that they are often proclaimed, especially by Member States (like Italy), as a perfect tool for efficiency in public spending is not sufficient to justify in light of the Directive a possible negative effect on cross-border procurement.

As for the enhancement of approximation of legislations as the major objective of the Directives, it has at least two consequences. The first is practi-

40. Arrowsmith – Kunzlich, cit. fn. 9, p. 32

cal and has to do with the discretion of Member States in the implementation of the Directives: since the scope is approximation of legislation, it would not be admissible for Member States to implement Directives using national provisions stricter than the Directives themselves.

The second consequence has to do with the model of the European economic constitution: while the prevalence of freedom of movement entails a model of anti-discrimination which leaves a wide margin of discretion to national legislation, with the only prohibition being to introduce limitations on free movement (be it direct or indirect), if approximation of legislation takes the lead, then the model turns into that of market integration which is, in fact, uniformity of rules throughout all of Europe.

Bibliography

Arrowsmith, S. – Kunzlik, P., (eds), Social and Environmental Policies in EC Procurement Law, Cambridge University Press, 2009;

Boyle, R., EU procurement green paper on the modernisation of EU public procurement policy: a personal response, in P.P.L.R. 2011, 5, NA171-184;

Bovis, Christopher, C., EU Procurement Law, Elgar, Cheltenham, 2012

Caranta, R. –Trybus, M., (eds), Green and Social Procurements in Europe, Copenhagen, Djoef, 2001;

Caranta, R., The Borders of EU Public Procurement Law, in D. Dragos – R. Caranta (eds), Outside the EU Procurement Directives – Inside the Treaty?, Copenhagen, Djoef, 2012, p. 25 – 60;

Comba, M. – Richetto, S., Horizontal Cross-Fertilization and Cryptotypes in EU Administrative Law, in Review of European Administrative Law, vol 5 (2012), pag. 153 – 165

Comba, M., Green and Social Considerations in Public Procurement Contracts: A Comparative Approach, in Caranta-Trybus, Green and Social Procurements in Europe, Copenhagen, Djoef, 2001, p. 299 – 319;

Poiares Maduro, M., We The Court. The European Court of Justice and the European Economic Constitution, Hart, Oxford, 1998;

Trybus, M., Public contracts in European Union Internal Market Law: Foundations and Requirements, in R. Noguellou – U. Stelkens, Droit comparé des Contrats Publics – Comparative Law on Public Contracts, Bruxelles, Bruylant, 2010, pages 81 – 121.

Contracting authorities, in-house services and public authorities cooperation

Martin Burgi[1]

I. Introduction

The Commission's reform of the Public Procurement Directives has raised high expectations among public procurement experts, especially regarding the codification of the hitherto unwritten exceptions of the application of EU public procurement law for vertical and horizontal cooperation between public authorities in Article 12 of the new Directive 2014/24/EU. Precisely this has been one of the most intensively debated topics throughout the entire legislative process.[2]

It is questionable whether the new rules will meet expectations. In order to prevent distortions of competition, the Commission's initial proposal went far beyond the guidelines stipulated by the Court of Justice. Unnecessary additional criteria and new indefinite legal terms were included even if it would have been easier to just fully incorporate the case law. Instead, legal uncertainty and barriers especially to horizontal cooperation were created, running

1. The author wishes to thank research assistant Laura Wittschurky, LMU München, for her valuable support with the preparation of the present article.

2. M. Burgi/F. Koch, 'In-House Procurement and Horizontal Cooperation Between Public Authorities', EPPPL 2012, p. 86. For example, 16 amendments concerning Article 12 were tabled in the Committee on the Internal Market and Consumer Protection alone, see European Parliament Plenary sitting document A7-0007/2013, 11.01.2013, pp. 53 ff.

counter to the Commission's self-imposed regulatory goal.[3] Moreover it was debatable whether the initially proposed rules were in keeping with EU primary law.[4] Changes made during the legislative proceedings are an improvement in this respect, but the question whether the new rules will be workable still arises.

The present article aims to describe as well as to evaluate two selected provisions of the new Directive 2014/24/EU, namely Article 2, which deals with the definition of contracting authorities, and the aforementioned Article 12.

II. Article 2 – Contracting authorities

Article 2 contains the definition of "contracting authorities" and insofar differentiates (in conjunction with Annex I) between two groups of contracting authorities: central and sub-central contracting authorities. Following up on this, the remaining rules prescribe several less strict requirements for sub-central contracting authorities. So higher thresholds apply to sub-central contracting authorities (Article 4 (c)), sub-central contracting authorities may set the time limit for the receipt of tenders by mutual agreement with the selected candidates (Article 26 (5), Article 28 (4)), and sub-central contracting authorities may use a prior information notice as a call for competition (Article 48 (2)).

In the Federal Republic of Germany, only the Federal Chancellery and the Federal Ministries come under the definition of central contracting authorities.[5] Predominantly, contracting authorities are sub-central – such as the German federal states and municipalities. For them, the lighter regime applies.

The differentiation between central and sub-central contracting authorities provided in Article 2 follows the WTO Agreement on Government Procurement (GPA)[6] by which the EU is bound. The GPA has opened the possibility to arrange a lighter regime for certain contracting authorities also previously. But until now the EU legislator made use of this option only concerning sectoral contracting authorities – there have been reservations against an exten-

3. See the recitals of the Directive 2014/24/EU.
4. M. Burgi/F. Koch, 'In-House Procurement and Horizontal Cooperation Between Public Authorities', EPPPL 2012, pp. 86 ff.
5. See Annex I.
6. OJ C 256/1, 03.09.1996.

sion.[7] By the new directive, the possibility is to be used to its full extent. The new provision leaves the Member States scope to establish regulations by which sub-central contracting authorities receive more liberties and greater flexibility. A complete subsumption of all contracting authorities under all mandatory standards of EU public procurement law as it was the case until now was certainly not in conformity with EU primary law.[8] However, it is open to question whether Article 2 will play a major role: Germany, for instance, has pronounced not to make use of the provided option.

In the context of the reform, the possibility of a more useful solution for the classification of contracting authorities than the chosen one between central and sub-central contracting authorities was opened up, namely, a differentiation depending on size or the number of procurement processes and thus between small and medium contracting authorities on the one side and large contracting authorities on the other side.[9] This would have had the advantage of a congruent differentiation between contractors. Regrettably, the EU legislator failed to take advantage of this chance.

III. Article 12 – Relations between entities within the public sector

1. General remarks

Considered as one of the core rules of the new directive,[10] Article 12 aims to codify the hitherto unwritten jurisdiction of the Court of Justice regarding vertical and horizontal cooperation between entities within the public sector. This again is intended to achieve clarification and to prevent different interpretation of the decisions of the Court of Justice and was in principle met with approval in the green paper.[11]

7. K. Wiedner/N. Spiegel 'Europäische Vergaberichtlinien: Die nächste Generation', in H-J. Prieß/N. Lau/R. Kratzenberg (eds.) Wettbewerb –Transparenz – Gleichbehandlung, Festschrift für Fridhelm Marx, 15 Jahre GWB Vergaberecht, (C.H. Beck, München 2013), 821 f.
8. M. Burgi 'Die Förderung sozialer und technischer Innovationen durch das Vergaberecht' NZBau 2011, 583.
9. M. Burgi 'Die Förderung sozialer und technischer Innovationen durch das Vergaberecht' NZBau 2011, 583; see also Stellungnahme Bundesverband der Deutschen Industrie, D 0532/1, 15.
10. M. Burgi 'Die Förderung sozialer und technischer Innovationen durch das Vergaberecht' NZBau 2011, 583.
11. See recitals (31) ff.; European Commission 'Green Paper on the modernisation of EU public procurement policy, Towards a more efficient European Procurement Market,

The Court of Justice case law in terms of relations between entities within the public sector is rather extensive. Building on its initial decisions concerning vertical cooperation (Teckal)[12] and horizontal cooperation (Stadtreinigung Hamburg),[13] the Court of Justice developed its jurisdiction further in about 15 subsequent cases. In view of this comprehensive and acknowledged, almost statutory jurisdiction, the necessity of a nearly three A4 pages codification is questionable.[14] In case the EU legislator had chosen a full adoption of the case law established over years by the Court of Justice, nothing would have remained to do but to include the approved criteria for vertical as well as horizontal cooperation into a less extensive provision on explicit exceptions to the Directive.[15]

However, the new directive takes another approach. Looking at the subdivision of Artcle 12, paragraph 1 concerns the "conventional" single in-house constellation in which a contracting authority awards a contract to a legal person it controls. Paragraph 2 also concerns the single in-house constellation, but where – conversely – the controlled legal person awards a contract to the controlling contracting authority or the controlled legal person awards a contract to another legal person controlled by the same contracting authority, thus to a sister company.

Paragraph 3 in turn deals with the so-called joint in-house procurement where several contracting authorities control the legal person jointly. There is criticism that in-house procurement is not centralised in only one prescription but fragmented in the three numbers of Article 12. It is not comprehensible why joint in-house in particular is dealt with separately of, especially in such a detailed fashion, and subjected to additional conditions.[16]

Paragraph 4 at least deals with horizontal cooperation that is cooperation between contracting authorities exclusively.

Synthesis of replies', in http://ec.europa.eu/internal_market/consultations/docs/2011/public_procurement/synthesis_document_en.pdf, last visited on September, 2013.

12. Case 107/98 Teckal [1999] ECR I-8121.
13. Case 480/06 Stadtreinigung Hamburg [2009] ECR I-4747.
14. M. Burgi/F. Koch 'In-House Procurement and Horizontal Cooperation Between Public Authorities' EPPPL 2012, 87.
15. M. Burgi 'Anwendungsbereich und Governanceregeln der EU-Auftragsvergabereformrichtlinie: Bewertung und Umsetzungsbedarf' NZBau 2012, 603 f.; M. Burgi/F. Koch 'In-House Procurement and Horizontal Cooperation Between Public Authorities' EPPPL 2012, 87.
16. M. BURGI/F. KOCH 'In-House Procurement and Horizontal Cooperation Between Public Authorities' EPPPL 2012, 88.

It is obvious that the extensive and circumstantial drafting of Article 12 is not in full accordance with the objectives pursued by the new directive, legal certainty and simplification.[17]

Article 12 is systematically included under the section "Exclusions" of Directive 2014/24/EU. That has provoked criticism, too: only what in principle applies can be excluded, but the EU's legislative competence to direct the application of public procurement rules on vertical as well as horizontal cooperation is disputed in some quarters.[18] Otherwise, the Court of Justice has not yet taken stand on this, plus an inclusion of Article 12 under section "Scope" would have necessitated a circuitous and detailed prescription.[19]

2. Significance of administrative cooperation, particularly in the current financial crisis

The administration has been pressured to economise for years. Naturally, this has even increased during the financial crisis. If it is true that public money can best be saved and thereby public debt in the Eurozone can best be reduced through cooperation,[20] pressure to economise translates into pressure to cooperate. Thus it will be reasonable not to curtail administrative cooperation by codifying it and making it subject to strict conditions as the initial Commission proposal did. This applies all the more since curtailed administrative cooperation will by no means lead to intensified public-private cooperation and hence cause an increase of the number of public procurements contended on the market. Quite the contrary: it will result in solo efforts to provide in-house. Public authorities – at both local and regional level – will perform their public tasks for themselves. It can be doubted whether this is politically desirable.[21]

17. See recitals of Directive 2014/24/EU.
18. Bundesrat-Drucksache 15/12, Nr. 10.
19. M. Burgi 'Anwendungsbereich und Governanceregeln der EU-Auftragsvergabereformrichtlinie: Bewertung und Umsetzungsbedarf' NZBau 2012, 603; see also T. Mestwerdt/D. Sauer 'Institutionalisierte Kooperationen öffentlicher Auftraggeber als kodifizierter Ausnahmetatbestand im Unionsvergaberecht', in H-J. Prieß/N. Lau/R. Kratzenberg (eds.), Wettbewerb –Transparenz – Gleichbehandlung, Festschrift für Fridhelm Marx, 15 Jahre GWB Vergaberecht, (C.H. Beck, München 2013), 391 ff.
20. T. I. SCHMIDT Kommunale Kooperation (Mohr Siebeck, Tübingen, 2005), 9 ff.
21. M. Burgi/F. KOCH 'In-House Procurement and Horizontal Cooperation Between Public Authorities' EPPPL 2012, 92.

3. Vertical cooperation

a. Regulation

Article 12 (1-3) regulates vertical cooperation, also referred to as in-house or institutionalised cooperation. Hardly any other issue has occupied the Court of Justice over the last few years as frequently as the inclusion or exclusion of public purchasing from providers controlled vertically by contracting authorities. The Court of Justice seems to have addressed all problems of interpretation. Hence the number of judgments by national courts as well as the amount of practice-focused essays on the subject has considerably decreased. But given the economic and technical complexity of this field of law, it will also come as no surprise if a need for legal advice, minor changes, and a certain number of legal proceedings persist.[22]

In the Teckal case, the Court of Justice decided on vertical cooperation for the first time and assumed that the award of a contract to a legal person was not subject to EU procurement law in case the contracting authority exercised over the legal person a control similar to which it exercised over its own departments and the legal person carried out its activities essentially for the controlling contracting authority.[23] These requirements, the criterion of organisational dependence and the criterion of economic dependence, are together designated as Teckal criteria.[24] If these qualifications are fulfilled, the contracting authorities will resort to accomplish their tasks with their own resources – there is no procurement, the purpose of the EU public procurement law does not take effect.

In the Stadt Halle case the Court of Justice decided that the criterion of organisational dependence was precluded in any case of the involvement of private entities within the legal person, no matter how insignificant the degree of involvement was.[25] The Court of Justice acknowledged this in subsequent judgments.[26]

The widely undisputed requirements established by the Court of Justice – the criterion of organisational dependence, the criterion of economic depend-

22. M. Burgi/F. Koch 'In-House Procurement and Horizontal Cooperation Between Public Authorities' EPPPL 2012, 87.
23. Case 107/98 Teckal [1999] ECR I-8121 paragraph 50.
24. See for example opinion of advocate general Trstenjak, Case 324/07 Coditel [2008] ECR I-8457 paragraphs 30, 31.
25. Case 26/03 Stadt Halle [2005] ECR I-1 paragraph 49.
26. Case 29/04 Stadt Mödling [2005] ECR I-9705 paragraphs 46-49; Case 324/07 Coditel [2008] ECR I-8457 paragraph 30; Case 573/07 Sea [2009] ECR I-8127 paragraph 46.

ence, and the criterion of the entire absence of any private participation – are now taken on by the directive, in doing so the criterion of the entire absence of any private participation (which the Court of Justice developed as an individual element of the criterion of organisational dependence) is dealt with as a discrete criterion.[27] Thereon, Article 12 (1-3) provides particulars of all three criteria.

aa. Reform: Control criterion

The Court of Justice pointed out already in the Teckal decision that an in-house case not subject to EU public procurement law could only be accepted in the event that the contracting authority exercised over the legal person to which the contract was awarded a control similar to the control the contracting authority exercised over its own departments.[28] Article 12 (1) Subparagraph 1 lit. (a) as well as (2) and (3) Subparagraph 1 lit. (a) recalls this criterion of organisational dependence.

Article 12 (1) Subparagraph 2 – also applicable to Article 12 (2) – concretises the control criterion to the effect that the contracting authority has to exercise a decisive influence over both strategic objectives and significant decisions of the controlled legal person. Here, too, the jurisdiction of the Court of Justice is taken up – the mentioned requirements originate from the decision on the Parking Brixen case verbatim.[29] Additionally, it is provided that the control may also be exercised by another legal person which is itself controlled by the contracting authority.

Article 12 (3) Subparagraph 2 specifies the control criterion as well. The requirement that the contracting authority has to exercise a decisive influence over strategic objectives and significant decisions is included here, too, but tailored to joint in-house situations in which several contracting authorities exercise control. The directive insofar provides that it will do if the contracting authorities exercise decisive influence over strategic objectives and significant decisions of the legal person jointly. This is based on the jurisdiction of the Court of Justice as well. In Coditel the Court decided that the jointly exerted influence met the requirements for in-house situations.[30]

27. See M. Söbbeke 'In-house quo vadis?' DÖV 2006, 999; P. Schleissing Möglichkeiten und Grenzen vergaberechtlicher In-House-Geschäfte (Nomos Verlag, Baden-Baden 2012), 118.
28. Case 107/98 Teckal [1999] ECR I-8121 paragraph 50.
29. Case 458/03 Parking Brixen [2005] ECR I-8585 paragraph 65.
30. Case 324/07 Coditel [2008] ECR I-8457 paragraph 50; see also Case 573/07 Sea [2009] ECR I-8127 paragraph 63.

Furthermore, Article 12 (3) Subparagraph 2 assumes for the control criterion that the decision-making bodies of the controlled legal person are composed of representatives of all participating contracting authorities. This, too, refers back to the case law of the Court of Justice. Namely the Econord case can be cited here – although it originates from 2012 and therefore followed the proposal. In the Econord case, the Court of Justice decided that in joint in-house situations the control criterion would only be met if the participating contracting authorities held capital in the legal person as well as played a role in its managing bodies.[31]

Beyond all this, the initial Commission proposal envisaged two additional criteria which could be summarized by the generic term "absent market orientation".[32] It required that the legal person not pursue any interests distinct from those of the participating contracting authorities (Article 12 (3) (c) of the initial Commission proposal) and not draw any gains other than the reimbursement or re-allocation of actual costs from the public contracts with the contracting authorities (Article 12 (3) (d) of the initial Commission proposal). These criteria were not in accordance with the jurisdiction of the Court of Justice. Indeed the Court actually dealt with the market orientation of the legal person – and the Commission referred to that. Article 12 (3) (c) of the initial Commission proposal originated from the decision in the Coditel case almost verbatim.[33] In its decision in the Sea case, the Court of Justice ruled out the existence of the control criterion because of the market orientation of the legal person.[34] And in its decision in the Stadtreinigung Hamburg case – which, certainly, did not concern a vertical but a horizontal cooperation – the Court of Justice commented on market orientation, too.[35] However, the criterion of market orientation was used only in the context of the individual cases. The Court of Justice did precisely not qualify the criterion as a general standard, level to which it was elevated by the initial Commission proposal.[36]

The final version of the new directive takes up only the requirement that the legal person does not pursue any interests which are not only distinct from

31. Case 182/11 Econord [2012], paragraph 33.
32. M. Burgi 'Anwendungsbereich und Governanceregeln der EU-Auftragsvergabereformrichtlinie: Bewertung und Umsetzungsbedarf' NZBau 2012, 604; M. Burgi/F. Koch 'In-House Procurement and Horizontal Cooperation Between Public Authorities' EPPPL 2012, 88.
33. Case 324/07 Coditel [2008] ECR I-8457 paragraph 38, see also paragraph 36.
34. Case 573/07 Sea [2009] ECR I-8127 paragraphs 65, 66.
35. Case 480/06 Stadtreinigung Hamburg [2009] ECR I-4747 paragraph 47.
36. M. Burgi 'Anwendungsbereich und Governanceregeln der EU-Auftragsvergabereformrichtlinie: Bewertung und Umsetzungsbedarf' NZBau 2012, 604.

but contrary to those of the controlling authorities. The requirement that the legal person does not draw gains other than the reimbursement or re-allocation of actual costs from the public contracts with the contracting authorities has not been retained. Considering that it will be sufficient by the essentiality criterion if the legal person carries out its activities essentially for the contracting authorities and hence insignificant additional activities for others than the contracting authorities carry no weight, it was illogical to require an absolute correlation of interests as well as a lack of revenues other than the reimbursement or re-allocation of funds for the performance.[37] On that score, the partial revocation of the criterion of "absent market orientation" by the final version of the new directive is to be welcomed.

bb. Reform: Essentiality Criterion

Likewise decided already in the Teckal judgment, the Court of Justice stated that an in-house case would only be accepted if, in addition to the control criterion, the controlled legal person carried out its essential activities for the controlling contracting authority.[38] Also this second Teckal criterion, the criterion of economic dependence, is taken on by Article 12 (1) as well as (2) and (3). But henceforth, a fixed percentage for the minimum proportion of activities carried out for the contracting authority will be established – a percentage which was originally fixed at 90% but then reduced to 80% upon the insistence of the Council. This ceiling will contribute to legal certainty but it leaves little scope for the consideration of the individual case. The Court of Justice had instead avoided the definition of a fixed percentage.[39]

Finally, it should be noted that Article 12 (5) lays down that the percentage of activities is proved by the average total turnover, or an appropriate alternative activity based measure for the three years preceding the contract award. In case that the turnover or alternative measure are not available for the preceding three years or no longer relevant, it is sufficient to show that it is credible.

37. M. Fruhmann 'Die neue Ausnahme für öffentlich-öffentliche Vergaben gemäß der Allgemeinen Ausrichtung des Rates', in H-J. Prieß/N. Lau/R. Kratzenberg (eds.) Wettbewerb –Transparenz – Gleichbehandlung, Festschrift für Fridhelm Marx, 15 Jahre GWB Vergaberecht, (C.H. Beck, München, 2013), 158 f.
38. Case 107/98 Teckal [1999] ECR I-8121 paragraph 50; see also R. Gruneberg/A. Wilden 'Höhere Hürden für In-House-Geschäfte – Verschärfung des Wesentlichkeitskriteriums' VergabeR 2012, 150 ff.
39. Case 340/04 Carbotermo [2006] ECR I-4137 paragraph 64; see also F. Marx 'Zur Neuregelung der „Wesentlichkeitsschwelle" für Inhouse-Geschäfte: If it ain't broke, don't fix it!' NZBau aktuell, Heft 10/2012, V.

cc. *Reform: Criterion of absent direct private participation*

In Article 12 (1-3), the new directive assumes for all the captured in-house constellations that in principle no direct private capital participation in the controlled legal person exists, but excludes non-controlling and non-blocking forms of private capital participation required by applicable national legislative provisions, in conformity with the Treaties, which do not exert a decisive influence on the legal person. Initially, the Commission proposal invariably presupposed the absence of any private participation. That original regulation was exposed to criticism precisely because of its inconsistency. Some national legislative provisions actually require the participation of private capital. For example, so-called Wasser- und Bodenverbände in some German federal states have compulsorily to involve private members.[40] The final version of the directive excluded just these very forms of private capital participation.

Likewise in contrast to the originally proposed draft, the final version does not comprise specifications for the criterion of absent direct private participation, in particular it does not set the critical date anymore. Furthermore, not expanded in the new directive at all are two constellations the Court of Justice was concerned with:[41] Firstly the situation in which a subsequent (mandatory or optional) opening to private capital is prescribed but does not come to effect during the ongoing contract, secondly situations of purposeful evasion. This, in turn, is an example of a case in which the EU legislator decided against a codification.

As mentioned before, the Court of Justice decided in the Stadt Halle case that any private involvement in the legal person ruled out that the contracting authority exercised over the legal person a control similar to the control over its own departments.[42] The criterion of absent private participation thus was developed as only one element of the control criterion whereas the directive absorbs it as a discrete criterion.

b. Critical remarks

Looking at the regulation of vertical cooperation in summary, mainly the criteria of "absent market orientation" for joint in-house, that was the requirement that the controlled legal person not pursue any interest distinct from

40. See for example § 4 of the Gesetz über die Emschergenossenschaft.
41. Case 573/07 Sea [2009] ECR I-8127; Case 29/04 Stadt Mödling [2005] ECR I-9705; see also R. Caranta 'The In-House Providing: The Law as It Stands in the EU', in M. Comba/S. Treumer (eds.) The In-House Providing in European Law, European Procurement Law Series vol. 1, (Djøf Publishing, Kopenhagen, 2010), 52.
42. Case 26/03 Stadt Halle [2005] ECR I-1 paragraph 49.

those of the participating contracting authorities and not draw any gains other than the reimbursement or re-allocation of actual costs from the public contracts with the contracting authorities, was to be criticised. Including these requirements, the initially proposal went partly beyond decisions of the Court of Justice and, moreover, used public procurement law to avoid competitive distortions – this one objective was prioritised over respect for the Member States' freedom to structure administrative cooperation in the range of joint in-house.[43]

The final version of the new directive has maintained only the condition that the controlled legal person pursues similar interests to those of the participating contracting authorities, but excludes joint in-house cooperation only in case that the interests pursued by the controlled legal person are contrary to (instead of distinct from) the interests pursued by the participating contracting authorities. The condition that the controlled legal person not draw any gains other than the reimbursement or re-allocation of actual costs has been deleted in its entirety. This is to be welcomed as a step in the right direction.

4. Horizontal cooperation

a. Court of Justice case law before and during the reform process

After the Court of Justice accepted vertical cooperation as an exceptional case not subject to EU public procurement law in the Teckal decision in 1999, the Court of Justice took yet another exception in the Stadtreinigung Hamburg decision in 2009: horizontal cooperation, also referred to as non-institutionalised cooperation. As follows from this decision, horizontal cooperation as an exemption from the application of EU public procurement law is subject to the following cumulative conditions:

- Performance of a common public interest task relating to the pursuit of objectives in the public interest,
- solely by public authorities, without the participation of private party,
- on a contractual basis instead of an institutionalised legal form.[44]

On December 19, 2012, the Court of Justice decided on horizontal cooperation again following a preliminary ruling from the Consiglio di Stato (Italy).[45]

43. M. Burgi 'Anwendungsbereich und Governanceregeln der EU-Auftragsvergabereformrichtlinie: Bewertung und Umsetzungsbedarf' NZBau 2012, 604.
44. Case 480/06 Stadtreinigung Hamburg [2009] ECR I-4747 paragraphs 37, 38, 44-47.

The underlying main proceedings concerned the Italian Province of Lecce which had directly awarded a contract to the local university. The university was to carry out a study and evaluation of the seismic vulnerability of hospital structures. It received no other revenues than the actual reimbursement and re-allocation of costs. Pursuant to the contract, the university was entitled to avail itself of the services of third parties to perform the tasks assigned to it.[46]

In its decision on the Lecce case, the Court of Justice firstly acknowledged the cumulative criteria for horizontal cooperation posted in the decision on the Stadtreinigung Hamburg case. Against this background, the Court of Justice then denied the existence of an inter-municipal cooperation not subject to EU public procurement in the underlying main proceedings. The Court of Justice questions that a common public task relating to the pursuit of both the Province of Lecce and the university was to be fulfilled because the public task concerned only one of the public authorities involved, namely the Provincia, whilst the role of the university was limited to that of a vicarious agent. Additionally the Court of Justice stated that the university was placed in a position of advantage vis-à-vis the competitive associations of engineers and architects which could possibly also have produced the studies.[47]

With its decision on the Piepenbrock case, the Court of Justice recently commented on horizontal cooperation once again following a preliminary ruling from the Higher Regional Court of Düsseldorf (Germany) which refers the question to the Court of Justice whether an inter-municipal cooperation is to be accepted in case that a municipality awards a contract concerning a barely ancillary public interest task to another municipality that is to receive no other revenues than the reimbursement and re-allocation of actual costs.[48]

In concreto, the underlying main proceedings were about the German County of Düren assigning the task of cleaning offices, administrative and school buildings to the City of Düren. The County of Düren was the owner of the premises to be cleaned though these were located in the area of the City of Düren. Referred to the contract, the City of Düren was entitled to avail itself of the services of third parties to perform the tasks assigned to it. And, in fact,

45. Case 159/11 Lecce [2012] ECR I-0000.
46. Case 159/11 Lecce [2012] ECR I-0000, paragraphs 12-21.
47. Case 159/11 Lecce [2012] paragraphs 37-40.
48. Case 386/11 Piepenbrock [2013], commented by F. L. Hausmann/G. Queisner 'In-House Contracts and Inter-Municipal Cooperation – Exceptions from the European Union Procurement Law Should be Applied with Caution' EPPPL 2013, 231 ff.

the City of Düren planned to avail itself of the services of the Dürener Reinigungsgesellschaft mbH, a 100% subsidiary of the City of Düren.[49]

In its decision the Court of Justice initially outlined anew that, as a general principle, EU public procurement law applied to contracts between entities within the public sector and that the legal status of the City of Düren as a public authority did not by itself absolve the County of Düren from abiding to EU procurement law. Thereafter, the Court acknowledged – as in the Lecce decision – the criteria for horizontal cooperation developed in the Stadtreinigung Hamburg decision. Referring to the underlying main proceedings, the Court then ruled out the existence of an inter-municipal cooperation not subject to EU public procurement law. Barely aiding public interest tasks were no qualified object of horizontal cooperation as an exception of the application of EU public procurement rules. Plus, the Court of Justice focused on the entitlement of the City of Düren to avail itself of the services of third parties to perform its tasks. These third parties achieved competitive advantages vis-à-vis competitors thereby.[50]

A closer look at the new regulation will now show what significant influence the Court of Justice case law has had on it.

b. Legislation

Article 12 (4) regulates horizontal cooperation and lays down three criteria for horizontal cooperation that only partially tie with the case law of the Court of Justice. It is about the following criteria:

- The contract establishes or implements a cooperation between the participating contracting authorities with the aim of ensuring that public services they have to perform are provided with a view to achieving objectives they have in common.
- The implementation of the cooperation is governed solely by considerations relating to the public interest.
- The participating contracting authorities perform on the open market less than 20% of the activities concerned by the cooperation.

Since the original version of Article 12 (4) drew criticism, these criteria have been amended during the legislation process. Plus, further criteria provided for by the original proposal have been deleted without substitution.

49. Case 386/11 Piepenbrock [2013] ECR I-0000, paragraphs 9-25.
50. Case 386/11 Piepenbrock [2013] ECR I-0000, paragraphs 39-41.

Originally Article 12 (4) required not only any cooperation but a genuine cooperation between the participating contracting authorities. It meant that the cooperation had to involve mutual rights and obligations of all participating contracting authorities. An actual reciprocal cooperation, a work-sharing cooperation, was requested. It was insofar not sufficient if only one of the public authorities involved performed the assigned task and whether the other only compensated. According to the original proposal, these "conventional" contractual relations comprehending the bare exchange of service and money did not justify the privilege by the exemption from EU public procurement law. But in practice, exactly this is the case in point. Especially smaller federal states or municipalities which are not able to provide more than financial services would thus have been a priori excluded from the possibility of horizontal cooperation and been forced to invite to tender.[51] The possibility of horizontal cooperation would have been curtailed by the criterion of genuine cooperation; synergetic effects, economisation, and the provision for elementary requirements by municipalities would have been compromised.

Neither the criterion of genuine cooperation could be said to have been developed by the case law of the Court of Justice. The Court merely required that public authorities agree upon the performance of a common public interest task to the pursuit of objectives in the public interest.[52] Moreover, the Court put emphasis on the freedom of public authorities to choose the form of cooperation.[53] Therefore, it is to be welcomed that the final version finds mere cooperation sufficient and does not expect a genuine cooperation any longer.

As a further, now deleted criterion, the original proposal required that the contract did not involve financial transfers between the contracting authorities other than the reimbursement or re-allocation of funds for the works, services, or supplies concerned and that there be no private capital participation in any of the contracting authorities involved.

The wording of the initial criterion of no other financial transfers than the reimbursement or re-allocation of funds for the performance originated from the Stadtreinigung Hamburg decision. In this case, the cooperation contract in fact did not involve financial transfers other than these corresponding to the reimbursement or re-allocation of actual costs. The Court of Justice indeed

51. M. BURGI/F. KOCH 'In-House Procurement and Horizontal Cooperation Between Public Authorities' EPPPL 2012, 90.
52. Case 480/06 Stadtreinigung Hamburg [2009] ECR I-4747 paragraph 47.
53. Case 480/06 Stadtreinigung Hamburg [2009] ECR I-4747 paragraph 47.

qualified this as a case of horizontal cooperation.[54] However, it did not elevate the absence of other financial transfers to a discrete criterion – this was only one individual aspect brought up. The same applies for the Court of Justice decisions in the Lecce and Piepenbrock, issued after the Commission adopted its proposal and although the Court of Justice was definitely aware of the proposal. Additionally, the criterion was a further hindrance to horizontal cooperation.

So the original proposal made high demands on the acceptance of horizontal cooperation by laying down additional criteria. The freedom to "make or buy" was curtailed more than required by Court of Justice case law. In contrast, the Court of Justice has frequently put emphasis on the relevance of the freedom to "make or buy".[55] Against this background, the deletion of this criterion is reasonable. Taking account of the fact that horizontal cooperation as an exemption from the application of EU public procurement law is intensely linked to organisational structures of the Member States, this is all the more the case. The original proposal affected these organisational structures and thus came into conflict with primary law. Since the organisational structures are reserved the Member States, it was questionable whether the original provision was covered by EU competences.

For example Germany – as well as a significant number of other Member States – is federally and municipally organised, therefore comprises federal states and self-administrated municipalities. Altogether, there are about 30,000 autonomous administration units all of which are contracting authorities in terms of EU public procurement law and thus all are subject to EU public procurement law in case they do not fulfil the requirements for horizontal cooperation.[56] The relevance of horizontal cooperation for precisely Germany can also be seen by the fact that the decisions in Stadtreinigung Hamburg and Piepenbrock both concerned German municipalities. Otherwise, in Member States which are not federally or municipally organised, there are not as much autonomous administration units which are contracting authorities in terms of EU public procurement law. Therefore, cooperation

54. Case 480/06 Stadtreinigung Hamburg [2009] ECR I-4747 paragraph 49.
55. Case 480/06 Stadt Halle [2005] ECR I-1 paragraph 48; Case 324/07 Coditel [2008] ECR I-8457 paragraph 48; Case 215/09 Oulun kaupunki [2010] ECR I-13749 paragraph 31.
56. Stellungnahme Bundes-Arbeitsgemeinschaft der Kommunalen IT-Dienstleister e.V., in http://www.forum-vergabe.de/fileadmin/user_upload/Stellungnahmen zum Gr%C3%BCnbuch_2011/Vitako-Stellungnahme_2018-04-2011.pdf, last visited on September, 2013.

cannot only take place under the strict requirements for horizontal cooperation here. However, whether a Member State is federally and municipally organised or not, originates from its autonomous decision. Pursuant to Article 4(II)(1) TEU, the EU shall respect the national identities of the Member States, inherent in their fundamental structures, political and constitutional, inclusive of regional and local self-government. The initial proposal answered this precisely not by having subjected federally and municipally organised Member States to worse conditions.[57] It is to be stressed again that the deletion is reasonable.

The final version of the new directive still makes horizontal cooperation subject to the criterion of market performance less than 20%. Participating contracting authorities have to perform on the market less than 20% of the activities concerned by the cooperation. This criterion does not acknowledge Court of Justice jurisprudence on horizontal cooperation but is in accordance with the Court of Justice jurisprudence on vertical cooperation in the shape of the criterion of essentiality. However, the acceptance of a correspondent criterion for horizontal cooperation, too, is coherent. A market orientation of the participating contracting authorities and subsequent distortions of competition can thus be avoided. This is as much more as the requirement developed by the Court of Justice that private undertakings not be placed in a position of advantage vis-à-vis competitors was not adopted one-to-one. The existing criterion of market performance less than 20% prevents the betterment of public undertakings vis-à-vis competitors. Both other criteria still required in the final version of the directive originate from Court of Justice case law and are considered reasonable.

c. Critical remarks

After the deletion of the needless further criteria, Article 12 (4) is to be considered coherent. Whilst the originally proposed provision went beyond the case law of the Court of Justice, comprised new indefinite terms (such as the above-mentioned criterion of "genuine cooperation"), came into conflict with primary law, and would have led to transposition problems due to its interference with national organisational structures, the current version does not create excessive obstacles to horizontal cooperation and is covered by both Court of Justice case law and EU primary law.

57. See also M. Burgi '"In-House" Providing in Germany', in M. Comba/S. Treumer (eds.) The In-House Providing in European Law, European Procurement Law Series vol. 1, (Djøf Publishing, KopenhagenCopenhagen, 2010), 78 ff.

5. Conclusions

The codification of vertical as well as horizontal cooperation may indeed prevent legal uncertainty and different interpretations of the case law of the Court of Justice. However, not only the most circumstantial codification will be able to eliminate every demarcation problem. Included indefinite legal terms (as for example "public interest") lead to new interpretation problems. Then again, the case law of the Court of Justice is established and broadly accepted (what intrinsically contributes legal certainty), even though detailed and necessarily case-by-case based (so that it is questionable whether a generalised codification really is realisable). Nevertheless, the Commission stated a broad acceptance pro codification in the Green paper.[58]

As regards vertical cooperation, it can be noted on the positive side that the final version of the directive has moved away from the including the criterion of "absent market orientation" for joint in-house. The same goes for horizontal cooperation, here again it is to be welcomed that the two additional criteria for horizontal cooperation that had been provided in the original proposal, namely the criterion of no other financial transfers than the reimbursement or re-allocation of actual costs as well as the criterion of the entire absence of any private capital involved in the participating contracting authorities, have been deleted without substitution, and moreover, that the regulation no longer requires a genuine cooperation but finds a mere cooperation sufficient. Most points of criticism regarding the proposed provision have thus been omitted from the provisions now in force.

Bibliography

Burgi, Martin, 'Anwendungsbereich und Governanceregeln der EU-Auftragsvergabereformrichtlinie: Bewertung und Umsetzungsbedarf' (2012) NZBau 601.

Burgi, Martin/Koch, Frauke, 'In-House Procurement and Horizontal Cooperation between Public Authorities' (2012) EPPPL 86.

58. COM (2011) 896 final, 36; European Commission, 'Green Paper on the modernisation of EU public procurement policy, Towards a more efficient European Procurement Market, Synthesis of replies', in http://ec.europa.eu/internal_market/consultations/docs/2011/public_procurement/synthesis_document_en.pdf, last visited on September, 2013.

Burgi, Martin, 'Die Förderung sozialer und technischer Innovationen durch das Vergaberecht' (2011) NZBau 577.

Burgi, Martin, '"In-House" Providing in Germany', in: Comba, Mario/Treumer, Steen (eds.), The In-House Providing in European Law, European Procurement Law Series vol. 1 (DJØF Publishing 2010).

Caranta, Roberto, 'The In-House Providing: The Law as It Stands in the EU', in: Comba, Mario/Treumer, Steen (eds.), The In-House Providing in European Law, European Procurement Law Series vol. 1 (DJØF Publishing 2010).

Fruhmann, Michael, 'Die neue Ausnahme für öffentlich-öffentliche Vergaben gemäß der Allgemeinen Ausrichtung des Rates', in: Prieß, Hans-Joachim/Lau, Niels/Kratzenberg, Rüdiger (eds.), Wettbewerb – Transparenz – Gleichbehandlung, Festschrift für Fridhelm Marx, 15 Jahre GWB (C.H. Beck 2013).

Gruneberg, Ralf/Wilden, Anke, 'Höhere Hürden für In-House-Geschäfte – Verschärfung des Wesentlichkeitskriteriums' (2012) VergabeR 149.

Hausmann, Friedrich Ludwig/Queisner, Georg, 'In-House Contracts and Inter-Municipal Cooperation – Exceptions from the European Union Procurement Law Should be Applied with Caution' (2013) EPPPL 231.

Marx, Fridhelm, 'Zur Neuregelung der „Wesentlichkeitsschwelle" für Inhouse-Geschäfte: If it ain't broke, don't fix it!' 2012 NZBau Heft 10, V.

Mestwerdt, Thomas/Sauer, Dirk, 'Institutionalisierte Kooperationen öffentlicher Auftraggeber als kodifizierter Ausnahmetatbestand im Unionsvergaberecht', in: Prieß, Hans-Joachim/Lau, Niels/Kratzenberg, Rüdiger (eds.), Wettbewerb – Transparenz – Gleichbehandlung, Festschrift für Fridhelm Marx, 15 Jahre GWB (C.H. Beck, 2013).

Schleissing, Philipp, Möglichkeiten und Grenzen vergaberechtlicher In-House-Geschäfte (Nomos Verlag 2012).

Schmidt, Thorsten Ingo, Kommunale Kooperation (Mohr Siebeck, 2005).

Söbbeke, Markus, 'In-house quo vadis?' (2006) DÖV 996.

Wiedner, Klaus/Spiegel, Nico, 'Europäische Vergaberichtlinien: Die nächste Generation', in: Prieß, Hans-Joachim/Lau, Niels/Kratzenberg, Rüdiger (eds.), Wettbewerb – Transparenz – Gleichbehandlung, Festschrift für Fridhelm Marx, 15 Jahre GWB (C.H. Beck, 2013).

Mapping the margins of EU public contracts law: covered, mixed, excluded and special contracts

Roberto Caranta

1. Introduction

In the past very few years the Court of Justice had to deal with a number of cases focusing on whether the arrangements at issue were to be classified as a procurement contract to which EU law does apply or not. Directive 2014/24/EU has provided further elements on the definition of 'public procurement contract' which go someway towards clarifying the scope of application of EU secondary law. Concerning instead mixed contracts having a procurement competent Directive 2014/24/EU has introduced a specific provision consolidating the case law which however leaves the door open to some doubts.

The positive definition of what a procurement contract is goes hand in hand with a list of excluded contracts, and especially excluded service contracts, which has been much tinkered with by Directive 2014/24/EU. Finally, while apparently doing away with the distinction between priority and non-priority services, the new Public sector directive has introduced a special 'light' regime for social and other specific service contracts.[1]

1. See also C.H. Bovis 'Highlights of the EU Procurement Reforms: The New Directive on Concessions' in Eur. Publ. Priv. Partnership Law Rev., 2014, 1.

2. The definition of public procurement contracts

Article 2 of Directive 2004/18/EC defines 'public contracts' as "contracts for pecuniary interest concluded in writing between one or more economic operators and one or more contracting authorities and having as their object the execution of works, the supply of products or the provision of services". 'Concessions' were defined along the same lines with the difference that the consideration for the works to be carried out or the services to be provided consists either solely in the right to exploit the work or service or in this right together with payment.[2]

The actual meaning of the provision was litigated in a number of cases. Helmut Müller concerned a somewhat complex arrangement.[3] The German federal agency responsible for managing public property (Bundesanstalt) put for sale some land which the purchaser was to develop in conformity with the urban-planning objectives of the competent local authority. The buyer was chosen by the federal agency in agreement with the municipality and the choice was challenged on the ground that public procurement rules had not been followed. The Court of Justice remarked first of all that the sale by a public authority of undeveloped land or land which has already been built upon does not constitute a public works contract within the meaning of Article 1(2)(b) of Directive 2004/18/EC. Indeed, such a contract requires that the public authority assume the "position of purchaser and not seller".[4]

Concerning instead the relationship between the public authority with town-planning powers and the purchaser of the land the Court of Justice held that the directive covers contracts for pecuniary interest and "does not refer to other types of activities for which public authorities are responsible".[5] This means that the contracting authority which has concluded a public contract – or members of the public in the pursuance of whose interests the contracting authority has acted[6] – "receives a service pursuant to that contract in return for consideration".[7] The exercise of urban-planning powers, however, has not

2. See R. Noguellou 'Scope and Coverage of the EU Procurement Directives' in M. Trybys, R. Caranta, G. Edelstam (eds) EU Public Contract Law. Public Procurement and Beyond (Bruxelles, Bruylant, 2014) 24 f.
3. Case C-451/08 Helmut Müller [2010] ECR I2673, see P. Eleftheriadis 'Planning Agreement as Procurement Contracts under the EU Procurement Rules'. Public Procurement L. Rev, 2011, 43.
4. Paragraph 41.
5. Paragraph 46.
6. Paragraph 49.
7. Paragraph 48.

the purpose of obtaining a contractual service.[8] Moreover, the mere fact that a public authority, in the exercise of its urban-planning powers, examines certain building plans presented to it, or takes a decision applying its powers in that sphere, does not satisfy the obligation that there be 'requirements specified by the contracting authority', within the meaning of Article 1(2)(b) of Directive 2004/18/EC laying down the definition of public works.[9]

In the more recent Libert case the applicable Flemish legislation laid down on developers an obligation to build some social housing units in the framework of land development projects. The Court of Justice held that the obligation referred to the placement of the said units on the market rather than to the building of public works and consequently ruled out the applicability of Directive 2004/18/EC.[10]

Reasonably enough the Commission took the opportunity provided by the reform process to try and clarify the scope of application of EU public contract law. At the same time, the decision to have a directive on concessions narrowed the scope of what has become Directive 2014/24/EU down to 'procurement'. Directive 2004/18/EC instead regulated the award of 'public contracts', including works concessions (but not service concessions).[11]

In this vein Recital 4 of 2014/24/EU indicates that "The increasingly diverse forms of public action have made it necessary to define more clearly the notion of procurement itself". The new provisions are however not intended to go beyond a clarification and, as such, they should "not broaden the scope of this Directive compared to that of Directive 2004/18/EC".

Accordingly, Article 1(2) of the Directive has introduced a new definition:

> Procurement within the meaning of this Directive is the acquisition by means of a public contract of works, supplies or services by one or more contracting authorities from economic operators chosen by those contracting authorities, whether or not the works, supplies or services are intended for a public purpose.[12]

8. Paragraph 57.
9. Paragraph 68.
10. Joined Cases C-197/11 and C-203/11 Libert [2013] ECR I0000, paragraph 114; the facts of the case had however been insufficiently clarified by the referring court.
11. See R. Noguellou 'Scope and Coverage of the EU Procurement Directives' above fn 2, 30 ff; see also S.E. Pommer 'Public Private Partneships' M. Trybys, R. Caranta, G. Edelstam (eds) EU Public Contract Law. Public Procurement and Beyond above fn 2, 300 ff.
12. The Commission's proposal had 'purchase' in the place of 'acquisition', which was in the end rightly preferred.

The definition of procurement brings an additional requirement – 'acquisition' – to the definition of public contract brought about by Article 2(5). This means that, in line with Loutraki and Müller, the mere sale of a public property falls outside the scope of the Public Sector Directive.[13] EU State aids rules might instead be relevant.[14]

One could of course challenge the wisdom of having two definitions rather that a comprehensive one. Indeed Article 2(5) reiterates the traditional and already recalled definition of 'public contracts' as "contracts for pecuniary interest concluded in writing between one or more economic operators and one or more contracting authorities [...]". Article 2(6) to (9) provide the definitions of 'public works contracts', 'works', 'public supply contracts', 'public service contracts'. These are mostly in line with the definitions provided in Directive 2004/18/EC, even if the terminology is somewhat different.[15]

The last part of Article 1(2) Directive 2014/24/EU is meant to dispel some doubts which had arisen in Germany as to whether some form of ownership transfer or direct economic benefit accruing to the contracting authority as an effect of the contract was required by the definition of public procurements: it is not.[16]

The notion of procurement contract is further clarified by Recital 4

> The Union rules on public procurement are not intended to cover all forms of disbursement of public money, but only those aimed at the acquisition of works, supplies or services for consideration by means of a public contract [...]. The notion of acquisition should be understood broadly in the sense of obtaining the benefits of the works, supplies or services in question, not necessarily requiring a transfer of ownership to the contracting authorities.

13. Joined Cases C145/08 and C149/08, Club Hotel Loutraki [2010] ECR I-4165; Case C-451/08 Helmut Müller [2010] ECR I2673.
14. Commission Communication on State aid elements in sales of land and buildings by public authorities (OJ 1997 C 209, p. 3).
15. It is to be noted that the specificity of the notion of 'procurement' as compared to the more general notion of 'contract' is lost in many linguistic version, like the Spanish one, which do not have a correspondingly specific word; on the different types of procurement see R. Noguellou 'Scope and Coverage of the EU Procurement Directives' above fn 2, 28 ff.
16. See the questions referred to the Court of Justice in Müller; the Court muddled up the issue holding that the contract "must be of direct economic benefit to the contracting authority": Case C-451/08 Helmut Müller [2010] ECR I2673, paragraph 49; see the discussion in R. Caranta 'General Report' in U. Neergaard, C. Jacqueson, G.S. Ølykke (eds.) Public Procurement Law: Limitations, Opportunities and Paradoxes. The XXVI FIDE Congress in Copenhagen 2014 (Copenhagen, DJØF, 2014) Vol. 3, 95 ff, and works referred therein.

Direct economic benefit to the contracting authority is therefore not a requirement for a procurement contract and Müller is no more good law under this respect (if it ever was, which I doubt).[17]

The new definition may help to bring some consistency in the case law. Helmut Müller may indeed be distinguished from the Auroux and Ordine degli Architetti delle Province di Milano e Lodi.[18] In the latter case, the beneficiary of a building permission had undertaken to build a work according to the specifications given by the contracting authority in lieu of paying duties due to the same contracting authority. This was therefore building licence coupled with works procurement.[19] The agreement relevant in Auroux provided the development of a leisure centre in successive phases, consisting inter alia in the construction of a multiplex cinema and commercial premises intended to be transferred to third parties and works intended to be transferred to the contracting authority (car park as well as access roads and public spaces). The Court of Justice regarded the construction of the leisure centre as a whole as corresponding to the requirements specified by the municipality.[20] While it could be disputed that buildings to be sold to third parties do amount to 'public works', some of the works envisaged clearly were public, and anyway it was provided that all areas and buildings not sold at a given date had to be transferred to the municipality. Here we have urban planning and decisions to develop (or re-develop) urban areas plus public works.[21]

Libert remains somewhat problematic. Basically developers were 'forced' to deliver affordable homes thus implementing a policy in the general interest designed by the public authority granting the building permission. It is however true that the authority did not provide any consideration, not even in the form of a discount on the duties the developer is to pay, as instead it was the case in Ordine degli Architetti delle Province di Milano e Lodi so that the pecuniary interest was probably lacking.[22]

17. Case C-451/08 Helmut Müller [2010] ECR I2673, paragraphs 48 ff.
18. Case C220/05 Auroux and Others [2007] ECR I385; Case C-399/98 Ordine degli Architetti and Others [2001] ECR I5409.
19. See also the analysis in Case C-451/08 Helmut Müller [2010] ECR I2673, paragraphs 50 ff.
20. Paragraph 42.
21. See also the analysis in Case C-451/08 Helmut Müller [2010] ECR I2673, paragraphs 52 ff.
22. Case C-399/98 Ordine degli Architetti and Others [2001] ECR I5409; this would have also distinguished Libert from Case C-576/10 Commission v the Netherlands [2013] ECR I-, where however the Court did not go into the qualification of the arrangement at issue.

What is still hard to reconcile with the case law and with the new definition is a Court of Justice judgment in an infringement procedure brought against Spain because of the conclusion of development agreements in the Valencia region.[23] The activities entrusted to the developer included the preparation of the development plan, the proposal and management of the corresponding land consolidation project, obtaining for the administration free of charge plots for public ownership and for the community's public land bank, management of the legal conversion of the plots concerned or even the equitable division of the costs and profits between the parties concerned as well as the transactions for financing and guaranteeing the cost of the investments, works, installations and compensation necessary for the execution of the project; the developer might also have been tasked to organise the public competition for the appointment of the building contractor to which the execution of the urban development works was to be entrusted. According to the Court of Justice, the Commission failed to demonstrate that the public works which are indeed among of the activities committed to the developer constituted the "main object of the contract".[24]

In this perspective it is however hard to believe that building a theatre shell was the main object of the contract concluded by the Municipality of Milan and challenged in Ordine degli Architetti delle Province di Milano e Lodi either. The Court of Justice is referring here albeit in an truncated way to the mixed contract doctrine which will be analysed in the next paragraph, all the way forgetting about the severability requirement which is an essential aspect that doctrine.

Unfortunately the use of 'acquisition' still leaves some uncertainty as to the extent of the definition. The problem is that contracting authorities at times buy for themselves, so to speak, other times they procure to the benefit of the general public or of section thereof for whose well-being they are responsible. The latter is the case with many procurement contracts (and concessions) and this is especially the case with service contracts. Just think of social service contracts.[25]

23. Case C-306/08 Commission v Spain [2011] ECR I-4541.
24. Paragraph 96; see also J.M. Gimeno Feliú – P. Valcárcel Fernández 'Spain' in U. Neergaard, C. Jacqueson, G.S. Ølykke (eds.) Public Procurement Law: Limitations, Opportunities and Paradoxes above fn 16, 713.
25. See also A. Tokár 'Institutional Report' in U. Neergaard, C. Jacqueson, G.S. Ølykke (eds.) Public Procurement Law: Limitations, Opportunities and Paradoxes above fn 16, 182 f.

Recital 4 also makes it clear that two more contract types will not normally be considered as procurement contracts, that is the contracts whose subject matter is the mere financing, in particular through grants, of an activity, and contracts concluded with all operators fulfilling certain conditions which are thus entitled to perform a given task, without any selectivity (such as for instance customer choice and service voucher systems). Voucher systems must be open, meaning that every economic operator having the required qualification may easily and at every time become part of the systems. Otherwise the rules on framework agreements should be used by analogy.[26]

The latter type of arrangements may be treated as 'simple authorisation schemes'. The same is also true – according to the more recent case law – with licences for horse-race betting operations.[27] Selectivity might however be the case in some of these schemes, without necessarily implying the application of public procurement rules in the absence of any 'acquisition' on the part of the contracting authority. Directive 2006/123/EC on services in the internal market might rather be the applicable law to the granting of some licences or authorisations.[28]

It is questionable whether this links with the public procurement case law based on Article 51 TFEU. Under this provision the rules relating to the freedom of establishment and the freedom to provide services do not extend to activities which in a Member State are connected, even occasionally, with the exercise of official authority. As a consequence, according to this case law, such activities are also excluded from the scope of public procurement directives which are designed to implement the provisions of the Treaty relating to the freedom of establishment and the freedom to provide services.[29]

On the on hand, the distinction between contracts and authoritative measures does not always run according to substantive requirements, the Court of Justice being happy with the form chosen by the Member State.[30]

26. R. Caranta 'General Report' above fn 16, 115 f.
27. Case C-203/08 Sporting Exchange [2010] ECR I-4695; Case C470/11 Garkalns SIA [2012] ECR I-; see the discussion in G.S. Ølykke 'Is the granting of special and exclusive rights subject to the principles applicable to the award of concessions? Recent development in the case law and their implication for one of the last sanctuaries for protectionism' Public Procurement L. Rev. 2013, 8 f.
28. On the directive see the contribution collected by U. Neergaard, R. Nielsen, L.M. Roseberry (eds) The Services Directive (Copenhagen, DJØF, 2008) 65; see also C. Barnard 'Unravelling the Services Directive' Common Market L. Rev. 2008, 323.
29. Case C-160/08 Commission v Germany [2010] ECR I-3713, paragraphs 73 f.
30. For discussion and references please refer to R. Caranta 'General Report' above fn 16, 87 ff.

On the other hand, when assessing whether official authority has been exercised, the Court may be very demanding.[31]

The need to distinguish contracts from unilateral administrative decisions leads us to the question of the possible legal means for entrusting the provision of services of general interest – SGIs and especially of services of general economic interest – SGEIs.

Article 1(4) and (5) of Directive 2014/24/EU are relevant here. According to Article 1(4) the provisions in the directive do not affect the freedom of the Member States to

> define, in conformity with Union law, what they consider to be services of general economic interest, how those services should be organised and financed, in compliance with the State aid rules, and what specific obligations they should be subject to. Equally, this Directive does not affect the decision of public authorities whether, how and to what extent they wish to perform public functions themselves pursuant to Article 14 TFEU and Protocol No 26.[32]

The reference to State aid rules is of great relevance since the legal act entrusting a SGEI may "take the form of a legislative or regulatory instrument or a contract".[33]

This is confirmed by Recital 5 which reassures Member States that nothing in the directive obliges them to contract out or externalise the provision of services that they wish to provide themselves or to organise by means other than public contracts; more specifically, the provision of services based on laws, regulations or employment contracts is not covered.[34]

31. See again Case C-160/08 Commission v Germany [2010] ECR I-3713, paragraphs 73 f.
32. See also Recital 7.
33. Communication from the Commission On the application of the European Union State aid rules to compensation granted for the provision of SGEI (2012/C 8/02), point 33; see more generally U. Neergaard 'Services of General (Economic) Interest and the Services Directive' in U. Neergaard, R. Nielsen, L.M. Roseberry (eds) The Services Directive above fn 28, 84 ff; G.S. Ølykke 'The definition of a 'Contract' Under Article 106 TFEU' in E. Szyszczak et al. (eds) Developments in Services of General Interest (The Hague, T.M.C. Asser Press, 2011), spec. 113 ff; N. Fiedziuk 'Putting Services of General Economic Interest up for Tender: Reflection on Applicable EU Rules' Common Market L. Rev. 2013, 99 f.
34. See also Recital 6.

A good procurement related instance for this is the Irish ambulances case.[35] The Eastern Regional Health Authority had directly entrusted the Dublin City Council to provide emergency ambulance services without putting up for tender the services in question. The Court of Justice noted that under the applicable domestic legislation both the Authority and the Council had the power to carry out emergency ambulance services. The Court therefore dismissed the action of the Commission holding it "conceivable that Council provides such services to the public in the exercise of its own powers derived directly from statute, and applying its own funds, although it is paid a contribution by the Authority for that purpose, covering part of the costs of those services".[36]

The European law maker has therefore left the rules on the entrustment of SGEIs the way they were restated in the Alumnia package (which is regrettable since this leaves a number of questions open).[37] This is confirmed by Article 12 of Directive 2014/24/EU which has affirmed the exclusion for contracts awarded on the basis of an exclusive right consistent with EU rules which was before provided for in Article 18 of Directive 2004/18/EC.

3. Mixed contracts

The Court of Justice refined its doctrine of mixed contracts in the Loutraki case.[38] At the roots of that case stood a decision by the Greek government to privatize a casino. The foreseen contract was a mixed contract including: a) an agreement under which the State would sell 49% of the shares in the company managing the casino to a 'single purpose limited company' (AEAS) to be set up by the successful tenderer; b) an agreement under which the AEAS would undertake to implement a development plan comprising the refurbishment of the casino and of two adjoining hotel units; c) an agreement under which AEAS would take over management of the casino business, in return

35. Case C532/03 Commission v Ireland [2007] ECR I11353; A. Brown ''The Commission Loses another Action against Ireland Owing to Lack of Evidence: A Note on Case C-532/03 Commission v Ireland' Public Procurement L. Rev. 2008 NA92.
36. Paragraph 35.
37. Please refer to R. Caranta 'General Report' above fn, 147 ff, and works referred therein.
38. Joined Cases C145/08 and C149/08, Club Hotel Loutraki [2010] ECR I-4165; an earlier case was Case C331/92 Gestión Hotelera Internacional [1994] ECR I1329, paragraphs 23 to 29.

for payment, having as its remuneration a percentage of the annual operating profits, and d) a provision to compensate AEAS in the event that another casino were to be lawfully established in the same geographical area during the period of validity of the contract (10 years). Concurring with the findings of the referring court, the Court of Justice concluded that the transaction at issue was a mixed contract comprising a sale of shares aspect, services (managing the casino) and works (refurbishment and development).[39] The Court held that basically the same rules apply to the legal classification of mixed contracts, irrespective of whether or not the aspect constituting the main object of a mixed contract falls within the scope of the directives on public contracts. According to the Court,

> in the case of a mixed contract, the different aspects of which are, in accordance with the contract notice, inseparably linked and thus form an indivisible whole, the transaction at issue must be examined as a whole for the purposes of its legal classification and must be assessed on the basis of the rules which govern the aspect which constitutes the main object or predominant feature of the contract.[40]

Having considered the transaction at issue as an inseparable whole,[41] the Court found the privatisation aspect to be the prevailing one, with the works and services being ancillary to the main object. As such, the contract could not be held to fall within the scope of the directives on public contracts.[42]

39. Paragraphs 46 f.
40. Paragraph 48; Case C3/88 Commission v Italy [1989] ECR 4035, paragraph 19; Case C331/92 Gestión Hotelera Internacional [1994] ECR I1329, paragraphs 23 to 26; Case C220/05 Auroux and Others [2007] ECR I385, paragraphs 36 and 37; Case C412/04 Commission v Italy [2008] ECR I619, paragraph 47; and Case C536/07 Commission v Germany [2009] ECR I10355, paragraphs 28, 29, 57 and 61, are referred to.
41. Paragraphs 51 ff; one could argue that the severability test was already present in the case law: Case C411/00 Felix Swoboda [2002] ECR I10567, paragraph 57, referred to contracting authorities artificially grouping in one contract services of different type: A. Tokár 'Institutional Report' above fn 25, 189.
42. Paragraphs 55 ff; the Court also refers to the Green Paper on public-private partnerships and Community law on public contracts and concessions (COM(2004) 327 final), where the Commission points out that it is necessary to ensure that privatisation does not in reality conceal the award to a private partner of contracts which might be termed public contracts or concessions (which is held not to be the case). As already recalled, the 'main object' criterion only was used in Case C-306/08 Commission v Spain [2011] ECR I-4541.

Another mixed contract case was Mehiläinen Oy.[43] Oulu City Council decided to set up a joint venture with a private partner to provide occupational health care and welfare services. The two partners intended activities to be chiefly and increasingly focused on private clients. However, for a transitional period of four years, they undertook to purchase from the joint venture the health services they were required to provide for their staff. The Court of justice again held that

> as regards a mixed contract, the different aspects of which are inseparably linked and thus form an indivisible whole, that contract must be examined as a whole for the purposes of its legal classification in the light of the rules on public contracts, and must be assessed on the basis of the rules which govern the aspect which constitutes the main object or predominant feature of the contract.[44]

Differently from Loutraki, this case turned on the severability of the different transactions involved in the agreement. In that context, the transitional arrangement was intended as a parting gift to the new venture. According to the Court of Justice, however, this did not mean that the services envisaged for the transitional period were not severable. Quite on the contrary, they could and should have been awarded through a procurement procedure.[45]

The Loutraki case law seems to have been codified in Article 3 of Directive 2014/24/EU. The provision bears the title of 'Mixed procurement'. 'Procurement' should in principle be understood as an 'acquisition' contract according to definition given in Article 1(2). If this is so, the provision will not be applicable to the Loutraki type of circumstances, in which the (main) object of the contract was a sale or privatisation of assets. In no way a sale can be seen as 'acquiring'. Of course this would deprive the provision of much of its potential usefulness. It is true that Recitals 11 and following rather refer to 'mixed contracts' than to 'mixed procurements' and it would be easier to proceed on the assumption that indeed the scope of Article 3 is correspondingly wider. The problem is that the French, German, Italian, and Spanish versions all have the same word both in the recitals and in the text of the directive (marché, Auftrag, appalti, contrato).

It seems therefore sensible to proceed on the basis of the assumption that Article 3 is indeed about mixed procurements, but it lays down rules which

43. Case C215/09 Mehiläinen Oy [2010] ECR I-13749.
44. Paragraph 36; Joined Cases C145/08 and C149/08, Club Hotel Loutraki [2010] ECR I-4165, paragraphs 48 and 49 are referred to.
45. Paragraphs 37 ff.

are applicable more generally to all mixed contract since they do correspond to the general principles laid down in the case law of the Court of Justice. In the end that the situation is still very much as it was before Loutraki.[46]

Article 3(2) is dedicated to mixed procurements in the traditional sense of mixes of works, supplies, and services. These contracts were already regulated in Directive 2004/18/EC whose provisions are basically repeated with the adjustements necessary after social and special services have taken the place of non-priority services.[47]

Concerning other mixed contracts Article 3(3) introduces a different regime according to whether the different parts of a given contract are objectively separable or not. This implies that contracting authorities are now expressly empowered to shape complex contractual arrangements provided that this does not translate in bringing the resulting contract outside the scope of application of the Public Sector Directive.

According to Recital 11, it should be clarified "how contracting authorities should determine whether the different parts are separable or not. Such clarification should be based on the relevant case-law of the Court of Justice". However the provisions of Directive 2014/24/EU do not provide any indication as to how to determine when the parts of a contract are objectively separable, and therefore we need to refer back to Recital 11. According to this recital, the determination should be carried out on a case-by-case basis; expressed or presumed intentions of the contracting authority to regard the various aspects making up a mixed contract as indivisible should not be sufficient, but

> should be supported by objective evidence capable of justifying them and of establishing the need to conclude a single contract. Such a justified need to conclude a single contract could for instance be present in the case of the construction of one single building, a part of which is to be used directly by the contracting authority concerned and another part to be operated on a concessions basis, for instance to provide parking facilities to the public.

Moreover, according to Recital 11, "It should be clarified that the need to conclude a single contract may be due to reasons both of a technical nature and of an economic nature". This might at first seem to recall the definition of 'work' to be found in Article 2(1)(7) which refers to 'an economic or tech-

46. See also the discussion of a number of mixed contracts which did not reach the Court of Justice in R. Caranta 'General Report' above fn 16, 119 ff, and the cases referred therein.
47. See below under § 5.

nical function'. A previous enactment of this provision was clarified by the Court of Justice in an infringement procedure brought against France.[48] The Court very much insisted on the idea of one and the same function.[49]

The reference to the 'nature' of the reasons to be found in Recital 11 seems however to go beyond the idea of 'function'. Moreover, the idea of 'function' may be appropriate for works, but we are dealing here with mixed contracts whose subject matter may be quite complex, including works and services, procurement and concessions, and so on. Reasons of economic nature alone may keep this contract together. It is submitted that even a parting gift as the one relevant in Mehiläinen Oy might easily make economic sense in making the business unit up for sale more attractive; therefore that case might have been decided differently.[50]

Even when a contract is objectively separable the special rules laid down in Article 16 apply in case of contracts having a defence or security-related component. These rules give contracting authorities a fairly large discretion in preferring the specific regime for defence and security procurement.[51] In case of mixed contracts having a utilities component, Articles 5 and 6 of Directive 2014/25/EU will apply. More specifically, under Article 5, the utilities directive will be the applicable law; if, however, the components of the contract concern different activities, the choice between awarding a single contract or awarding a number of separate contracts shall not be made with the objective of excluding the contract or contracts in question from the scope of application of any of the new directives (Article 6(1)).

If the different parts of a given contract are objectively separable the appropriate regime will be applicable to the components awarded as distinct contracts. Contracting authorities are however allowed to choose to award a single contract. In this case, under Article 3(4), Directive 2014/14/EU will be applicable quite independently from "the value of the parts that would otherwise fall under a different legal regime". If a mixed contract has a concession component (and therefore, by the way, it is not a mixed procurement, but a mixed contract), Directive 2014/24/EU will however be applicable only is so far the estimated value of the procurement part of the contract is equal to or greater than the relevant threshold.

Provided that the mixes of procurement and utilities, procurement and defence and security, and procurement and concession have all been specifical-

48. Case C-16/98 Commission / France [2000] ECR I-8315.
49. See paragraph 38.
50. Case C215/09 Mehiläinen Oy [2010] ECR I-13749.
51. See also Recital 13.

ly addressed, it is not easy to understand which other mixes should fall under the general rule of Article 3(4)? The answer is probably contracts mixing a procurement component with some excluded contracts different from those referred to in Articles 7 and 16, such as for instance covered and excluded legal or ambulance services.

Even so it is difficult to understand why, differently from the case of a mix of procurement and concession, here Directive 2014/24/EU should be applicable whatever the value of the procurement component. Besides the obvious consequence that this will lead contracting authorities to always separate the components of this contracts, this goes well beyond the legislative concern not to see the rules of the directive circumventing by adding other components to the procurement part.[52] In the text that was circulated in July 2013 the "mix with concession" case was introduced with the word 'thus' and was therefore just an instance of the more general rule on mixed procurements.[53] Today it seems rather an exception, which does not make much sense.

This said, basically the special utilities and defence and security regimes takes precedence over Directive 2014/24/EU, which however takes precedence over the concession directive and in case of mixed contract which includes components which are not regulated by EU public contracts law. This of course unless either the contracts are separated or can not objectively be separated.

If the latter is the case Article 3(6) provides that "the applicable legal regime shall be determined on the basis of the main subject-matter of that contract". This will be mainly relevant in case of objectively non-separable mixed procurement and concession contract or mixed covered and excluded procurement. When the non-covered procurement part of the contract turns out to be the main subject-matter of the contract, the rule providing for the prevalence of Directive 2014/24/EU will not apply, and either Directive

52. Recital 12.

53. "Where contracting authorities choose to award a single contract, this Directive shall, unless otherwise provided in Article 14a, apply to the ensuing mixed contract, irrespective of the value of the parts that would otherwise fall under a different legal regime and irrespective of which legal regime these parts would otherwise have been subject to.

Thus, in the case of mixed contracts containing elements of supply, works and service contracts and of concessions, the mixed contract shall be awarded in accordance with the provisions of this Directive, provided that the estimated value of the part of the contract which constitutes a contract covered by this Directive, calculated in accordance with the provisions of Article 5, is equal to or greater than the relevant threshold set out in Article 4".

2014/25/EU or the general principles of the TFEU will (on the assumption that the latter are applicable to excluded contract having certain cross-border interest as well, provided of course that these contracts are not regulated under different Treaty provisions, as it is the case with employment contracts).[54]

It is to be noted that unlike Article 3(2), Article 3(6) does not refer to the value, the main subject-matter of the contract having to be defined on the basis of both quantitative and qualitative parameters.

This might be for instance the case with legal assistance contracts covering both excluded and covered (albeit as special) services. Keeping all aspects of legal assistance in one contract makes technical and possibly economic sense, and the regime applicable will depend on which is the main subject-matter of the contract. One could opine that judicial representation is more relevant that simple advice unrelated to legal representation; indeed the former only requires a special qualification in many jurisdictions. Mixed ambulance services contracts, which will be discussed later, might also fall under Article 3(6) of Directive 2014/24/EU.

There is no reason why the very general provision laid down in Article 3(6) should not also apply by analogy to situations in which, as it was the case in Club Hotel Loutraki, one part of the contract, and possibly the most relevant part, does not fall under any EU public contract regime in the sense they are neither procurements (in either the public or the utilities or the defence and security sectors) nor concessions. This might be very relevant in situations in which the contracting authority is pursuing what were once called 'secondary objectives', and especially social ones, like in the case of works procurements passed to provide training and jobs to long-term unemployed.[55]

54. R. Caranta 'General Report' above fn 16, 124 f.

55. Please refer to R. Caranta 'Sustainable Procurement' in M. Trybys, R. Caranta, G. Edelstam (eds) EU Public Contract Law. Public Procurement and Beyond above fn 16, 170 f.

4. Excluded procurement contracts

The Classic Sector Directive traditionally couples a fairly wide definition of the contracts covered with a number of exclusions. Exclusions have to a considerable extent been reviewed by Directive 2014/24/EU.[56]

Articles 7 and 8 reiterate the customary exclusions for the contracts now covered under Directive 2014/25/EU and for those permitting the contracting authorities to provide or exploit public communications networks or to provide to the public one or more electronic communications services.

Article 9 covers what are now called public contracts awarded and design contests organised pursuant to international rules, with the exclusion of those involving defence or security aspects which are instead regulated under Article 17. The provision has been reworded and modified as compared to Article 15 of Directive 2004/18/EC. More specifically, the exclusion related to international agreement relating to the stationing of troops and concerning the undertakings of a Member State or a third country has been deleted. Moreover, the exclusion by reason of the application of the rules of international organisations has been much specified in Article 9(2) for the case the contracting authority is granted some aid by international organisations or financial institutions. The directive shall not apply to contracts fully financed by international organisations and financial institutions; in case the grant covers most of the costs, the parties will have to agree on applicable procurement procedures. By implication, if the grant covers less than half of the cost, EU law will be fully applicable.

As already recalled, the exclusion for contracts awarded on the basis of an exclusive right once provided for in Article 18 of Directive 2004/18/EC has been confirmed by Article 12 of Directive 2014/24/EU.

Articles 15 to 17 now deal with defence and security contracts, including mixed contracts having some defence and security part. The new provisions go well beyond what was Article 14 of Directive 2004/18/EC and take stock of the rules enacted in the meantime with Directive 2009/81/EC. So much so that they no more are branded as 'exclusions' but as rules pertaining to special situations.[57]

56. The older provisions have been analysed by R. Noguellou 'Scope and Coverage of the EU Procurement Directives' above fn 2, 27 f; the Commission's proposal was much closer to the older text.
57. See the detailed analysis by M. Trybus Buying Defence and Security in Europe: The EU Defence and Security Procurement Directive in Context (Cambridge, Cambridge University Press, 2014 forthcoming) Chapter 6.

While Article 17 of Directive 2004/18/EC expressly excluded service concessions from its coverage, the new public sector directive does not have any corresponding provision. True all concessions are now covered by Directive 2014/25/EU, and cases of conflicts are addressed in Article 3, which was already discussed. However recalling that directive in a specific exclusion as it was done with reference to both the utilities and defence and security ones would have made for a tidier system (and possibly further but marginally enraged those claiming that the directive is too long).

The apparent demise of the special treatment for non-priority services has impacted on the list of specific service contract exclusions once to be found in Article 17 Directive 2004/18/EC.[58] As a new entry among excluded services Article 10(d) provides a very long and detailed list of legal services, including both litigation and consultancy related to a litigation and other specific legal activities. The description of the exclusion leaves margins of uncertainty. For instance concerning legal advice given "where there is a tangible indication and high probability that the matter to which the advice relates will become the subject" to litigation. It is unclear what is the requirement here, and whether it is necessary that a dissatisfied economic operator has already manifested his/her intention to challenge the decisions taken by the contracting authority.[59]

The exclusion is conditioned on the services being provided by a lawyer belonging to the relevant professional organisation as defined under Article 1 of Directive 77/249/EEC, by a notary or by another professional designated by a court or tribunal in the Member State concerned.

The directive has here taken the lead from Strong Segurança,[60] a case concerning the award of a contract for surveillance and security services for the installations of Sintra municipality.[61] While affirming the case law which found the general principles of the TFEU applicable to contracts not covered or partially covered by the public procurement directives,[62] the Court of Jus-

58. See also S. Smith 'Articles 74 to 76 of the Public Procurement Directive: the new "light" regime for social, health and other services and a new category of reserved contracts for certain sociela, health and cultural services contracts' Public Procurement L. Rev. 2014, 159.
59. Such argument could for instance be derived by Case C340/04 Carbotermo and Consorio Alisei [2006] ECR I4137, paragraph 55.
60. Case C95/10 Strong Segurança [2011] ECR I-1865.
61. This exception was not in the Commission's proposal, being added by the European Parliament and then fine tuned in the legislative process.
62. See generally C. Risvig Hansen, Contracts not covered or not fully covered by the Public Sector Directive (Copenhagen, DJØF Publishing, 2012) and the works collect-

tice stressed that this does not mean that the provisions in the directive are applicable by analogy.[63] More specifically, Article 47(2) of Directive 2004/18/EC concerning the reliance by an economic operator on the capacities of other entities was not considered to be implied by the general principles of transparency and equal treatment.[64] The Court of Justice relied on its case-law to the effect that contracts relating to the services listed in Annex II B to Directive 2004/18/EC are specific in nature.[65] According to the Court,

> at least some of those services have particular characteristics that would justify the contracting authority taking into account, on a personalised and specific basis, the individual bid presented by the candidates. This is the case, for example, for 'legal services', 'personnel placement and supply services', 'education and vocational education services' or 'investigation and security services'.[66]

As it will be seen, most of the services recalled here by the Court of Justice are now to be awarded according to the light regime provided under Article 74, including legal services which are not excluded under Article 10(d).[67]

Other new entries among excluded service contracts, added at the request of the European Parliament, are civil defence, civil protection, and danger prevention services that are provided by non-profit organisations or associations (with the exception of patient transport ambulance services). This is somewhat perplexing, because the contracts in questions are not excluded per se, but only is so far as they are awarded to specific legal persons.

It is from the outset to be remarked that, unlike Article 77(2), Article 10(h) does not provide a definition of 'NPO'. For systematic reasons, however, it would seem that the first three requirements in Article 77(2) are relevant here as well.

In a number of Member States like for instance Germany and Italy these services are provided by non-profit organisation – NPOs acting on a charitable basis. The new directive had here to strike a careful balance taking into

ed in D. Dragos – R. Caranta (eds) Outside the EU Procurement Directives – Inside the Treaty? (Copenhagen, DJØF Publishing, 2013).

63. See the discussion in R. Caranta 'The Borders of EU Public Procurement law' in D. Dragos – R. Caranta (eds) Outside the EU Procurement Directives – Inside the Treaty? Above fn. 63, 51 f.
64. Paragraph 44.
65. The Court refers here to Case C-507/03 Commission v Ireland [2007] ECR I-9777, paragraph 25.
66. Paragraph 43.
67. Below, under § 5.

account a surprisingly rich specific case law. In the Ambulanz Glöckner case the Court of Justice held that the provision on the market and for remuneration from the users of emergency transport services and patient transport services constitutes an economic activity for the purposes of the application of the competition rules laid down by the Treaty.[68] The Commission took heed from Ambulanz Glöckner to bring two distinct infringement procedures against Italy and Ireland because of direct awards of ambulance services. The Irish ambulances case, which was already mentioned, is not of interest here since the Court of Justice held that the Commission had failed to prove that the arrangement at issue indeed amounted to a public procurement contract.[69] In the Italian ambulances case, however, the Court of Justice affirmed Ambulanz Glöckner holding that NGOs providing those service are indeed market operators. The direct award of a number of contract for healthcare transport services without a call for tenders in Tuscany was therefore found to be in breach of the internal market general principles.[70]

A few years later a new infringement procedure was brought this time against Germany due to the existence of a practice of awarding contracts for public emergency services in some Länder. The Court of Justice excluded that the activities in question could be considered to be connected, even occasionally, with the exercise of official authority, as such falling outside the scope of the Treaty and derivate law provisions.[71] In its pleading the Commission had distinguished between contracts awarded for public ambulance services characterised by the predominance of the value of transport services as compared with the value of health services, and contracts characterised instead by the predominance of the value of latter services. While the former fall under the full rigour of the regime of the directive, contracts characterised by the predominance of the value of health services were considered as non-priority services. The Court of Justice however did not elaborate on the distinction, since the Commission had failed to prove which was the predominant component of the contracts at issue.[72]

68. Case C475/99 Ambulanz Glöckner [2001] ECR I8089, paragraphs 21 and 22.
69. Case C532/03 Commission v Ireland [2007] ECR I11353; A. Brown 'The Commission Loses another Action against Ireland Owing to Lack of Evidence: A Note on Case C-532/03 Commission v Ireland' Public Procurement L. Rev. 2008 NA92.
70. Case C-119/06 Commission v Italy [2007] ECR I-168; see A. Brown 'Application of the Directives to Contracts to Non-for-profit Organisations and Transparency under the EC Treaty: A Note on Case C-119/06 Commission v Italy' Public Procurement L. Rev. 2008 NA96.
71. Case C-160/08 Commission v Germany [2010] ECR I-3713, paragraphs 94 ff.
72. Paragraphs 116 ff.

The recent conclusions of Advocate general Wahl in ASL 5 'Spezzino' go in the same direction.[73] This was again a direct award to some NGOs of ambulance service by one of the units of the Italian NHS. The Advocate general recalls that either the health or the transport component may be prevalent in an ambulance service contract. If the former is the case, these services will be considered as non-priority service as they are "health and social services" which are listed in Annex II B to directive 2004/18/EC.[74] Therefore, according to the Advocate general, in case emergency services are prevailing, Article 23 of the old directive will be applicable if the value of the contract is above threshold. If it is not, the general principle of non-discrimination will still apply.[75]

The new directive seems due to change this approach significantly. While Article 10(h) of Directive 2014/24/EU reflects the same distinction between health (emergency) and transport ambulance services, their legal regime has been shifted and made more flexible. Among the excluded services under Article 10(h) are civil protection, and danger prevention services that are provided by non-profit organisations or associations, including those covered by CPV code 85143000-3, which is the general label for ambulance services; Article 10(h) expressly excepts from the exception 'patient transport ambulance services'. This means that, while patient transport ambulance services are now covered by the directive, emergency ambulance services are excluded when provided by NPOs.[76] As a consequence, in some situations emergency ambulance services may no more be considered to fall under what was the regime for non priority services and are therefore fully outside the scope of the directive.[77]

At the same time, 'patient transport ambulance services' are listed in Annex XIV since all ambulance services (CPV code 85143000-3) in principle fall in between CPV codes from 85000000-9 to 85323000-9. As a consequence, they now qualify as special services under Article 74.[78]

73. Case C-113/13 ASL No 5 'Spezzino, delivered on 30 April 2014, judgement pending.
74. Paragraph 36.
75. Paragraph 44.
76. See also Recital 28.
77. It is therefore submitted that Advocate general Wahl in the ASL 5 'Spezzino' case was wrong in referring to the new directive as an additional argument to demonstrate that all ambulance services fall under the scope of the public procurement directives (paragraph 40).
78. See below § 5 of this chapter.

This requalification of ambulances services impacts the rules applicable to mixed contracts including both types of services. Article 3(2) providing that in the case of mixed contracts consisting partly of social and special services and partly of other services the main subject shall be determined in accordance with which of the estimated values of the respective services is the highest will not be applicable because emergency ambulance services are not special, they are excluded. Article 3(6) will instead be applicable, which, as was already shown, unlike 3(2) does not focus on the value of the different parts of the contract but rather on the main subject-matter of that contract.

Once again, legal, public security and rescue and other services which are not excluded services under Article 10 will normally be listed in Annex XIV as special services and therefore ruled under Articles 74 ff.[79]

Article 10(j) also excludes specific contracts for political campaign services when awarded by a political party in the context of an election campaign.

Finally, contracts for research and development services are no more listed as excluded service contracts in what has become Article 10 of Directive 2014/24/EU. They are one of the specific situations regulated in a separate chapter of the new Public Sector Directive.[80]

One last question concerning excluded contracts is whether the application of the general principles of the TFEU is also to be ruled out.[81] It seems reasonable to assume that the general principles will apply to excluded contracts unless they fall under some other specific regime or must be considered to be excluded by the scope of EU law as defined by the Treaties.[82]

Given how limited to the minimum is the 'light' regime foreseen in Article 74 ff, which will discussed below, one could well question whether it is possible to think of anything lighter but still complying with the general principles. While democracy and lobbying were obviously at play here, since the Commission's proposal was very much changed here, in that it did not foresee this exclusion case (and neither it foresaw the special-special regime laid down in Article 77), it is submitted that the rules will have been tidier if some contracts – such as legal services and civil defence, civil protection, and danger prevention services – had rather been treated as special contracts under Article 74.

79. See also Annex XIV.
80. See below Chapter X.
81. See also C. Risvig Hansen, Contracts not covered or not fully covered by the Public Sector Directive above fn 63, 103 ff.
82. R. Caranta 'General Report' above fn 16, 124 f, and works referred therein.

5. Social and other specific services

The Telaustria case law has been applied to non-priority services as well. In an infringement procedure arising from the direct award of services relating to the payment of social welfare benefits to An Post, the Irish postal service, the Court of Justice acknowledged that the Community legislature based itself on the assumption that non-priority service contracts are not of cross-border interest and therefore do not justify award EU-wide award procedure.[83] The Court was however fast in pointing out that it was common ground among the parties that "the award of public contracts is to remain subject to the fundamental rules of Community law, and in particular to the principles laid down by the Treaty on the right of establishment and the freedom to provide services".[84]

As already recalled, in Strong Segurança the Court of Justice affirmed the applicability of the general principles to the award of non-priority service contracts having cross-border interest while at the same time making it clear that this does not mean that the provisions in the directive are applicable by analogy.[85]

The time was ripe to reconsider the overall regime for non-priority services.[86] On the top of that, the Commission staff working paper on "Evaluation Report: Impact and Effectiveness of EU Public Procurement Legislation" suggested that the exclusion of certain services from the full application of the Public Sector Directive should be reviewed, extending the full application of this directive to a number of services.[87]

That said, certain categories of services are still considered to have a limited cross-border dimension, such as some social, health and educational services. According to Recital 114, "Those services are provided within a particular context that varies widely amongst Member States, due to different cultural traditions". This however does not translate into an outright exclusion from public procurement rules, but into the higher threshold of EUR 750.000.

The definition of these services is to be found in Article 74 of Directive 2014/24/EU which in turn refers to Annex XIV for a more precise description

83. Case C-507/03, Commission v Ireland [2007] ECR I-9777, paragraph 25.
84. Paragraph 27; Case C92/00 HI [2002] ECR I5553, paragraph 42 is referred to.
85. Case C-95/10 Strong Segurança [2011] ECR I-1865.
86. See C. Risvig Hansen, Contracts not covered or not fully covered by the Public Sector Directive above fn 63, 109.
87. See Recital 113; see also the analysis by S. Smith 'Articles 74 to 76 of the Public Procurement Directive' above fn 59, 160.

and CPV numbering. As a result of the tug-of-war between the EU institutions,[88] the list is quite long, and includes health, social and related services, administrative social, educational, healthcare and cultural services, compulsory social security services but also some surprising entry like tyre-remoulding and blacksmith services.[89]

With reference to compulsory social security services a footnote clarifies that "These services are not covered by the present Directive where they are organised as non-economic services of general interest. Member States are free to organise the provision of compulsory social services or of other services as services of general interest or as non-economic services of general interest". This links with Article 1(5) of the Directive, under which the directive itself "does not affect the way in which the Member States organise their social security systems".[90]

However, this is true not just of social security services but of a large number of services, such as education and training services or prison related services or investigation and security services which are all listed as well in Annex XIV. Indeed, as Recital 6 makes it clear, "non-economic services of general interest should not fall within the scope of this Directive".

Moreover, under Article 1(4), the Directive

> does not affect the freedom of Member States to define, in conformity with Union law, what they consider to be services of general economic interest, how those services should be organised and financed, in compliance with the State aid rules, and what specific obligations they should be subject to. Equally, this Directive does not affect the decision of public authorities whether, how and to what extent they want to perform public functions themselves pursuant to Protocol (No 26) on Services of General Interest and Article 14 TFEU.[91]

In the end, the special regime enacted with Articles 74 ff will be applicable only once a Member State has not just decided to treat a given service as a SGEI but also to outsource its provision through the award of a procurement contract rather than providing it in house. Directive 2014/23/EU will instead apply if a concession is the contract chosen to outsource the service. To give an instance, the 'light' award procedure will have to be followed only in

88. A. Schwab – A. Giesemann 'Mit mehr Regeln zu mehr Rechtssicherheit? Die Überarbeitung des europäischen Vergaberechts' Vergaberecht, 2014, 357 f.
89. See also Recitals 115 ff.
90. See also Recital 6.
91. See also Recital 6.

those Member States having 'privatised' prison related services. Moreover, as Recital 114 makes it clear

> Member States and public authorities remain free to provide those services themselves or to organise social services in a way that does not entail the conclusion of public contracts, for example through the mere financing of such services or by granting licences or authorisations to all economic operators meeting the conditions established beforehand by the contracting authority, without any limits or quotas, provided that such a system ensures sufficient advertising and complies with the principles of transparency and non-discrimination.

Under Article 75, and unless recourse to a negotiated procedure without prior publication would be allowed under Article 32, contracting authorities are given the choice to make known their intention of awarding a contract either by means of a contract notice following the model laid down in Annex V Part H, or by means of a prior information notice containing the information set out in Annex V Part I. Moreover, contracting authorities are called to publish contract award notices on a regular basis.[92]

Besides compliance with these rules on publicity, Member States are given wide berth as to how devise the procedures to award social and other special services contracts. This is why this regime is characterised as a 'light' one.[93] Indeed, having considered the importance of the cultural context and the sensitivity of these services, Member States are given wide discretion to organise the choice of the service providers in the way they consider most appropriate.[94]

Basically, under Article 76 domestic rules must comply with the general principles of transparency and equal treatment. The requirements for this 'light' regime are in the end the same which according to the case law which was already recalled are applicable to below the thresholds contracts and other contracts not covered or not fully covered by the directives having cross-border interest. The Commission interpretative communication on the 'Community law applicable to contract awards not or not fully subject to the

92. See also S. Smith 'Articles 74 to 76 of the Public Procurement Directive' above fn 59, 163 f.
93. See C.H. Bovis 'Highlights of the EU Procurement Reforms: The New Directive on Concessions' above fn 1; S. Smith 'Articles 74 to 76 of the Public Procurement Directive' above fn 59, 161.
94. Recital 114.

provisions of the "Public Procurement" Directives'[95] will provide the Member States with inspiration on how to draft the domestic rules implementing Article 76.[96]

Moreover the procedural rules applicable must take into account the specificities of the services in question, ensuring "quality, continuity, accessibility, affordability, availability and comprehensiveness of the services, the specific needs of different categories of users, including disadvantaged and vulnerable groups, the involvement and empowerment of users and innovation".[97] To this end award to the (lowest) price may be excluded to the benefit of quality and sustainability criteria for social services.[98]

Having introduced a fairly high threshold the new rules pose the question of the regime applicable to below the threshold contracts. According to Recital 114, in some circumstances, such as for instance Union financing for cross-border projects, these contracts could well present a cross-border interest which will entail the application of the principles of non-discrimination and transparency. The following recitals however go a long way in arguing that only above the EUR 750.000 threshold services do indeed present an interest for economic operators established in a Member State different from the one the contracting authority belongs to. For instance, according to Recital 115 "hotel and restaurant services are typically offered only by operators located in the specific place of delivery of those services"; however, "[l]arge hotel and restaurant service contracts above that threshold can be of interest for various economic operators, such as travel agencies and other intermediaries, also on a cross-border basis". Along the same lines is Recital 116 concerning legal services and Recital 117 referred to rescue services, firefighting

95. 2006/C 179/02; see U. Neergard 'Public Service Concessions and Related Concepts – the Increased Pressure from Community Law on Member States' Use of Concessions' Public Procurement L. Rev. 2007 387; A. Brown 'Seeing Through Transparency: the Requirement to Advertise Public Contracts and Concessions Under the EC Treaty' Public Procurement L. Rev. 2007, 1.
96. S. Smith 'Articles 74 to 76 of the Public Procurement Directive' above fn 59, 161, writes about 'detailed rules'; given the need for flexibility, it is however doubtful whether the domestic rules really need to go much beyond minimal requirements.
97. The list has rightly been considered as non-exhaustive: S. Smith 'Articles 74 to 76 of the Public Procurement Directive' above fn, 165.
98. See also Recital 114; see generally the chapter by D.C. Dragos – B. Neamtu 'Sustainable Public Procurement in the 2014/24/EU Directive' in this book.

services and prison services inasmuch as they are not excluded under Article 10 of the Directive.[99]

In principle, therefore, the Commission or any claimant will face very much an uphill fight in proving that a below the threshold social or special service presents a certain cross-border value.[100]

The recitals however present the interpreter with a conundrum. Recital 116 for instance states that

> [l]arge legal service contracts above that threshold can be of interest for various economic operators, such as international law firms, also on a cross-border basis, in particular where they involve legal issues arising from or having as its background Union or other international law or involving more than one country.

What about above the threshold legal services not presenting any one of those characteristics? The so far received wisdom is that above the thresholds contracts do have cross-border interest and must therefore be awarded according to the procedures laid down in the EU directives, but this could very well revoked into doubt in a number of cases, including those concerning some social or special services.[101] Indeed, in Strong Segurança the Court was quite sweeping in holding at least some services "have particular characteristics that would justify the contracting authority taking into account, on a personalised and specific basis, the individual bid presented by the candidates".[102]

Besides the general regime for reserved contracts provided in Article 20 and discussed in another chapter of this book,[103] Article 77 of Directive 2014/24/EU allows Member States to provide that contracting authorities may reserve the right for organisations to participate in procedures for the award of public contracts exclusively for specific health, social and cultural

99. Recital 117 is particularly trenchant in indicating that government services or the provision of services to the community, "would normally only be likely to present a cross-border interest as from a threshold of EUR 750 000 and should consequently only then be subject to the light regime".
100. See also S. Smith 'Articles 74 to 76 of the Public Procurement Directive' above fn 59, 166. And this besides on top of the usual uncertainties facing this concept: P. Telles 'The Good, the Bad, and the Ugly: The EU's Internal Market, Public Procurement Thresholds, and Cross-Border Interest' 43 Public Contract Law Journal 2013/1, 12 ff.
101. As P. Telles 'The Good, the Bad, and the Ugly' above fn 99, argues the EU has here traded purity for convenience and legal certainty.
102. Case C-95/10 Strong Segurança [2011] ECR I-1865, paragraph 43.
103. D. C. Dragos – B. Neamtu 'Sustainable Public Procurement in the 2014/24/EU Directive' belowin this book, at.

services listed in the first paragraph of the same provision with reference to their specific CPV codes.[104]

This possibility again was not foreseen in the Commission's proposal and added at the eleventh hour. According to Recital 118 this derogation is justified by the need to ensure the continuity of public services. This is not easy to understand, since the distinction between profit and non-for profit organisations could hardly be considered relevant when assessing the reliability of the service provider.

The legislative history tells us that the UK insisted to have this set aside regime to benefit organisations set up by former employees of the contracting authorities thus possibly making externalisation processes less contentious.[105]

This still does not by itself ensure the continuity of public services since legally speaking the contract has to be put for tender and could well be awarded to a different organisation.

The possibility to reserve certain service contracts to NPOs was anticipated in Sodemare,[106] a case which could have been mistaken to belong to the past.[107] The case concerned a statute of the Lombardy Region in Italy which allowed only NPOs to be awarded contracts concerning the provision of services in the framework of the social welfare system. Rejecting the arguments raised by a federation of Belgian commercial companies, the Court of Justice held that

> a Member State may, in the exercise of the powers it retains to organize its social security system, consider that a social welfare system of the kind at issue in this case necessarily implies, with a view to attaining its objectives, that the admission of private operators to

104. See also Recital 120 as to how these references must be read; see also S. Smith 'Articles 74 to 76 of the Public Procurement Directive' above fn 59, 167 f.
105. See also S. Smith 'Articles 74 to 76 of the Public Procurement Directive' above fn 59, 167.
106. Case C-70/95 Sodemare [1997] ECR-I, 3395.
107. And indeed it did not feature prominently in The Commission's Communication; "Implementing the Community Lisbon programme: Social services of general interest in the European Union" COM(2006) 177 final, at 2.2.1; see however "Guide to the application of the European Union rules on State aid, public procurement and the internal market to services of general economic interest and, in particular, to social services of general interest" (SEC(2010) 1545), a Commission staff working document acknowledging at paragraph 4.2.10 that Sodemare left open margins for preferential treatment of NPOs.

that system as providers of social welfare services is to be made subject to the condition that they are non-profit making.[108]

The 2011 Green Paper 'on the modernisation of EU public procurement policy' however rescued Sodemare from oblivion and paved the way for what has become Article 77 of Directive 2014/24/EU.[109]

Article 77(2) lays down in quite some details the requirements NPOs must meet to be allowed to take part into the award procedures for these reserved contracts.[110] They must pursue a public service mission linked to the delivery of the services concerned; they must reinvest any profit with a view to achieving the organisation's objective; however, where profits are distributed or redistributed, this should be based on participatory considerations; employee ownership or participatory principles must be at the basis of the structures of management or ownership of the organisation, and finally "the organisation has not been awarded a contract for the services concerned by the contracting authority concerned pursuant to this Article within the past three years".

The latter condition is very restrictive and logically difficult to understand. It can easily defeat the purported ratio of reserving this contract, since it does not only limit the possibility for NPOs to seek a constant flow of contracts, but makes the continuity of service simply impossible because no NPO can be awarded again the same service when under Article 77(3) the maximum duration of any contract is 3 years. The provision is again the result of an uneasy compromise between (some Member States in) the Council and the Commission. The latter accepted a special set-aside regime but wanted at least to avoid the situation in which the same organisation is always being awarded a given contract in a reserved competition.[111] This still has very little if not nothing to do with the 'continuity of public services' and one can fairly say that the recital "does not really provide an helpful explanation of why the provisions in Article 77 are in place".[112]

108. Paragraph 32.
109. Point 4.4 and question 97.1.2; that section was based on (SEC(2010) 1545), a Commission staff working document acknowledging at paragraph 4.2.10.
110. However, as it was pointed out, some of the terms used are not defined, which could lead to litigation: S. Smith 'Articles 74 to 76 of the Public Procurement Directive' above fn 59, 167.
111. It could in a non-reserved one: S. Smith 'Articles 74 to 76 of the Public Procurement Directive' above fn 59, 168.
112. S. Smith 'Articles 74 to 76 of the Public Procurement Directive' above fn 59, 167.

It is to be stressed again that in no way the provision allows for direct award. As it is the case with Article 20 as well, it only allows Member States to reserve participation to the award of given contracts to some categories of economic operators. As Advocate general Wahl pointed out in the ASL 5 'Spezzino' case, this will not vouchsafe direct award to NPOs.[113]

6. Conclusions (with specific reference to service procurements)

The EU law makers has tried hard to clarify the objective scope of application of the Public Sector Directive. The results do not always seem to match the effort and it is feared that more cases will be needed before issues such as mixed contracts are finally settled. More generally, a robust theory distinguishing the different instruments contracting authorities may use to entrust the provision of SGEIs is still missing and therefore it is not always clear whether public procurement law does apply to a given situation.

Concerning the award of service contracts, one could well wonder whether the distinction between priority and non priority services has really disappeared. It would rather seem that some services have moved from being under the full rigour of the directive to the 'light regime' provided for social and special services or, and more often, moved the opposite way. Moreover, some contracts have become excluded services in so far as they are awarded to NPOs. Finally, as it is the case with many legal services, they have been altogether excluded from the scope of application of Directive 2014/24/EU. In the main, the label has changed, but as the Correlation table (Annex XV) gives out, Annex XIV (social and special services) has to a large extent taken now the place of old Annex II (B).[114]

As an additional complication, the 'light regime' has been coupled with a special set aside system reserving the competition for the award of some contracts to (some) NGOs. One has to navigate in the vast sea of CPV codes to find out whether a given services is excluded, social or special, and/or such to be awarded under Article 77. It is submitted that this will lead some contracting authorities to try some kind of a choose the CPV code the best fit the procedure you want to follow game. And again more litigation will be the inevitable consequence of this over-complex regime.

113. Paragraph 42.
114. Even if we are cautioned by S. Smith 'Articles 74 to 76 of the Public Procurement Directive' above fn 59, 162, to check the CPV very carefully.

Bibliography

R. Caranta 'General Report' in U. Neergaard, C. Jacqueson, G.S. Ølykke (eds.) Public Procurement Law: Limitations, Opportunities and Paradoxes. The XXVI FIDE Congress in Copenhagen 2014 (Copenhagen, DJØF, 2014) Vol. 3.

D. Dragos – R. Caranta (eds) Outside the EU Procurement Directives – Inside the Treaty? (Copenhagen, DJØF Publishing, 2013).

N. Fiedziuk 'Putting Services of General Economic Interest up for Tender: Reflection on Applicable EU Rules' Common Market L. Rev. 2013, 99.

R. Noguellou 'Scope and Coverage of the EU Procurement Directives' in M. Trybys, R. Caranta, G. Edelstam (eds) EU Public Contract Law. Public Procurement and Beyond (Bruxelles, Bruylant, 2014).

C. Risvig Hansen, Contracts not covered or not fully covered by the Public Sector Directive (Copenhagen, DJØF Publishing, 2012).

S. Smith 'Articles 74 to 76 of the Public Procurement Directive: the new "light" regime for social, health and other services and a new category of reserved contracts for certain sociela, health and cultural services contracts' Public Procurement L. Rev. 2014, 159.

P. Telles 'The Good, the Bad, and the Ugly: The EU's Internal Market, Public Procurement Thresholds, and Cross-Border Interest' 43 Public Contract Law Journal 2013/1, 12.

A. Tokár 'Institutional Report' in U. Neergaard, C. Jacqueson, G.S. Ølykke (eds.) Public Procurement Law: Limitations, Opportunities and Paradoxes. The XXVI FIDE Congress in Copenhagen 2014 (Copenhagen, DJØF, 2014) Vol. 3.

Trybus, R. Caranta, G. Edelstam (eds) EU Public Contract Law. Public Procurement and Beyond (Bruxelles, Bruylant, 2014).

Exclusion, Qualitative Selection and Short-listing in the New Public Sector Procurement Directive 2014/24

Dr Albert Sanchez Graells

1. Introduction

Following the 2011 proposal of the European Commission for the adoption of a new set of public procurement Directives, and after intense negotiations at the Council, a Compromise Text was published on 12 July 2013[1] for submission to the European Parliament for a first reading,[2] with a view to the adoption of new public procurement rules by the end of 2013. The final text of the Directive was approved by the European Parliament on 15 January 2014 and its final official version has been published in the Official Journal of the European Union on 28 March 2014 as Directive 2014/24/EU of the European Parliament and of the Council of 26 February 2014 on public procurement and repealing Directive 2004/18/EC[3] (hereinafter, the 'new Directive'). The reform of legislation on public procurement was one of the twelve priority actions set out in the Single Market Act adopted in April 2011.[4] As the Com-

1. The most updated set of publicly accessible proposals is in the Compromise Text of the Council on 12 July 2013 register.consilium.europa.eu/pdf/en/13/st11/st11745.en13.pdf.
2. The European Parliament published a report on the original 2011 proposal on 11 January 2013 europarl.europa.eu/sides/getDoc.do?type=REPORT&mode=XML&reference=A7-2013-7&language=EN.
3. Directive of the European Parliament and of the Council on public procurement and repealing Directive 2004/18/EC, OJ L 94, 28/03/2014, p. 65–242.
4. Later followed by a Single Market Act II; ec.europa.eu/internal_market/ smact/index_en.htm.

mission made clear: 'the efficiency of public tendering has become a priority for all Member States, in view of the current budgetary constraints. We therefore need flexible, simple instruments which allow public authorities and their suppliers to conclude transparent, competitive contracts as easily as possible and at the best value for money'.[5]

Therefore, the main aims of the European Commission with its initial proposal were to simplify the current rules and to provide contracting authorities more flexibility in the carrying out of their procurement activities, without restricting the opportunities for competition and with a view to enhance access to small and medium enterprises (SMEs). In parallel, the European Commission also aimed to facilitate a qualitative improvement in the use of public procurement by ensuring greater consideration for social and environmental criteria such as life-cycle costs or the integration of vulnerable and disadvantaged persons.

On the basis of such a background to public procurement reform in the EU, this paper is concerned with the modifications that the new Directive contains in relation to the general principles (rectius, rules) for the choice of participants and award of contracts (section 2) and, more specifically, on the rules for the exclusion of economic operators (section 3), the qualitative selection of candidates and tenderers (section 4), and the short-listing of candidates, tenders and solutions (section 5), including the particular technique of technical dialogue (section 6). It will also offer some brief conclusions (section 7). The assessment is based on a comparison with the equivalent rules under current Directive 2004/18/EC, as well as on the problems and implementation difficulties that the author envisages in the new Directive, and always subject to the specific decisions of each Member State in the transposition of the new rules into their domestic public procurement systems – which shall bring into force the laws, regulations and administrative provisions necessary to comply with this Directive by 18 April 2016.

5. Press release, 'Modernising European public procurement to support growth and employment', IP/11/1580 europa.eu/rapid/press-release_IP-11-1580_en.htm?locale=en.

2. General principles (rectius, rules)

2.1. Cumulative compliance of criteria concerned with tenderers and their tenders, regardless of the order in which they are assessed

The new Directive creates a new Article 56 on general principles (rectius, general rules) for the choice of participants and the award of contracts that expands and modifies significantly the rules in current Article 44(1) of Directive 2004/18. Article 56(1) of the new Directive condenses the content of Article 44(1) of Directive 2004/18 and changes its drafting significantly in order to clarify that contracts can only be awarded where both the tenderer and its tender comply with all applicable requirements under the relevant procurement documents. This clarification may not have been necessary, as the application of the rules under Directive 2004/18 surely led to the same conclusion. By the change of drafting, it also suppresses the reference to a mandatory sequence of evaluation that required that 'Contracts shall be awarded [...] after the suitability of the economic operators not excluded [...] has been checked', which seemed to require that exclusion and qualitative selection of economic operators was conducted prior to the analysis of their tenders in accordance with award criteria. This is the logical sequence, in any case. Nonetheless, in order to clarify this flexibility, Article 56(2) of the new Directive expressly foresees, subject to Member States transposition decision to exclude it or to restrict it for certain types of procurement or specific circumstances, the possibility for contracting authorities to 'examine tenders before verifying the absence of grounds for exclusion and the fulfilment of the selection criteria' but, in such case, 'they shall ensure that the verification of absence of grounds for exclusion and of fulfilment of the selection criteria is carried out in an impartial and transparent manner so that no contract is awarded to a tenderer that should have been excluded [...] or that does not meet the selection criteria set out by the contracting authority'. This rule, which has no equivalent under Directive 2004/18, will only be applicable in connection with open procedures because in the rest of the procedures, a reversal of the sequence selection-award is not feasible.

This provision seems to anticipate itself the problems that such sequence can generate, given that contracting authorities will always have an incentive to 'twist' exclusion and selection criteria to be able to retain the best offer they have received. Moreover, unless the procurement is carried out under rare circumstances that make the assessment of the tender (both in technical and economic terms) simpler and quicker than the general assessment of the tenderers, there seems to be an advantage in proceeding first to exclude non-suitable or non-qualified tenderers in order to avoid the costs (in terms of time, at least) of evaluating their tenders. Moreover, the contracting authority can significantly reduce the cost of exclusion and selection analyses both for tenderers and for itself by resorting to the acceptance of the European Single Procurement Document and other facilitating measures under Article 59 of the new Directive (below section 4.5). Therefore, the practical impact of this new provision can be doubted, as contracting authorities may only find an advantage in the reversal of the assessment sequence in a limited number of open procedures and, even in those cases, they may want to avoid any potential challenge on the basis of discrimination derived from the ex post assessment of the tenderer that has submitted the best tender against exclusion grounds and qualitative selection criteria.

2.2. Exclusion possible at any point of the tender procedure

Still as a matter of general rules, Article 57(5) of the new Directive introduces a much needed clarification on the possibility or duty for contracting authorities to exclude economic operators at any moment during the procedure. This clarifies that exclusion grounds (both those that are mandatory as a matter of EU law, and those that Member States make mandatory in their jurisdictions) should be considered unwaivable [ie mandatory because they represent the 'public interest', unless some of them are configured in a discretionary manner by domestic law, as allowed for by art 57(4) new dir] and that contracting authorities should be aware of them and check for compliance throughout the tender procedure. Equally, contracting authorities are now given express legal support for the exclusion of tenderers at late stages of the tender procedure, therefore nullifying any claims based on the potential (legitimate?) expectations derived from not having been excluded at the beginning of the procedure. According to Article 57(5) of the new Directive, it is now clear that a contracting authority would not be going against its own prior acts and thus not be estopped from excluding tenderers previously admitted to (or not excluded from) the tender procedure.

More specifically, Article 57(5) of the new Directive establishes that contracting authorities 'shall at any time during the procedure exclude an economic operator where it turns out that the economic operator is, in view of acts committed or omitted either before or during the procedure,' convicted by final judgment of one of the qualified crimes of Article 57(1), or where the contracting authority is aware that the economic operator is in breach of its obligations relating to the payment of taxes or social security contributions and where this has been established by a judicial or administrative decision having final and binding effect [Art 57(2) new dir, and below section 3.1]. Moreover, 'contracting authorities may exclude or may be required by Member States to exclude an economic operator where it turns out that the economic operator is, in view of acts committed or omitted either before or during the procedure, in one of the situations referred to in paragraph 4'. Indeed, and as we shall see in further detail (below section 3), in some cases, contracting authorities are simply able to exclude, but not obliged to exclude, economic operators that have incurred in certain (mandatory) grounds for exclusion. Hence, this new provision is due to generate significant legal effects and may be open to litigation to test its boundaries against the general principles of equal treatment, protection of legitimate expectations and legal certainty –which can raise 'constitutional' law issues in some of the domestic jurisdictions.

2.3. Exclusion and rejection possible on the basis of non-compliance with (EU, domestic and international) social, labour and environmental law

Linked to the possibility that contracting authorities actually award the contract to a tenderer not having submitted the best tender (but for reasons other than lack of compliance with exclusion grounds or qualitative selection criteria, discussed above section 2.1), it is worth noting that Article 56(1) in fine of the new Directive opens the door to the use of public procurement decisions as a lever to promote enforcement of (or sanction the lack thereof) social, labour and environmental law – thereby strengthening the possibilities to use procurement for the pursuit of such 'secondary' or 'horizontal policies'.[6]

In more detail, the provision contemplates that 'Contracting authorities may decide not to award a contract to the tenderer submitting the most economically advantageous tender where they have established that the tender does not comply with the applicable obligations referred to in Article 18(2)' – that is, 'obligations in the fields of environmental, social and labour law established by Union law, national law, collective agreements or by the international environmental, social and labour law provisions listed in Annex X' – which can be modified by the Commission from time to time, according to Article 56(4) of the new Directive.

This should be connected to the provision of Article 57(4)(a) of the new Directive, which indicates that 'Contracting authorities may exclude or may be required by Member States to exclude from participation in a procurement

6. See S Arrowsmith, 'Horizontal Policies in Public Procurement: A Taxonomy,' (2010) 10(2) Journal of Public Procurement 149 and the various contributions to S Arrowsmith and P Kunzlik (eds) Social and Environmental Policies in EC Procurement Law (Cambridge, Cambridge University Press, 2009).

procedure any economic operator [...]: (a) where [they] can demonstrate by any appropriate means a violation of applicable obligations referred to in Article 18(2)' (further discussed below section 3.4). It is important to stress that such exclusion could take place at any moment (above section 2.2), which includes the exclusion right at the point of making an award decision.

In my view, both Article 56(1) in fine and 57(4)(a) of the new Directive serve exactly the same function – ie the strengthening of the social, labour and environmental aspects of the public procurement function, although in a manner that can seriously diminish its economic effectiveness and that can impose a burden difficult to discharge on contracting authorities (which could now be in a difficult position where they will need to assess tenderers' and tenders' compliance with an increased set of diverse rules of a social, labour and environmental nature). Indeed, both provisions aim at the same outcome, with the only apparent difference that Article 56(1) in fine is concerned with the tender specifically, whereas Article 57(4)(a) is concerned with the tenderer more generally – and, consequently, Article 57(4)(a) may be seen as a rule that looks at the past and present general compliance of the economic operator with social, labour and environmental law, whereas Article 56(1) in fine allows the contracting authority to make a prognosis of compliance and reject a tender if its future implementation would imply non-compliance with social, labour and environmental law requirements. In any case, their effectiveness will largely depend on the transposition decisions of the Member States and, ultimately, on the actual capacity of contracting authorities to engage in such possibly complex assessments of compliance with EU, domestic and international social, labour and environmental rules.

2.4. More scope for a power / duty to seek clarifications and additional information from tenderers

On a different note (but possibly related if the contracting authority needs further information to assess compliance with eg social, labour or environmental rules, above section 2.3), it is also relevant that Article 56(3) of the new Directive is extending the powers of contracting authorities to seek clarifications or additional information from candidates and tenderers. Currently, Article 51 of Directive 2004/18 simply foresees that contracting authorities 'may invite economic operators to supplement or clarify the certificates and documents' concerned with their personal situation – ie the documents and certificates concerned with the (lack of) grounds for exclusion and compliance with qualitative selection criteria (including their suitability to pursue a professional activity, their economic and financial standing, their technical and/or professional ability, or their systems to ensure compliance with quality assurance and environmental management standards).[7] Under the rest of the rules of Directive 2004/18, clarifications are only allowed in competitive dialogues and always provided that 'this does not have the effect of modifying substantial aspects of the tender or of the call for tender and does not risk distorting competition or causing discrimination' [art 28(7) dir 2004/18].[8]

On its part, Article 56(3) of the new Directive goes well beyond the current rules and empowers contracting authorities to adopt a more proactive role. Specifically, this provision foresees that 'Where information or documentation to be submitted by economic operators is or appears to be incomplete or erroneous or where specific documents are missing, contracting authorities may, unless otherwise provided by the national law implementing this Directive, request the economic operators concerned to submit, supplement, clarify or complete the relevant information or documentation within an appropriate time limit, provided that such requests are made in full compliance with the principles of equal treatment and transparency'. This should be seen as a codification of the case law of the Court of Justice of the European Union (CJEU) concerned with the duty of good administration[9] in the area of public procurement and need to be read in conjunction with its interpretation of the limits imposed by the principles of transparency and equal treatment.[10] Despite being concerned with the tender phase rather than the selection of candidates itself, the closest 'precedent' to the rule in Article 56(3) of the new Directive should be found in the Slovensko Judgment, where the CJEU clearly indicated that EU procurement law 'does not preclude a provision of national law [...] according to which, in essence, the contracting authority may ask tenderers in writing to clarify their tenders without, however, requesting or accepting any amendment to the tenders. In the exercise of the discretion thus enjoyed by the contracting authority, that authority must treat

7. Interestingly, the Court of Justice of the European Union has strengthened this possibility in its recent Judgments Case C-599/10 Slovensko [2011] ECR I-10873, and C-336/12 Manova [2013] ECR nyr.
8. For discussion of the rules under Directive 2004/18 and their implementation, see A Sanchez Graells, "Rejection of Abnormally Low and Non-Compliant Tenders in EU Public Procurement: A Comparative View on Selected Jurisdictions", in M Comba & S Treumer (eds), Award of Contracts in EU Procurement, European Procurement Law Series, Vol. 5 (Copenhagen, DJF, 2013) p. 289-293.
9. J Mendes, 'Good Administration in EU Law and the European Code of Good Administrative Behaviour', EUI Working Paper Law 2009/09 cadmus.eui.eu/handle/1814/12101.
10. See Case T-19/95 Adia interim v Commission [1996] ECR II-321, and Case T-195/08 Antwerpse Bouwwerken v Commission [2009] ECR II-4439.

the various tenderers equally and fairly, in such a way that a request for clarification cannot appear unduly to have favoured or disadvantaged the tenderer or tenderers to which the request was addressed, once the procedure for selection of tenders has been completed and in the light of its outcome'.[11] After the proposal for the new Directive was already being discussed, the CJEU clarified that Slovensko provided "guidance in relation to tenders [that] can also be applied to applications filed at the screening stage for candidates in a restricted procedure",[12] hence suppressing any doubts as to the applicability of the rule throughout the tender procedure and not only in any specific phase. Even more specifically, it clarified that "a contracting authority may request the correction or amplification of details of such an application, on a limited and specific basis, so long as that request relates to particulars or information, such as a published balance sheet, which can be objectively shown to pre-date the deadline for applying to take part in the tendering procedure concerned", but bearing in mind that "this would not be the case if the contract documents required provision of the missing particulars or information, on pain of exclusion".[13]

Moreover, an interpretation of this clause in view of the CJEU case law may result in a positive obligation to contact tenderers and seek clarification or additional information (given that contracting authorities do not have an unfettered discretion not to exercise their power to seek clarification[14]), at least under certain conditions, such as when 'the circumstances of the case, of which [the contracting authority] is aware, suggest that the ambiguity probably has a simple explanation and is capable of being easily resolved'.[15] Therefore, Article 56(3) of the new Directive should be welcome inasmuch as it can contribute (through the interpretation to be given to it by the CJEU) to the development of a common (minimum) standard of 'good administration' in public procurement across all EU Member States – regardless of the requirements of their domestic codes of administrative procedure or similar provision.

11. Case C-599/10 Slovensko [2011] ECR I-10873, para 41.
12. Case C-336/12 Manova [2013] ECR nyr, para 38.
13. Ibid, paras 39 and 40.
14. Case T-211/02 Tideland Signal v Commission [2002] ECR II-3781.
15. Case T-195/08 Antwerpse Bouwwerken v Commission [2009] ECR II-4439, para 56.

3. Grounds for the exclusion of economic operators

3.1. Extension of the grounds for mandatory exclusion of economic operators: an emphasis on the fight against fraud and corruption

Article 57 of the new Directive alters and extends the grounds for mandatory exclusion currently foreseen in Article 45 of Directive 2004/18. According to Article 57(1) of the new Directive, the current four grounds for mandatory exclusion of economic operators convicted by final judgment are maintained, which include the following offences: i) participation in a criminal organisation, ii) corruption (see also below here and section 3.2), iii) fraud, and iv) money laundering. The references to the statutory instruments where these offences are regulated have been updated, but the regime remains substantially identical. However, Article 57(1) and 57(2) of the new Directive significantly extend the remit of the grounds for mandatory disqualification.[16]

Firstly, in connection with corruption, the ground is extended beyond the 'EU definition' of this offence[17] and will now cover 'corruption as defined in the national law of the contracting authority or the economic operator' [art 57(1)(b) new dir]. This will not be without difficulty, given the variety of criminal laws that might need checking, but it seems in line with the requirements of Article IV:4(c) of the revised version of the 2011 WTO Agreement on Government Procurement (GPA),[18] which mandates that contracting authorities conduct 'covered procurement in a transparent and impartial manner that: (c) prevents corrupt practices' and which makes explicit reference to the

16. However, there is a very scant (if not non-existent) explanation for these relevant changes in the recitals of the new Directive, which number (100) simply states that 'Public contracts should not be awarded to economic operators that have participated in a criminal organisation or have been found guilty of corruption, fraud to the detriment of the Union's financial interests, terrorist offences, money laundering or terrorist financing. The non-payment of taxes or social security contributions should also lead to mandatory exclusion at the level of the Union. Member States should, however, be able to provide for a derogation from these mandatory exclusions in exceptional situations where overriding requirements in the general interest make a contract award indispensable. This might, for example, be the case where urgently needed vaccines or emergency equipment can only be purchased from an economic operator to whom one of the mandatory grounds for exclusion otherwise applies'.
17. See T Medina Arnaiz, 'The Exclusion of Tenderers in Public Procurement as an Anticorruption Mean' nispa.org/files/conferences/2008/papers/200804200047500. Medina_exclusion.pdf and S Williams, 'The mandatory exclusions for corruption in the new EC procurement directives' nottingham.ac.uk/pprg/documentsarchive/fulltextarticles/sope_exclusions_in_proc.pdf.
18. See wto.org/english/tratop_e/gproc_e/gp_gpa_e.htm.

United Nations Convention against Corruption.[19] Therefore, the scope of this ground for mandatory exclusion seems to have been significantly broadened (at least potentially, and depending on the actions of the Member States to adopt aggressive anti-corruption legislation) (see also below section 3.2). Such broadening can even result in a certain extraterritoriality in the application of this ground for exclusion when national criminal laws concerned with corruption cover instances of bribery of third country officials following the OECD Convention on Combating Bribery.[20]

Secondly, in relation to terrorism, two new mandatory grounds for exclusion are created for terrorist financing [art 57(1)(e) new dir] and for terrorist offences or offences linked to terrorist activities [art 57(1)(d) new dir].

Thirdly, a new ground for mandatory exclusion is created to tackle child labour and other forms of trafficking in human beings, as defined in the corresponding EU instruments [art 57(1)(f) new dir].

Fourthly, lack of payment of taxes or social security contributions becomes a ground for mandatory disqualification 'where this has been established by a judicial or administrative decision having final and binding effect in accordance with the legal provisions of the country in which it is established or with those of the Member State of the contracting authority' [art 57(2) new dir]. This makes mandatory the grounds for discretionary exclusion currently foreseen in Articles 45(2)(e) and 45(2)(f) of Directive 2004/18 where there is a final and binding jurisdictional or administrative decision – and, otherwise, it will remain a discretionary ground for exclusion under Article 57(2)II of the new Directive (below section 3.2).[21]

Lastly, Article 57(1) in fine of the new Directive clarifies the provisions in Article 45(1) in fine of Directive 2004/18 and extends the obligation to exclude the economic operator on the basis of any of the prior grounds for exclusion 'where the person convicted by final judgment is a member of the administrative, management or supervisory body of that economic operator or has powers of representation, decision or control therein'. The only excep-

19. See unodc.org/unodc/en/treaties/CAC/.
20. oecd.org/corruption/oecdantibriberyconvention.htm. See also the 2009 OECD Recommendation for Further Combating Bribery of Foreign Public Officials in International Business Transactions, oecd.org/daf/anti-bribery/oecdantibriberyrecommendation2009.htm.
21. This may resolve some of the problems raised in case C-358/12 Consorgio Stabile Libor Lavon Pubblici [2014] ECR nyr, where Italian rules imposing a very harsh treatment aganinst minor delays in the payment of social security contributions were considered adequate and proportionale.

tion to this rule concerns the lack of payment of taxes and social security contributions, but this seems open to contention. In my opinion, at least where lack of payment is related to the activities of the economic operator, the rule should apply despite the legal person not being the one directly convicted or the direct addressee of the jurisdictional or administrative decision confirming the breach of tax or social security rules.

It is also worth stressing that, similar to what is already provided for in Article 45(1)III of Directive 2004/18, Article 57(3) of the new Directive foresees that 'Member States may provide for a derogation from the mandatory exclusion [...] on an exceptional basis, for overriding reasons relating to the public interest such as public health or protection of the environment'. In this regard, I would submit that the interpretation of the concept of 'general interest' developed by the CJEU in the area of free movement (of goods, in relation to art 36 TFEU and the so called Cassis rule of reason[22]) may be of relevance for the interpretation and construction of such potential derogations. Moreover, in the case of the lack of payment of taxes and social security contributions, Article 57(3) in fine of the new Directive authorises Member States to create an (additional) derogation 'where an exclusion would be clearly disproportionate, in particular where only minor amounts of taxes or social security contributions are unpaid or where the economic operator was informed of the exact amount due following its breach of its obligations relating to the payment of taxes or social security contributions at such time that it did not have the possibility of taking measures [addressed at sorting out the situation ...] before expiration of the deadline for requesting participation or, in open procedures, the deadline for submitting its tender'.[23] In order to ensure consistency of such a de minimis exception to the mandatory rule established in Article 57(2) of the new Directive, a common definition of what constitutes 'minor amounts' seems necessary. Otherwise, this is an issue likely to end up being referred to the CJEU for a preliminary interpretation, which answer may be almost impossible for the Court to provide, unless it is clearly willing to create a judicial de minimis threshold for this ground of exclusion.

22. For a first description and numerous references to the relevant CJEU case law, see section 6 on 'Justifications for barriers to trade' in the Commission's 2010 Guide to the application of Treaty provisions governing the free movement of goods ec.europa.eu/enterprise/policies/single-market-goods/files/goods/docs/art34-36/new_guide_en.pdf.
23. This is also clearly a reaction to the situation that gave rise to the Judgment in C-358/12 Consorgio Stabile Libor Lavon Pubblic [2014] ECR nyr.

3.2. Extension of the discretionary grounds for exclusion of economic operators

Following the current distinction in Article 45(2) of Directive 2004/18, which establishes additional exclusion grounds that contracting authorities can decide to apply at their discretion, Articles 57(2)II and 57(4) of the new Directive extend the current list of discretionary grounds for the exclusion of economic operators that contracting authorities may decide to use (or may be required by their Member State to use) to exclude any economic operator from participation in a procurement procedure. With some drafting modifications, but with fundamentally the same content, the list provided in Articles 57(2)II and 57(4) covers the current grounds of exclusion on the basis of: i) bankruptcy, judicial administration or assimilated situations, including being part of ongoing proceedings, ii) demonstrated grave professional misconduct, which renders its integrity questionable,[24] iii) lack of payment of taxes or social security contributions not established by a jurisdictional or administrative decision having final and binding effect (otherwise, the exclusion ground becomes mandatory, above section 3.1), and iv) serious misrepresentation in supplying the information required for the verification of the absence of grounds for exclusion or the fulfilment of the selection criteria, or withholding of such information. Furthermore, and similarly to what happened with mandatory exclusion grounds, Article 57(4) of the new Directive extends and broadens the list of situations in which an economic operator can (or must) be excluded.

Firstly, given the creation of new rules on the European Single Procurement Document (ie the submission of self-declarations) rather than the supply of full evidence supporting the inexistence of grounds for exclusion and compliance with qualitative selection criteria (art 59 new dir and below section 4.5), the ground concerned with misrepresentation and withholding of

24. Article 57(4)(c) of the new Directive refers to situations 'where the contracting authority can demonstrate by appropriate means that the economic operator is guilty of grave professional misconduct', merging the current provisions of Directive 2004/18 in Articles 45(2)(c) 'has been convicted by a judgment which has the force of res judicata in accordance with the legal provisions of the country of any offence concerning his professional conduct' and 45(2)(d) 'has been guilty of grave professional misconduct proven by any means which the contracting authorities can demonstrate'. Actually, the list (partially) suppresses the content Article 45(2)(c). This seems to exclude the grounds for exclusion for non-grave professional misconduct sanctioned by a final judgment under Article 45(2)(c). However, given the absence of a common definition of 'grave professional misconduct' the practical effects of such a change remain doubtful.

information is extended to cover situations where the economic operator is 'not able to submit the supporting documents required pursuant to Article 59' [art 57(4)(h) new dir]. This establishes a iuris et de iure presumption that the economic operator that cannot supply the required supporting documentation has gravely misrepresented its suitability and qualification to be awarded the contract and seems a natural extension of this grounds for exclusion – which, in my opinion, should however constitute a mandatory ground for exclusion (below section 4.5).

Secondly, as already mentioned (above section 2.3), contracting authorities can exclude economic operators where they can demonstrate by any appropriate means violations of applicable obligations established by Union law or national law compatible with it in the field of social and labour law or environmental law or of the international social and environmental law provisions listed in Annex X [arts 18(2) and 57(4)(a) new dir]. Other than the considerations related to the use of public procurement as a lever to reinforce compliance with such 'secondary policies', this new ground for exclusion raises the issue of the standard of diligence that the contracting authority must discharge in order not to be negligently unaware of the existence of such violations. Given that there are different standards for different exclusion grounds, these are issues that are prone to litigation and that will likely require interpretation by the CJEU. In my view, any means of proof should suffice to proceed to such exclusion, but the violation should be of a sufficient entity as to justify the exclusion under a proportionality test (similarly to what the new Directive proposes in terms of lack of payment of taxes or social security contributions, or 'grave' professional misconduct), since exclusion for any minor infringement of social, labour or environmental requirements may be disproportionate and, ultimately, not in the public interest if it affects the level and intensity of competition for the contracts.

Thirdly, the new Directive creates a new (limited) ground for the exclusion of infringers of competition law. Indeed, contracting authorities can now exclude economic operators where they have 'sufficiently plausible indications to conclude that the economic operator has entered into agreements with other economic operators aimed at distorting competition' [art 57(4)(d)]. This should be read in connection with the OECD's July 2012 Recommendation on Fighting Bid Rigging in Public Procurement[25] and with the many actions undertaken by national competition authorities of some of the Member States to better liaise with contracting authorities and entities, and to advocate for

25. oecd.org/competition/cartels/fightingbidrigginginpublicprocurement.htm.

competition law compliance in the public procurement setting. In my opinion, this new ground for exclusion is excessively limited and, given the gravity of bid rigging, it should be a ground for the mandatory exclusion of the offenders.[26] As a matter of diligence (and subject to applicable domestic rules), in these cases, the contracting authority seems likely to be under a duty to report this behaviour to the national competition authority and to cooperate as much as necessary with the ensuing competition law investigation.

Fourthly, the new Directive creates yet another ground for exclusion based on poor past performance by the economic operator. Under this new ground, contracting authorities can exclude economic operators that have 'shown significant or persistent deficiencies in the performance of a substantive requirement under a prior public contract, a prior contract with a contracting entity or a prior concession contract which led to early termination of that prior contract, damages or other comparable sanctions' [art 57(4)(g)]. The introduction of past performance as an exclusion ground responds to the requests made for a long time by practitioners and brings the EU system closer to that of the US. Remarkably, this provision may overturn the practice and case law that prevented contracting authorities to take past performance into consideration. In my opinion, even if good past performance should not be taken into consideration either for selection or award purposes (because of the effect it has in entrenching the incumbents),[27] it seems sensible to introduce its use for 'negative' purposes in order to allow contracting authorities to (self)protect their interests by not engaging contractors prone not to deliver as expected. This seems particularly proportionate in view of the rules on 'self-cleaning' that allow contractors to compensate such poor past performance by showing that they have implemented changes to avoid them recurring (below section 3.3).

26. For further discussion, see A Sanchez Graells, 'Prevention and Deterrence of Bid Rigging: A Look from the New EU Directive on Public Procurement', in G M Racca and C R Yukins (eds), Integrity and Efficiency in Sustainable Public Contracts (Brussels, Bruylant, 2014) p. 137-157.

27. Indeed, 'the past acquisition of significant experience in the field of [providing services to public authorities] and, more specifically, to the [contracting authority], cannot under any circumstances be taken into account by the contracting authority when selecting tenders if the principles of equal treatment and non-discrimination are to be respected'; Case T-59/05 Evropaïki Dinamiki (DG AGRI) [2008] ECR II-157 para 104. Similarly, although in less explicit terms, see Case T-183/00 Strabag Benelux [2003] ECR II-135 para 79; and Case T-495/04 Belfass [2008] ECR II-781 para 76.

Interestingly, a (soft) corruption-related new ground for exclusion is also created.[28] Further to the ground for mandatory exclusion of economic operators engaged in (hard) corruption (above section 3.1), contracting authorities can exclude economic operators where they have 'undertaken to unduly influence the decision-making process of the contracting authority, to obtain confidential information that may confer upon it undue advantages in the procurement procedure or to negligently provide misleading information that may have a material influence on decisions concerning exclusion, selection or award' [art 57(4)(i) new dir]. To be sure, some or all of these activities may be caught by the definition of corruption under domestic laws and, consequently, could substantively overlap with the mandatory ground for exclusion in Article 57(1)(b) of the new Directive (above section 3.1). However, the mandatory ground for exclusion is only triggered if the economic operator has already been convicted by final judgment. Consequently, the virtuality of Article 57(4)(i) of the new Directive resides in allowing the contracting authority to immediately exclude any economic operator engaged in (quasi)corruption or that has otherwise tried to tamper with the integrity of the tender procedure. As a matter of diligence (and subject to applicable domestic rules), in these cases, the contracting authority seems likely to be under a duty to report this behaviour to the competent authorities or courts and to push for criminal prosecution.

Finally, and strengthening the general remarks contained in the recitals of previous generations of procurement directives,[29] the new Directive has also created two complementary grounds for the exclusion of tenderers in cases of conflict of interest, either generally [arts 24 and 57(4)(e)], or as a result of the

28. This would have been strengthened if the intermediate drafts of the Compromise Text published in July 2012 had changed Article 15 on the principles of procurement to read 'Contracting authorities shall treat economic operators equally and without discrimination and shall act in a transparent and proportionate *manner that avoids or remedies conflicts of interest and prevents corrupt practices'* (emphasis added). See register.consilium.europa.eu/pdf/en/12/st12/st12878.en12.pdf. However, this is not the drafting retained in the latest version of the Directive.
29. As criticised by H-J Prieß, 'Distortions of Competition in Tender Proceedings: How to Deal with Conflicts of Interest (Family Ties, Business Links and Cross–Representation of Contracting Authority Officials and Bidders) and the Involvement of Project Consultants' (2002) 11 Public Procurement Law Review 153 and S Treumer, 'Technical Dialogue and the Principle of Equal Treatment – Dealing with Conflicts of Interest after Fabricom' (2007) 16 Public Procurement Law Review 99. See also A Sanchez Graells, Public Procurement and the EU Competition Rules (Oxford, Hart Publishing, 2011) 305-309.

prior involvement of candidates or tenderers in the preparation of the procedure [arts 41 and 57(4)(f)]. Indeed, the contracting authority can exclude economic operators 'where a conflict of interest within the meaning of Article 24 cannot be effectively remedied by other less intrusive measures',[30] or 'where a distortion of competition from the prior involvement of the economic operators in the preparation of the procurement procedure, as referred to in Article 41, cannot be remedied by other, less intrusive measures'. These provisions should allow contracting authorities to ensure the integrity of the procurement process, despite the fact that the conflict of interest will also affect themselves (or members of their staff) and, consequently, these may end up being provisions which disappointed tenderers use in order to challenge their lack of application, rather than provisions directly and positively applied by the contracting authorities themselves – depending, of course, on the institutional robustness of the specific contracting authority concerned (and the litigation environment in any given Member State).

3.3. Self-cleaning and corporate compliance programs

As a novelty, and in order to allow 'for the possibility that economic operators can adopt compliance measures aimed at remedying the consequences of any criminal offences or misconduct and at effectively preventing further occurrences of the misbehaviour' [rec (102) new dir], Article 57(6) of the new Directive establishes rules on self-cleaning[31] and promotes the adoption of corporate compliance programs. Under the rules of Article 57(6), any economic operator that should be excluded under any of the grounds in 57(1) or 57(4)[32] can provide evidence to the effect that measures it has taken are sufficient to demonstrate its reliability despite the existence of a relevant ground

30. It is worth noting that, according to Article 24.II of the new Directive, 'The concept of conflicts of interest shall at least cover any situation where staff members of the contracting authority or of a procurement service provider acting on behalf of the contracting authority who are involved in the conduct of the procurement procedure or may influence the outcome of that procedure have, directly or indirectly, a financial, economic or other personal interest which might be perceived to compromise their impartiality and independence in the context of the procurement procedure.'
31. S Arrowsmith, H-J Prieß and P Friton, 'Self-Cleaning as a Defence to Exclusions for Misconduct – An Emerging Concept in EC Public Procurement Law?' (2009) 18 Public Procurement Law Review 257.
32. Exclusion on the grounds of lack of payment of taxes or social security contributions is not included due to the fact that the only 'compensatory' measures accepted in the new Directive are payment of the arrears or entering into a binding agreement to do so (below section 3.4).

for exclusion and, if such evidence is considered as sufficient by the contracting authority, the economic operator concerned shall not be excluded.

The new Directive includes a list of compensatory measures that, as a minimum, shall include proof that the economic operator 'has paid or undertaken to pay compensation in respect of any damage caused by the criminal offence or misconduct, clarified the facts and circumstances in a comprehensive manner by actively collaborating with the investigating authorities and taken concrete technical, organisational and personnel measures that are appropriate to prevent further criminal offences or misconduct'. Furthermore, the discretion retained by the contracting authority to assess the sufficiency of the self-cleaning measures adopted by the economic operator is modulated by the requirement that they 'shall be evaluated taking into account the gravity and particular circumstances of the criminal offence or misconduct'. As a specific requirement of the duty of good administration and the obligation to provide reasons for any decision adopted in a procurement procedure, '[w]here the measures are considered to be insufficient, the economic operator shall receive a statement of the reasons for that decision' – which, in my opinion, shall be amenable to judicial review under the applicable rules of each Member State.

Oddly, the new Directive restricts the possibility of implementing self-cleaning measures for economic operators that have 'been excluded by final judgment from participating in procurement procedures [which] shall not be entitled to make use of [this] possibility [...] during the period of exclusion resulting from that judgment in the Member States where the judgment is effective'. This shows a lack of trust in self-cleaning measures and imposes exclusion as an irreversible sanction in the Member State adopting that decision (but, oddly, not in other Member States), which can sometimes disproportionately reduce competition (as well as creating a dual standard applicable in 'domestic' and 'cross-border' participation in procurement by that operator). Therefore, in my opinion, self-cleaning should also be available in these cases, which may justify a particularly tough approach to the evaluation of the sufficiency of the measures implemented by the economic operator. At least, an escape clause should exist in these cases to waive, substitute or defer the exclusion on grounds of public interest if having the economic operator excluded actually harms the interests of the contracting authority (which may be the case in highly concentrated or specialised markets).

3.4. Harmonisation of minimum rules on maximum exclusion periods

Following the current position in Articles 45(1) and 45(2) of Directive 2004/18, Article 57(7) of the new Directive requires that Member States specify the implementing conditions for the exclusion of economic operators by law, regulation or administrative provision and always having regard for EU law. However, it establishes new minimum rules concerning maximum exclusion periods. Indeed, Member States shall 'determine the maximum period of exclusion if no [self-cleaning] measures [...] are taken by the economic operator to demonstrate its reliability. Where the period of exclusion has not been set by final judgment, that period shall not exceed five years from the date of the conviction by final judgment in the cases referred to in paragraph 1 and three years from the date of the relevant event in the cases referred to in paragraph 4' of that same article 57 of the new Directive.

In the specific case of (mandatory or discretionary) exclusion due to lack of payment of taxes or social security contributions, the exclusion seems to be subject to an indefinite period that will only finish once the economic operator settles the outstanding debt or enters into arrangements to do so. This derives from Article 57(2) in fine which determines that these grounds for exclusion 'shall no longer apply when the economic operator has fulfilled its obligations by paying or entering into a binding arrangement with a view to paying the taxes or social security contributions due, including, where applicable, any interest accrued or fines'.

In my opinion, such different treatment for these specific exclusion grounds seems unwarranted and other exclusion grounds that indicate the existence of similarly ongoing infringements (such as those concerned with infringements of social, labour and environmental law, or those concerning bankruptcy and administration) should also be subjected to indefinite exclusion until the economic operator complies with the relevant legislation. This result may be achieved anyway depending on the domestic rules applicable to continued infringements, but some further clarification and harmonisation could be desirable in order to keep the level playing field. Moreover, rules on the recognition of domestic exclusion decisions in the rest of the Member States could also be necessary, although this can be indirectly achieved by the European Single Procurement Document (below section 4.5).

4. Qualitative selection criteria

4.1. Numerus clausus? of selection criteria and minimum ability levels

Article 58(1) of the new Directive consolidates and somehow clarifies the requirements in Articles 41(1) and 41(2) of Directive 2004/18 as regards the fact that selection criteria can exclusively relate to: i) the suitability to pursue the professional activity concerned, ii) the economic and financial standing, and iii) the technical and professional ability of the economic operator; and that, in any case, the requirements shall be limited to 'those that are appropriate to ensure that a candidate or tenderer has the legal and financial capacities and the technical and professional abilities to perform the contract to be awarded. All requirements shall be related and proportionate to the subject-matter of the contract'.

However, Article 58(1) of the new Directive is not free from interpretive difficulties, since it seems to aim to establish a numerus clausus or exhaustive list of selection criteria when it indicates that 'Contracting authorities *may only* impose criteria referred to in paragraphs 2, 3 and 4 of this Article on economic operators as requirements for participation' (emphasis added). However, this is not consistent with the open-ended wording of such paragraphs (see below sections 4.2 to 4.4) and would contradict the existing case law of the CJEU, which establishes that contracting authorities have wide discretion to set the specific requirements that they consider adequate for the evaluation of the suitability of candidates to perform the contract.[33] Therefore, regardless of the specific drafting, it seems clear that there is actually no numerus clausus of selection criteria,[34] as long as they refer to the suitability to pursue the professional activity concerned, the economic and financial standing, or the technical and professional ability of the economic operator (are related and proportionate to the subject-matter of the contract, and are kept to a minimum in order to take into account the need to ensure genuine competition[35]).

33. Joined Cases 27 to 29/86 CEI and Bellini [1987] ECR 3347 paras 13-5. See also S Arrowsmith, The Law of Public and Utilities Procurement, 2nd edn (London, Sweet and Maxwell, 2005) 725-30, and P Trepte, Regulating Procurement. Understanding the Ends and Means of Public Procurement Regulation (Oxford, Oxford University Press, 2004) 99.
34. Cf Arrowsmith, The Law of Public and Utilities Procurement, above n 32, 732-3, and P Trepte, Public Procurement in the EU. A Practitioner's Guide, 2nd edn (Oxford, Oxford University Press, 2007) 341-2, who considered that the equivalent lists under Articles 45(2) and 46 of Directive 2004/18 imposed a numerus clausus "The reasons [for the exclusion of tenderers on grounds of their general unsuitability] are exhaustive, as demonstrated in the early case of Transporoute" [with reference to Case 76/81 Transporoute [1982] ECR 417]. However, the discussion between acceptable criteria and admissible means of proof or documentary requirements is bound to create confusion in any case.
35. This last caveat has been suppressed in the new Directive, but was included in the original 2011 proposal by the European Commission and, in my view, gave all rules on selection criteria a much more pro-competitive spin and imposed stricter proportionality requirements; A Sanchez Graells, 'Are the Procurement Rules a Barrier for Cross-Border Trade within the European Market? A View on Proposals to Lower that

In any case, where contracting authorities want to establish minimum capacity levels, they have to comply with Article 58(5) of the new Directive [which carries forward the requirements of art 44(2) dir 2004/18] and 'indicate the required conditions of participation which may be expressed as minimum levels of ability, together with the appropriate means of proof, in the contract notice or in the invitation to confirm interest'.

4.2. Suitability to pursue the professional activity concerned

This is now regulated in Article 58(2) of the new Directive, which recasts and keeps the rules of Article 46 of Directive 2004/18 substantially unchanged. In this regard, it may simply be worth noting that, in relation to service contracts, contracting authorities may face difficulties in cases of breach of the Services Directive[36] by Member States that impose excessive professional requirements.

4.3. Economic and Financial Standing and its Capping

Article 58(3) of the new Directive provides substantive guidance on the requirements concerned with the economic and financial standing of the economic operator and goes beyond Article 47 of Directive 2004/18, which was limited to regulating the means of proof that could be furnished and had to be accepted by the contracting authority [something now regulated in art 60(3) new dir]. Interestingly, Article 58(3) of the new Directive focuses on requirements of minimum yearly turnover, which is one of the criteria more widely used in practice.

According to this provision, 'contracting authorities may impose requirements ensuring that economic operators possess the necessary economic and financial capacity to perform the contract' and, in particular, 'may require [...] that economic operators have a certain minimum yearly turnover, includ-

Barrier and Spur Growth' in Tvarnø, Ølykke & Risvig Hansen (eds), EU Public Procurement: Modernisation, Growth and Innovation, (Copenhagen, DJØF, 2012) p. 107-133. In any case, this procompetitive requirement should be seen as an (implicit) extension of Article 18(1) of the new Directive, which expressly consolidates the principle of competition by mandating that: 'The design of the procurement shall not be made with the intention of [...] artificially narrowing competition. Competition shall be considered to be artificially narrowed where the design of the procurement is made with the intention of unduly favouring or disadvantaging certain economic operators'.

36. Directive 2006/123/EC of 12 December 2006 on services in the internal market [2006] OJ L 376/36. See ec.europa.eu/internal_market/services/services-dir/guide/index_en.htm.

ing a certain minimum turnover in the area covered by the contract. In addition, contracting authorities may require that economic operators provide information on their annual accounts showing the ratios, for instance, between assets and liabilities. They may also require an appropriate level of professional risk indemnity insurance'.

More importantly, the new Directive introduces a cap on economic and financial standing requirements that is particularly addressed to foster SME participation. Indeed, 'The *minimum yearly turnover* that economic operators are required to have *shall not exceed two times the estimated contract value,* except in duly justified cases such as relating to the special risks attached to the nature of the works, services or supplies. The contracting authority shall indicate the main reasons for such requirement in the procurement documents' (emphasis added). However, in order to avoid this becoming the de facto standard requirement, it is still important to stress that contracting entities and authorities still have to comply with the requirement of article 58(1) of the new Directive, so that – within that limit – the specific requirements set still are 'strictly proportionate to the subject-matter of the contract', taking into account the need to ensure genuine competition.

This rule must be adjusted where the contract is tendered in lots and, in that case, the cap to double the value 'shall apply in relation to each individual lot. However, the contracting authority may set the minimum yearly turnover that economic operators are required to have by reference to groups of lots in the event that the successful tenderer is awarded several lots to be executed at the same time'. In cases of framework agreements and dynamic purchasing systems, this cap should be calculated on the basis of expected maximum size of specific contracts.

4.4. Technical and professional ability and a hidden rule on conflicts of interest

Similarly to the changes introduced in relation to the economic and financial standing (section 4.3), Article 58(4) of the new Directive goes beyond the documentary requirements in Article 48 of Directive 2004/18 [now in art 60(4) new dir] and lays down some substantive requirements concerned with the technical and professional ability of economic operators. Generally, this provision indicates that 'contracting authorities may impose requirements ensuring that economic operators possess the necessary human and technical resources and experience to perform the contract to an appropriate quality standard' and, in particular, may require 'economic operators have a sufficient level of experience demonstrated by suitable references from contracts performed in the past.'. Even more specifically, and consolidating the current rule in Article 48(5) of Directive 2004/18, Article 56(4) in fine stresses that '[i]n procurement procedures for supplies requiring siting or installation work, services or works, the professional ability of economic operators to provide the service or to execute the installation or the work may be evaluated with regard to their skills, efficiency, experience and reliability'.

Interestingly enough, Article 58(4) includes a rule against conflicts of interest disguised as a requirement of professional ability (which seems to stretch the concept, at least if taken on its ordinary meaning).[37] Indeed, it establishes that 'A contracting authority may assume that an economic operator does not possess the required professional abilities where the contracting authority has established that *the economic operator has conflicting interests which may negatively affect the performance of the contract*' (emphasis added). This development should be welcome, as it aims to cover a significant gap in the regime of Directive 2004/18, which has no rules concerned with the existence of conflicts of interest (despite mentioning them in the recitals),[38] but more clarification should have been provided as to the type of conflicts of interest that justify the exclusion of the economic operator on the basis of its lack of professional ability. In that regard, it is important to stress that Article 24 of the new Directive defines 'conflicts of interest' for other purposes,[39] indicating that it 'shall at least cover any situation where staff members of the contracting authority or of a procurement service provider acting on behalf of the contracting authority who are involved in the conduct of the procurement procedure or may influence the outcome of that procedure have, directly or indirectly, a financial, economic or other personal interest which might be perceived to compromise their impartiality and independence in the context of the procurement procedure'. However, the conflicts of interest that can affect economic operators are not necessarily identical, nor their mirror image and, consequently, some further clarification will be necessary.

37. This would have been easier to achieve and strengthened if an alternative drafting of Article 18(1) on the principles of procurement had been retained. See above n 27.
38. See footnote 28 above and accompanying text.
39. Member States shall ensure that contracting authorities take appropriate measures to effectively prevent, identify and remedy conflicts of interests arising in the conduct of procurement procedures so as to avoid any distortion of competition and ensure equal treatment of all economic operators.

4.5. Means of proof and a revolution on paper: the European Single Procurement Document, self-declarations and other facilitating measures

Article 60 of the new Directive regulates in minute detail the certificates, statements and other means of proof that contracting authorities can require in order to check for the absence of grounds of exclusion (above sections 3.1 and 3.2) and compliance with qualitative selection criteria (above sections 4.2 to 4.4.) and makes it clear that, together with Article 62 on quality assurance standards and environmental management standards,[40] it sets a numerus clausus of documentation that can be required from economic operators. Such documents are fundamentally the same foreseen in Articles 45(3), 47 and 48 of Directive 2004/18, which are moved to several annexes in the new Directive. Therefore, there are limited changes in that respect.

Nonetheless, Article 59 of the new Directive introduces a significant attempt to flexibilise documentary requirements and to reduce red tape in public procurement by means of the European Single Procurement Document (ESPD) (ie a collection of self-declarations) and other facilitating measures.[41] Under this new system, economic operators will be able to submit an ESPD 'consisting of an updated self-declaration as preliminary evidence in replacement of certificates issued by public authorities or third parties confirming' that they are not affected by exclusion grounds, that they meet selection and short-listing criteria (as applicable) and that they will be able to produce hard documentary evidence of such circumstances without delay, upon request of the contracting authority [art 59(1)]. Indeed, the ESPD 'shall consist

40. Article 62 of the new Directive fundamentally consolidates the rules in Articles 49 and 50 of Directive 2004/18, with some updates to the standards referred to and with some changes in drafting, the only of which seems relevant is that contracting authorities must now only accept other evidence of equivalent quality assurance standards and environmental management standards where the economic operator concerned has no access to such certificates, or no possibility of obtaining them within the relevant time limits for reasons that are not attributable to that economic operator. This seems to reduce the scope for the submission of equivalent certificates in some instances and could be unduly restrictive of competition. However, this effect will largely depend on the interpretation given to this 'waiver clause'. In view of the limited changes in Article 62 of the new directive, it will not be discussed further. The same applies to Article 64, which deals with official lists of economic operators and is substantially identical to the current rules under Article 52 of Directive 2004/18 – although, admittedly, the new Directive has aimed to simplify the drafting.
41. For further discussion, including the now abandoned proposal for the creation of a European Procurement Passport, see Sanchez Graells, 'Are the Procurement Rules a Barrier for Cross-Border Trade within the European Market? (2012) 121-126.

of a formal statement by the economic operator that the relevant ground for exclusion does not apply and/or that the relevant selection criterion is fulfilled and shall provide the relevant information as required by the contracting authority. The ESPD shall further identify the public authority or third party responsible for establishing the supporting documents and contain a formal statement to the effect that the economic operator will be able, upon request and without delay, to provide those supporting documents'.[42] In order to try to increase the advantages of the ESPD, it is conceived as a 'reusable' instrument, so that '[e]conomic operators may reuse an ESPD which has already been used in a previous procurement procedure, provided that they confirm that the information contained therein continues to be correct'.

The contracting authority will then be free to request submission of such documents at any point of the process where this appears necessary to ensure the proper conduct of the procedure and, in any case, shall require them from the chosen contractor prior to awarding the contract, unless it already possesses these documents or can obtain these documents or the relevant information by accessing a national database [art 59(4)]. In that regard, it is worth stressing that, as a complementary facilitating measure, Article 59(5) of the new Directive foresees that: 'economic operators shall not be required to submit supporting documents or other documentary evidence where and in so far as the contracting authority has the possibility of obtaining the certificates or the relevant information directly by accessing a national database in any Member State that is available free of charge, such as a national procurement register, a virtual company dossier, an electronic document storage system or a prequalification system. [...] For [that] purpose [...] Member States shall ensure that databases which contain relevant information on economic operators and which may be consulted by their contracting authorities may also be consulted, under the same conditions, by contracting authorities of other Member States'.[43]

42. Moreover, where the contracting authority can obtain the supporting documents directly by accessing a database pursuant to Article 59(5), the self-declaration shall also contain the information required for this purpose, such as the internet address of the database, any identification data and, where applicable, the necessary declaration of consent.
43. As a complement, and according to Article 59(6) of the new Directive, 'Member States shall make available and up-to-date in e-Certis a complete list of databases containing relevant information on economic operators which can be consulted by contracting authorities from other Member States. Upon request, Member States shall communicate to other Member States any information related to the databases referred to in this Article'. Moreover, according to Article 61(1), 'With a view to facili-

It should be recalled that failure to provide the required documentation in support of the self-declarations submitted by the economic operator will constitute a discretionary ground for exclusion [art 57(4)(h), above section 3.2], which the contracting authority can apply any time [art 57(5), above section 2.2]. In that regard, the system seems too lenient towards the failure to support any of the prior declarations. Under the initial 2011 proposal, it would generate an impediment to award under Article 68, now suppressed. Indeed, it is hard to understand why contracting authorities would be free to award the contract to an economic operator that cannot support its own self-declarations and how that would not infringe the principles of transparency, equal treatment and non-distortion of competition. In my view, this should constitute a case of mandatory exclusion of the economic operator concerned, unless there were good reasons beyond its control that prevented it from submitting the required documentation.

More generally, in my view, this rather revolutionary proposal (revolutionary at least for countries with 'traditional' administrative procedure regulations) for the acceptance of the ESPD (rectius, 'mere' self-declarations) clearly has the potential to reduce the costs of participating in the tender for unsuccessful bidders (increasing the incentive to participate), but generates a relatively small advantage for successful bidders (only a time gain, and of an uncertain length at that), increases the length of the procedure (there is no regulation concerning the time that the authority must give the successful tenderer to produce the requested documents prior to award) and generates a risk of potential award to non-compliant bidders that would require second or ulterior awards (with the corresponding difficulties regarding the need to ensure that other bidders keep their offers open, new award notices, etc).[44]

tating cross-border tendering, Member States shall ensure that the information concerning certificates and other forms of documentary evidence introduced in e-Certis established by the Commission is constantly kept up-to-date'.

44. These risks are identified in the Commission, Impact Assessment of the Proposal for a Directive of the European Parliament and of the Council on Public Procurement 70 [SEC(2011) 1585 final] ec.europa.eu/internal_market/publicprocurement/modernising_rules/reform_proposals_en.htm, but simply dismissed on the hope that self-declarations would bring a significant reduction of time and costs and a potential automatisation of selection and award procedures. In my view, the analysis conducted in the impact assessment is overly optimistic, eg: "If measures reducing the information obligations placed on firms were to be implemented (e.g. through generalising the "winning bidder provides" provisions), this could theoretically reduce the efficiency of the evaluation process for contracting authorities and entities if, in some cases, a firm identified as a winner fails the evidentiary tests (and the contracting au-

In order to complete this proposal, I think that it would be necessary to set speedy but reasonable time limits to produce the requested documents and to strengthen the consequences of failing to produce supporting evidence for the self-declarations, which should not only be an impediment to award, but also be clearly identified as a ground for mandatory exclusion – and maybe expressly set it as a head of damage that allows contracting authorities to recover any additional expenses derived from the need to proceed to a second-best, delayed award of the contract (without excluding the eventual enforcement of criminal law provisions regarding deceit or other types of fraud under applicable national laws). Also, rules on annulment of the awarded contract and other sanctions are needed for those instances where the discovery of the falsity of the documents occurs after contract award – since this case is not fully covered by the provision of Article 73(b) of the new Directive, which only requires that contracting authorities have the possibility to terminate a public contract during its term, where it turns out that 'the contractor has, at the time of contract award, been in one of the situations referred to in Article 57(1) and should therefore have been excluded from the procurement procedure'. Hence, if the self-declaration that the economic contractor has been unable to support is not concerned with Article 57(1), there is not even an indirect way to challenge (at least clearly) the award of the contract despite the infringement of Article 59(4) of the new Directive. In my opinion, challenges under domestic contract rules governing misrepresentations or falsity in private documents should be available in this case, but it would have been desirable that the new rules included a specific termination clause in this case in Article 73.

thority or entity would have to go to their second choice or repeat the process). From the information available, such instances are not that common, and in most cases contracting authorities and entities should save time by accepting self-certification of compliance from bidders who ultimately do not win the contract. Also, if more firms feel able to bid, competition could increase, which could lead to greater price savings or improvements in quality for the contracting authority or entity." The premise that instances where the winner fails to meet the evidentiary tests are rare simply cannot be imported from an ex ante full control scenario to an ex post verification paradigm. In my view, the increase in risks based on strategic behaviour by bidders and the potential difficulties in meeting short submission deadlines prior to award of the contract are just not comparable with the current situation – at least, unless stronger consequences are attached to failing to provide the requested documentation or, more clearly, in cases of falsity of declarations.

4.6. More precise rules governing reliance on the capacities of other entities

Article 63 of the new Directive maintains the functional approach in Directive 2004/18 and consolidates the rules on reliance on the capacities of other entities that are now scattered in Articles 47(2), 47(3), 48(3) and 48(4) of the Directive. It continues to make it clear that, as long as it is appropriate for a particular contract, any economic operator can 'rely on the capacities of other entities, regardless of the legal nature of the links which it has with them' to which aim it 'it shall prove to the contracting authority that it will have at its disposal the resources necessary, for example, by producing a commitment by those entities to that effect'. Equally and under the same conditions, 'a group of economic operators [...] may rely on the capacities of participants in the group or of other entities'.[45] However, the new Directive goes beyond these general rules and imposes more specific (and restrictive) criteria concerning reliance on other operators for certain requirements.

Firstly, with regard to criteria relating to the educational and professional qualifications or to the relevant professional experience, economic operators may only rely on the capacities of other entities where the latter will perform the works or services for which these capacities are required.

Secondly, the contracting authority shall verify whether the other entities on whose capacity the economic operator intends to rely fulfil the relevant selection criteria or whether there are grounds for their exclusion. Consequently, an entity which does not meet a relevant selection criterion, or in respect of which there are grounds for exclusion, may be excluded (ie may not be relied upon). In the precise terms of Article 63(1) '[t]he contracting authority shall require that the economic operator replaces an entity which does not meet a relevant selection criterion, or in respect of which there are compulsory grounds for exclusion. The contracting authority may require or may be required by the Member State to require that the economic operator substitutes an entity in respect of which there are non-compulsory grounds for exclusion.'

Thirdly, Member States may provide that in the case of works contracts, service contracts and siting or installation operations in the context of a supply contract, contracting authorities may require that certain critical tasks be performed directly by the tenderer itself or, where the tender is submitted by a group of economic operators, by a participant in that group.

45. Interestingly, Article 19 of the new Directive provides specific rules for groups of operators.

Finally, where an economic operator relies on the capacities of other entities with regard to criteria relating to economic and financial standing, the contracting authority may require that the economic operator and those entities be jointly liable for the execution of the contract.

In my view, the first two additions are sensible and aim to prevent instances where reliance on third party capabilities is merely formal. However, the same cannot be said from the other two requirements. On the one hand, there is no good reason to require that the conduct of critical tasks be carried out by the main contractor, given that it is already assuming full liability for such tasks. Imposing a requirement that the task is actually carried out by the main contractor can have the effect of excluding other tenderers that could actually fulfil the contract relying on the capabilities of third parties and, consequently, runs contrary to the functional approach in the current Directive, goes beyond the terms of Article 19 of the new Directive[46] and, ultimately, of the case law of the CJEU on teaming and joint bidding.[47] On the other hand, and on a related note, the last requirement of joint liability for the execution of the contract can make it very difficult to reach subcontracting agreements or similar arrangements for the reliance on third parties for the partial execution of a minor part of the contract. Moreover, it can result in complicated structures of side letters of indemnity that raise the legal costs linked to participation. In my opinion, in relation with both requirements, the contracting entity should be satisfied with the liability of the main contractor and, if need be, 'self-protect' through requirements for adequate professional risk indemnity insurance under Article 58(3) of the new Directive.

5. Short-listing or reduction of numbers of candidates, tenders and solutions

The content of Article 44(3) Directive 2004/18 has been moved to Article 65 of the new Directive and the content of Article 44(4) Directive 2004/18 has been moved to Article 66. There are no changes in these rules, other than

46. Indeed, it only requires that 'in the case of public service and public works contracts as well as public supply contracts covering in addition services or siting and installation operations, legal persons may be required to indicate, in the tender or the request to participate, the names and relevant professional qualifications of the staff to be responsible for the performance of the contract in question'.
47. Sanchez Graells, Public Procurement and the EU Competition Rules (2011) 276-280.

some minor drafting changes and an update of the cross-references to other Articles in the Directive.

Grosso modo, the rules continue to allow for contracting authorities to limit the number of candidates that they will invite to tender or to negotiate in procedures other than open (and negotiated without prior publication). In that case, they have to establish the minimum (and maximum) number of candidates they intend to invite (at least five in the restricted procedure and three in the competitive procedure with negotiation, in the competitive dialogue procedure and in the innovation partnership). Contracting entities must 'indicate, in the contract notice or in the invitation to confirm interest, the objective and non-discriminatory criteria or rules they intend to apply' to short-list candidates [art 65(2) new dir]. Once the short-listing is completed, they must invite a number of candidates at least equal to the minimum number and where the number of candidates meeting the selection criteria and the minimum levels of ability is below that minimum, they may continue the procedure by inviting the candidates with the required capabilities but 'the contracting authority shall not include economic operators that did not request to participate, or candidates that do not have the required capabilities' [art 65(2) in fine new dir]. Similar rules apply to the reduction of the tenders to be negotiated or the solutions to discussed but, at any rate, in the final stage, the number arrived at shall make for genuine competition insofar as there are enough solutions, qualified candidates or tenderers [art 66 new dir]. By sticking to the same rules, the new Directive does not resolve the problems that, in my opinion, a strict interpretation of these rules may generate (such as short-listing that only leaves one tenderer out).[48]

6. Technical dialogue as a particular way of short-listing

Articles 30 and 31 of the new Directive regulate in rather obscure terms the 'technical dialogue' in which contracting authorities can engage with candidates invited to participate in a competitive dialogue or a tender for an innovation partnership. The procedures are basically subjected to very minimum requirements whereby contracting authorities need to establish their needs and (if known) minimum technical requirements in the tender documents [arts 30(2) and 31(1)] and, subsequently, can engage in the (technical) dia-

48. For discussion, Sanchez Graells, Public Procurement and the EU Competition Rules (n 37) 262-265.

logue with the candidates that have been invited after checking that they meet the necessary selection/shortlisting criteria [arts 30(3) and 31(3)] and run rounds/stages of technical discussions and negotiations in order to reduce the number of solutions/proposals they are willing to continue analysing and negotiating, until a single set of technical specifications (or innovation plans, so to call them) is selected [arts 30(4) and 31(4)]. In case they want to avail themselves of this 'staged' (technical) dialogue, they must proceed to a reduction of the solutions to be further pursued in each round 'by applying the award criteria defined in the contract notice or in the descriptive document'[49] and 'the contract notice or the descriptive document [...] shall indicate [that the contracting authority] will use this option' [arts 30(4) and 31(5)]. In any case, regardless of conducting it in a staged or in a single-stage manner, the contracting authority shall continue the dialogue until it can identify the solution or solutions which are capable of meeting its needs [arts 30(5) and, implicitly, 31(5)]. Needless to say, discarding solutions (at the single stage or in any of the intermediate) generates effects that are not dissimilar from an exclusion of the candidate and, consequently, that decision should be subjected to the same procedural guarantees.[50]

Particularly, in order to ensure the integrity of the technical dialogue process, contracting authorities shall ensure equality of treatment among all participants and, in particular, they shall not provide information in a discriminatory manner which may give some participants an advantage over others. They must also comply with the requirements of Article 21 regarding protection of confidential information[51] and shall not reveal to the other participants

49. And, in the case of the innovation partnership, 'contracting authorities shall in particular apply criteria concerning the candidates' capacity in the field of research and development and of developing and implementing innovative solutions', as per Article 31(6) of the new Directive.
50. For discussion on the theoretical possibility of an obligation to admit participants to compete based on a solution different from the one they suggested, see S Arrowsmith and S Treumer, "Competitive dialogue in EU law: a critical review", in ibid (eds.), Competitive Dialogue in EU Procurement, 2nd edn (Cambridge, Cambridge University Press, 2012) 3 and ff.
51. 'Unless otherwise provided in this Directive or in the national law to which the contracting authority is subject, in particular legislation concerning access to information, and without prejudice to the obligations relating to the advertising of awarded contracts and to the information to candidates and tenderers [...] the contracting authority shall not disclose information forwarded to it by economic operators which they have designated as confidential, including, but not limited to, technical or trade secrets and the confidential aspects of tenders'. On the issue of protection of confidential information, see the recent Judgments in Case C-629/11 P Evropaïki Dynamiki v Com-

solutions proposed or other confidential information communicated by a candidate participating in the dialogue without its agreement (which shall not take the form of a general waiver but shall be given with reference to the intended communication of specific information) [arts 30(4) and 31(6)].

7. Conclusions

As this brief overview of the novelties and changes brought about by the new Directive on the rules concerning exclusion, qualitative selection and short-listing has shown, the new texts aim to generate some simplification and flexibilisation of the current rules. The new Directive has also tried to clarify and improve the drafting of the current Directives and to consolidate requirements and avoid duplication where possible.

The search for flexibility and simplification is particularly clear concerning the rules that aim to make exclusion of economic operators a dynamic activity (section 2.2), that increase the scope and power for contracting authorities to seek clarifications and source additional information from tenderers (section 2.4), that allow for an evaluation of the effectiveness of self-cleaning measures adopted by economic operators that should otherwise be excluded (section 3.3), or that allow for a 'certificate-less' qualitative selection of candidates, subject to an ex post verification of the self-declarations submitted by means of the newly created European Single Procurement Document (ESPD) (section 4.5). However, such flexibility does not come without risks and contracting authorities must tread lightly if they want to avoid challenges based on potential abuses of their (increased) administrative discretion. Moreover, the extent and weight of the obligations derived from the principle of good administration are expanding and this needs being duly taken into consideration.

There are also several indications of a clearer integration of public procurement and competition rules (such as the possibility to exclude bid riggers, section 3.2) which should be seen as a natural result of the consolidation of the principle of competition in Article 18(1) of the new Directive; as well as clear evidence of the increasing will to use of public procurement as a lever to ensure compliance with social, labour and environmental rules, in a classic example of pursuit of secondary (or horizontal) considerations in procure-

mission (ESP-ISEP) [2012] ECR nyr, and Joined Cases T-339/10 and T-532/10 Cosepuri Soc. Coop. pA v European Food Safety Authority (EFSA) [2013] ECR nyr.

ment (section 2.3). This shows that, despite the search for simplification, the (asymmetrical) integration of public procurement and other economic and non-economic policies by necessity depicts a more complicated scenario that requires further professionalism and capacity building in the Member States, as well as more cooperation between contracting authorities and other competent authorities, such as national competition or environmental agencies.

All in all, in my view, EU public procurement regulation continues becoming more and more sophisticated (and complicated), the new Directive does not solve all problems and creates some new ones and, consequently, public procurement litigation will continue playing a key role in the clarification of the applicable rules.

Bibliography

S Arrowsmith, The Law of Public and Utilities Procurement, 2nd edn (London, Sweet and Maxwell, 2005).

S Arrowsmith, 'Horizontal Policies in Public Procurement: A Taxonomy,' (2010) 10(2) Journal of Public Procurement 149.

S Arrowsmith, H-J Prieß and P Friton, 'Self-Cleaning as a Defence to Exclusions for Misconduct – An Emerging Concept in EC Public Procurement Law?' (2009) 18 Public Procurement Law Review 257.

S Arrowsmith and P Kunzlik (eds) Social and Environmental Policies in EC Procurement Law (Cambridge, Cambridge University Press, 2009).

S Arrowsmith and S Treumer, "Competitive dialogue in EU law: a critical review", in ibid (eds.), Competitive Dialogue in EU Procurement, 2nd edn (Cambridge, Cambridge University Press, 2012) 3 and ff.

T Medina Arnaiz, 'The Exclusion of Tenderers in Public Procurement as an Anticorruption Mean' nispa.org/files/conferences/2008/papers/200804200047500.Medina_exclusion.pdf.

J Mendes, 'Good Administration in EU Law and the European Code of Good Administrative Behaviour', EUI Working Paper Law 2009/09 cadmus.eui.eu/handle/1814/12101.

H-J Prieß, 'Distortions of Competition in Tender Proceedings: How to Deal with Conflicts of Interest (Family Ties, Business Links and Cross–Representation of Contracting Authority Officials and Bidders) and the Involvement of Project Consultants' (2002) 11 Public Procurement Law Review 153.

A Sanchez Graells, Public Procurement and the EU Competition Rules (Oxford, Hart Publishing, 2011).

A Sanchez Graells, 'Are the Procurement Rules a Barrier for Cross-Border Trade within the European Market? A View on Proposals to Lower that Barrier and Spur Growth' in Tvarnø, Ølykke & Risvig Hansen (eds), EU Public Procurement: Modernisation, Growth and Innovation, (Copenhagen, DJØF, 2012) p. 107-133.

A Sanchez Graells, "Rejection of Abnormally Low and Non-Compliant Tenders in EU Public Procurement: A Comparative View on Selected Jurisdictions", in M Comba & S Treumer (eds), Award of Contracts in EU Procurement, European Procurement Law Series, Vol. 5 (Copenhagen, DJF, 2013) p. 289-293.

A Sanchez Graells, 'Prevention and Deterrence of Bid Rigging: A Look from the New EU Directive on Public Procurement', in G M Racca and C R Yukins (eds), Integrity and Efficiency in Sustainable Public Contracts (Brussels, Bruylant, 2014) p. 137-157.

P Trepte, Regulating Procurement. Understanding the Ends and Means of Public Procurement Regulation (Oxford, Oxford University Press, 2004).

P Trepte, Public Procurement in the EU. A Practitioner's Guide, 2nd edn (Oxford, Oxford University Press, 2007).

S Treumer, 'Technical Dialogue and the Principle of Equal Treatment – Dealing with Conflicts of Interest after Fabricom' (2007) 16 Public Procurement Law Review 99.

S Williams, 'The mandatory exclusions for corruption in the new EC procurement directives' nottingham.ac.uk/pprg/documentsarchive/fulltextarticles/sope_exclusions_in_proc.pdf.

Public Procurement Award Procedures in Directive 2014/24/EU

Pedro Telles and Luke R. A. Butler[1]

1. Introduction

The purpose of this Chapter is to explore changes to contract award procedures instituted by Directive 2014/24/EU. The Chapter will re-examine the traditional open and restricted procedures, the more recent competitive dialogue procedure and the new competitive procedure with negotiation as well as innovation partnerships. Concerning existing procedures (open, restricted and competitive dialogue), discussion will focus on the changes that have or should have been introduced. The new competitive procedure with negotiation and innovation partnership necessitates more detailed critical examination. It will be demonstrated that although some of the changes answer the call for simplification,[2] many challenges remain and new challenges have been introduced, particularly concerning the new procedures.

This Chapter is divided into the following Sections. Section 2 examines the nature of the procedures according to a proposed taxonomy of standard and special procedures. Section 3 examines the standard procedures comprising the open and restricted procedures. Section 4 examines special procedures comprising the competitive dialogue, competitive procedure with negotiation and innovation partnership. Section 6 offers some provisional conclusions.

1. Lecturers at the Universities of Bangor and Bristol, respectively.
2. An objective also mentioned in Recitals 84, 86 and 114 to Directive 2014/24/EU and assumed by the European Commission. See Commission, Public Procurement Reform – Fact Sheet 1 (2014).

2. Nature of Procedures under Directive 2014/24/EU

The number of public procurement procedures that can be used has expanded over the years, in particular, as a result of the 2004 and 2014 revisions. In addition to the traditional open, restricted and negotiated procedures, the 2004 reform formally introduced competitive dialogue.[3] The 2014 reform has instituted a new competitive procedure with negotiation[4] and the innovation partnership.[5] The multiplication of procedures necessitates defining their nature as their different characteristics have an impact on which subsidiary rules are applicable or how legislative limitations should be overcome. As such, it can be argued that the procedures contained in Directive 2014/24/EU may be characterised as standard, special or exceptional depending on the freedom that contracting authorities exercise in their choice as to the relevant procedure.

Procedures may be characterised as standard when the contracting authority can use them in any circumstances and for any type of contract covered by the Directive. By contrast, procedures have a special nature when they can be chosen only according to specific grounds for use. Finally, procedures are deemed exceptional when they function as a final alternative enabling a contract award when all else fails. This proposed taxonomy of procedures implies that only the open and restricted procedures are to be classified as standard. Competitive dialogue,[6] the competitive procedure with negotiation and the innovation partnership require specific grounds for use and, as such, are

3. Article 29 Directive 2004/18/EC.
4. Article 29 Directive 2014/24/EU.
5. Article 31 Directive 2014/24/EU.
6. For a detailed discussion concerning the nature of competitive dialogue under Directive 2004/18/EC, see S Arrowsmith and S Treumer, 'Competitive Dialogue in EU Law: A Critical Review' in S Arrowsmith and S Treumer (eds) Competitive Dialogue in EU Procurement (CUP 2012), 36-58. For the view that the competitive dialogue is a standard procedure, see M Farley, 'Directive 2004/18/EC and the competitive dialogue: A case study on the application of the competitive dialogue procedure to the NHS LIFT' (007) 2 EPPL, 62; and S Arrowsmith, The Law of Public and Utilities Procurement (2nd edition, Sweet & Maxwell, London 2005) 632-635. For a view that the competitive dialogue is a special procedure, see Commission, Explanatory note on competitive dialogue, 2005, 2. Considering the procedure under Directive 2004/18 as exceptional in nature, see S Treumer, 'The field of application of the competitive dialogue' (2006) 6 PPLR, 313; S E Hjelmborg et al., Public Procurement Law: the EU Directive on Public Contracts (Djof, Copenhagen, 2006), 283; and P. Delelis, Le Dialogue Compétitif (2007) 3 Revue du Tresor, 280.

deemed special procedures.[7] Finally, the negotiated procedure without prior notice remains a procedure of final resort if none of the other procedures are suitable. The latter cannot be identified as a regulated procedure as such, rather constituting an authorisation to contracting authorities to devise a method of awarding a contract according to circumstances prescribed by the Directive. As such, this procedure is not examined for the purposes of this Chapter.

Interestingly, whilst Member States previously exercised freedom to decide whether or not to introduce new procedures like the competitive dialogue,[8] this is no longer possible under Directive 2014/24/EU which requires that all the special procedures mentioned above must be transposed.[9] Importantly, however, Member States remain free to adapt such procedures through national legislation.[10]

3. Standard Procedures

Directive 2014/24/EU has instituted certain changes to both the open and restricted procedures in accord with the simplification objective and stated aims to make them more flexible and increase market access.[11] These changes can be organised into two main categories: reducing timescales and reducing bureaucracy. Timescales have generally been shortened by approximately 30.[12] Bureaucracy is to be reduced through the introduction of the European Single Procurement Document,[13] self-certification for prospective tenderers[14] and a

7. With regard to the innovation partnership, Article 31(1) provides an indication of its nature in its reference to the need for an innovative product, service or works that "cannot be met by purchasing products, services or works already available on the market" and also Article 2(1)(22) which defines innovation for the purposes of the Directive. As such, the procedure cannot be used if whatever is proposed does not meet such definitions. For a discussion of the definition of "innovation" under the Directive, see Section 3 of Butler's Chapter in this book.
8. Article 29(1) Directive 2004/18/EC.
9. Article 24 (1) Directive 2014/24/EU.
10. Portugal had made such adaptations with regard to the competitive dialogue procedure. See P Telles, 'Competitive Dialogue in Portugal' in S Arrowsmith and S Treumer (eds) Competitive dialogue in EU Procurement (n 6) 370.
11. Commission, Procurement Reform Fact Sheet 2 – Simplification for tenderers (2014).
12. G Fletcher, 'Minimum time limits under the new Public Procurement Directive' (2014) 3 PPLR, 94-102, 94.
13. Article 59 Directive 2014/24/EU.
14. Ibid.

single stage variant in the case of the open procedure.[15] With the exception of the single stage variant, all other changes are arguably of an evolutionary rather than revolutionary character and should be considered as a much needed "refresh" to modernise the procedures.

3.1. Common Aspects for the Open and Restricted Procedures

3.1.1. Reduced bureaucracy and paperwork

Article 59 of Directive 2014/24/EU mandates that contracting authorities must accept the European Single Procurement Document,[16] which substantially equates to a self-declaration produced by a candidate as constituting prima facie evidence they are not subject to any of the exclusion grounds contained in Article 57 and that they comply with the selection criteria set by Articles 58 and 65. In the UK, for example, the use of self-declarations to verify non-application of the exclusion grounds is relatively common. To this extent, Directive 2014/24/EU simply provides a clearer legal basis for such an approach. However, it is likely that changes will arise from the use of self-declarations with regard to selection criteria (suitability, financial and technical ability). Until now, contracting authorities have generally requested detailed evidence to be provided for analysis. Again, drawing on the UK's experience, this approach has motivated the notoriously onerous "prequalification questionnaire" requirements which must be complied with for every procurement procedure. By restricting the request of selection information to a self-declaration, Directive 2014/24/EU, in effect, reduces a barrier to entry that had been highlighted as a key deterrent to supplier participation in public procurement.[17]

By removing this barrier to public procurement participation, it is expected that the total number of companies taking part in public procurement will increase, in turn, increasing the overall transaction costs for each contracting authority using the open procedure in expectation of more tenders. In addition, overall transaction costs for the market are also expected to increase

15. Article 27 Directive 2014/24/EU.
16. This should be read in conjunction with Article 61 which creates an online repository of certificates (e-Certis) that should be accessible to contracting authorities and is also expected to reduce the burden imposed on suppliers.
17. Both by trade bodies and independent research, at least in the UK. See for example, Confederation of British Industry, Getting a better purchase – CBI public sector procurement report (2014), 15; Federation of Small Businesses, Local government procurement report (2013) 7-8, 93 and Welsh Government, Barriers to procurement research, (2008) 9-15.

due to increased participation rates. In correspondence, if it is assumed that the number of public contracts available in the market does not increase in relative proportion, it is expected that there will be a larger number of unsuccessful bidders which could also increase recourse to remedies.

Although the authors agree that this is a welcome evolution and that artificial barriers to public procurement participation should be reduced, it would have been appropriate to consider the implications of this measure and propose solutions for them. For example, early intervention at the tender documents stage is necessary. Shorter and clearer documentation enables potential suppliers to take an informed decision as to whether or not to proceed without making the investment of time and effort to formulate a tender.[18] In addition, a push for alternative dispute resolution mechanisms that do not involve litigation could have been considered such as a procurement ombudsman or similar independent authority. With greater autonomy afforded to suppliers, there ought to be effective mechanisms in place to enable clearer determinations to be made and issues to be resolved which are appropriate and proportionate to the nature of the decision-making and stage of tendering.

In addition to the above, Directive 2014/24/EU now requires contracting authorities to provide tender documents online and free of charge.[19] Anecdotal evidence seen by the authors in Portugal and Spain in the past indicates that charging for tender documents was a common practice used by contracting authorities to restrict access to suppliers interested in the contract opportunity.

3.1.2. Minimum yearly turnover requirements (turnover cap)

A second major change to the standard procedures concerns the introduction of Article 58(3) which imposes a cap on turnover requirements limited to twice the value of the contract. Excessive turnover requirements have been widely used by contracting authorities as an easy filter to exclude participants in procedures. This had a pernicious effect on SMEs[20] (in particular, start-ups) more directly as their turnover numbers will always be smaller than larger companies, putting them at a disadvantage. It could be argued that

18. Such was piloted in Wales for contracts below the EU thresholds in the Winning in Tendering project undertaken by Bangor University during 2012 and 2013 (unpublished). In total, over 15 contracts from three different contracting authorities were awarded under this pilot.
19. Article 53 Directive 2014/24/EU, although this principle is subject to restrictions (see Article 22(1)).
20. Recognised in Recital 83 of Directive 2014/24/EU.

turnover requirements are discriminatory in, and of themselves, not least because they are a blunt instrument to achieve exclusion and one which is generally completely unconnected to the contract itself. By capping turnover requirements, Directive 2014/24/EU may provide an implicit recognition of their prima facie incompatibility with EU law.

However, it should be observed that Article 58(3) does allow for contracting authorities to set higher turnover requirements but imposes the burden of proof on the contracting authority to justify why such turnover is required for that particular contract. It remains to be seen whether contracting authorities will comply with the spirit of the Directive in facilitating market access or continue to demand higher turnover requirements to restrict access to smaller providers.

Although the turnover cap is a welcomed addition, and exceptions notwithstanding, the fact is that excessive turnover requirements were being used for a reason, in effect, limiting the number of participants, in particular in the open procedure. The underlying reasons for such requirements have not been fully addressed by the reduction in transaction costs through the single-stage variant, discussed below. The reality is that contracting authorities wish to avoid analysing too many tenders as well as the increased risk of litigation due to the higher number of aggrieved participants. As such, it would not be surprising if contracting authorities remained committed to finding new ways of limiting market access during the selection stage. For example, in order to achieve essentially the same aim, contracting authorities could demand ever higher insurance values,[21] participation or performance bonds,[22] or impose harsher technical requirements. All these options (and more) remain available to contracting authorities interested committed to limiting the number of participants in procedures. In addition, this is likely to be further exacerbated as the nature of funding arrangements become increasingly more complex as well as methods of measuring economic standing, for example, other financial requirements not directly connected with turnover values such as financial ratios or overall leverage values.

3.2. Open Procedure

3.2.1. Reduced timescales

Directive 2014/24/EU reduces the duration of certain stages of the open procedure, allowing for the procedure to be carried out more expeditiously than

21. Common in the UK and an area in which a more integrated approach by the Directive would have been welcome.
22. Common in Spain and Portugal, for example.

had previously been possible. For example, whereas under Directive 2004/18/EC the minimum time limits for receipt of bids stood at 52 days,[23] under Directive 2014/24/EU it is now only either 35 days[24] (for paper tenders) or 30 days (in electronic format).[25] It should be noted, however, that the average duration of tenders in the EU, irrespective of procedure, is much longer than the advertised minimum targets, averaging 123 working days in 2013.[26]

In the event that a prior information notice is used in accordance with Article 48, it is now possible to reduce the advertising period to 15 days,[27] whereas under Directive 2004/18/EC the norm was either 36 or 22 days for exceptional cases.[28] By using a prior information notice, the contracting authority may effectively halve the actual duration of the open procedure, although the time spent on the preparatory phases of the procurement will be higher due to the use of the prior information notice.[29] In addition to these reductions, under Article 27(3), it is now possible to accelerate the open procedure in cases of urgency, an option that was formerly only available for the restricted procedure under Directive 2004/18/EC.[30] However, Directive 2014/24/EU does not clarify what constitutes grounds for urgency. According to Recital 46 of Directive 2014/24, the state of urgency need not be one of extreme urgency brought about by events unforeseeable for, and not attributable to, the contracting authority.[31] This contrasts with the circumstance of "extreme urgency" permitting the use of the negotiated procedure without prior publication.[32] As the concept of urgency is an exception to the regular dead-

23. Article 38(2) Directive 2014/24/EU.
24. Article 27(1) Directive 2014/24/EU.
25. Article 27(4) Directive 2014/24/EU.
26. Spend Network, Tender time frames: <http://tt.spendnetwork.com/index.html> accessed May 15 2014. For reference, the UK Government aims to conduct open procedures in less than 120 working days. See, Government Procurement, Government sourcing: A new approach using, LEAN (2012) 3-6.
27. Article 27(2) Directive 2014/24/EU.
28. Article 38(4) Directive 2004/18/EC.
29. Which needs to be advertised at least 35 days before the contract notice and up to a maximum of 12 months in advance.
30. Article 38(3). See generally, S Arrowsmith, The Law of Public and Utilities Procurement (n 6) 457-460.
31. G Fletcher, 'Minimum time limits under the new Public Procurement Directive' (n 12) 96.
32. For a discussion of the concept of urgency and and its application under this ground in previous Directives, see S Arrowsmith, The Law of Public and Utilities Procurement (n 6) 617-620).

lines, it is open to argue that the contracting authority may, itself, give rise to the situation of urgency, for example, by delaying commencement of the procedure on purpose, although case law on the negotiated procedure without prior publication may suggest that such reasons are unlikely to be tolerated.[33] Further, Recital 46 merely states that urgency needs to be "duly substantiated" but does not prescribe any specific threshold that must be met. Recital 46 also requires that the general time-limits must be "impracticable". This differs from an objective impossibility and provides a further indication that any such determination could incorporate a considerable degree of discretion and subjective decision-making by contracting authorities.

Reducing timescales for the open procedure is a reasonable measure when seeking to reduce transaction and opportunity costs imposed on both procurers and the market. However, there is a balancing act to be undertaken given that too significant a reduction could potentially affect competition.[34] When timescales are too short, it is very difficult for suppliers to find the opportunity and prepare a bid on time. As such, very short timescales may be used by contracting authorities with an anti-competitive motivation, precisely for the purposes of reducing the scope of potential bidders or to skew a tender in favour of a preferred supplier.[35] Further, this negative effect is felt particularly by SMEs which generally suffer disproportionately from transaction costs due to the lack of resources and dedicated expert procurement staff.

Notwithstanding, the reduction in timescales is to be welcomed, although for simple contracts or contracts near the lower end of threshold values, it might have been preferable to have reduced the timescales further, particularly, in tenders where suppliers are not required or expected to submit a detailed qualification document.

3.2.2. "Single stage"

One of the criticisms levelled at the open procedure over the years has been the excessive bureaucracy the procedure entails and is one which has contrib-

33. Ibid.
34. A similar argument is made by G Fletcher, 'Minimum time limits under the new Public Procurement Directive' (n 12) 94.
35. It is particularly interesting to note that under Articles 40 and 41, companies consulted before the launch of a tender and involved in the drafting of the tender specifications can take part in the procurement as long as it does not distort competition, nor violate non-discrimination or transparency. In the event that a single supplier or a limited number of suppliers are consulted, is hard to imagine that such access will not distort competition.

uted, in significant part, to the procedure's perceived excessive duration. In part, this is due to the two successive stages that need to be completed before the award: selection and tender. Until now, all participants in an open procedure submitted the selection information at the start of the procedure. All selection information submissions were then assessed in accordance with the prescribed selection criteria identified at the start, followed by the analysis of tenders. The two-stage approach increases the transaction costs which, although beneficial for complex contracts, make it unwieldy for contracts with limited complexity or lower values. In this area, the biggest innovation introduced by Directive 2014/24/EU is to be found in Article 56(2). This article allows contracting authorities to award the contract without checking candidates against the selection criteria set in the tender documents. Under this model, after selecting the preferred bidder, the contracting authority will then assess the winning tenderer's documentation only. In effect, this amounts to cutting out a full stage of the procedure as it does not constitute a "selection stage" in itself, nor is it subject to the minimum time limits imposed by article 27(1) as these apply to the receipt of tenders only. In addition, after identifying the preferred bidder, nothing in the Directive precludes the contracting authority from using the standstill period to require the necessary information from tenderers, thus shortening the procedure further.

In this "single stage" version, the open procedure is significantly shorter and with lower transaction costs for everyone involved as only the prospective winner submits the selection information. The most interesting point about this option is that it reorients the focus back on the quality of the tender instead of tenderer qualities without necessarily downgrading the importance of the latter. One of the risks attending the traditional open procedure is the potential to assess tenders under the influence of the bidder's results in the selection stage when the same panel is used.

Some potential issues with this new version of the open procedure should be noted, however. First, it imposes on the contracting authority the risk and work of collating the selection information itself under certain circumstances, for example, under Article 59(5), namely when accessing databases containing the necessary information. In consequence, part of the transaction cost savings afforded by the new model could be consumed by forcing the contracting authority to find that information. In other words, there is a transfer of the transaction cost from the supplier to the contracting authority.

Second, this new model of checking the qualifying information raises the risk that the preferred bidder will not comply with the necessary requirements as set in the tender documents. As this fact will only be confirmed later in the procedure where the emphasis is to award the contract as soon as possible, it is possible that contracting authorities will simply turn a blind eye to lack of compliance, at least for minor, non-material non-compliance (howsoever determined) which does not increase the likelihood of the contract being successful. A legalistic view of such possibility would imply that any non-compliance should lead to exclusion. However, for minor compliance faults, this is unlikely to happen due to the sunk costs in the procedure and the fact the preferred bidder has the best bid (as only the best bidder has its documents checked). It could be argued that this would constitute a violation of equal treatment. However, in this circumstance, only one tenderer is scrutinised and the effective exclusion of other tenderers from the competition (having not submitted the best bid) means that such tenderers are not in a comparable position. As long as all candidates could potentially be treated equally in the same situation, then equal treatment would be ensured. A question would remain, however, in relation to suppliers that never submitted a tender on the basis of their determination that they would not be able to comply with the selection criteria. The answer might be that as they never submitted a tender (and thus have not borne the cost of developing one) they are not in the same situation and as such do not warrant equal treatment in this sense.

Contracting authorities can, and should, take measures to reduce the risk of companies submitting tenders without complying with the selection criteria. For example, they should list the criteria clearly and the consequences for lack of compliance i.e. exclusion from, or cancellation of, the procedure. Keeping both options open is important to minimise the risk of collusion where all tenderers (with the exception of the worst tender) are then unable to comply with some of the selection criteria.[36] Additionally, particularly for larger or more complex contracts, contracting authorities could consider requiring performance or participation bonds to balance risk,[37] although even this approach carries risks.

3.3. Restricted Procedure

3.3.1. Reduced timescales

The restricted procedure received only minor changes to its operation under Directive 2014/24/EU, mostly connected to reducing timescales but with exception of a specific change related to sub-central contracting authorities. Re-

36. This approach has been successfully piloted in Wales for contracts below EU thresholds by the Winning in Tendering project between 2012 and 2013 (unpublished).
37. These are common in some Member States (e.g. Portugal and Spain) but are not widespread practice elsewhere (e.g. UK).

quests to participate may now be time limited to 30 days[38] instead of the previous 37 days,[39] while tenders have also been reduced from 40 days[40] to 30 days.[41] In instances in which electronic means have been used, tendering timescales can be further reduced to 25 days[42] a reduction from 35 days.[43] In the instance in which a prior information notice[44] is used, the period for receiving tenders can be reduced to only 10 days[45] in comparison with the current limit of 36 days.[46] With further regard to the use of the prior information notice, the same concerns and limitations raised above for the open procedure are of equal, and perhaps even greater, application. As the restricted procedure is a procedure used for more complex contracts, offering suppliers only 10 days to submit tenders seems to impose a significant limitation upon tender preparation. Further, it could offer the possibility for contracting authorities to facilitate the discreet disclosure of discriminatory information to a preferred supplier during the prior information notice period and still appear to comply with the Directive by giving only 10 days for the tender submission.

The exception mentioned above is the possibility granted in Article 28(4) for sub-central contracting authorities to agree with the selected candidates the duration of the tender stage. It is unclear if the agreement must be obtained from all candidates, although the use of the expression "mutual agreement" appears to imply that an agreement from all must be required. It should also be observed that Directive 2014/24/EU does not impose a need for explicit agreement to be obtained, opening the possibility for contracting authorities to require only implicit consent. For example, it could state as a condition of participation in the restricted procedure that by submitting a request to participate, the supplier is consenting to a certain duration of the tender stage. Another example could be where the contracting authority informs suppliers that the tender stage duration is a certain period unless they express their disagreement within 24 or 48 hours. Further, it might even be raised that perhaps the time limits may not be identical for all tenderers and that each tenderer may be given its own deadline as technically both the contracting au-

38. Directive 2014/24/EU Article 28(1).
39. Directive 2004/18/EC Article 38(3).
40. Directive 2004/18/EC Article 38(3).
41. Directive 2014/24/EU Article 28(2).
42. Directive 2014/24/EU Article 28(5).
43. Directive 2004/18/EC Article 38(6).
44. The notice can now be used as a call for competition if the conditions set by Article 48 are met.
45. Directive 2014/24/EU Article 28(3).
46. Directive 2004/18/EC Article 38(4).

thority and each tenderer are in "mutual agreement". In any case, the above could potentially increase legal uncertainty and the possibility of discrimination (factual and/or legal) between tenderers in practice.

Whilst the reductions in timescales appear reasonable and sensible, the shortened timescales pertaining to the prior information notice may seem excessive. Restricted procedures tend to be used for larger and more complex contracts and where suppliers will ordinarily need more time to prepare bids. Further, shorter timescales will foster close relationships between suppliers and procurers as suppliers will want to know as soon as possible the prescribed dates for bids, thereby potentially facilitating corruption or discrimination in favour of suppliers with preferential access. In addition, such tight timescales may have the impact of either foreclosing the market as suppliers may be forced to invest in developing the bid without knowing if they have made it to the tender stage. In alternative, this may disadvantage suppliers which are not in a position to take that risk and may not be able to prepare a tender in the short "official" tender stage. There is also the risk that suppliers will simply not even bother taking part in the procedure at all due to those short timescales. Finally, SMEs are generally disproportionately affected by transaction and opportunity costs in comparison with larger organisations. By shortening the window for submitting full tenders, this may lead SMEs to avoid taking part in the procedure and thus function as a new mechanism to control the number of participants in the procedure, in particular, if the European Single Document and self-declaration by tenderers makes it more difficult.

4. Special Procedures

According to Article 26 of Directive 2014/24/EU, contracting authorities are able to use competitive dialogue,[47] the new competitive procedure with negotiation[48] and innovation partnerships[49] to award contracts as long as certain grounds for use are met. All three must be transposed into national legislation.[50]

The competitive procedure with negotiation and competitive dialogue share the same grounds for use, whereas the innovation partnership appears to

47. Directive 2014/24/EU Article 26(4).
48. Ibid.
49. Directive 2014/24/EU Article 26(3).
50. Directive 2014/24/EU Article 26(3) and (4).

be applicable in situations where close cooperation between the parties is envisaged over a long-term relation and need requires the development of products or services which are not otherwise available on the market.[51] A cursory glance at the three procedures, regulated in successive articles of the Directive, creates an instant impression that all three procedures are very similar. Each has its own specificities but there is more by way of commonality than distinction between them. As such, the underlying rationale for providing two or three very similar procedures with similar grounds for use might be questioned.[52] It can be argued in favour of the new setup that by having multiple different procedures for use in the same situations, contracting authorities have more choice at the time of selecting a procedure. However, there are opposing arguments. It may be that having two or three similar procedures for the same situations will actually confuse procurers and lead to non-adoption as it leaves officials open to criticism should a procedure fail or the results are not as good as anticipated. Further, it may be that the current national or local practice will prevail. For example, competitive dialogue is popular in countries such as the UK and France and so it is possible that contracting authorities within these Member States may prefer to keep on using the tools to which they have become accustomed. In other countries like Portugal, where competitive dialogue has been unsuccessful and where a version of the competitive procedure with negotiation has existed since the 1990s for the award of service concessions, it is expected that use of the competitive dialogue option will remain practically non-existent.

4.1. Competitive dialogue

Competitive dialogue is primarily regulated in Article 30, with the exception of the grounds for use (Article 26) and confidentiality (Article 21). The gen-

51. Directive 2014/24/EU Recital 49. See also P Cerqueira Gomes, 'The Innovative Innovation Partnerships Under the 2014 Public Procurement Directive' (2014) 23 PPLR 209, 210, citing also at fn 12 M. Steinicke, The Public Procurement Rules and Innovation, in EU Procurement Directives – Modernisation, Growth and Innovation – Discussions on the 2011 proposals for Procurement Directives (Jurist- og Økonomforbundets Forlag, 2012), 260
52. Competitive dialogue has previously been used for the procurement of innovation, particularly in the health sector. See P Telles, 'Competitive Dialogue and Innovation: The Case of the Spanish Health Sector', in G Piga and S Treumer (eds) The applied law and economics of public procurement (Routledge 2013) 28-49 and G Simonsen, M Rolfstam, 'Public Procurement of healthcare innovation in the ScanBalt area' 2013 <http://vbn.aau.dk/files/173630136/Simonsen_Rolfstam_2013.pdf> last accessed May 5 2014.

eral purpose of competitive dialogue appears to remain unchanged, namely that for certain contracts where the solution is not clear in advance, it is possible for contracting authorities to discuss with candidates any and all topics related to a contract. As with the open and restricted procedure, the changes to competitive dialogue are relatively minor and essentially relate to the grounds for use which, as will be discussed, below appear to have been widened as well as the possibility of conducting the dialogue with a single supplier.[53] It could be said that Directive 2014/24/EU is a missed opportunity with regard to the changes or improvements which were needed to make the procedure more useful and easier to use.

4.1.1. Grounds for use

Directive 2004/18/EC introduced competitive dialogue as a means to award complex contracts. Since its inception, the objective scope and nature of the procedure has been subject to extensive academic discussion.[54] This was mostly due to the fact that Article 1(11)(c) of Directive 2004/18/EC demanded the contract to be "particularly complex" without providing a clear definition of what constitutes such a contract. However, whilst there has been substantially no or limited jurisprudence on this particular procedure, this could also constitute a possible indication that, where it has been used in practice, the procedure has not proven to be problematic. The perceived risks surrounding the grounds for use may have impaired uptake of the procedure in some Member States such as Portugal[55] but this reputation has not lead to significant litigation in Member States where it has been extensively used, for example, in the UK and France.[56]

Under Directive 2014/24/EU, competitive dialogue is no longer limited to situations of particular complexity but can be used for the award of contracts

53. In case no others have been deemed suitable according to the selection criteria, Article 65(2) Directive 2014/24.
54. For the view that the procedure has an exceptional nature and that its grounds for use should be interpreted restrictively, S E Hjelmborg et al., 'Public procurement law: the EU directive on public contracts' (n 6) 283 and Delelis, 'Le Dialogue Compétitif' (n 6) 280. For the view that the grounds for use of the procedure are more flexible, see S Arrowsmith and S Treumer, 'Competitive Dialogue in EU Law: A Critical Review' (n 6) 36 – 49.
55. See P Telles, 'Competitive Dialogue in Portugal' (n 10) 380 and P Telles, 'Competitive Dialogue in Portugal' (2010) 1 PPLR, 1-32.
56. See S De Mars and R Craven, 'An Analysis of Competitive Dialogue in the EU' in S Arrowsmith and S Treumer (eds) Competitive Dialogue in EU Procurement (n 6) 152.

on the same grounds as the competitive procedure with negotiation specified in Article 26(4). The new grounds for use are reasonable, while appearing clearer and more straightforward than had previously been the case. Although these grounds for use do not resolve perceived or actual problems inherent in the procedure itself, they do remove part of the uncertainty that might have affected the procedure's adoption in some Member States. As such, they may help increase its use. However, it must be taken into account that the grounds for use are shared in their entirety with the competitive procedure with negotiation. As these procedures are alternatives to one another, it is possible that, in fact, the adoption rate of competitive dialogue will diminish rather than increase due to competition from the new competitive procedure with negotiation.

Directive 2014/24/EU is generous with regard to the prescribed grounds for use of the competitive dialogue (and the competitive procedure with negotiation) and covers two completely different scenarios: one where the grounds for use are primary or direct; the other where the grounds are secondary or indirect.[57] With regard to the first scenario, the procedure can be used as a matter of first recourse whereas in the second it can be use in the instance in which a previously open or restricted procedure has failed for specific reasons.

Regarding the primary or direct grounds for use, Article 26(4)(a) states that the procedure can be used for the award of works, supplies or services when: (i) the needs of the contracting authority demand adaptation of readily available solutions; (ii) they include design or innovative solutions; (iii) due to the nature, legal and financial complexity of the contract; or (iv) technical specifications cannot be defined in sufficient detail.[58] These grounds are alternative rather than cumulative. Therefore, a contracting authority may be able to justify the use of the procedure based upon any one or more bases. In comparison to the grounds for use of competitive dialogue in Articles 29, 1(11)(c) and Recital 31 of the Directive 2004/18/EC,[59] it is clear that (iii) and (iv) are adaptations of pre-existing grounds whereas (i) and (ii) are complete-

57. On the division of the grounds for use into categories (adaptation; design; complexity; technical specifications), see J Davey, 'Procedures involving negotiation in the new Public Procurement Directive: key reforms to the grounds for use and the procedural rules' (2014) 3 PPLR 103-111, 109.
58. These grounds are detailed in the definitions included in Annex VII.
59. Although Directive 2014/24/EU includes in its own Recitals some examples of projects that could be tendered via the competitive procedure with negotiation or the competitive dialogue, e.g. Recitals 42 and 43.

ly new, perhaps constituting a recognition of the flexibility needed in more contracts than expressly anticipated in Directive 2004/18/EC. In addition, Directive 2014/24/EU contains no reference either to particular complexity (Article 29) or objective impossibility (Article 1(11)(c)). This new state of affairs can only be considered as a positive development, particularly in the interests of simplification and legal certainty.[60] Although it can be said that Article 26(4)(a)(iii) appears to be similar to the previous requirement of Article 1(11)(c) of Directive 2004/18/EC, it does not in fact require a degree of particular complexity as had previously been the case.

For use of competitive dialogue and the competitive procedure with negotiation under primary grounds, contracting authorities will still have to justify the choice of procedure. Notwithstanding the fact there is no objective impossibility requirement, it has been argued this test needs to be objective.[61] The authors would contend that, as had previously been the case, this is very difficult to do in practice. A strategic use of pre-market engagement would solve most of the issues that can be tackled with the competitive dialogue, albeit with less transparency or safeguards. Under Directive 2014/14/EU, the test should essentially be subjective in nature: the contracting authority must justify why, in that specific situation, it needs to use either of these procedures. This should not depend on any external unit of measurement or comparison, i.e what the reasonable contracting authority would do in that situation. By "subjective", it is meant the actual situation being faced at that moment by that specific contracting authority. In any event, the authors are of the view that the availability of broader grounds will enable easier reliance on any of the requirements set forth in Article 26(4)(a).

Concerning the secondary grounds for use, these can be found in Article 26(4)(b) and arise in situations where only irregular or unacceptable tenders are submitted in the course of an open or restricted procedure. In this instance, it appears that the contracting authority has two options: it can either issue a further invitation to those tenderers for a competitive procedure with negotiation without putting out a notice or re-advertise the contract as a competitive procedure with negotiation. Perhaps surprisingly, only the first option is specifically referred to in Article 26(4)(b). This gives cause for question for

60. For the view that the new grounds for use do achieve the stated aim of simplification and flexibility, see generally J Davey, 'Procedures involving negotiation in the new Public Procurement Directive: key reforms to the grounds for use and the procedural rules' (n 57).
61. For the view that an objective test is still required, see J Davey, 'Procedures involving negotiation in the new Public Procurement Directive (n 57) 105-106.

two reasons. Firstly, it is not clear why the competitive procedure with negotiation is allowed to proceed without a notice when Article 26(1) and (5) specifically state that a notice must be used. Secondly, it is not clear why it is permitted to use the competitive procedure with negotiation without notice (the more substantial exception to the principle of transparency) as opposed to a procedure with notice (a lesser incursion on transparency). In fact, if all the tenders are unacceptable and/or irregular, it is not clear why those tenderers should be given a privileged "second chance" with competition closed to potential bidders that did not have an unacceptable or irregular bid in the first instance. When examining the conditions under which tenders should be considered unacceptable[62] or are otherwise irregular,[63] in accordance with the second paragraph of Article 26(4)(b), it is clear that the situations leading to the classification of being unacceptable or irregular should not warrant the preferential treatment of closing off the competition to other bidders. Finally, in the specific case of a candidate being excluded due to lack of qualifications, it appears unlikely that such candidate will be able to secure such requirements in short order.

Whereas the primary or direct ground for use appears to be a step in the right direction when compared to Directive 2004/18/EC, the secondary or indirect grounds for use could have perhaps been given more careful attention. The possibility of allowing a new competition (whether competitive dialogue or competitive procedure with negotiation) with a contract notice could have gone some way to potentially resolving this issue.

4.1.2. Non-discrimination and Confidentiality

As was the case under Directive 2004/18/EC, competitive dialogue continues to raise issues surrounding non-discrimination and confidentiality.[64] Article 30(3) states that equal treatment must be observed and that information should not be provided to candidates in a discriminatory manner. Further, the same paragraph adds that any confidential information cannot be disclosed without prior authorisation from the respective candidate. Under Directive

62. For example, not having required qualifications or excessive price.
63. For example, for corruption or collusion, lack of compliance, late submission or abnormally low prices.
64. S Charveron, 'Competitive dialogue threatens PFI' (2007) 18 Construction Law, 29, A Brown, 'The impact of the new procurement directive in large public infrastructure projects: competitive dialogue or better the devil you know' (2004) 4 PPLR, 173; S Treumer, 'Competitive Dialogue' (2004) 13 PPLR, 178; and S Arrowsmith and S Treumer, 'Competitive Dialogue in EU Law: A Critical Review' (n 6) 64-66.

2004/18/EC, it was debatable as to whether or not contracting authorities might ask for a blanket authorisation to disclose before launching a procedure, for example, as a condition for participation. [65] According to Article 30(3) of Directive 2014/24/EU, it is simply illegal to impose such an authorisation as a condition for participation.

This change of approach to the confidentiality clause through a draconian and overly formalistic prohibition on communication (unless agreed), benefits candidates to the detriment of the procedure's utility. It is argued that its adoption demonstrates a clear lack of understanding as to how the procedure works and how it has been used over the last ten years, namely, to design and establish a common set of specifications on which candidates can base their tenders. This has been the practice in Spain, Italy and, to a certain extent, the UK.[66] Either in situations where the contracting authority has no solution for its problem or where it has an idea but is unsure on the best solution, the reality is that candidates are in effect competing to shape the contracting authority's opinion and influence the draft of the technical specifications. In effect, contracting authorities have been using competitive dialogue to "crowd source" the tender specifications.[67] This modus operandi was quite common over the last decade and represented the most useful (and easy) way to organise competitive dialogue. In addition, from the perspective of competition, such a model avoids two important pitfalls in public procurement. The first concerns the "dialogue" that some suppliers want to have with contracting authorities before launch of a procedure particularly the open and restricted procedures where technical specifications and award criteria are clearly set in advance. It is perhaps ironic to think that suppliers may complain against confidential information being shared during a competitive dialogue but may be interested in passing the same information to the contracting authority during preliminary market consultations before the launch of an open or restricted

65. For a view in favour, see S Arrowsmith and S Treumer, 'Competitive Dialogue in EU Law: A Critical Review' (n 6) 66. For a view that this would create a new selection criterion not foreseen in articles 45 through 52 of the Directive 2004/18, see M K Larsen, 'Competitive Dialogue' in Nielsen and Treumer (eds), The new EU public procurement directives (Djøf 2005) 76-77 and S De Mars and F Olivier, 'Competitive dialogue in France' in S Arrowsmith and S Treumer (eds) Competitive Dialogue in EU Procurement (n 6) 292-295.
66. S Arrowsmith and S Treumer, 'Competitive Dialogue in EU Law: A Critical Review' (n 6) 72–78.
67. P Telles, 'Competitive Dialogue in Spain, in S Arrowsmith and S Treumer (eds) Competitive Dialogue in EU Procurement (n 6) 413-416.

procedure as to influence tender specifications.[68] The second is that by insisting on a model where each candidate will present a tender based on their own design and assuming that no "cross-pollination" occurs, then, in effect, all candidates except the one with the contracting authority's preferred solution are wasting their time and money in the dialogue. Although Article 30(6) states that final tenders have to be based on the solutions presented by participants in the dialogue, in reality, there will be no or limited competition as the contracting authority will sooner or later identify a preferred solution (officially or not) and reach its determination well in advance of the end of the dialogue.

4.1.3. Negotiations with Preferred Bidder

Article 29(7) of Directive 2004/18/EC allowed the contracting authority to clarify certain aspects of the preferred bidder offer as long as the discussions did not modify essential aspects of the tender or procedure. The drafting of this provision generated debate as to what would fall within the legitimate scope of discussion for the purposes of clarification. Article 30(7) of Directive 2014/24/EU introduces two small albeit important changes: (i) what were previously deemed as "clarifications" are now defined as "negotiations"; and (ii) financial commitments of tenderers are now expressly identified.

The first change indicates an evolution of what kinds of discussions the contracting authority and preferred bidder may entertain. It would appear that moving from "clarifications" to "negotiations" entails an enlarged scope for changes to the bid submitted. Article 30(7) of Directive 2014/24/EU states that the contracting authority may start negotiations with the preferred bidder with the aim of confirming financial commitments or any other terms as long as such negotiations do not modify essential aspects of a tender, tender requirements or distort competition. It can be argued that this change reflects the perspective of some authors that the preferred bid needs to be negotiated to obtain the best possible result from the procedure and to reduce bid costs.[69] This is arguably a naive view of competition and one that leaves the door open for suppliers to claw back any promises made either in the dialogue or in the bid submitted in a moment where there is zero competitive pressure from other tenderers. Although it is possible for the contracting authority to

68. Which is now explicitly allowed for in Article 40 of Directive 2014/24/EU.
69. S Arrowsmith, The Law of Public and Utilities Procurement (n 6) 660-663; R Craven, 'Competitive Dialogue in the UK' in S Arrowsmith and S Treumer (eds) Competitive Dialogue in EU Procurement (n 6) 244-264.

negotiate hard at this stage, the reality is that it is generally starting from a weaker negotiation position. In terms of costs, it has as many sunk costs as the winner but crucially a much higher reputation cost to shoulder in case the procedure is aborted. The "nuclear" option of returning to the second bidder is sometimes not even possible at all, as these discussions may drag for months and the second best bidder may have simply demobilised. Further, even if it is possible to do so, by definition, the second best bid is always worse than the winning bid, again putting the contracting authority in a difficult negotiation position. It could be argued that it even leaves the contracting authority in a worse bargaining position, as the second bidder knows it is the last chance before cancellation, thus having an even stronger starting position than the original winner. Although some contracting authorities under the right conditions and right advice will be able to navigate this scenario, many more will not have the resources (person hours, knowledge) available to do so.

Further, opening the door for further discussion with the preferred bidder actually gives the dialogue participants the incentive to go as low as possible at tender stage to ensure access to this negotiation phase. That constitutes yet another incentive for tenderers to view the dialogue stage as scarcely relevant and not commit resources until final tenders are to be submitted.[70] Article 30(7) (as 29(7) Directive 2004/18/EC did before it) states that only the contracting authority may request the start of negotiations. However, this is of limited use when it is considered that the preferred bidder may confirm financial commitments at this stage. In effect by allowing negotiation on financial issues, Directive 2014/24/EU is putting contracting authorities in a very difficult negotiating position. As was seen in Portugal with the open procedure with a negotiation phase, inviting third parties such as banks (which are not tenderers and, as such, not bound by the terms of the tender) to confirm their financial commitments to large complex projects invites them to move the goal posts when there is no, or limited, competitive pressure. Additionally, it can be argued that once negotiations are declared open, it will be very difficult for the contracting authority to block out requests and suggestions from the tenderer. Moreover, once negotiations have started, the supplier has the incentive of protracting those negotiations for as long as possible until it gets what it wants because the contracting authority will be the party under pressure to finalise the contract. This type of approach may be said to explicate

70. This has been observed in Spain. See for example, P Telles, 'Competitive Dialogue in Spain' (n 67) 418.

the perceived excessive cost[71] and duration[72] of competitive dialogue procedures reported in the UK which averaged 430 working days[73] and which is absent from countries like Spain where the average has been shorter than a calendar year.[74]

Finally, when faced with difficulties arising from discussions with the preferred bidder, contracting authorities (and the actual personnel involved) face the possibility of reputation risk arising from failure and sunken costs and so will likely more easily concede to demands rather than abort the procedure. In other words, the lack of competitive pressure at this stage leaves the preferred bidder with the upper hand.

4.1.4. Unresolved Issues

4.1.4.1. Payment of solution development

Under Article 29(8) of Directive 2004/18/EC, it was possible for the contracting authority to specify prices or make payments to the participants in the dialogue stage as compensation for development work. Contracting authorities were under no obligation to do so. Unsurprisingly, there are no confirmed reports of their widespread use other than in France,[75] evidence they were seldom used in Denmark,[76] and evidence that they were not used at all in Poland,[77] Portugal,[78] Spain[79] or the UK.[80] Directive 2014/24/EU could have introduced a significant change in the regulation of competitive dialogue by imposing the requirement that solutions be paid for, a reality that has been uncommon in practice. For instance, with regard to the innovation partnership discussed below, Article 31 provides that contracting authorities should bear

71. R Craven, 'Competitive Dialogue in the UK' (n 69) 262.
72. Ibid, 263.
73. Cabinet Office, Accelerating Government Procurement (February 2011) 3. It is not entirely clear if the 430 days identified referred to working days, although the stated objective of turning around competitive dialogues in 130 days indicates that this is the case.
74. P Telles, 'Competitive Dialogue in Spain' (n 67) 270.
75. S De Mars and F Olivier, 'Competitive Dialogue in France' (n 65) 303-304.
76. S Treumer, 'Competitive Dialogue in Denmark' in S Arrowsmith and S Treumer (eds) Competitive Dialogue in EU Procurement (n 6) 366.
77. A Gorczynka, 'Competitive Dialogue in Poland' in S Arrowsmith and S Treumer (eds) Competitive Dialogue in EU Procurement (n 6) 442.
78. P Telles, 'Competitive Dialogue in Portugal' (n 10) 397.
79. P Telles, 'Competitive Dialogue in Spain' (n 67) 419.
80. R Craven, 'Competitive Dialogue in the UK' (n 69) 256.

the development costs.[81] Paying for the development of solutions (even if not the full cost) signals to the market that the contracting authority is serious about the process by "putting money on the table", mitigating (to some extent) fears that it is looking only for free consultancy under the guise of a competitive dialogue. These arguments have been made in practice in Portugal in the past in relation to the competitive procedure with negotiation where the contracting authority decided to pay for the bid development costs for losing bidders up to a certain value.[82] As a consequence, there had been a reported reduction in litigation due to the fact that payments could not be made before the contract was awarded i.e. after the standstill period had passed. In essence, suppliers are forced to make the choice between cutting their losses and taking the payment or risk delaying any payment as a result of having to go through the judicial process.

4.1.4.2. No reduction in transaction or opportunity costs

Competitive dialogue is perceived to be a lengthy procedure imposing high transaction and opportunity costs to all involved. Some of these are necessary and inherent in complex contracts in which projects often involve high-risk exposure and complex management. However, Directive 2014/24/EU has done very little to reduce the transaction costs for the parties involved, although it should be emphasised that part of the responsibility for reducing such costs lies with Member States and their transposition.[83] For example, the time limit to receive requests for participation remains at 30 days. As indicated above, it is still possible to discuss important contract elements with the preferred bidder without any competition leverage still present.[84] Further, dia-

81. Article 31(2) which requires payment in appropriate instalments according to the successive phases of the research and innovation process.
82. This information had been collected and collated during Ph.D research for one of the author's Ph.D theses (Telles) and which has taken the form of unpublished semi-structured interviews. See P. Telles, Competitive Dialogue in Portugal and Spain. Ph.D Theses, submitted to the University of Nottingham (2011).
83. For instance, the UK has analysed how competitive dialogue has been used and published guidance aiming to improve practice. See HM Treasury, Review of Competitive Dialogue (November 2010) and Cabinet Office, Accelerating Government Procurement, (February 2011). In addition, the new Crown Commercial Service includes standard operating procedures for competitive dialogue. Available at: <https://ccs.cabinetoffice.gov.uk/about-government-procurement-service/lean-capability/lean-sourcing/lean-sourcing-standard-solution> last accessed 14 May 2014.
84. Although, as discussed in Section 4.2 below, this does not happen under the competitive procedure with negotiation.

logues can still run for as long as the contracting authority wishes. It would have been preferable to impose upon the contracting authority the need to identify a deadline for the dialogue stage,[85] in conjunction with a clear exclusion of negotiations with the preferred bidder, something which Directive 2014/24/EU does enable for the competitive procedure with negotiation.[86]

4.1.4.3. Non-binding dialogue stage

Another issue that could have been resolved in Directive 2014/24/EU would have been to make any discussions, particularly interim solutions presented, binding as well as providing a mechanism to force candidates that have not been eliminated during the dialogue to present a bid after the dialogue is concluded. Under the current system, any "offer" made by suppliers during the dialogue stage is not binding and can be changed during the dialogue or at tender stage. It is therefore perhaps no surprise that suppliers do not provide all the information (especially price) during the dialogue and retain such information for the tender stage. In consequence, the dialogue stage may not be as useful as could otherwise be the case, as suppliers can simply offer any information without being bound by that information. However, considering a commitment during the dialogue as a firm commitment also carries risks not least in reducing the procedure's flexibility. A compromise might be to provide that if successive stages are present and used, the information used to make the decision would be binding for the remaining tenderers in the dialogue stage. After all, the information provided at that moment has been considered definitive enough to make a decision whether or not to exclude the tenderer. However, such approach would not solve the problem in situations where no successive stages are used.

4.2. Competitive Procedure with Negotiation

Directive 2014/24/EU includes a "new" public procurement procedure called the competitive procedure with negotiation. In reality, this is not an entirely new procedure but simply a new name for the negotiated procedure with prior notice or at least of one of the ways in which such could be undertaken. This procedure is also very similar to an award procedure already in existence in Portugal called the open procedure with negotiation phase.[87]

85. Such a deadline could be subject to interim review and possible extension in exceptional cases where this is necessary (subject to appropriate justification).
86. Discussed in Section 4.2 below.
87. P Telles, 'Competitive Dialogue in Portugal' (n 10) 1-32.

A primary observation regarding this procedure is that it has the ostensible appearance of the kind of negotiation procedure which contracting authorities have been looking for since the 1990s and is, perhaps, what competitive dialogue should have been in 2004.[88] This assumption then begets the question introduced at the start of this Part of the Chapter, namely why is it that competitive dialogue is made available alongside this procedure? It is open to question precisely what point there is in offering two very similar procedures for the same or substantially the same situations, as discussed earlier with regard to the grounds for use. In the interests of simplification and "economies of scale", it would have been preferable to have only one instead of both.[89]

4.2.1. General characteristics

The grounds for use of the procedure have been discussed in Section 4.1.1. above. In terms of characteristics, the competitive procedure with negotiation follows a three-stage design comprising selection, initial tenders and negotiation of subsequent tenders. Suppliers apply to take part in the procedure. Suppliers are then selected before being invited to present the initial and subsequent bids. During the negotiation phase, contracting authorities may reduce the number of participants before awarding the contract.[90] As indicated above, this is not an entirely new structure as it is identical to the open procedure with negotiation which exists in Portugal and similar to the practice of negotiated procedures in general.[91]

4.2.2. Selection stage

The procedure commences with a notice that must include the needs and characteristics required, award criteria and minimum requirements.[92] As with competitive dialogue, the contracting authority will have to provide procurement documents at the start of the procedure including the imposition of minimum requirements,[93] These documents should provide "sufficient detail to tenderers to make an informed decision," which appears to indicate that a

88. S Arrowsmith and S Treumer, 'Competitive Dialogue in EU law: A Critical Review' (n 6) 8-25.
89. In support of this argument, see J Davey, 'Procedures involving negotiation in the new Public Procurement Directive' (n 57) 109.
90. Article 29(6) Directive 2014/24/EU.
91. S Arrowsmith and S Treumer, 'Competitive Dialogue in EU law: A Critical Review' (n 6) 16-25.
92. Article 29(1) Directive 2014/24/EU.
93. Ibid.

higher level of detail is required. This suggests that such a level of information is closer to the requirements set for the open and restricted procedure than competitive dialogue.

As with the restricted procedure, competitive dialogue and the innovation partnership to be discussed below, contracting authorities are entitled to restrict the number of suppliers to select, in this case to at least three.[94] This appears to be a reasonable compromise. A procedure in which multiple iterations from each bid were expected would not be well served by a completely open field of competition equivalent to that anticipated under the open procedure. By allowing the limitation of suppliers for selection purposes, Directive 2014/24/EU ensures that the transaction costs are limited for the contracting authority. Further, the market will not have to bear unnecessary transaction costs. Similarly, from the supplier's perspective, the internal market is not well served by multiple companies investing time and money on a project that only a limited few will have a realistic chance of winning. However, such reduction could limit opportunities for SMEs as the selection requirements tend to favour larger suppliers.

4.2.3. Initial bids stage

According to Article 29(2), selected bidders are to be invited to present an initial bid and have 30 days in which to do so. There is no indication in the Directive as to how detailed these initial bids should be e.g. whether in complete form or simple bid outline. In the interests of economy and simplicity, it would appear that contracting authorities are entitled to set in advance the level of detail they expect in the bid at this stage. In most cases, an outline bid will be sufficient to commence negotiations, for example, in situations where an innovative solution is required, although the risks attending the procurement of an innovative solution may necessitate a detailed initial bid to instil sufficient confidence to get the proposal off the ground. In other cases, it may be preferable to require a detailed bid, for example, where the contracting authority intends to use the no-negotiation option included in Article 29(4), which allows the contracting authority to award the contract immediately after receiving the first set of bids without conducting any negotiations.

Concerning the benefits and drawbacks of requiring complete or outline initial bids, attention should focus on the higher transaction costs imposed by requiring more detailed initial bids against the benefits which this approach may bring to the parties, although typically the contracting authority tends to

94. Article 65 (2) Directive 2014/24/EU.

extract the greater benefit from this approach. First, it focuses the discussion on the points that are central to the contract and avoids wasting time on subsidiary or secondary concerns thereby potentially making for a shorter procedure and expedited award. Second, it anchors the discussion by forcing suppliers to commit themselves at the start, thus conferring an advantage on the contracting authority concerned to establish its mandate as early as possible. In proposing an outline bid, a supplier may steer the negotiations on the topics that are yet to be discussed and settled, whereas if negotiations start from a complete bid it is more difficult, though not impossible, to move prior commitments. Even though such changes are indeed possible,[95] a competent negotiator acting on behalf of the contracting authority will be able to extract concessions from the supplier in return.

4.2.4. Negotiation stage

The negotiation phase of the competitive procedure with negotiation is to be carried out under similar rules or limitations as concerns the competitive dialogue. Everything relevant may or should be negotiated;[96] equal treatment of tenderers is to be ensured;[97] no confidential information may be passed from one tenderer to another;[98] and exclusions during this stage are possible.[99] In this respect, the sense is that Directive 2014/24/EU has largely copied and pasted the dialogue stage into this procedure, replacing the word "discussions" with "negotiations", thus leading to the issue raised at the start of this Section, namely that if both procedures share the same grounds for use and are quite similar, the basis for maintaining two discrete procedures is unclear.

There are, however, certain specificities to the negotiation phase that distinguish it from the discussion phase of competitive dialogue. For example, the contracting authority should give sufficient time to tenderers to re-submit tenders during the negotiation phase when the technical specifications change.[100] The possibility of providing enough time for tender preparation could be deduced from the 30 day minimum deadline for initial tenders but the Directive has expressly provided for this possibility in Article 29(5) (and not for the competitive dialogue). There is also a limit on discussing or nego-

95. With the exception of minimum requirements and award criteria which are not negotiable. See Article 29(3).
96. Article 29(3) Directive 2014/24/EU.
97. Article 29(5) Directive 2014/24/EU.
98. Article 29(5) Directive 2014/24/EU.
99. Articles 29(6) and 66 Directive 2014/24/EU.
100. Article 29(5) Directive 2014/24/EU.

tiating the minimum requirements. As the minimum requirements need to be set at the start of the procedure, prohibiting a discussion of such requirements ensures that negotiations will not be entirely free, thus avoiding a situation in which final bids solve a different problem to that originally advertised. As the minimum requirements are mandatory and imposed upon tenders, this limitation can be seen as reflecting the Nordecon case.[101] In consequence, a tender that does not meet the minimum requirements cannot be accepted for negotiation by changing those same minimum requirements. The question remains unresolved, however, if the non-compliant tender may be made compliant via negotiations, perhaps by applying the principle of proportionality or if it must be excluded as a non-compliant bid.

However, the general trend is that contracting authorities are left with the same flexibility as they have had in relation to the competitive dialogue over the last 10 years. The contracting authority will define how this stage should be run subject to certain overarching obligations such as equal treatment and confidentiality. This is not necessarily to be criticised as it provides the flexibility contracting authorities have been requesting. Nevertheless, the flexibility afforded by the lack of prescriptive rules provides a corresponding measure of legal uncertainty. Some contracting authorities (or more specifically, the individuals tasked with leading the procedure) are generally uncomfortable exercising the judgment call on the design of, and reasons for, a particular negotiation format. The perception, and often reality, is that where there is uncertainty, there is risk. As such, it would not be surprising to see contracting authorities that successfully used competitive dialogue in the past embracing this new competitive procedure with negotiation. After all, the differences between both are minor and the newer procedure does allow for "negotiations". For contracting authorities that have never embraced competitive dialogue for reasons such as perceived risk and uncertainty (even discounting that the grounds for use are now clearer), it seems unlikely that they will adopt this procedure quickly, at least until practice emerges on how to run the negotiation phase. In this regard, the authors expressly advocate the broad publication and dissemination of guidance and information sharing among contracting authorities.

Another issue meriting consideration, in particular, with regard to equal treatment and confidentiality, concerns the limitations imposed upon contracting authorities during the negotiation stage. In a procedure in which suppliers develop and refine tenders already submitted (as opposed to the com-

101. Case C-561/12 Nordecon v Rahandusministeerium [2013] WLRD (D) 470.

petitive dialogue, for example, in which new solutions are developed), it makes perfect sense to impose confidentiality and equal treatment in no uncertain terms. Any information passed from one tenderer to another confers a comparative advantage or disadvantage in what is effectively a zero-sum game. As such, Directive 2014/24/EU prohibits the contracting authority from imposing a blanket authorisation on sharing information. The logic of this assessment changes if, in reality, the competitive procedure with negotiation ends up being used in scenarios for which competitive dialogue has proven so popular over the last decade, namely to design technical specifications that will be used at the final tender stage. Flexibility is already built into the procedure as the Directive only imposes limits on the discussions of minimum requirements and award criteria. Everything else appears to fall within the legitimate bounds of discussion and negotiation, thus in theory, allowing the procedure to be run as the competitive dialogue has been until now. In such case, participants will no longer be engaged in a zero-sum game thereby favouring a more flexible view of confidentiality requirements. In this instance, bidders are competing to influence the technical specifications and, as such, have an incentive in sharing the information necessary for inclusion in the final technical specifications. After all, technical specifications are generally public by nature.

4.2.5. Final tender stage

Directive 2014/24/EU makes no reference to the fine-tuning of tenders and discussions with the preferred bidder at the final tender stage. Absent explicit authorisation, the conclusion could be that neither are permitted at all or, more likely, that the position is equivalent to that under the open and restricted procedure. By contrast, it is interesting to observe that competitive dialogue still includes specific rules allowing for the fine-tuning of tenders and discussions with the preferred bidder.[102] In this regard, it is unclear why the Directive would choose two different ways to conclude two similar procedures with common grounds for use and similar structure. One argument might be that since tenders are negotiated and solutions only discussed, it is expected that all the relevant issues have been settled by the time the final tenders are received. However, the same arguments made with regard to competitive dialogue in favour of flexibility can also be offered in relation to competitive negotiation, i.e. reducing transaction costs or securing financial commitments only at this stage. It is arguable that such flexibility should not

102. See Section 4.1.3. above.

be permitted in the competitive procedure with negotiation phase. The absence of effective competition at this stage means that there is little deterrent to prevent the preferred bidder's interest in "clawing back" concessions made in the final tender. It would perhaps be preferable for all-important discussions to occur while there is competitive pressure and lower costs which have already been sunk. For the sake of consistency, it would have also been preferable to have the same solution in both the competitive dialogue and competitive negotiations. In the authors' view, the approach taken under the competitive procedure with negotiation is the preferable one.

4.2.5.1. Risks arising from the competitive procedure with negotiation

The competitive procedure with negotiation as stipulated in Directive 2014/24/EU exposes certain potential risks in its practical application. This procedure demands competent negotiation skills from contracting authorities and may impact the principle of competition. As contracting authorities have not traditionally been permitted to negotiate (at least in contracts significantly above thresholds) there will be a steep learning curve for the officials involved that may not lead to the best outcomes being achieved.[103] In addition, good project management skills will become essential in order to avoid procedures becoming unnecessarily protracted, an experience already encountered in relation to competitive dialogue.[104]

The second risk is connected with the duration of procedures and tender commitments. As indicated above, with regard to the competitive procedure with negotiation, it is possible that the contracting authority will require only outline tenders and not full tenders from the point of commencement. If that is the case, it is not clear how to determine whether the changes introduced during the negotiations are not actually violations of commitments made in the outline tenders or made in any interim tender during the negotiation stage. In both cases, there is a risk that the "horse trading" involved in any negotiation may imply changes to tenders received. Directive 2014/24/EU provides an indication in this regard in permitting the negotiations to cover anything except the award criteria or the minimum requirements. By contrast, everything else can be negotiated and changed, including the terms of the outline tenders. This is not simply a matter of legalistic or academic abstraction, as the longer the negotiation stage lasts, the more likely it is that the original as-

103. L Chever and J Moore, 'Negotiated procedures overrated? Evidence from France questions the Commission's approach in the latest procurement reforms' (2012) 4 EPPPL, 228-241.

104. P Telles, 'Competitive Dialogue in Spain' (n 67) 416-418.

sumptions made by tenderers become out-dated. In consequence, if the tenders submitted are indeed negotiable and suppliers are not bound by them until the final tender is submitted, it must be questioned to what extent suppliers will take the starting and interim bids seriously. This problem has previously been associated with competitive dialogue,[105] where discussions are not taken seriously precisely because they do not constitute firm commitments.

As indicated above, there is also a risk that the minimum requirements may change as the procedure progresses. It may be that the situation has simply changed and the original minimum requirements no longer make sense or that temptation (and sunken costs) may incline the contracting authority to abandon or downplay those requirements. It may not be legitimate to do so but the likelihood of tenderers complaining against such change as time goes on reduces accordingly also likely, in part, to sunken costs.[106] However, in the instance in which all remaining tenderers are in agreement with the change then such threat is removed, irrespective of the fact that an eliminated tenderer or candidate might have been prejudiced by such change and will not know about it.

A final risk for this procedure is the possibility that it will be used to "crowd-source" technical specifications that will be used for the final tenders, as happened in relation to the competitive dialogue over the last decade.[107]

It is extremely difficult to gauge at present whether practice in relation to this procedure will organically evolve in the directions hypothesised in this Section. Much may be learned from the evolution of competitive dialogue as one of the models adopted in various EU Member States over the last decade.

4.3. Innovation Partnership

During consultations on Directive 2014/24/EU, stakeholders recommended greater use of procedures suited for innovative procurement such as competitive dialogue, design contests and, in particular, the negotiated procedure.[108] Whilst there exists a certain ambivalence on the part of contracting authorities

105. Ibid, 411-416.
106. Time limits for remedies may also play a part, for example, if the change occurred well before the award and stand still period.
107. See Section 4.1.2. above.
108. Commission Staff Working Paper, 'Impact Assessment Accompanying the document Proposal for a Directive of the European Parliament and of the Council on Public Procurement and the Proposal for a Directive of the European Parliament and of the Council on procurement by entities operating in the water, energy, transport and postal sectors', SEC(2011) 1585 final, 65.

as to how to tailor procurement processes accordingly,[109] the Impact Assessment indicated that 48% of contracting authorities seek innovative products, solutions or services in their tender documents on at least some occasions; 7% indicate an aim to do so as much as possible and 10% indicate that they do so regularly.[110] As will be discussed in this Section, in addition to incorporating slight modifications to the grounds for use of existing procedures, Directive 2014/24/EU has gone one step further in instituting a tailor-made innovation partnership procedure under Article 31.

Described as the Directive's "most important novelty",111 the innovation partnership mandates, under a single procedure, the purchase of both research and development ("R&D") solutions and resulting supplies, services or works which cannot be met by solutions already available on the market.[112] In this regard, the procedure deviates from the historical tendency of the public sector Directives to require discrete treatment of R&D and resultant purchases through the award of separate procedures, although the extent to which the innovation partnership may be said to achieve purposes not otherwise possible through use of existent procedures is at least questionable enough to raise the necessity of a discrete procedure. [113] Specifically, the innovation partnership has been identified as comprising three key phases. Under the first phase, an award procedure is conducted in accordance with the Directive to choose the partner or partners that will subsequently participate in the innovation phase of the contract awarded.[114] The second phase occurs after the award of the contract under which an innovative solution is developed as a matter of contract execution.[115] The final phase concerns the placing of orders for the purchase of results constituting the outcome of the innovation phase, again, as part of contract execution.[116] This Section examines the key features of the innovation partnership procedure.

109. For a discussion in this regard, see Section 2 of Butler's Chapter in this book.
110. Impact Assessment, (n 108) 61.
111. A R Apostol, 'Pre-commercial procurement in support of innovation: regulatory effectiveness?' (2012) 6 PPLR 213, 221.
112. Recital 49 and Article 31(1) Directive 2014/24/EU.
113. See generally Butler's Chapter in this collection.
114. P Cerqueira Gomes, 'The Innovative Innovation Partnerships Under the 2014 Public Procurement Directive' (51) 210.
115. Ibid.
116. Ibid.

4.3.1. Choice of Procedure

Directive 2014/24/EU does not specify any explicit grounds for use of the innovation partnership procedure per se.[117] However, as indicated in Section 2 above, on the taxonomy proposed in this Chapter, the innovation partnership may be said to be a special procedure for use where R&D development is necessary i.e. in those instances in which there is no available solution on the market.[118] In this regard, contracting authorities must apply national procedures adjusted to be in conformity with the Directive.[119] The previous Section has touched upon national experiences of adjusting (or not) to forms of negotiated procedure such as competitive dialogue. In light of this experience, the absence of specified grounds for use may provide a further incentive (or excuse) for Member States to simply copy and paste the procedure into national law.[120] It is suggested that in order for the procedure to gain traction, Member States must make suitable adaptations (howsoever determined) that allow contracting authorities on the ground to acculturate. The procedure will only gain credence if it is seen as an option capable of local implementation; otherwise the procedure may simply generate a perception of a symbolic but otherwise practically redundant inclusion. The extent to which options are available to use the procedure and whether the procedure will be taken up is another matter.

4.3.2. Participation in an Innovation Partnership

The innovation partnership may be said to provide greater visibility of the contracting authority's search for innovative products. The Impact Assessment observed that simply allowing for variants or alternative solutions does not signal to potential suppliers that the contracting authority is looking for an innovative solution[121] whereas the innovation partnership allows contracting authorities to clearly indicate their interest in such proposals while retaining broad competition.[122] The innovation partnership relies exclusively on the contracting authority's own initiative to identify need and request participa-

117. On the conditional use of the competitive procedure with negotiation and competitive dialogue, see Section 4.1.1. above.
118. Article 31(1) Directive 2014/24/EU.
119. Article 26(1) Directive 2014/24/EU.
120. This is particularly likely in Member States such as the UK which signals a commitment to a "copy-out" method of transposition.
121. It appears that variants are rarely requested in practice in any event. For a discussion in this regard, see Section 7 of Butler's Chapter in this book.
122. Impact Assessment (n 108) 191.

tion by issuing a contract notice.[123] In response, any economic operator may submit a request to participate by providing the requested information for qualitative selection.[124] The minimum time limit for receipt of requests to participate must be 30 days from the date on which the contract notice is sent.[125] Contracting authorities may limit the number of suitable candidates to be invited to participate in the procedure.[126] Only those economic operators invited by the contracting authority following the assessment of the information provided may participate in the procedure.[127]

The status of the innovation partnership as a special procedure is confirmed by the fact that in the procurement documents, the contracting authority must identify the need for an innovative product, service or works that cannot be met by purchasing products, services or works already available on the market.[128] It must indicate which elements of this description define the minimum requirements to be met by all tenders.[129] The information provided must be sufficiently precise to enable economic operators to identify the nature and scope of the required solution and decide whether to request to participate in the procedure.[130]

Ultimately, the contracting authority may decide to set up the innovation partnership with one partner or with several partners conducting separate R&D activities.[131] It should be observed that Recital 49 states that contracting authorities should not use innovation partnerships in such a way as to prevent, restrict or distort competition. In this regard, Recital 49 further states that in certain cases, setting up innovation partnerships with several partners could contribute to avoiding such effects. However, it is submitted that anti-competitive behaviour may continue to result even with the inclusion of several partners. It has been observed that the innovation partnership procedure could have an anti-competitive effect by locking in to a single supplier absent a stipulation as to limits of time or volume of purchases.[132] A number of sup-

123. Article 31(1) Directive 2014/24/EU.
124. Ibid.
125. Ibid.
126. Ibid. In accordance with Article 65(2) which provides that there is a minimum of three candidates in the innovation partnership.
127. Ibid.
128. Ibid.
129. Ibid.
130. Ibid.
131. Ibid.
132. S Bedin, HT.618 – Consultation on the draft R&D&I-Framework, Section 2.3. Public procurement of research services, addressed to the European Commission, Direc-

pliers could similarly be locked in. Further, as will be discussed below with regards to target setting and termination, participation of multiple partners presents its own difficulties and potential distortive effects. Directive 2014/24/EU does not contain any specific provisions relating to the review of innovation partnerships once the partnerships are set up, or with a view to the admittance of new members. It is therefore at least arguable that innovation partnerships may display certain behaviours increasingly characteristic of framework agreements and which should necessitate similar or equivalent safeguards. This could include the imposition of an equivalent time limited duration (of 4 years) or other suitable time limit which may be subject to review.[133]

4.3.3. Qualitative Selection

In selecting candidates, contracting authorities must, in particular, apply criteria concerning the candidates' capacity in the field of R&D and of developing and implementing innovative solutions.[134] The reference to "in particular" confirms that Article 58 containing the general provisions on selection criteria continue to apply with regard to this procedure. Article 58 indicates that selection criteria may relate to "suitability to pursue the professional activity" and "technical and professional ability".[135] Beyond this general provision, it is clear that the assessment of selection criteria under the innovation partnership procedure envisages a more specific assessment of capacity. It has been observed that the Directive clearly felt the need to explain that capacity in the field of R&D and innovative solutions could be taken into account when selecting economic operators without being discriminatory.[136] However, it has also been argued that this provides for more legal certainty than would be given by the general criteria set out in Article 58 thus constituting a step for-

torate-General for Competition, 16 February 2014. Available at: <http://ec.europa.eu/competition/consultations/2013_state_aid_rdi/sara_bedin_en.pdf > accessed 5 May 2014. See also S Corvers, R Apostol, C Mair and O Pantilimon, Comments on the procurement section in the ongoing DG COMP open consultation on the Draft Union Framework for State aid for Research, Development and Innovation, Corvers Procurement Services BV, 3. Available at: <http://ec.europa.eu/competition/consultations/2013_state_aid_rdi/corvers_en.pdf> accessed 5 May 2013.

133. Article 33(1) Directive 2014/24/EU.
134. Article 31(6) Directive 2014/24/EU.
135. Article 58(1)(a) and (c) Directive 2014/24/EU, respectively.
136. P Cerqueira Gomes, 'The Innovative Innovation Partnerships Under the 2014 Public Procurement Directive' (n 51) 210, fn14.

ward in its recognition that purchasing innovation demands different selection criteria due to the necessity of specialised knowledge in the field.[137]

It is questionable whether this additional provision is necessarily productive of more legal certainty. Firstly, clarity is not aided by the absence of any definition of R&D.[138] Secondly, potential issues arise in relation to relatively new suppliers to the market (e.g. start-ups) proposing a solution but which may lack the experience to demonstrate capability. It has been observed that the initial proposal for the Directive made reference not only to the tenderer's capacity but also to their experience whereas Directive 2014/24/EU has omitted reference to experience, allowing contracting authorities to select start up companies that generally have the capacity but not the experience of a large company.[139] Notwithstanding, it is not clear to what extent experience can still be an operative factor. Thirdly, in any event, it is conceivable that economic operators (whether start-ups or well-established operators) that may be able to evidence R&D capacity may not necessarily be able to evidence capacity related to the development and implementation of innovative solutions and vice versa. Directive 2014/24/EU does not clearly demarcate the boundaries between R&D and something which is developed, implemented or commercialized.[140] The potential for legal uncertainty in this area is also perhaps acknowledged by the fact that, in contrast to Directive 2014/24/EU, specific guidance has been issued in relation to the assessment of technical and/or professional ability under the Defence and Security Procurement Directive, in which such capacity is a particular focus.[141]

It has also been observed that another potentially problematic issue concerns the fact that the preferred supplier is selected before the market has started R&D and without firm evidence of who will be able to develop the best solution.[142] Instead, selection is based on antecedent qualification criteria

137. Ibid.
138. For a discussion in this regard, see Section 4 of Butler's Chapter in this book.
139. P Cerqueira Gomes, 'The Innovative Innovation Partnerships Under the 2014 Public Procurement Directive' (n 136).
140. See generally Section 3 of Butler's Chapter in this book.
141. See Article 42 of Directive 2009/81/EC of the European Parliament and of the Council of 13 July 2009 on the coordination of procedures for the award of certain works contracts, supply contracts and service contracts by contracting authorities or entities in the fields of defence and security, and amending Directives 2004/17/EC and 2004/18/EC [2009] OJ L 216/76. For guidance on this provision, see Directorate General Internal Market and Services, Guidance Note, Security of Supply, Directive 2009/81/EC on the award of contracts in the fields of defence and security, 8-9.
142. S Bedin, HT.618 – Consultation on the draft R&D&I-Framework (n 132).

such as financial capacity (e.g. minimum turnover) and technical capacity (e.g. prior customer references).[143] On this basis, it has been suggested that there is a risk of lock-in, thereby precluding competition at a point in which there is no substantial proof that the preferred supplier will be able to develop a more suitable solution than other providers.[144] Consequently, there is a risk that offers are not compared on the basis of which offer can deliver the most suitable solution (in the absence of evidence of any results that will come from the R&D) but rather based on other selection criteria and negotiation.[145]

Therefore, contracting authorities are afforded considerable discretion with regard to qualitative selection under the innovation partnership procedure.

4.3.4. Structure of the Innovation Partnership Procedure

After initial selection, the innovation partnership must be structured in successive phases.[146] The structuring of the innovation partnership is arguably as crucial as the dialogue stage in a competitive dialogue in ensuring the optimal end result. These phases are not defined except that they must follow the "sequence of steps in the research and innovation process".[147] It has been observed that the absence of any stipulation as to detail of these phases provides a measure of flexibility.[148] However, it is important to recognize that there are, nevertheless, inherent limitations that will impact on the structuring of the partnership. One significant limitation is that performance levels and maximum costs must be agreed before the commencement of the innovation process, a determination that has been identified as providing "less flexible boundaries".[149] This aspect is considered in more detail below. Suffice to state for present purposes, the obvious difficulty of prospectively determining performance and maximum costs aside, these considerations are likely to be important operative factors in the minds of officials when designing the phases, setting targets and potentially even determining the number of viable or suitable partners.

143. Ibid.
144. Ibid.
145. Ibid.
146. Article 31(2) Directive 2014/24/EU.
147. Ibid.
148. P Cerqueira Gomes, 'The Innovative Innovation Partnerships Under the 2014 Public Procurement Directive' (n 51) 212.
149. Ibid, 213.

With regard to the research and innovation process, this may include the manufacturing of the products, the provision of the services or the completion of the works.[150] However, the sequence of steps in the research and innovation process is not clear. The Directive does not define research, or, more specifically, R&D nor prototyping and manufacturing processes. Further, it has not been made clear in Article 31 or elsewhere in the Directive whether these steps correspond to Pre-Commercial Procurement ("PCP") phases.[151] It appears anomalous to provide guidance on the PCP model but no guidance on the corresponding use of such pre-commercial procurement phases under the innovation partnership procedure. Comparable guidance on the R&D phase under the innovation partnership procedure could prove useful to contracting authorities.

4.3.4.1. Proportionality of duration and value to the degree of innovation

An integral aspect of maintaining the structure of a partnership is to ensure, as far as possible and practicable, proportionality of time and cost. This aspect is expressly identified in Article 31 in two subsections. Firstly, Article 31(2) provides that the innovation partnership must aim at the development of an innovative product, service or works (as well as the results), provided that they correspond to the performance levels and maximum costs agreed between the contracting authorities and the participants.[152] Secondly, Article 31(7) provides that the duration and value of the different phases must reflect the degree of innovation of the proposed solution and the estimated value of supplies, services or works must not be disproportionate in relation to the investment required for their development. These references appear to indicate a primary focus on proportionality of cost (by phase and overall) above duration.

In this regard, Article 31 is more circumscribed than previous provision made in the 2011 Draft proposal, for example.[153] The latter provided that the

150. The 2013 draft provided that the partnerships shall be structured in successive stages following the sequence of steps in the research and innovation process possibly up to the manufacturing of the supply or the provision of the services (italics added). See Article 29(2) of Proposal for a Directive of the European Parliament and of the Council on public procurement (Classical Directive) (First reading), Brussels, 12 July 2013, 11745/13.

151. For a discussion in this regard, see Sections 3 and 4 of Butler's Chapter in this book and citations therein.

152. See also Recital 49 Directive 2014/24/EU.

153. Proposal for a Directive of the European Parliament and of the Council on public procurement, COM(2011) 896 final, Brussels, 20 December 2011.

partnership's duration and value should "remain within appropriate limits, taking into account the need to recover the costs, including those incurred in developing an innovative solution, and to achieve an adequate profit".[154] It had been observed that such additional provision seemed overly prescriptive.[155] For example, it would be difficult to determine what is meant by the fact that duration and value should "remain within appropriate limits", the types of costs that would form the basis of assessment and what constitutes an "adequate profit".[156] More fundamentally, these factors appear to relate exclusively to financial considerations such as cost recovery and profit when the provision requires that value (which is not technically specified in monetary terms) should reflect the degree of innovation. To this extent, Article 31 is therefore less prescriptive but the earlier prescriptions in the Draft provide an insight into the difficulties of objectively determining proportionality. Notwithstanding, it is suggested that these issues could never be fully resolved within the Directive itself, not least because such assessments concern intangible notions reminiscent of the kinds of assessments necessary to determine a "particularly complex" contract under the competitive dialogue. For this reason, the final text incorporates references which are even more generic. In any event, these factors are unlikely to be able to form a basis for challenge post-award. However, a public procurement challenge aside, it has been observed that the nature of such forms of partnership mean that it can be extremely difficult to value the resources put into a partnership by the contracting authority and contractor such as to ensure a balance which prevents illegal state aid.[157] As indicated above, the Directive appears to suggest that such an assessment can be undertaken with relative ease as the contracting authority is required to achieve proportionality in terms of structure, duration and value.[158]

154. Article 29(4) Draft Proposal (n 153)
155. See for example, A Semple, 'Mixed offerings for sustainability in new EU Directives'. Available at: <http://www.procurementanalysis.eu/resources/Mixed+offerings+for+sustainability+in+new+EU+Directives.pdf> accessed 15 May 2014.
156. Ibid.
157. For a useful discussion from the perspective of assessing compatibility of partnerships with State aid rules, see T Inden and K N Olesen, 'Legal Aspects of Public Private Innovation' (2012) 7(4) EPPPL 258-267.
158. Article 31(7). Experience suggests that even the use of specific calculation models used to quantify this balance (e.g. drawing up a "state aid account") do not solve the problem of how to value (i.e. qualify and quantify) the inputs and outcomes of a partnership. See T Inden and K N Olesen, 'Legal Aspects of Public Private Innovation' (n 157) 264.

It has also been observed that the Innovation partnership is "poorly drafted" on the duration and cost aspect, allowing significant discretion in deciding the value and duration of any contract.[159] It is possible but difficult to envisage how the EU legislator could realistically regulate the cost variable. However, with regard to duration, there is a conceivable risk of market foreclosure as contracting authorities could potentially set up "innovation partnerships" to get around time limits imposed on framework agreements, for example. It is recalled that Recital 49 emphasises the fact that innovation partnerships should not be used to prevent, restrict or distort competition but there are no specific requirements identified in Article 31 itself concerning reporting, monitoring, review or time-limits on innovation partnerships.

Perhaps one of the most significant questions concerns uncertainty as to why Directive 2014/24/EU seeks to require (or presumes) a necessary correspondence between the estimated value of the contract and the investment required for development. It is axiomatic that the end result should reflect the cost but this fails to take account of the reality that costs incurred in development will not necessarily bear in direct proportion to the overall contract value. Further, issues such as intellectual property inevitably factor into account on either side of the contracting equation and, as a result of which, it may be very difficult to argue that there is or will be proportionality in the short, medium and long term.

A final aspect that remains unclear is whether investment required for development is confined to investments made by the contracting authority within the framework of the innovation partnership or whether it includes investments previously made by the private partner, or both.[160] It has been suggested that if this could conceivably incorporate investments outside the terms of the innovation partnership, contracting authorities may have significant discretion to award large value contracts of lengthy duration for the purchase of R&D results.

4.3.4.2. Target Setting and Termination

Article 31 makes specific reference to post-award considerations, in particular, to target setting and termination of the partnership. Such provision confirms the somewhat anomalous character of the innovation partnership within

159. A R Apostol, 'Pre-commercial procurement in support of innovation: regulatory effectiveness?' (n 111) 222.
160. S Corvers, R Apostol, C Mair and O Pantilimon, Comments on the procurement section in the ongoing DG COMP open consultation on the Draft Union Framework for State aid for Research, Development and Innovation (n 132).

the overall legislative scheme of the Directive in its coverage not only of the procurement function but also aspects of contract management.

With regard to target setting, Directive 2014/24/EU provides that once an economic operator is admitted to the partnership, the partnership must set intermediate targets to be attained by the partners and provide for payment of the remuneration in appropriate instalments.[161] Based on those targets, the contracting authority may decide after each phase to terminate the innovation partnership or, in the case of an innovation partnership with several partners, to reduce the number of partners by terminating individual contracts.[162] Termination is possible provided the contracting authority has indicated those possibilities and the conditions for their use in the procurement documents.[163]

It has been observed that intermediate targets will play a decisive role in evaluating partner capacity/performance and that given the "evaluative nature" of these targets they should be as objective and proportionate as possible in order to comply with general principles of EU procurement law.[164] However, the provisions on targets generate significant legal and practical uncertainty, in the same way that the relative bargaining positions of suppliers and contracting authorities may be destabilized under the competitive dialogue and competitive procedure with negotiation. A fundamental issue concerns the boundaries of target setting and design.[165] For instance, it is unclear how such targets will be formulated e.g. in terms of performance, cost, other or a combination. Further, whilst it appears that there must be relative agreement on those targets, it is not clear to what extent the contracting authority will ultimately dictate their terms. A host of issues may also arise where multiple partners are involved. Firstly, the possibility cannot be excluded that multiple partners contracting on similar terms may collectively exercise control over targets, weakening the position of the contracting authority. Secondly, it is not clear whether certain targets will be applicable to all partners. Thirdly, there could be potential for variability in the form, content and application of targets between partners. Fourthly, it is also unclear to what extent contracting authorities will utilise those targets as a basis for comparison of performance by partners. Fifthly, it cannot be excluded that partners may evolve at different speeds and which may result in certain partners being giv-

161. Article 31(2) Directive 2014/24/EU.
162. Ibid.
163. Ibid.
164. P Cerqueira Gomes, 'The Innovative Innovation Partnerships Under the 2014 Public Procurement Directive' (n 51) 213.
165. Ibid 211.

en more time to develop solutions so as to reach any collectively agreed performance levels. Such a possibility may be foreseen, for example, where partnerships comprise both start-ups and established companies. It is unclear whether a legalistic view of equal treatment would prevent such variation. Sixthly, similar to the provisions for competitive procedure with negotiation and competitive dialogue, Article 31 contains no interstitial provision, for example, to review targets, allow for independent scrutiny or verification of those targets, or record requirements of performance. Further, there is an additional risk that any targets may be subject to ad hoc revision. Finally, if there are several partners but certain individual contracts are terminated, aggrieved partners may look to examine requirements imposed on other partners to determine whether the basis for termination is justifiable. It may also be particularly difficult for terminated partners to verify the application of such targets in the absence of requirements of the kind identified above.

It has been observed that whilst the result of the innovation partnership must have a direct connection to the subject matter of the contract giving effect to the initial aim, there is a potential risk that the outcome exceeds the concrete public need described in the procurement documents.[166] In response, it has been suggested that it would be appropriate, and arguably required, under the EU law principle of transparency for the contracting authority to publish not only the results of the final product, service or goods, but also the intermediate targets.[167] In light of the above, it is possible to envisage issues regarding the manner, form, detail and timing of publication. Notwithstanding, this kind of proposal evidences the need for some measure of transparency in light of their potential effects.

A number of other issues may also arise in relation to termination. For instance, provision is only made for termination on the contracting authority's election but Article 31 is otherwise silent on the partner's rights, if any, including in the instance of mutual termination. This aspect is likely to be governed exclusively by national law. Further, whilst Directive 2014/24/EU repeatedly emphasises the importance of protecting confidential information during the process of participation in negotiations, Article 31 is silent on the issue of exploitation of confidential information (e.g. know how or even intellectual property) obtained during the course of a now terminated contract in continuing on-going contracts with other partners. The only reference is to a requirement that the contracting authority must not reveal to the other part-

166. P Cerqueira Gomes, 'The Innovative Innovation Partnerships Under the 2014 Public Procurement Directive' (n 51) 214.

167. Ibid.

ners solutions proposed "or other confidential information communicated by a partner in the framework of the partnership" without that partner's agreement.[168] Given that the terminated participant is no longer a partner, it is not clear to what extent, if at all, any confidentiality obligation continues.

Finally, the provisions on payment of remuneration in appropriate instalments are also vague. It has been observed that this provision is "regrettably inflexible" because remuneration in instalments may not be suitable for all types of partnership, particularly, where the supplier receives funding for its R&D work from other sources.[169] However, if the amount or timing of instalments is an issue, for example, the reality will be that most suppliers entering an innovation partnership must appreciate that adaptations will need to be made in order to meet schedules and practices of the contracting authority. More fundamentally, it is submitted that by at least forcing a requirement to provide payments, the Directive ensures that contracting authorities do not look for free R&D, a position relatively common under the competitive dialogue in which it was often provided that development costs "may" be paid but rarely, if ever, were paid.

The issue of R&D instalment payments also raises broader questions concerning the risk of State aid under Article 107 TFEU. The longstanding assumption (increasingly challenged) is that the award of a public contract in accordance with the EU procurement Directives will not prima facie raise the issue of compatibility with EU State aid rules, provided any conferred economic advantage does not go beyond normal market conditions.[170] However, it has been argued that the drive towards added flexibility under Directive 2014/24/EU may increase the risk of State aid in public procurement, a risk which is exacerbated in procedures which permit extensive negotiations, the use of public funds to develop proprietary technology and the use of non-economic award criteria.[171] In this regard, the innovation partnership has been identified in emphatic terms as "the perfect cover to circumvent rules control-

168. Article 31(6) of Directive 2014/24/EU which further provides that: [...] such agreement shall not take the form of a general waiver but shall be given with reference to the intended communication of specific information.
169. A Semple, 'Procuring innovation – will the new Directives help?' <http://www.procurementanalysis.eu/resources/Procuring+innovation_new+directives.pdf> accessed 15 May 2014.
170. For a discussion of this position generally, See A Sanchez-Graells, 'Public procurement and state aid: reopening the debate?' (2012) 6 PPLR, 205-12 and citations therein.
171. Ibid, 209.

ling R&D State aid".[172] Specifically, it has been argued that where public procurement activities refer to future services, works or goods reliant on contracting authority funding or sponsoring through R&D, there risks potential for not only short term anti-competitive effects concerning interim payments for R&D development but also deferred anti-competitive effects in relation to future goods or services once developed.[173] These effects may be of acute significance from a State aid and competition law perspective if the the goods, works or services are not for exclusive use by the public buyer.[174] In this instance, at the outset, a contractor may gain a first mover advantage which prevents the development of competition in private markets.[175] To this extent, it is submitted that the Directive could have played a more substantial role in providing early detections and monitoring of anti-competitive effects e,g. reporting requirements on R&D funding, interim review of innovation partnerships and their duration.[176]

In light of the above, it should be emphasised that target-related performance (including performance-based termination) and payment by instalment requires careful planning and management. It follows that contracting authorities will need to ensure that they have the relevant expertise in place to deal with multiple legal and practical permutations at the execution stage. This should not be any different to the staff requirements or expectations of contracting authorities embarking on a competitive dialogue or competitive procedure with negotiation. However, it is clear that the innovation partnership introduces new variables that cannot simply be treated as matters of post-award contract execution falling outside the Directive's scope; rather, these are aspects which must comply with the specific provisions of the Directive and EU law more generally, in particular, principles of equal treatment and transparency.

4.3.4.3. Intellectual Property Rights and Risk Management

An inevitably recurring theme in the context of negotiated forms of procurement concerns the balance of interests between contracting authorities and economic operators in the trade-off. A key aspect in this regard relates to the

172. Ibid 211.
173. A Sanchez-Graells, 'Public procurement and state aid: reopening the debate?' (n 171) 211-12 and citations at fn26 and 27.
174. Ibid 212.
175. Ibid.
176. Such requirements could also assist assessments of compliance with the State aid rules (as well as any basis for exemption from their application).

management of risk.[177] This issue is particularly important with respect to intellectual property rights ("IPRs") and other technical "know-how". The Impact Assessment stated that the Innovation partnership "should provide for the necessary IPR transfer and protection arrangements depending on individual circumstances".[178] However, Article 31 simply requires the contracting authority to "define the arrangements applicable to intellectual property rights" i.e. without reference to determining acquisition, transfer or subsequent protection. A number of observations can be made in this regard. Firstly, this provision means that ultimately the terms of acquisition (as well as transfer and protection) are left to the discretion of the contracting authority.[179]

Secondly, given that Article 31 does not define the scope of the innovation partnership by reference to the sharing of benefits between the contracting authority and economic operators,[180] Article 31 does not necessarily preclude the possibility that a partnership may be implemented irrespective of the sharing of IPRs between the contracting authority and the private partner.[181] It has been argued that often the contracting authority will not need acquire the intellectual property right itself but solely the right to exploit the asset under an IP licence.[182] Further, it has been suggested that by allowing IPR retention by the private partner, the State will provide a competitive incentive for the private sector reinforcing the apparent spirit of Recital 49. It is beyond the scope of the Chapter to hypothesise the possible IPR and licensing options that may be available. Suffice to state that the (commercial) reality is that most forms of partnership will necessitate arrangements that will require at least one form of IPR acquisition, transfer, licensing or protection.

177. On the issue of risk in the procurement of innovation generally, see Report of Expert Group to the European Commission, 'Risk management in the procurement of innovation: Concepts and empirical evidence in the European Union' (2009). Available at: <http://ec.europa.eu/invest-in-research/pdf/download_en/risk_management.pdf> 15 May 2014.
178. Impact Assessment (n 108) 63.
179. Article 31(6) Directive 2014/24/EU. See also P Cerqueira Gomes, 'The Innovative Innovation Partnerships Under the 2014 Public Procurement Directive' (51) 215
180. This should be contrasted with Article 14 Directive 2014/24/EU discussed in Sections 3 and 4 of Butler's Chapter in this book.
181. A R Apostol, 'Pre-commercial procurement in support of innovation: regulatory effectiveness?' (n 111) 222.
182. P Cerqueira Gomes, 'The Innovative Innovation Partnerships Under the 2014 Public Procurement Directive' (52) 215-216.

Thirdly, Article 31 is silent on the issue of IPR management at discrete phases. For instance, Article 31 does not regulate how the relevant IPR should be acquired when the partnership comes to an end. It has been suggested that acquisition could possibly occur after the award of the contract or even after the achievement of an intermediate target.[183] The 2011 Draft Proposal provided that a contracting authority may decide after each stage to terminate the partnership and launch a new procurement procedure for the remaining phases, "provided that it has acquired the relevant intellectual property rights".[184] This provision has been omitted from the final text raising the question as to whether or not it is possible to terminate the partnership and launch a new procedure irrespective of the issue of IPR acquisition. In any event, the operating assumption appears to be that the contracting authority obtains the IPR under an innovation partnership. On any interpretation, the above indicates the importance of IPR not only in structuring the initial partnership with a partner but also in informing any decision to terminate a partnership and subsequently award contracts to other partners. Further, as indicated above in the context of the discussion of target setting and performance, Directive 2014/24/EU in unclear on the use to which information may be put by the contracting authority which was acquired during the course of a partnership and which is now terminated. Similar uncertainty exists in relation to the use of IPRs and other technical know-how in this regard.

A final issue concerns the potential risk of State aid. It has been argued that because the Directive does not specifically require that the contracting authority must acquire all intellectual property rights generated by the partner to achieve a prescribed intermediate target, a partner could benefit from having obtained public funds which it could then use in the development of other innovative solutions thereby unfairly impacting competition.[185] Further, as indicated above, the final text does not include any condition that the contracting authority must acquire the relevant intellectual property rights before terminating a partnership.

Notwithstanding the issues identified above, it is submitted that whilst Article 31 contains only a limited reference to IPR, at the very least such provision commits contracting authorities to a determination on IPR whilst also providing the flexibility needed to decide on if, and how, it wants IPR to be shared. An important issue will concern the nature and scope of IPR ar-

183. Ibid 215.
184. Article 29(2) Draft Proposal (n 153).
185. P Cerqueira Gomes, 'The Innovative Innovation Partnerships Under the 2014 Public Procurement Directive' (n 184).

rangements as well as any permissible amendments to those arrangements throughout the duration of a partnership. It is clear that IPR will need to become a focal point for planning procurement exercises.

4.3.5. Negotiation under the Innovation Partnership Procedure

As indicated in the introduction to Section 4 above, the Directive's successive provisions on the competitive procedure with negotiation, competitive dialogue and innovation partnership suggest that all have certain commonalities. Although designated as a discrete "procedure" alongside the other procedures, the innovation partnership does not formally prescribe a procedure comparable to competitive negotiation with publication or competitive dialogue. Whether the innovation partnership should correspond with the competitive procedure with negotiations is unclear in light of the omission of a reference to this procedure in the final text. The 2011 Draft Proposal expressly referred to the award of the contract in accordance with Article 27 (on the competitive procedure with negotiation).[186] Yet, the Impact Assessment identified the encouragement of iterative rounds of negotiation with suppliers under the Innovation partnership and relates such negotiations to the experience with comparable procedures, specifically identifying competitive dialogue.[187] Article 31 does not cross-reference the competitive negotiation with publication procedure. This could reflect an underlying uncertainty as to how any negotiation or dialogue is to proceed under the innovation partnership. However, in light of the earlier indications in the Draft Proposal and observations below, it may be inferred that the innovation partnership procedure utilizes a form broadly equivalent to the competitive procedure with negotiation.[188]

In this regard, Article 31 contains a number of provisions in relation to the conduct of negotiations. Firstly, Article 31 qualifies that the minimum requirements and the award criteria must not be subject to negotiations.[189] Secondly, unless otherwise provided for in Article 31, contracting authorities must negotiate with the tenderers the initial and all subsequent tenders submitted by them to improve their content, except for the final tender.[190] In contrast to Article 29(1) concerning the competitive procedure with negotiation,

186. Article 29(3) Draft Proposal (n 153).
186. Article 29(4) Directive 2014/24/EU.
187. Impact Assessment (n 108) 61-2.
188. In support of this view, see P Cerqueira Gomes, 'The Innovative Innovation Partnerships Under the 2014 Public Procurement Directive' (n 51) 210.
189. Article 31(3) of Directive 2014/24/EU.
190. Article 31(3) of Directive 2014/24/EU.

Article 31 does not provide for the possibility for contracting authorities to award contracts on the basis of the initial tenders without negotiation. Thirdly, during the negotiations, contracting authorities must ensure the equal treatment of all tenderers.[191] This requires that contracting authorities must not provide information in a discriminatory manner which may give some tenderers an advantage over others.[192] Further, contracting authorities must inform all tenderers whose tenders have not been eliminated through the process of negotiation in writing of any changes to the technical specifications or other procurement documents other than those setting out the minimum requirements.[193] Following those changes, contracting authorities must provide sufficient time for tenderers to modify and re-submit amended tenders, as appropriate.[194] These provisions are broadly equivalent to those under Article 29 on the competitive procedure with negotiation. Fourthly, negotiations may take place in successive stages in order to reduce the number of tenders to be negotiated by applying the specified award criteria in the contract notice, in the invitation to confirm interest or in the procurement documents.[195] The contracting authority must indicate whether it will use that option by specifying such in the contract notice, the invitation to confirm interest or in the procurement documents.[196] Finally, contracting authorities must not reveal to the other participants confidential information communicated by a candidate or tenderer participating in the negotiations without its agreement.[197]

To this extent, many of the same of observations identified in Section 4.2 above in relation to the competitive procedure with negotiation are applicable mutatis mutandis to negotiation under the innovation partnership procedure.

4.3.6. Award Criteria

Article 31 provides that contracts awarded under the innovation partnership must be awarded on the sole basis of the award criterion of the best price-quality ratio, thus excluding simply the lowest price, in accordance with Article 67.[198] Article 67 provides that the best price-quality ratio must be assessed

191. Article 31(4) Directive 2014/24/EU.
192. Ibid.
193. Ibid.
194. Ibid.
195. Article 31(5) Directive 2014/24/EU.
196. Ibid.
197. Article 31(4) Directive 2014/24/EU. The Directive's provisions on confidentiality are contained in Article 21.
198. Recital 49 and Article 31(1) Directive 2014/24/EU.

on the basis of criteria which may comprise inter alia quality including "innovative characteristics".[199] Again, whilst providing a measure of flexibility, there is no discernable indication as to how such criteria could be objectively formulated and applied. When considered in light of the discretion afforded to contracting authorities to assess innovation capacity for the purposes of qualitative selection, there exists potential for considerable subjectivity in decision-making across the procurement phases.

4.3.7. Correspondence of the Innovation Partnership to Innovation Objectives

The innovation partnership procedure clearly aims for greater procedural flexibility and which is reflected by the generality of its terms. However this Section has focused on some of the legal and practical issues which may be encountered in setting up and managing such a partnership and which could ultimately result in innovation objectives not being achieved. An identification of the practical issues of implementation augments the case for careful and strategic adjustment of national laws (or, at the very least, national policies) to flesh out the procedural content of Article 31.

Beyond the practical aspects, it could be argued in more general terms that the innovation partnership procedure does not stimulate contracting authorities to act as demanding first customers of innovative solutions. It has been observed that Directive 2014/24/EU is poorly drafted with regard to the subsequent purchase of products and services resulting from R&D.[200] The procedure does not appear to be limited to the direct purchase of first products or services (i.e. goods and services which have not yet been commercialized and for which the contracting authority is the first customer)[201] but also appears to permit contracting authorities to buy developed products or services after such have been commercialized.[202] Consequently, it has been argued that contracting authorities will not be incentivized to act as first customers to pull innovative products or services onto the market in accordance with the objective identified in Recital 49 but may, in fact, create obstacles to competition,[203] even to the extent of favouring national based technology suppliers

199. Article 67(2)(a) Directive 2014/24/EU.
200. A R Apostol, 'Pre-commercial procurement in support of innovation: regulatory effectiveness?' (n 111) 222.
201. Ibid 219.
202. Ibid 222.
203. Ibid.

and national industry.[204] This Section has also identified the broader State aid implications regarding the potential deferred anti-competitive effects which may be incurred if the results of the innovation partnership procedure are not for exclusive use by the public buyer. Overall, therefore, there are concerns not only about the limitations of the innovation partnership procedure in either locking suppliers in or conferring first mover advantages but also at the end game in relation to who will be permitted to use the results and in what markets, public or private or both. On this view, it has been suggested that contracting authorities are unlikely to apply the procedure in light of the resulting legal uncertainty.[205]

However, Article 31 does not preclude the terms of any individual innovation partnership from being limited to the purchase of first products and services. Much also depends on the extent of any freedom or restrictions specified under IPR arrangements. In reality, it remains to be seen to what extent innovation partnerships will be used given that they require contracting authorities to commit, at least formally, to buying commercial end-products before knowing whether suppliers can deliver. It is possible that contracting authorities may simply favour well-established suppliers that may be perceived to provide a greater assurance (if not guarantee) of success to the detriment of SMEs and other new market entrants.[206] It is beyond the scope of this Chapter to examine claims that innovation partnerships will crowd out mainstream types of R&D investments in Europe.[207] Nevertheless, it does raise the broader issue identified in the Chapter on innovation featured in this book, namely

204. S Corvers, R Apostol, C Mair and O Pantilimon, Comments on the procurement section in the ongoing DG COMP open consultation on the Draft Union Framework for State aid for Research, Development and Innovation (n 132).
205. Ibid.
206. S Bedin, HT.618 – Consultation on the draft R&D&I-Framework (n 125).
207. It is claimed that because innovation partnerships use the purchasing of R&D (representing approximately €2.5 billion each year) such partnerships prevent mainstream R&D grants and private R&D investments (representing approximately €200 billion each year). The argument runs that long-term innovation partnerships only permit the companies financing their R&D through that specific procurement contract to sell final end-products to the contracting authority for large scale deployments. By contrast, companies simultaneously pursuing the R&D phase of the innovation partnerships developing solutions through other types of R&D resource (e.g. company financing and R&D grants etc) will be excluded from selling to the contracting authority conducting the innovation partnership. For consideration of this point, see S Corvers, R Apostol, C Mair and O Pantilimon, Comments on the procurement section in the ongoing DG COMP open consultation on the Draft Union Framework for State aid for Research, Development and Innovation (n 132).

the extent to which EU public procurement law can be said to cohere within the overarching EU policy framework on R&D and innovation.[208]

Notwithstanding, it is suggested that there is a need for cautious optimism. As a model, the innovation partnership procedure may not be viable for use by smaller local authorities without the staff and expertise to set up and manage such partnerships. However, there are clear examples across the EU in which large contracting authorities have been prepared to engage in substantial forms of joint and cross-border procurement.[209] A strategic use of innovation partnerships is, therefore, entirely feasible provided that there is sufficient appetite for, and confidence in, their use. Critical to their use is a need for national legislators and contracting authorities to work within the existing parameters of what is legally certain even if there are aspects of inherent uncertainty. This could be aided by the publication of additional guidance on the innovation partnership procedure,[210] although the authors echoe caution expressed in the Impact Assessment, namely that guidance is no real substitute for certainty within the rules themselves. Further, it is quite conceivable that contracting authorities may err on the side of caution and continue to utilise forms of competitive dialogue or competitive negotiation to achieve substantially the same ends on the basis of at least some understanding of the legal parameters of those procedures. Ultimately, contracting authorities will need to be convinced that "value-added" will be realised through the use of this distinct partnership procedure.

5. Conclusions

As indicated in the introduction, Directive 2014/24/EU aims to introduce flexibility and simplification into public procurement in the EU. With regard to procurement procedures, there have been limited changes to the open and restricted procedures, mostly due to an honest desire to reduce the transaction costs and timescales involved. The biggest change introduced to these procedures was the possibility of running the open procedure as a single stage vari-

208. See Section 2 of Butler's Chapter in this book.
209. It has been suggested that the innovation partnership procedure seems likely to be of most use to EU Member States with developed publica administrations and high innovation profiles such as Denmark, Finland, Germany and Sweden. See P Cerqueira Gomes, 'The Innovative Innovation Partnerships Under the 2014 Public Procurement Directive' (n 51) 214.
210. This view is supported by Gomes (n 51) 216.

ant which should allow for much shorter procedures. Taking into consideration the long history and tradition of these procedures, these changes appear to constitute reasonable modifications in accord with their intended function and do not purport to radically alter their purpose. However, an important qualification concerns the short timescales under which the restricted procedure can now be used in circumstances of urgency.

Competitive dialogue could have been revised in Directive 2014/24/EU to provide a procedure more in tune with the realities of its use in practice. Other than getting rid of the hardly problematic "particularly complex" test, the Directive has not made radical changes. In fact, in the authors' view, the few changes introduced actually render the procedure less interesting and relevant than before while leaving many operational uncertainties present.

Of greater interest are the two new procedures included in the Directive: the competitive procedure with negotiation and innovation partnership. The competitive procedure with negotiation shares the exact same grounds as the competitive dialogue and most of its internal structure. In fact, other than referring to "negotiations", a cursory reading of Article 29 could leave the distinct impression that one was reading an article prescribing the competitive dialogue procedure! A central contention of the Chapter has been to question the rationale for instituting two similar procedures? This issue is exacerbated when considering the fact that both can also be used to procure innovation, a province of the innovation partnership which does not appear to be exclusive. Again, similar to competitive dialogue, the competitive procedure with negotiation continues to throw up a number of operational uncertainties.

Finally, it is apposite that the innovation partnership should be described as a "novelty". A "novelty' can connote both the positive quality of something being new and original as well as the negative sense of something that is intended to amuse as a result of its unusual design but which soon wears off. The procedure marks a shift from an historical preoccupation of the Directives to separate R&D and resultant purchases which, in turn, necessitate two distinct award procedures. This has been a cause of consternation for many contracting authorities and suppliers keen to ensure that, where practicable, those involved in development can ultimately follow through to deliver the resulting solution without the additional cost and risk involved in straddling two procedural realms. The innovation partnership provides a means of follow through from R&D to subsequent purchases in a single procedure. However, only time will tell whether it represents "value added" for contracting authorities and suppliers over and above the existent competitive dialogue and additional competitive procedure with negotiation. Whilst the objective to stimulate and facilitate innovation is a noble one, this Chapter has highlighted considerable legal and practical uncertainty with regard to the institutional set up of innovation partnerships, not least with regard to target setting and related performance, management in terms of proportionality of cost and duration, IPRs and termination. These discrete issues are also magnified by broader questions regarding the potential for innovation partnerships to act either as closed shops which prevent, restrict or distort competition or give rise to issues of State aid.

Bibliography

A R Apostol, 'Pre-commercial procurement in support of innovation: regulatory effectiveness?' (2012) 6 PPLR, 213.

S Arrowsmith, The Law of Public and Utilities Procurement (2nd edition, Sweet & Maxwell, London 2005).

S Arrowsmith and S Treumer, 'Competitive Dialogue in EU Law: A Critical Review' in S Arrowsmith and S Treumer (eds) Competitive Dialogue in EU Procurement (CUP 2012).

A Brown, 'The impact of the new procurement directive in large public infrastructure projects: competitive dialogue or better the devil you know' (2004) 4 PPLR, 173.

P Cerqueira Gomes, 'The Innovative Innovation Partnerships Under the 2014 Public Procurement Directive' (2014) 23 PPLR, 209.

S Charveron, 'Competitive dialogue threatens PFI' (2007) 18 Construction Law, 29.

L Chever and J Moore, 'Negotiated procedures overrated? Evidence from France questions the Commission's approach in the latest procurement reforms' (2012) 4 EPPPL, 228.

R Craven, 'Competitive Dialogue in the UK' in S Arrowsmith and S Treumer (eds) Competitive Dialogue in EU Procurement (CUP 2012).

J Davey, 'Procedures involving negotiation in the new Public Procurement Directive: key reforms to the grounds for use and the procedural rules' (2014) 3 PPLR, 103.

P. Delelis, Le Dialogue Compétitif (2007) 3 Revue du Tresor, 280.

S De Mars and F Olivier, 'Competitive dialogue in France' in in S Arrowsmith and S Treumer (eds) Competitive Dialogue in EU Procurement (CUP 2012).

S De Mars and R Craven, 'An Analysis of Competitive Dialogue in the EU' in S Arrowsmith and S Treumer (eds) Competitive Dialogue in EU Procurement (CUP 2012).

M Farley, 'Directive 2004/18/EC and the competitive dialogue: A case study on the application of the competitive dialogue procedure to the NHS LIFT' (007) 2 EPPL, 62.

G Fletcher, 'Minimum time limits under the new Public Procurement Directive' (2014) 3 PPLR, 94.

A Gorczynka, 'Competitive Dialogue in Poland' in S Arrowsmith and S Treumer (eds) Competitive Dialogue in EU Procurement (CUP 2012).

S E Hjelmborg et al., Public Procurement Law: the EU Directive on Public Contracts (Djof, Copenhagen, 2006).

T Inden and K N Olesen, 'Legal Aspects of Public Private Innovation' (2012) 7(4) EPPPL 258.

M K Larsen, 'Competitive Dialogue' in Nielsen and Treumer (eds), The new EU public procurement directives (Djøf 2005).

A Sanchez-Graells, 'Public procurement and state aid: reopening the debate?' (2012) 6 PPLR, 205-12.

P Telles, 'Competitive Dialogue in Portugal' (2010) 1 PPLR, 1.

P Telles, 'Competitive Dialogue in Portugal' in S Arrowsmith and S Treumer (eds) Competitive Dialogue in EU Procurement (CUP 2012).

P Telles, 'Competitive Dialogue in Spain, in S Arrowsmith and S Treumer (eds) Competitive Dialogue in EU Procurement (CUP 2012).

P Telles, 'Competitive Dialogue and Innovation: The Case of the Spanish Health Sector', in G Piga and S Treumer (eds) The applied law and economics of public procurement (Routledge 2013).

S Treumer, 'Competitive Dialogue' (2004) 13 PPLR, 178.

S Treumer, 'The field of application of the competitive dialogue' (2006) 6 PPLR, 313.

Framework agreements, dynamic purchasing systems and public e-procurement

François Lichère and Sara Richetto[1]

1. Introduction

Framework agreements, dynamic purchasing systems and part of the e-procurement provisions (electronic auctions and electronic catalogues) take place in the 2014/24 directive in a specific chapter called "Techniques and instruments for electronic and aggregated procurement" (chapter II). Such a specific chapter did not exist in the 2004/18 directive. It did not mean however that the provisions regarding these techniques and instruments were absent: they were simply included either in chapter V relating to the "procedures" for framework agreements and dynamic purchasing systems or in chapter VII regarding the "conduct of the procedure" for the whole electronic techniques and processes. To set a specific chapter for all three of them and call it techniques and instruments makes sense despite the absence of definition of what is a technique and what is an instrument: as already noticed,[2] they are not akin to "procedures" since they may be used in different procedures such as open and restricted procedures, competitive dialogue or negociated procedures. In other terms, they can be found – or not – along with the different

1. Respectively Professor at Aix-Marseille University and practising lawyer. Francois Lichere deal with by the introduction, the conclusion and section 9 and 10 while Sara Richetto deal with by the introduction, the conclusion and section 2 to 8 of this chapter.
2. See F. Lichere, New award procedures, in M. Trybus, R. Caranta, G. Edelstam (eds.), EU public contract law, Broylant 2014, p. 81.

award processes that may be put in place by contracting authorities. To classify them in the "conduct of the procedure" chapter would not make much sense either: framework agreements, dynamic purchasing systems, electronic auctions, electronic catalogues do not necessarily take place in the conduct of the procedure since they are options opened to contracting authorities. What is less obvious is to have added in the title of chapter 2 "for electronic and aggregated procurement" as it leads to believe that framework agreements are only made for aggregated procurement and/or electronic procurement. Although it is true that aggregated procurements pave the way to a wide use of framework agreement,[3] they are not reserved at all to such a case since many contracting authorities used them alone. And although an electronic technique – such as electronic auction – may be used in conjunction with a framework agreement, it is not necessarily so. In other words, we would not have been shocked if the European legislator had constricted the title of the chapter to "techniques and instruments of procurement".

Chapter II also aims at regulating the now so called "aggregated procurement" which encompasses "Centralised purchasing activities and central purchasing bodies", "Occasional procurement" and "Procurement involving contracting authorities from different Member States", all of them being dealt with by Gabriella Racca in the next chapter of this book.

However, other aspects of e-procurement, those which refer to the use of electronic means in the award process, are to be found not in chapter II but in chapter III of directive 2014/24 which deals with the "conduct of the procedure" and it is rightly so since electronic means are made compulsory as it will be seen below.

As is well known, the use of electronic communications plays a key role in the process of modernization of public procurement.

Since the '90s, many companies have been using electronic data interchange (EDI) to purchase order, invoice goods and to send other information.[4] In this period, the expression 'e-Procurement' was first used in e-commerce studies as one business information system employing information technologies (e.g. Internet, Electronic data interchange, electronic mail and electronic funds transfer).[5]

3. See G. Racca, next chapter of this book.
4. B. Lin – C.B. Jones 'Management implications of electronic data interchange' in Int. Business School Computing Quarterly 1993.
5. W. Witting 'A strategy for improving public procurement' in 9th International Anti Corruption Conference, Papers IACC, 1999.

E-Procurement means not only technology but also innovation of internal proceedings and of network relationships between suppliers and other organizations. Its main goals are represented by: cost-effectiveness, efficiency, transparency, dematerialization, competition governance and automation of purchase proceedings.[6]

In early 2000s, the opinion spread that e-Procurement can also help public authorities to purchase goods and services quickly and efficiently. It could help suppliers to identify opportunities and participate in tenders at lower cost. Thus, e-Procurement could increase the efficiency and effectiveness of public procurement as a whole.[7] And directive 2004/18 included provisions to this regard.

However, the introduction of electronic means in the purchase process raises a number of questions: the first one is if and how the use of electronic means as standard communication system could change public procurements. The second question is whether and to what extent the new regime of electronic means may really be transposed in the Member States' legislations along the lines laid down by the new EU Directive.

Framework agreements and dynamic purchasing systems were also first regulated in the directive 2004/18 in order to secure what already existed in practice and, to some extent, in the legal text as well.[8] Therefore this chapter deals with topics that are not in themselves innovations made by the new directive but rather gain some precisions and clarifications.

The aim of this chapter is to assess what will be the consequences of the introduction of new provisions on framework agreements, dynamic purchasing systems and electronic means in public procurements and what are the differences between the previous directives regime and the new provisions, while at the same time stating what are the benefits accrued to those Member States which have already implemented them. Since the new provisions on e-Procurement appear to carry greater weight than the provisions on framework agreements and dynamic purchasing systems, they will be treated first.

6. S.R. Croom 'The impact of web-based procurement on the management of operating resources supply' in Journal of Supply Chain Management 2000.
7. S. Arrowsmith 'Electronic reverse auctions under the EC public procurements rules: current possibilities and future prospects' in Public Procurement Law Review 2002, 302 ff.; see also M. Burgi – H. Goelnitz 'Die Modernisierung des Vergaberechts als Daueraufgabe' in Die öffentliche Verwaltung 2009, 833.
8. For instance, France has long been regulating framework agreements in the form of framework agreements with all terms defined in it.

2. Requirements for conducting public procurement using electronic means under the Directive 2014/24/EU

In order to analyse the new provisions on electronic means, it seems important to go back to the various actions undertaken by EU authorities to implement the use of electronic means in public procurements.

2.1. E-Procurement was first regulated in Europe by Directives 2004/18/EC and 2004/17/EC. They aimed at adapting public procurement rules to the modern administrative needs of a changing economic context. The 2004 directives provided the rules and principles governing e-Procurement. This includes first the general rules and principles relevant to all communications in the procurement process; second, the new purchasing technique based on the use of electronic means (e.g. dynamic purchasing systems and electronic auctions).[9]

Nowadays the rules laid down in 2004 are not enough. Technology is constantly evolving and those directives did not regulate in detail the use of all such methods. The old public procurement directives chose a pragmatic approach focusing on the obligation not to restrict the operators' access to the tendering procedures in order to help contracting authorities determine if the chosen means of communication were generally available and satisfied the requirement of the directives.

2.2. Trying to keep the pace of technological change, since 2004 the EU Commission has implemented a number of actions to boost the take-up of e-Procurement in Europe.

In 2005, it presented the rules and principles governing e-Procurement under Directives 2004/18/EC and 2004/17/EC,[10] underlining the tools for communication by electronic means which should be non-discriminatory, generally available and interoperable with the information and communication technology products (ICT) in general use.

Interoperability refers to the capability of ICT system to exchange information or services satisfactorily; the requirement of interoperable electronic

9. See generally F. Lichère 'New Award Procedures' in M. Trybus, R. Caranta, G. Edelstam (eds) EU Public Contract Law. Public Procurement and Beyond (Bruxelles, Bruylant, 2014) 100 ff.
10. Commission Staff Working Document: Requirement for conducting public procurement using electronic means under the new public procurement Directives 2004/18/EC and 2004/17/EC, SEC(2005) 959.

tools means that the chosen tools must be able to function and to interact with commonly used equipment and applications.

According to the European Commission, contracting authorities should take appropriate steps to document the progress of award procedures conducted by electronic means. This requirement should be referred to at every stage of the procurement process conducted electronically, maintaining at the same time the original version of all documents and a true and faithful record of all exchanges with economic operators.

2.3. In March 2010 the European Commission launched the Europe 2020 Strategy to prepare the EU economy for the challenges of the next decade.[11] The Digital Agenda for the Europe is one of the seven flagship initiatives of the Europe 2020 Strategy and it was set out to define the key enabling role of the use of ICT.

In the European Commission Communication for a Digital Agenda for Europe,[12] the Commission identified the seven most significant obstacles for the ICT implementation, making clear the need for a comprehensive and united policy response at European level.

The obstacles are:

a) a fragmented digital market which prevents EU citizens from enjoying the benefits of a digital single market;
b) lack of interoperability: weaknesses in standard-setting, public procurement and coordination between public authorities prevent digital services and devices used by Europeans from working together as well as they should;
c) rising cybercrime and risks of low trust in networks: Europeans need feeling that they can fully rely upon their network;
d) lack of investments in networks: more needs to be done to facilitate investments in the new very fast open and competitive internet networks;
e) insufficient research and innovation efforts: Europe continues to under-invest, fragment its efforts, under-use the creativity of SMEs and fail to convert the intellectual advantage of research into the competitive advantage of market-based innovations. The suboptimal character of current research and innovation efforts has to be addressed by leveraging more private investment, better coordinating and pooling of resources, 'lighter and faster' access of digital SMEs to Union research funds, joint research

11. Commission Communication: EUROPE 2020 – A strategy for smart, sustainable and inclusive growth – COM(2010) 2020.
12. Commission Communication: A Digital Agenda for Europe- COM(2010) 245 final.

infrastructures and innovation clusters and the development of standards and open platforms for new applications and services;

f) lack of digital literacy and skills: In Europe there is a growing professional ICT skills shortage and a digital literacy deficit. This requires a coordinated reaction, with Member States and other stakeholders at its centre;

g) missed opportunities in addressing societal challenges: some of Europe's societal challenges (such as: climate change and other pressures on our environment, an ageing population and rising health costs, developing more efficient public services and integrating people with disabilities, digitising Europe's cultural heritage and making it available to this and future generations, etc.) could be solved using ICT.

The key actions to tackle these problems consist in:

- opening up access to content. Public authorities should play their part in promoting markets for online content, for example, making public sector information available on transparent, effective, nondiscriminatory terms;
- making online and cross-border transactions straightforward, trough a revision of the eSignature Directive with a view to provide a legal framework for cross-border recognition and interoperability of secure eAuthentication systems;
- building digital confidence;
- reinforcing the interoperability between ICT products and services to build a digital society;
- investing in research and development.

2.4. After a few months, the EU Commission proposed a second eGovernment Action Plan[13] which aimed to realize the ambitious vision according to which, starting from 2015, all European public administrations will use eGovernment to increase their efficiency and effectiveness and to constantly improve public services in a way that caters for users' different needs and maximises public value.

The EU Commission stated that: "Businesses should be able to sell and provide services and products all across the EU, through easy electronic public procurement and the effective implementation of the Services offering

13. Commission Communication: The European eGovernment Action Plan 2011-2015-Harnessing ICT to promote smart, sustainable & innovative Government-COM(2010) 743 final.

single points of contact to businesses for their interactions with government. Two major initiatives have been set up in both areas over the last two years:

- SPOCS 'Simple Procedures Online for Cross-border Services' aims at removing the administrative barriers that European business face when wanting to offer their services abroad, by supporting the implementation of next generation points of single contact and the associated eProcedures.
- PEPPOL 'Pan-European Public eProcurement On-Line' aims to pilot an EU-wide interoperable public eProcurement solution allowing entrepreneurs to perform the full public procurement cycle online, from ordering to invoicing and access to catalogues. This will reduce administrative burden; increased transparency and potentially large costs savings are the expected gains from such implementation. Based on the results of the above initiatives, the envisaged actions should be: a cross-border and interoperable eProcurement infrastructure based on the results of the PEPPOL large scale pilot; and the development of a 'second generation' of points of single contact along with an extension of the Services Directive to other areas of business. This would mean that by 2015 businesses in Europe will be able to sell goods and provide services to public administrations in other countries just as easily as they currently do to those in their home country".

The actions on this priority will focus on using ICT and enabling organisational changes to deliver better, less intrusive, more sustainable and faster public services, by reducing the administrative burden, improving organisational processes and promoting a sustainable lowcarbon economy.

Notably, SPOCS is a large scale pilot project launched by the EU Commission in May 2009 that aims to overcome the obstacles in the existing system, acting as intermediaries between service providers and the national public administrations. The main goals are essentially information dissemination and case management/processing.[14]

PEPPOL is instead a pilot project partly funded jointly by EU Commission and the PEPPOL Consortium members.[15] It was inititated in 2008 to simplify electronic procurement across the borders by developing technology standards that could be implemented across all governments within Europe.

14. http://www.eu-spocs.eu
15. http://www.peppol.eu/

PEPPOL does not provide an e-Procurement platform but rather the interoperability bridges needed to connect the platforms already existing in Member States. It provides a set of technical specifications that can be implemented in existing eProcurement solutions and services to make them interoperabile across Europe.[16]

2.5. In 2011 the EU Commission set up an expert group bringing together individuals who have direct experience in the development of the eProcurement capacity or particular expertise in analysing, advising or representing public purchasers or suppliers who participate in on-line public procurement.[17]

Various areas of e-Procurement were under the scope of the expert group's work, such as eSubmission, authentication/identification, eSignatures, Dynamic Purchasing Systems (DPS), eTendering, eCatalogues, Document formats, encryption/decryption, integrity of data, confidentiality issues before the opening of the tenders.

The Group issued a report containing clear recommendations to Commission services, on steps to be taken to support the eProcurement infrastructure throughout the single market.[18]

The eTeg report's starting point is the definition of an ideal eTendering operation, to which eProcurement platform managers and services providers should consider converging in the medium term so as to set out eProcurement procedures that are streamlined, user-friendly, interoperable and widely accessible across borders.

In particular, the report provides high level strategic advice, covering:

- the need for EU eProcurement governance and the Member States national strategies towards EU goals;
- the need for all procurement players to refer to standards for interoperability, legal compliance, security, transparency and accessibility;
- support for a new generation of eProcurement platforms;

16. The OpenPEPPOL Association was set up on 1st September 2013 after successful completing of the PEPPOL project which saw PEPPOL specifications being implemented in several Europe countries solving interoperability issues for electronic procurement.
17. EU Commission, Terms of reference: Expert group on pre-awarding eProcurement- 29 July 2011.
18. The eTendering Expert Group Report, in Golden book of e-Procurement Good Practice, 11 March 2013.

- the need for wider dissemination of information on procurement opportunities;
- the need to reduce the burden on economic operators when accessing platforms; the need for a platform to enforce an adequate security policy;
- freedom for contracting authorities to set up their own digital signature policies, on the provision that no access barriers are raised for foreign tenderers;
- operational and technical advice on how to design, choose and use eProcurement system.

2.6. In 2012 the EU Commission also defined a strategy for e-Procurement.[19]

In particular, the Commission presented the strategic importance of electronic procurement and set out the main actions through which it intended to support the transition towards full e-Procurement in the EU.

According to the EU Commission, eProcurement can significantly simplify the way procurement is conducted, reduce waste and deliver better procurement outcomes (lower price, better quality) by stimulating greater competition across the Internal Market. It can also contribute to address two of the main challenges the European economy is facing today: the need to maximise the efficiency of public expenditure in a context of fiscal constraints and the need to find new sources of economic growth.

From the economic point of view, eProcurement has the potential to bring significant efficiency gains in this large market: eProcurement can help improving the transparency and the access to procurement opportunities, especially for SMEs, thus stimulating cross-border competition, innovation and growth in the Internal Market. It can achieve significant cost reductions also by reducing the duration of procurement procedures.

The Commission observed that implementation of eProcurement solutions inevitably incurs some up-front costs, but experience shows that these costs can be recouped in a relatively short period of time.

The strategy set-out in this Communication builds on the eProcurement provisions contained in the legislative proposals adopted by the European Commission in December 2011.

The proposal on the public procurement contracts foresees a gradual transition towards full electronic means of communication. In addition, the EU Commission promoted e-CERTIS, which is a support instrument for the various parties involved in public procurements. It is an information system

19. Commission Communication: A strategy for e-Procurement, COM (2012) 179 final.

which helps the user to identify the documentation that is required in the EU Member States in the public contract formation and execution phases. It will list the certificates and statements that may be required for qualification of a bidder in procurement and will set the equivalence criteria across Member States.

Last but not least, the proposals support sharing of information and best practices and greater cooperation through the use of the Internal Market Information System (IMI), a secure online application that allows the competent authorities in the EEA to communicate quickly and easily with their counterparts abroad.

The phased approach to eProcurement implementation is designed to give all stakeholders time to meet the operational challenges, whilst ensuring that the pace of change accelerates and that all Member States follow the same overall timetable. The objective is to avoid the coexistence of parallel electronic and paper-based procedures that significantly increase costs for both contracting authorities and economic operators.

The Commission urges Member States to adopt the necessary preparatory work as soon as possible to ensure timely compliance with these provisions.

2.7. The Commission's objectives for e-procurement have recently been reinforced in its "Communication on End-to-End E-Procurement". This communication develops the theme of significant savings and benefits for growth arising from e-procurement and introduces the concept of "end-to-end" e-procurement.This concept refers to the entire process from electronic publication of tender notices to electronic payment of selected contractors.

This communication focuses on four issues. The first is modernising public administration – e-procurement has more significant benefits in addition to cost savings and increased efficiency.

The second focus issue in the most recent communication is SME participation in public procurement.

The third issue is E-invoicing. E-invoicing in public procurement is already mandatory in a few Member States. Other Member States are taking positive steps towards the use of e-invoicing in public procurement. This has contributed to the fragmentation of the single market and has increate the cost and complexity of e-invoicing in cross-border public procurement.

Finally, the fourth issue examined is the state of play in e-procurement. E-notification and e-access to procurement documents are widespread across the EU, though in some member states they are not used for all procedures and purchases.[20]

3. Definition of electronic means and rule of communication in the Directive 2014/24/UE

3.1. Article 2 of Directive 2014/24/UE defines 'electronic means' as "electronic equipment for the processing (including digital compression) and storage of data which is transmitted, conveyed and received by wire, by radio, by optical means or by other electromagnetic means".

Article 22 provides that all communication and information exchange under this Directive are performed using electronic means of communication.

Under the 2004 Directives the rules on the use of e-communications established that e-communications were "on par" with traditional forms of communication, whereas under the new directive, e-communication will become mandatory form of communication for many aspects of the procurement process.

Under 2014/24 Directive, different means of communication are admitted as exceptions only. This is so in the following situations: (i) due to the specialised nature of the procurement, that requires specific tools, devices or file formats that are not generally available; (ii) the applications supporting file formats that are suitable for the description of the tenders use file formats that cannot be handled by any other open or generally available applications; (iii) the use of electronic means of communication would require specialised office equipment that is not generally available to contracting authorities; (iv) the procurement documents require the submission of physical or scale models which cannot be transmitted using electronic means.

In those cases, the Directive asks contracting authorities to state the reasons for their requirements.

The standard method to communicate is "written", which must be understood as any expression consisting of words or figures which can be read, reproduced and subsequently communicated, including information transmitted and stored by electronic means.

20. Communication from the Commission to the European Parliament, the Council, The European Economic and Social committee and the committee of the Regions, "end-to-end e-procurement to modernise public administration", COM (2013) 453 final, 26/6/2013.

Oral communication may be used in respect of communications other than those concerning the essential elements of a procurement procedure, provided that the content of the oral communication is documented to a sufficient degree. The essential elements are represented by procurement documents, requests for participation, confirmations of interest and tenders. In these cases, oral communication shall be documented by appropriate means, such as written or audio records or summaries of the main elements of the communication.

The aim of the lawmaker is to ensure an adequate level of transparency that allows for a verification of whether the principle of equal *treatment* has been adhered to.

Article 22(5) is a new provision which provides that notwithstanding the general rule that contracting authorities must specify e-communication tools which are "products in general use", contracting authorities may, where necessary, require the use of tools and devices which are not generally available, provided that the contracting authority offers an alternative means of access. The suitable alternative means of access are specified as being where the contracting authority:

(i) offers unrestricted and full direct access free of charge by electronic means to these tools and devices from the date of the contract notice or from the date when the invitation to confirm interest is sent;
(ii) ensures that tenderers having no access to the tools and devices concerned, or no possibility of obtaining them within the relevant time limits, may access the procurement procedure through the use of "provisional tokens" made available free of charge online;
(iii) or supports an alternative channel for electronic submission of tenders.

There was no equivalent to these detailed rules on the use of e-communication tools in the 2004 Directives, which simply stated that in order for electronic tools to be used they had to be "nondiscriminatory, generally available and interoperable with ICT products in general use". However, as the use of ICT tools will now be mandatory under the new directives there is a need for alternative arrangements to cater for the circumstances where these general requirements are not available or are inapplicable to a particular procurement process.[21]

21. R. Bickerstaff, "E-Procurement under the new EU procurement Directives" (2014) 3 Public Procurement Law Review 134-147.

Providing that electronic means have to be used for the receipt of tenders and the request for participation, Annex IV of the Directive 2014/24/EU lays down the requirements relating the tools and devices for this process.

In particular, they must guarantee that:

a) the exact time and date of the receipt of tenders, requests to participate and the submission of plans and projects can be determined precisely;
b) no-one can have access to data transmitted under these requirements before the relevant time limits;
c) only authorised persons may set or change the dates for opening data received;
d) during the different stages of the procurement procedure or of the design contest, the access to all data submitted, or to part thereof, must be possible only for authorised persons;
e) only authorised persons must give access to data transmitted and only after the prescribed date;
f) data received and opened in accordance with these requirements must remain accessible only to persons authorised to acquaint themselves therewith;
g) where the access prohibitions or conditions referred to under points (b), (c), (d), (e) and (f) are infringed or there is an attempt to do so, it may be reasonably ensured that the infringements or attempts are clearly detectable.

On the one hand, this provision wants to ensure access to informations; on the other hand it intends to safeguard the integrity of data and the confidentiality of tenders.

In addition to the requirements set out in Annex IV, Article 22 provides for some rules which shall be applied to tools and devices for the electronic transmission and receipt of tenders and for the electronic receipt of requests to participate: (a) information on specifications for the electronic submission of tenders and requests to participate, including encryption and time-stamping, shall be available to interested parties; (b) Member States, or contracting authorities acting within an overall framework established by the Member State concerned, shall specify the level of security required for the electronic means of communication in the various stages of the specific procurement procedure.

Annex IV of the new directives is a welcome simplification of the corresponding Annex 12 contained in the 2004 Directives. In fact the rules have been simplified to such an extent that it is now no longer clear why there is any need for a separate annex. In particular, the old rule which could be interpreted as requiring all tenders and requests to participate to be signed by an electronic signature conforming to the Electronic Signatures Directive has been removed, as has the requirement that access to tenders and requests to partecipate required "simultaneous action" by authorised persons.[22]

3.2. Recital 52 of Directive 2014/24/UE makes it clear that: "Electronic means of information and communication can greatly simplify the publication of contracts and increase the efficiency and transparency of procurement processes. They should become the standard means of communication and information exchange in procurement procedures, as they greatly enhance the possibilities of economic operators to participate in procurement procedures across the internal market".

The great difference with Directive 2004/18/EC is the mandatory nature of communications in electronic form.

The above mentioned Recital 52 states that the transmission of notices in electronic form, the electronic availability of the procurement documents and the fully electronic communication, meaning communication by electronic means at all stages of the procedure, including the transmission of requests for participation and, in particular, the transmission of the tenders (electronic submission) should be made mandatory and the use of other means of communication should be limited to exceptional cases.

This is different from the past, where the electronic means were considered au par with traditional means of communication and information exchange and contracting authorities were allowed to make use of electronic means provided they complied with the principles of equal treatment, non discrimination and transparency.

The new Public Sector Directive provides that the use of electronic means should be mandatory and that Member States and contracting authorities should remain free to go further if they so wish. The requirements imposed by EU Directives represent a minimum which Member States may well overshoot. It thus allows for 'gold plating'.[23]

22. R. Bickerstaff, 'The New Directives' Rules on E-communication Mechanisms in Public and Utilities Procurement" (2004) 13 Public Procurement Law Review 277.
23. M.E. Comba – S. Richetto 'Minor contracts: Outside the Directives and Outside the Treaties? Comparative analysis on public procurement below the thresholds in Europe, in D. Dragos – R. Caranta (eds) Outside the EU procurement Directives- inside the Treaty? (Copenhagen, DJØF, 2012) 362 ff.

The central question is whether Member States may provide for standards which are higher than those laid down in a EU directive only when the directive so expressly provides; or if they may do so even when they are not expressly empowered to do so.

From reading Recital 52, it would seem that when the EU lawmakers want to give Member States the power to go beyond what is required by the Directive, they make express reference to it. By implication, when nothing is said, Member States have to toe the line chosen in the EU provisions.

The new Public Sector Directive on public procurement provides that the electronic means used must not entail discriminations and must be generally available and interoperable with the ICT products in general use. However, the obligation to use electronic means at all stages of the public procurement procedure would neither be appropriate where the use of electronic means would require specialised tools or file formats that are not generally available nor where the communications concerned could only be handled using specialised office equipment.

For that purpose, it should be important to ensure interoperability between different technical formats or processes by standardisation, which means making the use of specific standards mandatory.

4. Saving time

In its 2012 Communication,[24] the Commission identified the most important eProcurement benefits in the simplification, quickness and efficiency of the procedure; this was repeated in Directive 2014/24/EU.[25]

First of all, the new directive gives contracting authorities the power to reduce the time limit of the procedures not only when there is an extreme urgency,[26] but every time they use electronic means.

24. EU Commission Communication: A strategy for eProcurement – COM(2012) 179 final, 20 April 2012.
25. According to Recital 52 of Directive 2014/24/UE "Electronic means of information and communication can greatly simplify the publication of contracts and increase the efficiency and transparency of procurement processes".
26. See Recital 46: "contracting authorities should be allowed to shorten certain deadlines applicable to open and restricted procedures and to competitive procedures with negotiation where the deadlines in question would be impracticable because of a state of urgency which should be duly substantiated by the contracting authorities. It should be clarified that this need not be an extreme urgency brought about by events unforeseeable for and not attributable to the contracting authority".

In particular, Directive 2014/18/EU provided the application of electronic means in the contest of electronic commerce and internal market. Moreover electronic means should be used for reducing the minimum periods where electronic means are used, subject, however, to the condition that they are compatible with the specific mode of transmission envisaged at Community level.

Article 36 established that in the case of restricted procedures and negotiated procedures with publication of a contract notice, where urgency renders impracticable the standard time limits laid down by the Directive, notices must be sent either by telefax or by electronic means.

According to Recital 80, in order to make procedures faster and more efficient, time limits for participation in procurement procedures should be kept as short as possible without creating barriers to access for economic operators from across the internal market and in particular SMEs.

The EU Parliament and the Council tackle the question of "time savings" under different points of view: a) the time limit for publication of notices; b) the time limit for receipt of tenders, and c) the importance of informations' update for the contracting authorities' decisions.

Concerning the time limit for publication of notices, Article 51 of Directive 2014/24/EU provides that prior information notices, contract notices and contract award notices shall be drawn up, transmitted by electronic means to the Publications Office of the EU and published by the same Publications Office or by the contracting authorities in the event of a prior information notice published on a buyer profile. In addition, contracting authorities may publish this information on the Internet on a 'buyer profile'.

The new directive imposes the transmission of notices by electronic means and the publication not later than five days after they are sent. This provision is novel because the previous provisions let contracting authorities choose to send the notices by electronic means or by other means, providing that only notices sent by electroning means should be published no later than five days after they were sent (rather than twelve days stated for other means).[27]

Moreover, according to Article 53, contracting authorities shall offer by electronic means unrestricted and full direct access free of charge to the procurement documents from the date of publication of a notice in compliance with Article 51 or the date on which an invitation to confirm interest was sent.

27. Directive 2004/18/EC, Article 36; Directive 2004/17/EC, Article 45.

The aim of this provision consists in ensuring transparency and equal treatment of all economic operators interested in the procedure.

Only in exceptional cases, where unrestricted and full direct access free of charge by electronic means to certain procurement documents cannot be offered for one of the reasons set out in the second subparagraph of Article 22 (oral communication) or in the second subparagraph of Article 21 (to protect the confidential nature of the information), contracting authorities may transmit procurement documents by other means.

Concerning the time limit for the receipt of tenders, the new Public Sector Directive provides that in order to ensure the transparency and traceability of the procurement process, all stages should be duly documented and all tenders throughout the procedure should be submitted in writing.

The transmission of tenders by electronic means (electronic submission) should be made mandatory even if it is clarified that mandatory use of electronic means of communications pursuant to this Directive should not, however, oblige contracting authorities to carry out electronic processing of tenders, nor should it mandate electronic evaluation or automatic processing.

Furthermore, according to Recital 80, when fixing the time limits for the receipt of tenders and requests to participate, contracting authorities should consider the complexity of the contract and the time required to draw up tenders, even if this entails setting time limits that are longer than the minimum provided for under this Directive.

The 'complexity of the contract' is the criterion to set an adequate time limit for the receipt of tenders which was already adopted by previous directives on public procurements.

The 2004 Directives set a 52 days minimum time limit for the receipt of tenders starting from the date on which the contract notice was sent, in the case of open procedures and a 40 days minimum time limit starting from the date on which the invitation was sent, in the case of restricted procedures.

Only when notices were drawn up and transmitted by electronic means, the time limits for the receipt of tenders in open procedures, and the time limit for the receipt of the requests to participate in restricted and negociated procedures and the competitive dialogue, could have been shortened by seven days.

The time limits for the receipt of tenders could be further reduced by five days where the contracting authority offered unrestricted and full direct access by electronic means to the contract documents and any supplementary documents from the date of publication of the notice.

The mandatory use of electronic means of information and communication and electronic transmission of communications provided under Directive

2014/24/UE further reduces the minimum time limits for the receipt of tenders. It shall be 35 days from the date on which the contract notice was sent to contracting authority for open procedures and, in restricted procedures, the minimum time limit for receipt of requests to participate shall be 30 days from the date on which the contract notice or, where a prior information notice is used as a means of calling for competition, the invitation to confirm interest was sent to contracting authority; in this case the minimum time limit for the receipt of tenders shall be 30 days from the date on which the invitation to tender was sent. The same deadline applies to competitive procedures with negociation and competitive dialogues. These deadlines may be reduced by five more days where the contracting authority accepts that tenders may be submitted by electronic means.

Moreover, in order to ensure an efficient public procurement system, the decisions of contracting authorities should be based on recent information, in particular as regards exclusion grounds, given that important changes can intervene quite rapidly.[28]

The Commission should promote measures that could facilitate easy recourse to up-to-date information electronically, such as strengthening tools offering access to virtual company dossiers, or means of facilitating interoperability between databases or other such flanking measures.

Therefore, the Commission has been empowered to adopt delegated acts to amend the technical details and characteristics set out in Annex IV to take account of technical developments and where technological developments render continued exceptions from the use of electronic means of communication inappropriate or, exceptionally, where new exceptions must be provided for because of technological developments.[29]

5. Safety and confidentiality of electronic means

5.1. Article 22(6) of the Directive lays down some rules which apply to tools and devices for the electronic transmission and receipt of tenders and for the electronic receipt of requests to participate. One of these rules provides that Member States, or contracting authorities acting within an overall framework established by the Member State concerned, shall specify the level of security required for the electronic means of communication in the various stages of

28. Recital 85 of 2014/24/UE Directive.
29. Directive 2012/24/UE, Article 22(7).

the specific procurement procedure; that level shall be proportionate to the risks attached.

According to Recital 57 of Directive 2014/24/UE, before specifying the level of security required for the electronic means of communications to be used at the various stages of the award procedure, the Member States and contracting authorities should evaluate the proportionality between, on the one hand, the requirements aimed at ensuring correct and reliable identification of the senders of the communication concerned as well as the integrity of its content, and, on the other hand, the risk of problems such as in situations where messages are sent by a sender different from the one indicated.

The central issue concerns the correct and reliable identification.

In particular, where Member States, or contracting authorities acting within an overall framework established by the Member State concerned, conclude that the level of risks of public procurement procedure is such that advanced electronic signatures as defined by Directive 99/93/EC of the European Parliament and of the Council are required,[30] contracting authorities shall accept advanced electronic signatures supported by a qualified certificate, taking into account whether those certificates are provided by a certificate services provider on a trusted list provided for in EU Commission Decision 2009/767/EC,[31] and created with or without a secure signature creation device subject to compliance with the following conditions:

(i) the contracting authorities shall establish the required advanced signature format on the basis of the formats established in Commission Decision 2011/130/EU[32] and shall put in place necessary measures to be able to process these formats technically;

30. Under Article 2(2) of Directive 99/93/EC "advanced electronic signature means an electronic signature which meets the following requirements:
(a) it is uniquely linked to the signatory;
(b) it is capable of identifying the signatory;
(c) it is created using means that the signatory can maintain under his sole control; and
(d) it is linked to the data to which it relates in such a manner that any subsequent change of the data is detectable".
31. Commission Decision 2009/767/EC of 16 October 2009.
32. Commission Decision 2011/130/EU of 25 February 2011 establishing minimum requirements for the cross-border processing of documents signed electronically by competent authorities under Directive 2006/123/EC of the European Parliament and of the Council on services in the internal market.

(ii) where a tender is signed with the support of a qualified certificate that is included on a trusted list, the contracting authorities shall not apply additional requirements that may hinder the use of those signatures by tenderers.

Decision 2009/767/EC sets out measures to facilite the use of procedures by electronic means through the point of single contact under Directive 2006/123/EC on services in the internal market which, inter alia, imposes an obligation on Member States to carry out risk assessments before requiring these electronic signatures from service providers and establishes rules for the acceptance by Member States of advanced electronic signatures based on qualified certificates, created with or without a secure signature creation device.

However, Decision 2009/767/EC does not deal with formats of electronic signatures in documents issued by competent authorities, that need to be submitted by service providers when completing the relevant procedures and formalities.

Consequently, in 2011 the EU Commission established the minimum requirements for the cross-border processing of document signed electronically by competent authorities under Directive 2006/123/EC on services in the internal market. The aim of the Decision 2011/130/EU is to allow greater automation and improve the cross-border interoperability of electronic procedures. In order to allow service providers to complete their procedures and formalities across borders by electronic means, it is necessary to ensure that at least a number of advanced electronic signature formats can be technically supported by Member States when they receive documents signed electronically by competent authorities from other Member States.[33]

The use of electronic means in public procurement contracts raises the contentious issue of the signature of electronic tenders.

In Italy, for example, the question is partially solved by the laws in force, which assimilate electronic advanced signature to autograph signature.[34]

33. Article 1 of Decision 2011/130/UE provides that: "Member States shall put in place the necessary technical means allowing them to process electronically signed documents that service providers submit in the context of completing procedures and formalities through the Points of Single Contact as foreseen by Article 8 of Directive 2006/123/EC, and which are signed by competent authorities of other Member States with an XML or a CMS or a PDF advanced electronic signature in the BES or EPES format, that complies with the technical specifications set out in the Annex".
34. See D. Lgs. 7 March 2005, n. 82, Article 20.

Directives 2004/18/EC and 2004/17/EC[35] provided that in electronic public procurements, contracting authorities should require that economic operators confirm and sign their tenders by electronic means.

A central question in the Italian case law is whether it is lawful for a contracting authority to exclude economic operators who didn't use advanced electronic signature to confirm their tenders.

According to Italian courts, in such cases, the exclusion is not only lawful but it is also due under the general principles laid down in the 2004 directives on public procurement. In particular, Italian courts consider the electronic signature necessary for the presentation of the tenderers and also for the contract award.[36]

Even if the EU measures on electronic means asked all Member States to encourage the use of standard and non-discriminatory instruments, the identification systems used in e-Procurement procedures often risk to lead to discrimination.

Therefore Article 22(6) of Directive 2014/24/EU leaves Member States the power to require advanced electronic signatures or to disregard the risks attached to the specific procurement procedure.

5.2. Directive 2014/24/EU underlines the role of the confidentiality of information and the possible need to protect the particularity sensitive nature of informations. In those exceptional cases, contracting authorities are allowed not to use electronic means of communication.[37]

Article 22 provides that contracting authorities are not obliged to require electronic means of communication in the submission process when the use of means of communication other than electronic means is necessary either because of a breach of security of the electronic means of communications or for the protection of the particularly sensitive nature of information requiring such a high level of protection that it cannot be properly ensured by using electronic tools and devices that are either generally available to economic operators or can be made available to them by alternative means of access.

So, the exception is allowed only in order to protect particularly sensitive informations; in all the other cases, contracting authorities shall have recourse to electronic means of communication.

35. Transposed in the Italian law system by D. Lgs. 12 April 2006 n. 163.
36. Cons. Stato, IV, 11 April 2007, n. 1653 and T.A.R. Puglia-Bari, I, 24 May 2012, n. 1019.
37. Recital 54 of Directive 2014/24/EU.

5.3. Referring to the protection of personal data, Article 86 of Directive 2014/24/EU provides that Member States shall ensure the confidentiality of the information which they exchange. The competent authorities of all Member States concerned shall exchange information in compliance with personal data protection rules provided for in Directives 95/46/EC[38] and 2002/58/EC.[39]

Directive 2002/58/EC concerning the processing of personal data and the protection of privacy in the electronic communications sector adapted the previous rules to developments in the markets and technologies of electronic communication services, in order to provide an equal level of protection of personal data and privacy for users of publicly available electronic communication services, regardless of the technologies used.

According to Recital 5, the successful cross-border development of these services is partly dependent on the confidence of users that their privacy won't be at risk.

To this end, the new Public Sector Directive provides that, when drawing up technical specifications, contracting authorities should take into account EU law requirements in the field of data protection law, in particular in relation to the design of the processing of personal data.[40]

6. New electronic techniques

As already said, articles 33 and ff. of Directive 2014/24/UE concern the techniques and instruments for electronic and aggregated procurement and in particular: framework agreements, dynamic purchasing systems, electronic auctions, electronic catalogues, centralised purchasing activities and central purchasing bodies.

Those instruments were already provided by Directive 2004/18/EC.[41]

In particular, in view of the rapid expansion of electronic purchasing systems, and to enable contracting authorities to take full advantage of the possi-

38. Directive 95/46/EC on the protection of individuals with regard to the processing of personal data and on the free movement of such data.
39. Directive 2002/58/EC on the processing of personal data and the protection of privacy in the electronic communications sector (Directive on privacy and electronic communications).
40. Recital 77 Directive 2014/24/EU.
41. See F. Lichère 'New Award Procedures' above fn., and C.H. Bovis EU Public Procurement Law 3rd (Cheltenham, Elgar, 2012) 112 ff.

bilities afforded by these systems, the 2004 Directives introduced some specific rules in order to ensure that electronic procurement operate in full accordance with the principles of equal treatment, non-discrimination, transparency and competition.

In order to take into account the different circumstances, Directive 2004/18/UE allowed Member States to choose whether contracting authorities could use dynamic purchasing systems and/or electronic auctions.

Since 2004 the use of the techniques of electronic auctions has increased but also new electronic purchasing techniques developed such as electronic catalogues.The 2014/24/EU directive clarifies certain aspects of electronic auctions and regulates for the first time electronic catalogues.

6.1. Electronic auctions

Electronic auctions are techniques of procurements where new prices, revised downwards, and/or new values concerning certain elements of tenders are presented.

Electronic auctions have become an important instrument of public procurement since 2004, and especially so since they seem to guarantee full transparency in the choice of tenderer. They may be chosen by contracting authorities as a method of conducting part of the award phase of an open, restricted or negociated procedure with a notice call for competition.[42] In the same circumstances, an electronic auction may be held on the reopening of competition among the parties to a framework agreement and on the opening of competition for contracts to be awarded under the dynamic purchasing system.

Referring to the use of electronic auctions, some German authors underlined that the tenders which may be evaluated automatically ("automatisch bewertet werden können") are peculiar because of the automatic evaluation, that is without an intervention and/or a decision by a contracting official ("ohne Eingreifen und/oder Beurteilung seitens des öffentlichen Auftragebers"), without the agency of contracting authority.[43] This method represents a sort of electronic negociation between contracting authorities and economic operators which can promote the effectiveness of public action.[44]

42. S. Arrowsmith The Law of Public and Utilities Procurement 2nd (London, Sweet & Maxwell, 2011) 1188 and ff.
43. H. Pünder 'Elektronische Auktion' in H. Pünder – Schellenberg (hers.) Vergaberecht (Baden Baden, Nomos, 2011) 353 ss.
44. A. Masucci 'Le aste elettroniche e la modernizzazione delle procedure di aggiudicazione' in Giorn. Dir. Amm. 2013, 317.

The new Public Sector Directive introduces some novel elements:

- it is not left to the Member States to allow contracting authorities to use electronic auction; any contracting authority is now allowed to do so.
- Electronic auction are defined in article 35 as a repetitive electronic process, which occurs after an initial full evaluation of the tenders, enabling them to be ranked using automatic evaluation methods.[45]
- Electronic auctions are typically not suitable for certain public contracts having as their subject matter intellectual performances, because only the elements suitable for automatic evaluation by electronic means, without any intervention or appreciation by the contracting authority, namely elements which are quantifiable so that they can be expressed in figures or percentages, may be subject to electronic auctions. This provision is not new but recital 67 provides that "It should, however, also be clarified that electronic auctions may be used in a procurement procedure for the purchase of a specific intellectual property right. It is also appropriate to recall that while contracting authorities remain free to reduce the number of candidates or tenderers as long as the auction has not yet started, no further reduction of the number of tenderers participating in the electronic auction should be allowed after the auction has started." The wording of the article has not been changed but the recital aims at proving that certain intellectual property purchases may be subject to electronic auctions since a strict interpretation of directive 2004/18 may have led to forbid electronic auctions for any intellectual property purchase.
- Directive 2014/24 establishes when a tender should be considered admissible and instead when it should be unacceptable. According to Article 35(5): "A tender shall be considered admissible where it has been submitted by a tenderer, who has not been excluded pursuant to Article 57 and who meets the selection criteria, and whose tender is in conformity with the technical specifications without being irregular or unacceptable or unsuitable.

  In particular, tenders which do not comply with the procurement documents, which were received late, where there is evidence of collusion or corruption, or which have been found by the contracting authority to be

45. This definition is slightly different from the definition of directive 2004/18 : "an electronic auction is a repetitive process involving an electronic device for the presentation of new prices, revised downwards, and/or new values concerning certain elements of tenders, which occurs after an initial full evaluation of the tenders, enabling them to be ranked using automatic evaluation methods."

abnormally low, shall be considered as being irregular. In particular tenders submitted by tenderers that do not have the required qualifications, and tenders whose price exceeds the contracting authority's budget as determined and documented prior to the launching of the procurement procedure shall be considered as unacceptable.

A tender shall be considered not to be suitable where it is irrelevant to the contract, being manifestly incapable, without substantial changes, of meeting the contracting authority's needs and requirements as specified in the procurement documents. A request for participation shall be considered not to be suitable where the economic operator concerned is to be or may be excluded pursuant to Article 57 or does not meet the selection criteria set out by the contracting authority pursuant to Article 58".

This provision seems to be a reminder of general rules on tenders established by 2004 Directives.

- All tenderers having submitted admissible tenders shall be invited simultaneously to participate in the electronic auction.
- 2014 Directive does not repeat the general rule stated by the previouse directives according which contracting authorities may not have improper recourse to electronic auctions in such a way as to prevent, restrict or distort competition or to change the object matter of the contract. However we can suppose that this general rule persists up to now. In fact, Recital 49 and 61 repeat the same rule referring respectively to innovative products or services or works and to framework agreements. So this rule can be considered a general principle, applicable to all the provisions of the 2014 directive.

Referring to the residual provisions, the new Public Sector Directive follows the 2004 Directives providing that, throughout each phase of an electronic auction, the contracting authorities shall instantaneously communicate to all tenderers at least sufficient information to enable them to ascertain their relative rankings at any moment.

After closing an electronic auction, contracting authorities shall award the contract on the basis of the results of the electronic auction.

6.2. Electronic catalogues

Electronic catalogues are a format for the presentation and organisation of informations in a manner that is common to all the participating bidders and which lead to electronic treatment.

Contracting authorities should be able to require electronic catalogues in all available procedures where the use of electronic means of communication is required. Electronic catalogues help to increase competition and streamline public purchasing, particularly in terms of savings in time and money.

According to Recital 12 of Directive 2004/18/EC, where competition was reopened under a framework agreement or where a dynamic purchasing system was being used, a tender could take the form of the tenderer's electronic catalogue if the latter uses the means of communication chosen by the contracting authority.

The new Public Sector Directive implements this information system laying down some rules to ensure that the use of the new techniques complies with this Directive and with the principles of equal treatment, non-discrimination and transparency.

According to Article 36, where the use of electronic means of communication is required, contracting authorities may require tenders to be presented in the format of an electronic catalogue or to include an electronic catalogue. Member States may render the use of electronic catalogues mandatory in connection with certain types of procurement.

Electronic catalogues shall be established by the candidates or tenderers with a view to participating in a given procurement procedure in accordance with the technical specifications and format established by the contracting authority. Furthermore, electronic catalogues shall comply with the requirements for electronic communication tools as well as with any additional requirements set by the contracting authority.

Electronic catalogues may be used:

- for the presentations of tenders, when contracting authorities state so in the contract notice or in the invitation;
- for the submission of tenders, in order to conclude a framework agreement with more than one economic operator;
- to award contracts based on a dynamic purchasing system.

7. eProcurement and thresholds

Article 4 of Directive 2014/24/EU lays down the different thresholds above which the directive itself does apply.

The first question is if and to what extent the regime laid down in the directive and more specifically the mandatory regime for electronic means may apply to below the threshold public procurements.

This depends on whether the use of electronic means is seen as corresponding to a general principle of EU law or not. As it is well known, the

Commission Interpretative Communication of 2006 stated that the application of the rules on public procurements should be applied to contracts below the threshold only in order to guarantee the application of EU Treaty principles of equal treatment and non-discrimination (which imply an obligation of transparency).[46]

According to Recital 52 of Directive 2014/24/EU "Electronic means of information and communication can greatly simplify the publication of contracts and increase the efficiency and transparency of procurement processes"; moreover, under Recital 53 "Contracting authorities should, except in certain specific situations, use electronic means of communication which are non-discriminatory, generally available and interoperable with the ICT products in general use and which do not restrict economic operators' access to the procurement procedure".

Therefore it seems wrong to conclude that the mandatory use of those instruments aims at ensuring the application of TfEU principles. Instead, we can say that when electronic means are used, the EU rules and principles should be complied with.

Despite this, under the previous regime on public procurement, IT solutions were seen as strategic to better enforce non-discrimination and transparency principles, particularly in List B services and below the threshold contracts.

According to recent research:

- the majority of Member States uses web sites or portals for the publication of below threshold contract notices;
- some Member States have already endorsed pre-qualification services to avoid the evaluation of the participation requirements;
- many Member States have identical rules for electronic procurement for above and below the threshold contracts.[47]

46. Commission Interpretative Communication on the Community law applicable to contract awards not or not fully subject to the provisions of the Public Procurement Directives, 2006/C 179/02; see generally D. Dragos – R. Caranta (eds.) Outside the EU Procurement Directives – Inside the Treaty?, Copenhagen, DJØF, 2012; C. Risvig Hansen, Contracts not covered or not fully covered by the Public Sector Directive (Copenhagen, DJØF Publishing, 2012).
47. G. Racca 'The role of IT solutions in the Award and Execution of Public Procurement below the Threshold and List B Services: overcoming E-Barriers' in D. Dragos – R. Caranta (eds.) Outside the EU Procurement Directives – Inside the Treaty?, above fn, 385 f.

It would in the end seem that Member States do not have to apply the rules on eProcurement laid down by Directive 2014/24/EU to below the threshold contracts. Each Member State may still decide whether to apply electronic means; if it so decides the general principles of equal treatment and non-discrimation will have to be complied with.

8. Statistical data

From a comparative approach in order to understand the importance of this phenomenon that seems to be increasing in the last few years, it is useful to provide some quantitative data on the development of electronic public procurement contracts.

In 2012, it was considered that eProcurement were used in only 5-10% of procurement procedures carried out across the EU.[48]

By comparison, a full online procurement market place has already been achieved in South Korea, which is said to have generated savings of US$ 4.5 billion (about 8% of total annual procurement expenditure) annually by 2007; in Brazil 80% of public procurement is carried out electronically. The EU is lagging behind both its own targets and internationally.

In the Communication of 2012, the EU Commission pointed out that contracting authorities and entities that have already made the transition to e-Procurement commonly report savings between 5 and 20%.

Given the size of the total procurement market in the EU, each 5% saved could return around €100 billion to the public purse.

E-Procurement also delivers significant environmental benefits by reducing paper consumption and transport, as well as the need for costly archiving space with its attendant energy consumption. The economic and environmental benefits of e-Procurement thus go hand-in-hand – contributing to the sustainable growth objective of the EU 2020 Strategy. Moreover, the Digital Agenda for Europe and the eGovernment Action Plan 2011 – 2015 highlights the importance of connecting e-Procurement capacities across the Internal Market.

The EU Commission butressed the economic case for e-Procurement observing that there are numerous examples of successful e-Procurement solutions already in operation across Europe.

48. EU Commission Communication: A strategy for eProcurement – COM (2012)179 final, 20 April 2012.

Following the introduction of e-Procurement, Portuguese hospitals were able to achieve price reductions of 18% on their procurement contracts. In aggregate, the switch-over to e-Procurement in Portugal is estimated to have generated savings of between 6% and 12% of total procurement expenditure. Most of the savings were due to lower prices resulting from higher competition, although administrative savings were also achieved.

In Wales – the Welsh e-Procurement programme – delivered benefits of £58 million (December 2011), three years after it was launched. The investment costs of setting up the programme were recouped in only one year. So far, £18 billion of contracts were advertised electronically.

UGAP (Union des groupements d'achats publics) – the French central purchasing body – estimates that the progressive switch to e-Procurement reduced the administrative burden for buyers by 10% (e.g. through faster analysis of bids and easier access to documents) and by another 10% for the legal services involved (as less legal control was required when e-Procurement is used).

A study of 400 local authorities in the Netherlands shows that switching to eprocurement generates process cost savings of over € 8.500 per tender. This is based on using electronic means from the publication of notices through to submission, but does not include automatic evaluation. Two of the key factors contributing to these cost savings are: time reduction – per procedure, and reduced printing and postage costs.

In Norway, the survey indicates that the use of e-Procurement: increased participation by foreign firms (22% of respondents) and by SMEs (30% of respondents), resulted in a larger number of bids per tender (74% of respondents), reduced purchase costs (70% of respondents) and reduced the time spent on each tender by more than 10% (73% of participants).[49]

In Italy, since 1 January 2013, public administrations should use electronic means for buying goods and services in public procurements below the threshold and, alternatively, they should use digital market set up by: i) the Economics and Finance Ministry; (ii) the Regional authorities; iii) the contracting authorities themselves.[50]

This provision seems to be in contrast with the general principle of "noncompulsary application" of electronic means to contracts below the threshold, above-mentioned in paragraph 7 of this paper.

49. These examples were obtained by the European Commission through direct contact with various public authorities and stakeholders; contrast the French situation as described by F. Lichère 'New Award Procedures' above fn, 102 f.

50. D.L. 7 May 2012, n. 52, Art. 7.

In that context, the digital market appears very fragmented in the EU and it has been implemented differently in each jurisdiction. It is important to overcome the barriers that continue to hamper the interoperability between Member States, to allow the transition towards full e-Procurement in the EU.

9. Framework agreements

As already observed, framework agreements were recognized as important tools in the 2004/18 directive and first regulated at the time. However, "regulated" may be a pitfall in those circumstances as the directive was in many ways very permissive by refusing to state too many conditions for their use. Contrary to what existed for example in France where framework agreements were allowed only "when, for economic, technical or financial reasons, the ordering rate or scope of the requirements to be met cannot be completely finalised in the contract", directive 2004/18 did not require specific situations in which a framework agreement would be allowed. The only constraint related to the duration of the contract limited to 4 years with some exceptions.

This somewhat flexible approach can be seen as an exception to the duty for contracting authorities to define precisely their needs as set out in Article 42(1) of the 2014/24 directive with regards to technical specification.[51] Indeed, a framework agreement means "an agreement between one or more contracting authorities and one or more economic operators, the purpose of which is to establish the terms governing contracts to be awarded during a given period, in particular with regard to price and, where appropriate, the quantity envisaged." In other words, the lack of precision regards the timing of the purchase. But as a framework agreement does not necesseraly set all the terms of the subsequent contracts, it may also lack precision towards the substance of the needs.

The 2014/24 directive aims at improving the system of framework agreements. The main idea is enshrined in Recital 60 of the directive which states that "The instrument of framework agreements has been widely used and is considered as an efficient procurement technique throughout Europe. It should therefore be maintained largely as it is. However, certain aspects need to be clarified, in particular that framework agreements should not be used by contracting authorities which are not identified in them. For that purpose, the

51. "The technical specification shall lay down the characteristics required of a works, service or supply."

contracting authorities that are parties to a specific framework agreement from the outset should be clearly indicated, either by name or by other means, such as a reference to a given category of contracting authorities within a clearly delimited geographical area, so that the contracting authorities concerned can be easily and unequivocally identified. Likewise, a framework agreement should not be open to entry of new economic operators once it has been concluded. This implies for instance that where a central purchasing body uses an overall register of the contracting authorities or categories thereof, such as the local authorities in a given geographical area, that are entitled to have recourse to framework agreements it concludes, that central purchasing body should do so in a way that makes it possible to verify not only the identity of the contracting authority concerned but also the date from which it acquires the right to have recourse to the framework agreement concluded by the central purchasing body as that date determines which specific framework agreements that contracting authority should be allowed to use."

Article 33(2) of the directive transposes this objective into concrete terms in a way which is significantly different from the recital.[52] Another precision with regard to the parties to the framework agreement deals with the possibility to open up the framework agreement to new economic operators. Contrary to a dynamic purchasing system, a framework agreement is, as a matter of principle, a closed system: once put in place, no other economic operator can enter the framework for its duration. However, Article 72 now introduces possible modifications of a public contract and also – explicitly – of a framework agreement and its point (d)(ii) admits that, in some circumstances such as insolvency or restructuring, a new firm may enter without any new competitition. This provision cannot be seen nonetheless as a true exception to the "closed" system since it is more akin to a substitution of an economic operator under strict conditions rather than to a real opening up of the framework agreement.

In our views, the main novelties regarding framework agreements are to be found elsewhere. They regard the award process of the subsequent contracts (i.e. the contracts awarded on the basis of the framework agreement) and the duration of the framework agreement.

Regarding the award process of the subsequent contracts, the directive maintains the distinction that has existed since 2004 between framework agreements concluded with one operator and framework agreements con-

52. "Those procedures may be applied only between those contracting authorities clearly identified for this purpose in the call for competition or the invitation to confirm interest and those economic operators party to the framework agreement as concluded."

cluded with several. Regarding the former, there is of course no duty to re-tender for the subsequent contract award. For the latter, i.e. framework contracts concluded with several economic operators, one must still distinguish between a framework agreement where not all the terms are laid down in it – that we can call incomplete – and a framework agreement where all the terms are laid down – let's call it complete. In the case of an incomplete framework agreement, the new directive reconducts the "mini competition" system put in place in 2004: the parties to the framework agreement are subject to a new competition in order to choose the best tender. In other words, competition for the subsequent contract must be put in place when not all the terms are laid down in the framework agreement and for the purpose directive 2014/24 sets the same conditions than the 2004/18 one.[53]

But new provisions regarding complete framework agreement concluded with several economic operators are introduced: in the 2004/18 directive, it was only mentioned that, in such a case, "Contracts based on framework agreements concluded with several economic operators may be awarded (...) by application of the terms laid down in the framework agreement without reopening competition". First of all, this hypothesis is made more precise since, from now on, it supposes that the framework agreement sets out "the objective conditions for determining which of the economic operators, party to the framework agreement, shall perform them", the latter conditions being

53. 33(5) : "The competitions referred to in points (b) and (c) of paragraph 4 shall be based on the same terms as applied for the award of the framework agreement and, where necessary, more precisely formulated terms, and, where appropriate, other terms referred to in the procurement documents for the framework agreement, in accordance with the following procedure:
(a)
for every contract to be awarded, contracting authorities shall consult in writing the economic operators capable of performing the contract;
(b)
contracting authorities shall fix a time limit which is sufficiently long to allow tenders for each specific contract to be submitted, taking into account factors such as the complexity of the subject-matter of the contract and the time needed to send in tenders;
(c)
tenders shall be submitted in writing, and their content shall not be opened until the stipulated time limit for reply has expired;
(d)
contracting authorities shall award each contract to the tenderer that has submitted the best tender on the basis of the award criteria set out in the procurement documents for the framework agreement."

indicated in the procurement documents for the framework agreement. The duty to set "objective conditions" reinforces the principle of transparency and, therefore, the principle of equal treatment. Unfortunately the directive is not very forthcoming on examples. The articles at stake are silent and Recital 61 gives an example which is not, in itself, very enlightening: "The objective conditions for determining which of the economic operators party to the framework agreement should perform a given task, such as supplies or services intended for use by natural persons, may, in the context of framework agreements setting out all the terms, include the needs or the choice of the natural persons concerned". One commentator gives as an example what she calls the "cascade model": the terms imply that the contracting authority must first consult economic operator number one, if that one cannot deliver the contracting authority will consult the second economic operator and so on.[54] We are not sure that such an example, which may occur in practice, is in line with the very purpose of a framework agreement: although it supposes a subsequent contract, a framework agreement is legally speaking a contract and therefore legally binding at least for the economic operators. To say that an economic operator "cannot deliver" the given task implies that it has the choice of not fulfilling its obligations which would compromise the very existence of this tool. A good example of objective criteria could be what we might call the "random process": the contractor is "chosen" by public drawing of lots. Another objective criterion could be the "swivelling process": the economic operators are numbered and each time the contracting authority needs the implementation of the framework agreement it will call number one then number two etc. The "alphabetical process", by which the order is determined by the name of the economic operator is also envisaged.[55]

But the main novelty regarding complete framework agreements with several economic operators lies in the possibility for the contracting authority to opt for a mini competition rather than a no competition system for certain parts of the subsequent contract award, including for certain lots (Article 33(3)(b)). This "additional flexibility", as Recital 61 puts it, appears to be a little bit blurred at first sight: if all the terms of the framework agreement are

54. Carina Risvig Hamer, 'Regular Purchases and Aggregated Procurement:The Changes in the New Public Procurement Directive Regarding Framework Agreements, Dynamic Purchasing Systems and Central Purchasing Bodies', P.P.L.R. 2014, n°4, p. 202.

55. See the French « Guide des bonnes pratiques en matière de marchés publics», § 7.2.1. http://www.legifrance.gouv.fr/affichTexte.do?cidTexte=JORFTEXT000025364925 (accessed June 17, 2014).

laid down in it, why can there be a new competition for the subsequent contract? Recital 61 gives the rationale of this option when requiring the contracting authority to set the objective criteria of choice between a no competition system and the mini competition system: "Such criteria could for instance relate to the quantity, value or characteristics of the works, supplies or services concerned, including the need for a higher degree of service or an increased security level, or to developments in price levels compared to a predetermined price index". In other words, the mini competition can take place when there are objective circumstances that justify to retender certain aspects of the framework agreement. The contracting authority therefore retains a significant discretion between imposing the complete framework agreement terms if it does not enter in a mini competition for the subsequent contract award or to modify certain terms of it if it does.

The second main novelty lies in the clarification of the duration of the framework agreement. Regarding the duration of the framework agreement itself, the 2024/14 directive maintains the duration of 4 years by principle, rejecting the proposal from the Parliament to extend it to 5 years,[56] and the possibility of a longer duration "in exceptional cases duly justified, in particular by the subject of the framework agreement".[57] The clarification comes out of Recital 62 in the following way: such cases "might for instance arise where economic operators need to dispose of equipment the amortisation period of which is longer than four years and which must be available at any time over the entire duration of the framework agreement". A French case law also ruled that 5 years was not excessive in the case of a contract whose subject matter was the maintenance and exploitation of heating, air conditioning and demisting at the musée du Louvre[58] whereas the maintenance of computers would not justify a longer duration.[59]

As far as the duration of the subsequent contract is concerned, the articles of the 2014/24 directive remain silent. But Recital 62 adds that "the duration of the individual contracts based on a framework agreement does not need to coincide with the duration of that framework agreement, but might, as appro-

56. See the report of the Parliament 11 January 2013 http://www.europarl.europa.eu/document/activities/cont/201301/20130115ATT59102/20130115ATT59102EN.pdf (accessed June 17, 2014).
57. artArticle .33(1) of the 2014/24 directive and art.Article 32(2) of the 2004/18 Directive.
58. TA Paris, 22 mars 2010, Société IDEX Énergies, req. no 1003599/3-5.
59. Ministerial answer to question from a senator, Q no 00114, JO Sénat 15 July 2012, Response 1 november 2012.

priate, be shorter or longer. In particular, it should be allowed to set the length of individual contracts based on a framework agreement taking account of factors such as the time needed for their performance, where maintenance of equipment with an expected useful life of more than four years is included or where extensive training of staff to perform the contract is needed". This is in line with the doctrine of the Commission[60] but its presence in the Recital gives a little more legal certainty to the practice. One issue nevertheless remains: the Recital only gives its view on the possibility for the subsequent contract to be longer than the framework agreement as long as it has been awarded within the time limit of the framework agreement but it does not expand on the duration of the contract itself. One could think that as a general rule, those contracts are subject to no specific requirement as the directive is silent on the duration of public contracts. But one should bear in mind that framework agreements are an exception to the duty of contracting authorities to set out precisely their needs and the counterpart of this flexibility lies in the limitation of the duration of the framework agreement. It is likely that the subsequent contract that would be performed partially or totally after the end of the framework agreement must be very limited in time so as to avoid too long a period without competition. Indeed, the Commission admits a possibility of entering into a subsequent contract one year before the expiration of the framework agreement which could extend to one year after the expiration.[61] It it unlikely that a longer extension would be permitted.

Another new flexibility concerns the withdrawal of the requirement in directive 2004/18 which stated that "where a framework agreement is concluded with several economic operators, the latter must be at least three in number, insofar as there is a sufficient number of economic operators to satisfy the selection criteria and/or of admissible tenders which meet the award criteria". From now on, a framework can be awarded to two economic operators.

More generally flexibility of framework agreements has increased thanks to the possibility of modifications as set out in Article 72. As there is no difference between public contracts and framework agreements to this regard, the rules are to be found below in the chapter of this book dealing with modifications, written by Steen Treumer.

60. Commission's explanatory note on framework agreements, document CC/2005/03_rev 1 of July 14, 2005,
61. Ibid.

10. Dynamic purchasing systems

Dynamic purchasing systems may be seen as a variant of framework agreements.[62] It is so as they also allow contracting authorities to postpone the moment of purchase. However, many differences can be spotted: they are reserved for commonly used purchases, they shall be operated as a completely electronic process, they shall be open throughout the period of validity of the purchasing system to any economic operator that satisfies the selection criteria. These characteristics have not been altered by the new directive. However, Recital 63 makes it clear – although in indirect terms[63] – that, contrary to framework agreements, dynamic purchasing systems have not become very popular among practitioners since their introduction in 2004. Simplification and clarification appear to be the main objectives of Directive 2014/24 to enhance their use. As a measure of simplification, the new directive transforms the award of dynamic purchasing systems from an open procedure to a restricted procedure. By doing so, it avoids the requirement of the indicative tender which has been identified as one of the major burdens associated with dynamic purchasing systems both for the contracting authorities who must evaluate it and for the economic operators who must provide it without being sure to have the minimum capacity for completing the contract. The abolition of the indicative tender also makes sense since its status was unclear: being a request, it should be submitted, but, being indicative, was it legally binding? It could have been that indicative tenders were legally binding only in the sense that they could be changed but for the better.[64]

Another simplification lies in the possibility for the contracting authorities to set a minimum time limit for receipt of tenders of 10 days from the date on which the invitation to tender is sent whereas it was 15 days in the 2004/18 Directive. The counterpart for them results in the duty to assess the request to participate in accordance with the selection criteria within 10 working days following their receipt, that deadline may be prolonged to 15 working days in individual cases where justified, in particular because of the need to examine

62. F. Lichère 'New Award Procedures' in M. Trybus, R. Caranta, G. Edelstam (eds) EU Public Contract Law. Public Procurement and Beyond (Bruxelles, Bruylant), 2014.
63. "There is also a need to adjust the rules governing dynamic purchasing systems to enable contracting authorities to take full advantage of the possibilities afforded by that instrument".
64. Guillaume Delaloy, 'La mise en place d'un SAD', VII.330.2.3, in O. Guézou and F. Lichère (eds), Droit des marchés publics et contrats public spéciaux, Editions du Moniteur, 2012.

additional documentation or to otherwise verify whether the selection criteria are met.

In addition, no charges may be billed prior to or during the period of validity of the dynamic purchasing system to the economic operators interested in or party to the dynamic purchasing system.

As far as flexibility is concerned, the new directive deletes the obligation to limit the dynamic purchasing system to 4 years and, by doing so, introduces another difference with framework agreements. But such a difference can be easily justified since dynamic purchasing systems are open systems, allowing new economic operators to enter throughout their entire period of validity.

Another flexibility aims at improving SMEs' access, these operators being often excluded from large-scale dynamic purchasing systems. Article 34(1) provides that a dynamic purchasing system "may be divided into categories of products, works or services that are objectively defined on the basis of characteristics of the procurement to be undertaken under the category concerned. Such characteristics may include reference to the maximum allowable size of the subsequent specific contracts or to a specific geographic area in which subsequent specific contracts will be performed". This latter sentence is interesting as it allows for a maximum size of the subsequent contracts, approaching the American Small Business Act system. It is unclear however how this possibility will interact with the possibility of defining lots.

Finally a new provision – that cannot be classified either in the simplification category or in the flexibility one – regards the duty to indicate in the procurement documents not only the nature, the necessary information concerning the dynamic purchasing system, including how the dynamic purchasing system operates, the electronic equipment used and the technical connection arrangements and specifications as did the 2004/18 directive but also the estimated quantity of forecasted purchases. However it remains uncertain whether this indication might become legally binding, even in the case of an important difference between the indication and the final purchase amount.

11. Conclusion

This paper discussed the implications of the single digital market on public procurement: the challenges stemming from the new directive, good practices of public contracting, the major impacts of eProcurement and of framework agreement and dynamic purchasing systems, namely on transparency and public savings.

The new Public Sector Directive foresees a gradual transition towards full electronic means of communication. Electronic means will become mandatory for some phases of the procurement process and for some actors by the transposition deadlines, either from 18 April 2016 or later on in the following cases.

First of all it would be mandatory for Central Purchasing Bodies by 18 april 2016 unless Member states postpone it to 18 April 2017 maximum. All other contracting authorities will be required to perform all procurement procedures using electronic means of communication, except in duly justified circumstances, by 18 April 2016 unless Member states postpone it to 18 October 2018, except where use of electronic means is mandatory pursuant to Articles 34, 35 or 36, Article 37(3), Article 51(2) or Article 53.

The directive encourages interoperability between e-Procurement systems and contains provisions designed to ensure that suppliers encounter no technical barriers when bidding on different systems. To this purpose, it empowers the Commission to adopt delegated acts in a number of specific areas to render mandatory the use of specific technical standards.

Those technical standards for electronic communication aim to ensure the interoperability of technical formats, processes and messaging in procurement procedures conducted using electronic means of communication taking into account technological developments.

The EU lawmaker asks every Member State to transpose the directive regime in its domestic law, in the hope that Member States could overcome existing legal and practical obstacles.

According to Directive 2014/24/EU a joint action at European and at national level will be needed to determine the conditions for the use and the implementation of electronic means.

Perhaps it would be too ambitious to expect a quick implementation of complete e-Procurement because of the fragmentation of the different domestic systems but the difference between the previous and the present regime consists in the fact that the new Public Sector Directive strongly promotes IT solutions.

These electronic new duties make a balance to the increased flexibility offered by the new directive with regard to framework agreements and dynamic purchasing systems. It remains uncertain whether this flexibility will allow the latter to become as popular as the former.

Bibliography

S. Arrowsmith 'Electronic reverse auctions under the EC public procurements rules: current possibilities and future prospects' in Public Procurement Law Review, 2002.

S. Arrowsmith The Law of Public and Utilities Procurement 2nd (London, Sweet & Maxwell), 2011.

C.H. Bovis EU Public Procurement Law 3rd (Cheltenham, Elgar), 2012

M. Burgi – H. Goelnitz 'Die Modernisierung des Vergaberechts als Daueraufgabe' in Die öffentliche Verwaltung, 2009.

M.E. Comba – S. Richetto 'Minor contracts: Outside the Directives and Outside the Treaties? Comparative analysis on public procurement below the thresholds in Europe, in D. Dragos – R. Caranta (eds) Outside the EU procurement Directives- inside the Treaty? (Copenhagen, DJØF), 2012.

S.R. Croom 'The impact of web-based procurement on the management of operating resources supply' in Journal of Supply Chain Management, 2000.

Ph. De Géry, Passation des accord-cadres, Passation des marchés fondés sur l'accord-cadre, Régime juridique des accord-cadres, Régime juridique des marchés à bon de commande, in O. Guézou and F. Lichère (eds), Droit des marchés publics et contrats public spéciaux, Editions du Moniteur, 2013.

G. Delaloy, 'La mise en place d'un SAD', VII.330.2.3, in O. Guézou and F. Lichère (eds), Droit des marchés publics et contrats public spéciaux, Editions du Moniteur, 2012.

F. Lichère 'New Award Procedures' in M. Trybus, R. Caranta, G. Edelstam (eds) EU Public Contract Law. Public Procurement and Beyond (Bruxelles, Bruylant), 2014.

B. Lin – C.B. Jones 'Management implications of electronic data interchange' in Int. Business School Computing Quarterly, 1993.

A. Masucci 'Le aste elettroniche e la modernizzazione delle procedure di aggiudicazione' in Giorn. Dir. Amm., 2013.

H. Pünder 'Elektronische Auktion' in H. Pünder – Schellenberg (hers.) Vergaberecht (Baden Baden, Nomos), 2011.

G. Racca 'The role of IT solutions in the Award and Execution of Public Procurement below the Threshold and List B Services: overcoming E-Barriers' in D. Dragos – Caranta (eds.) Outside the EU Procurement Directives – Inside the Treaty?, (Copenhagen, DJØF Publishing), 2012.

C. Risvig Hansen, Contracts not covered or not fully covered by the Public Sector Directive (Copenhagen, DJØF Publishing), 2012.

C. Risvig Hamer, 'Regular Purchases and Aggregated Procurement:The Changes in the New Public Procurement Directive Regarding Framework Agreements, Dynamic Purchasing Systems and Central Purchasing Bodies', P.P.L.R. 2014, n°4, p. 199-208

W. Witting 'A strategy for improving public procurement' in 9th International Anti Corruption Conference, Papers IACC, 1999.

Joint Procurement Challenges in the Future Implementation of the New Directives

Gabriella M. Racca

1. Introduction

The need to improve efficiency and effectiveness in public procurement markets requires the promotion of collaborative procurement arrangements and the use of framework agreements in order to modernize the procurement system.[1] Aggregation of demand can yield considerable positive effects for contracting authorities and suppliers including economies of scale, increased buying power on the part of public authorities and a possibility for them to pool skills and expertise and to share the procurement related costs and risks. A coherent strategy of lots in framework agreements might favour the development of SMEs and promote the entrance of new economic operators in the relevant market, preventing an excessive concentration of contracts in favour of larger undertakings. Such evolution, together with increased skills of procurement officials, can foster transparency, equal treatment and accountability.

Widespread fragmentation of procurement entities across the public sector is still present.[2] An overall vision on how to organize and exploit the strategic

1. OECD Centralised Purchasing Systems in the EU, January 11, 2011, at www.oecd-ilibrary.org/governance/centralised-purchasingsystems-in-the-european-union_-5kgkgqv703xw-en.
2. The contracting authorities and entities concluding contracts outside of the scope of the Public Procurement Directives must comply with the fundamental principles of the EU Treaty in general and the principle of non-discrimination on grounds of na-

power of public spending is still missing.[3] This leads to a fragmentation of contracts of limited value below the European thresholds, being a first key factor that limits the creation of a European procurement market. According to the Green Paper, only 1.6 percent of public contracts are awarded to operators from other Member States.[4] From a transaction cost viewpoint, the signing of hundreds of thousands of low-value contracts can possibly result in large price variations for very similar products resulting in considerable inefficiency. Consequently, a new complex approach for a complete and comprehensive vision of the possible strategies of Collaborative Procuring policies and Framework Agreements strategies is required.[5]

The Europe 2020 Strategy requires a more efficient use of public funds by improving the conditions for business to innovate and supporting the shift towards a resource-efficient and low-carbon economy. Directive 2014/24/EU has introduced simplified rules and procedures with the aim of opening EU

tionality in particular, where those contracts are of certain cross-border interest. Case C-324/98 Telaustria Verlags GmbH v Telekom Austria AG [2000] ECR-I 10745; Joined Cases C-147/06 and C-148/06, SECAP SpA v Comune di Torino [2008] ECR I-3565, for procurement below the threshold with a certain cross-border interest. Case C-412/04, European Commission v Repubblica italiana [2008] ECR I-619. See also: G. M. Racca, 'The role of IT solutions in the award and execution of public procurement below threshold and list B services: overcoming e-barriers' in D. Dragos – R. Caranta (eds.) Outside the EU Procurement Directives – inside the Treaty?, (Copenhagen, DJØF, 2012), 373 et seq.

3. A high percentage of the total amount of public procurements is awarded without complying with most of the rules set by European Directives, and value of approximately 4 percent is below threshold. Organisation for Economic Co-operation and Development, 'Public Procurement in EU Member States – The Regulation of Contract Below the EU Thresholds and in Areas not Covered by the Detailed Rules of the EU Directives', May 27, 2010, 13 et seq, in http://www.oecd-ilibrary.org governance/public-procurement-in-eu-member-states_5km91p7s1mxv-en, where on explain that "an evaluation of the Public Procurement Directives carried out by Europe Economics for the European Commission and published in 2006 concluded that only about 20% of the total amount of public procurement was covered by the detailed rules of the Directives, while the remainder would be covered by exceptions to the Directives, such as certain defence procurements and below threshold procurement". Racca G. M., 'The role of IT solutions in the award and execution of public procurement below threshold and list B services: overcoming e-barriers', above fn. 2, 376.
4. Commission EU 'Green paper on the modernisation of EU public procurement policy – towards a more efficient European procurement market', COM(2011) 15 final, January 27, 2011.
5. Edler J. – Georghiou L., 'Public procurement and innovation – resurrecting the demand side', in Research Policy, 2007, 36(7): 949-963.

markets (especially for SME). It aims, among other objectives, to overcome barriers to aggregation of public demand of goods, services and works and to foster cooperation between public entities, preventing any distortion of competition.

A special Chapter on "Techniques and instruments for electronic and aggregated procurement" has been introduced.[6] It allows national contracting authorities, and contracting authorities from different EU Member States, to engage in public-public cooperation following various models. The opening of new models of joint procurement could foster cross-border participation but also requires means to tackle the problem of persisting differences among Member States' national procurement systems and solutions to barriers faced by economic operators seeking to participate in electronic procedures, particularly across the borders. A significant and effective aggregation can be achieved through framework agreements. An innovative use of electronic instruments that could foster transparency and accountability[7] will assure citizens' monitoring of the quality of the public spending and which is an important imperative in times of economic crisis. Aggregated procurement undoubtedly constitutes an important future challenge for innovation in public procurement award procedures.[8]

Joint procurement and electronic tools implemented by central purchasing bodies (CPBs) for the award of framework agreements changes the perspective of public procurement and opens up new forms of strategic sourcing which individual procuring entities may find difficult to fully understand and comprehend.

Such change requires the adoption of common standards and interoperable systems as well as procedures conducted by electronic means in the performance phase too. Central purchasing bodies (CPB) are best equipped to ensure such development through use the use of the most innovative e-procurement platforms. Such bodies could also assure effective translation given that language remains a significant barrier to cross-border procurement. Equally, joint procurement presents an opportunity to introduce greater scru-

6. Directive 2014/24/EU, Art. 33-39.
7. On this point, see G. M. Racca, 'The electronic award and execution of public procurement', in Ius Publicum Network Review, available at http://www.ius-publicum.com/repository/uploads/17_05_2013_19_31-Racca_IT_IUS-PUBLICUM-_EN.pdf.
8. See G. M. Racca, 'Aggregate Models of Public Procurement and Secondary Consideration: An Italian Perspective', in R. Caranta and M. Trybus (eds.), The law of green and social procurement in Europe, (Copenhagen, DJØF, 2010), 165.

tiny within procurement systems, providing ways to apply more objectivity in selecting suppliers, supporting better governance and assuring the quality of the performance required.[9]

2. Collaborative procurement in Europe

National governments, local authorities and public organizations, utilities and agencies at any level are normally endowed with contractual autonomy and can purchase independently, according to international, European, and national rules. This means that a considerable mix of individual procuring efforts can be utilised within a public administration.[10] Entities that carry out single procuring procedures often cannot assure the required professional skills and procurement training.[11] Many small procurement units do not have highly trained professionals with necessary skills. Further, the risks and transaction costs of a huge number of award procedures may become very high.

This widespread fragmentation of procuring entities hinders an overall vision of public purchasing power and becomes an obstacle to complete and comprehensive procurement strategies.[12] The promotion of value achieved through forms of collaborative procurement and professionalism might change the perspective on public procurement, allowing the achievement of a deeper knowledge of the different market conditions and characteristics[13] and of the possibility to orient innovation or promote sustainability policies.

9. Commission (EC) 'Evaluation of the 2004 Action Plan for Electronic Public Procurement Accompanying document to the Green Paper on expanding the use of e-Procurement in the EU' SEC(2010) 1214 final October 10, 2010, 7. G. M. Racca, 'Collaborative procurement and contract performance in the Italian healthcare sector: Illustration of a common problem in European procurement', in P.P.L.R., 2010, 119.
10. M. Burgi, 'In-house providing in Germany', in M. Comba and S. Treumer (eds.), The In-House Providing in European Law, (Copenhagen, DJØF Publishing), 2010, 71-93.
11. G. M. Racca, 'Collaborative procurement and contract performance in the Italian healthcare sector: Illustration of a common problem in European procurement', cit.above fn. 10, 119-133. The value of these single award procedures can be very limited if we consider, for example, a small rural community. On the contrary, this value can also be very high for an urban city hospital.
12. Edler J. – Georghiou L., 'Public procurement and innovation resurrecting the demand side' above fn. 5, 949.
13. Commission EU, 'European code of best practices facilitating access by SMEs to public procurement contracts' SEC(2008) 2193, June 25, 2008.

The previous rules on public procurement were mainly concentrated only on single award procedures by individual procuring entities. Nonetheless, several Member States coordinated a number of procuring activities in order to deliver the 'best value' in public spending. Over the years, awareness of the efficiency of joint procurement increased and was finally introduced in the European legal framework, thus facilitating a quicker growth of these new opportunities and strategies in public procurement. The previous Directives provided a number of tools for the aggregation of demand, including central purchasing bodies (CPBs) and other instruments that may be used for this purpose.[14] Procuring entities can coordinate their activities by simply sharing their experiences or coordinating certain phases of the procurement procedure. Procurements can be awarded on the basis of a contract of cooperation between several procuring entities through a 'contractual model' of cooperation.[15] Collaborative purchasing arrangements between municipalities in a specific geographical area, formally and permanently established, are not unusual in a number of EU Member States, and which have recently taken off in Italy.[16] Such arrangements are especially feasible for goods and services that are commonly in demand in any municipality, such as food, fuel, and energy.[17]

14. Different kinds of agreement between contracting entities. G. M. Racca 'Collaborative procurement and contract performance in the Italian healthcare sector': illustration of a common problem in European procurement' above fn. 10; S. Arrowsmith, 'Framework Purchasing and Qualification Lists under the European Procurement Directives' in P.P.L.R., 1999, 115-146 and 168-186; J. Chard, G. Duhs, J. Houlden, (2008) 'Body beautiful or vile bodies? Central purchasing in the UK', in P.P.L.R., 2008, NA26; C. R. Yukins, 'Use and Regulation of Electronic Reverse Auctions in the United States', in S. Arrowsmith (ed.), Reform of the UNCITRAL model law on procurement: Procurement regulation for the 21st century, Danvers: Thomson Reuters/West.
15. See G. M. Racca, 'Le modalità organizzative delle aziende sanitarie in relazione all'attività contrattuale e le prospettive di razionalizzazione degli acquisti connessi alla prestazione dei servizi sanitari pubblici', in A. Pioggia – M. Dugato – G. M. Racca – S. Civitarese Matteucci (eds.), Oltre l'aziendalizzazione del servizio sanitario, (Milano, Franco Angeli, 2008), 264-297. This normally leads to a sum of separate procuring procedures or the sum of lots included into them, sometimes with a common elaboration of technical specifications and the estimation of aggregate requirements. Cooperation can also lead to informal agreements for the exchange of information on highly standardized products and their prices.
16. Italian D.L. 24 April 2014, Article 9, converted in law 23 June 2014 No. 89.
17. OECD, Centralised Purchasing Systems in the EU, above fn. 1.

In Europe, CPBs are created to purchase goods, services or works or other contracting authorities without having to comply with the public procurement rules.[18] The Directives provide discretion to Member States to choose whether to create CPBs and the choice of how to use these instruments.[19] Ordinarily, the aim is to achieve economies of scale and to limit the transaction costs. The new Directives define different models for such activity, underlining certain advantages especially in sharing the risks of innovative procurements.

In this regard, joint procurement and the professionalization of public procurement have become two of the most important challenges for public purchasers and for the suppliers.

Joint procurement is regarded as a fundamental step in optimising professional skills, since it allows Member States to address the present fragmentation and dispersion of these skills.[20] The increasing complexity of the award procedure can only be addressed through a number of different legal, economic and technical skills that a small or medium-sized procuring entity cannot afford. This should lower the increasing legal risk of dealing with protests and complaints during both the award of framework agreements and the procedure for call-offs and mini-competitions.

Moreover collaborative procurement can significantly improve the use of IT tools.[21] A CPB can use these instruments for the digitalization of procuring documents and, in particular, to implement new procedures of selecting

18. DG internal policies of the UE 'The Applicability of Internal Market rules for Inter-Communal Co-operations' September 2006. According to Article 1, para. (10) European Parliament and Council of Directive 18/2004 [2004] O.J. L134/114 A/18/EC a "central purchasing body" is a contracting authority which: – acquires supplies and/or services intended for contracting authorities or – awards public contracts or concludes framework agreements for works, supplies or services intended for contracting authorities.
19. Directive 2004/17/EC, Recita No. 23.
20. OECD, Centralised Purchasing Systems in the EU, cit above fn. 1.
21. C. R. Yukins, 'Use and regulation of electronic reverse auctions in the United States', above fn. 15. As is known, the provisions inside in the EU directives have to implemented by Member States. Directive 2014/24/EU requires national transposition within 24 months from the date of entry into force of the directive itself (see directive 2014/24/EU, cit., Article 90). Yet, Member States may postpone the application of "rules applicable to communication" ex Article 2, § 1 until 18 October 2018, except where use of electronic means is mandatory pursuant to Articles 34, 35 or 36, Article 37(3), Article 51(2) or Article 53, respectively on dynamic purchasing systems, electronic auctions, electronic catalogues, electronic means of communication to be used in all procurement procedures conducted by a central purchasing body, electronic transmission of notices and electronic availability of procurement documents.

bidders such as e-auctions, framework agreements, dynamic purchasing systems as well as build archives of award data.[22]

At the European level, the presence of a number of barriers faced by public organizations buying innovations is increasingly evident. These barriers include a lack of coordination among CPBs as well as a lack of understanding as to how purchasing power can drive innovation at both national and European level. To address this issue, the EU[23] is promoting European public procurement networks[24] as strategic means of cooperation.

22. In view of the large volumes purchased by these organizations, it has been considered that these techniques can help increase competition and streamline public purchasing. L. Albano – L. Carpineti – F. Dini, L. Giamboni, F. Russo, G. Spagnolo, 'Riflessioni sull'impatto economico degli istituti innovativi del codice dei contratti pubblici relativi a lavori, servizi e forniture', in Quaderni CONSIP, 2007, IV, 13 et seq.
23. Commission EU, DG Enterprise and Industry, 'The lead market initiative' (2009).
24. For significant examples of such networks, see the projects launched within the Competitiveness and Innovation Programme. The legal basis for such networks is the Decision No. 1639/2006/EC of the European Parliament and of the Council, of 24 October 2006, establishing a Competitiveness and Innovation Framework Programme (2007 to 2013). Specifically, the call under which the networks have been launched is the Call for Proposals, "Supporting Public Procurement Of Innovative Solutions: networking and financing procurement" (ENT/CIP/11/C/N02C011), and the financed project are: "HAPPI", which establishes long-term collaboration between healthcare purchasing organisations across Europe in order to identify "ageing well" and innovative health products, services and solutions and to put in place joint cross-border procurement for the benefit of healthcare organisations (about "HAPPI", see http://www.happi-project.eu/); "FIRED-uP", with the aim of creating the conditions in which the procurement of new solutions can occur, "by engaging with the market, developing specifications, and addressing legal and operational risk factors", and by launching a competitive dialogue procedure through which one of the two partners, the London Fire Brigade, will award a framework agreement split in lots on behalf of other contracting authorities (about FIRED-uP, see http://www.fired-up.eu/). "PRO-LITE", with the aim to support the development of guidance for public sector authorities on how they can consolidate their procurement power to create economies of scale, procure innovatively and drive the European economies, also through delivering common specifications – across member states – for lighting requirements (about "PRO-LITE", see http://www.prolitepartnership.eu/); "EcoQUIP", with the aim to support public procurers in purchasing new/improved solutions in order to offset the additional risks and costs of innovation procurement, enable collaboration to create a critical mass of demand and test the feasibility and options for a future EU support scheme; in this context, the project will give birth to an 'Innovation Procurement Leaders Group' of hospitals that have competence in innovation procurement and the capacity to pioneer new approaches to collaborative procurement (about "EcoQUIP" see http://www.ecoquip.eu/); "InnoBuild", whose main objective is to improve the process by which contracting public authorities and entities are acquiring

The instruments for establishing and regulating the activities of CPBs differ across EU Member States. Some CPBs in the EU have the legal status of a publicly-owned limited company.[25] In other cases, a public-private partnership is established. The question of how activities are funded using such methods becomes more and more complex. This is a key point whenever

goods and services, developing a joint public procurement strategy and then implementing this joint procurement for sustainable high tech building projects for senior citizens (about "InnoBuild" see http://www.innobuild.eu/); "Innobooster inLIFE", with the aim to support public procurers in purchasing new and improved solutions in the field of energy efficiency and resource scarcity, through defining technical specifications for innovative solutions and formulating a business-case regarding the procurement of innovation (about "Innobooster inLIFE" see http://www.bbg.gv.at/ index.php?id=1028); "SPEA", with the aim of undertaking a joint procurement between the three partners, for the purchasing of innovative solutions in the area of energy efficiency in municipal buildings in the three partner cities (about "SPEA" see http://www.speaproject.eu/en/spea); "SYNCRO", with the aim to develop a smart road system with measures that range from road and/or car sensors to smart data collection, proposing itself to be a business opportunity for SMEs to access a transnational tender through the launch of transnational public procurement of innovative solutions promoting high tech ITS solutions (about "SYNCRO" see http://www.syncromobility.eu/); "PPI Platform", with the objective to structure and coordinate networking, capacity building, dissemination and use of public procurement as a mechanism for procurement of innovation. To achieve the overall objective, the project has created a European Procurement and Innovation Platform consisting of a highly interactive public website supported and complemented by guidance tools, events, training and staff exchange to support public procurement of innovative solutions (about "PPI Platform" see https://www.innovation-procurement.org).

25. Hansel (Finland), Consip (Italy), and SKI (Denmark) are all non-profit limited companies that are partially or totally owned and controlled by their countries' ministries of finance.25 SKI has, in addition, a second owner that is the Association of Local Authorities, which owns 45 percent of the company. UGAP (France) is a public body with legal personality and no share capital, fully controlled by the State. Others are public bodies, or agencies or public–private partnerships such as NHS Supply Chain in the UK which has considerable economic independence and a relationship with the German-owned logistics business, DHL. OECD, Centralised Purchasing Systems in the EU, citabove fn. 1. See also G. M. Racca – R. Cavallo Perin, 'Organizzazioni sanitarie e contratti pubblici in Europa: modelli organizzativi per la qualità in un sistema di concorrenza', in A. Pioggia – S. Civitarese Matteucci – G. M. Racca – M. Dugato (eds.) I servizi sanitari: organizzazione, riforme e sostenibilità. Una prospettiva comparata, Santarcangelo di Romagna, 2011, 193. In the same book there are more detailed article concerning Joint Procurement in UK (by D. Casalini), France (by S. Ponzio), Germany, Spain (by M. Pignatti) and US (by M. Mattalia and M. Consito).

CPBs are funded through fees as service charges. [26] Procurements can be designed such that procuring entities pay a fee when call-offs (second-round efforts) are made, or fees are paid by suppliers when they invoice through framework agreements. Service charges enable CPBs to make profits which can be reinvested to improve the quality of their services. Further, national rules can define whether they can operate only in specific sectors, act as wholesalers in predetermined product categories,[27] or arrange framework agreements in the capacity of intermediary.[28] The mandates given to CPBs may be different and specify whether the framework agreements have to be considered mandatory or voluntary for the procuring entities. Some countries require adherence to CPBs contracts as mandatory with the aim to encourage and strengthen collaborative procurement.[29] The new Directive offers Member States the possibility to oblige recourse to such methods, even if only for just some categories of public contracts to specific CPBs (Directive 2014/24/EU, Article 37(1)). A more flexible approach is often adopted, leaving procuring entities with a choice to adhere to a non mandatory framework contract of a CPB, based on the evaluation that better conditions are unlikely to be found in the market.

This requires an in-depth knowledge of the specific market, appropriate organizational design and a strategic system for local, regional, national and European procurement. When the requirements are broadly similar, sometimes CPBs face highly concentrated supply markets amongst multi-national

26. OECD, Centralised Purchasing Systems in the EU, above fn. 1, 11, where it is noted that the service fee is based on the invoiced turnover generated under the framework agreement and normally amounts to between 0.6% and 2%.
27. See ECD Centralised Purchasing Systems in the EU, cit. above fn. 1, particularly on Italy, Hungary, Finland and Denmark experiences the operations of Consip (Italy) and KSzF (Hungary) are regulated quite in detail, while the CPBs in the Nordic countries are given more freedom to plan and manage their operations. As an example, the regulatory instrument in Hungary governing the operations of KSzF prescribes in detail the product areas and public sector bodies covered and specifies whether the framework agreements are mandatory or voluntary as well as the financing mechanism. No similarly detailed regulations exist in countries such as Denmark, Finland and Sweden. There, CPBs may basically decide for themselves on the products and service areas that are subject to framework agreements, the financing models, the type of framework agreements to use including call-off systems and, in particular, the organisation, staffing, market relationships and design of all of the steps in the procurement process.
28. OECD, Centralised Purchasing Systems in the EU, above fn. 1.
29. OECD, Centralised Purchasing Systems in the EU above fn. 1.

suppliers and it seems unefficient to set up hundreds of award procedures.[30] The limit to free competition considered to be a risk involved in the aggregation of purchases can be overcome[31] through the provision of different kind of lots for size and type of products when the market conditions require it.

2.1. Joint Procurement as public-public cooperation

In 2011, the EU Commission identified the need to distinguish what is meant by public-public cooperation with the aim to clarify when the EU Public Procurement Directives apply and when they do not for the benefit of contracting authorities wishing to cooperate.[32] As highlighted by the ECJ case law, joint procurement can follow different organizational models, which the EU Commission qualifies as "non-institutionalized/horizontal co-operation" (without creating a jointly controlled 'in-house' entity) to jointly fulfil public tasks.[33] The Court has stressed that EU law does not require contracting authorities to use any particular legal form in order to jointly carry out their public service tasks.[34] On this basis, contracting authorities may establish horizontal co-operation amongst themselves, which involves the conclusion of agreements, not covered by EU public procurement law, if at least the following conditions are met: the arrangement involves only contracting authorities; there is no participation of private capital; the agreement is aimed at real co-operation for the joint performance of a common task, as opposed to a normal public contract[35]; and the cooperation is governed only by considerations relating to the public interest.[36]

30. S. Williams, T. Chambers, S. Hills, F. Dowson, 'Buying a better word: sustainable public procurement', 2008, available at http://www.forumforthefuture.org/projects/buying-a-better-world.
31. G. M. Racca, 'Professional Buying Organisations, Sustainability and Competition in Public Procurement Performance' proceeding at 4th International Public Procurement Conference, Seoul, August 26-28, 2010,
32. EU Commission, Commission staff working paper concerning the application of EU public procurement law to relations between contracting authorities ('public-public cooperation'), 4 October 2011, SEC(2011) 1169 final, 3.
33. EU Commission, Commission staff working paper concerning the application of EU public procurement law to relations between contracting authorities ('public-public cooperation'), above fn. 34, 12.
34. Case C-480/06, Commission v Germany, [2009] ECR I-04747, par. 47.
35. EU Commission, Commission staff working paper concerning the application of EU public procurement law to relations between contracting authorities ('public-public cooperation'), above fn. 34, 13. Case C-480/06 Commission v Germany [2009] ECR I-4747, par. 38. On the basis of the Hamburg-judgment, the aim of cooperation is to

As recalled, the new Directive highlights the difference between individual contracting authorities and any forms of PP cooperation (Public-to-Public) (voluntary, contractual, corporate) and better defines the role of CPBs as wholesaler or intermediary. In this legal framework contracting authorities may, without applying the procedures provided in the new Directive, "award a public service contract for the provision of centralised purchasing activities to a central purchasing body" (Directive 2014/24/EU, Article 37(4)).

The Court of Justice[37] has dealt with the risk of public-public collusion[38] related to the concentration of public purchasing power. The Court of Justice excluded such risks considering that such coordination is for the benefit of citizens. Moreover, a lots strategy can avoid the risks of awarding too few and too large contracts. Correctly addressed, Public-Public cooperation can result in a "positive collusion" for the benefit of competition. It can drive the market according to public interest and encourage sharing risks and costs of innovations among a number of contracting authorities. However, aggregated purchasing also requires more transparency since the use of contractual tools such as Framework Agreements can determine risks for integrity as happens in the US with the IDIQ (indefinite delivery – indefinite quantity) "umbrella contract".[39] In the EU, risks of discrimination were related to the award of Framework Agreements, particularly in the UK Healthcare sector.[40]

The substantial challenge of collaborative procurement is to overcome language and legal barriers among Member States. Cross-border cooperation among CPBs might be an important tool to foster competition and participation of economic operators from different Member States and of innovative SMEs.

jointly ensure the execution of a public task which all the cooperation partners have to perform.

36. EU Commission, Commission staff working paper concerning the application of EU public procurement law to relations between contracting authorities ('public-public cooperation'), above fn. 34.
37. Case C-205/03P, Federación Española de Empresas de Tecnología Sanitaria (FENIN) v EC Commission in [2006] ECR I-6295; Case C-113/07, Selex v EC Commission – Eurocontrol, [2009] ECR I-2207. in C-113/07 P.
38. Case C-113/02, EC Commission v Kingdom of the Netherlands, [2004] ECR I-9707.
39. See C. R. Yukins, 'Are IDIQs Inefficient? Sharing Lessons with European Framework Contracting', in P.C.L.J., 2008, 545. G. I. Gordon – G. M. Racca, 'Integrity Challenges in the EU and U.S. Procurement Systems', in G. M. Racca – C. Yukins, Integrity and Efficiency in Sustainable Public Contracts, Bruylant, 2014, 117-145.
40. Case C- 406/08, Uniplex (UK) Ltd v NHS Business Services Authority, ECR I-00817.

3. New perspectives of Joint Procurement in the recent provisions

The issue of joint procurement is addressed in a special Chapter on "Techniques and Instruments for Electronic and Aggregated Procurement" (Articles 33 to 39 of Directive 2014/24/EU). Electronic and aggregated procurement are the two main instruments to innovate award procedures.

A combination of these two elements may also be considered of utmost relevance for the purpose of improving procurement efficiency and competition (Directive 2014/24/EU, Recital 69). From a legal, economic or technical viewpoint, IT-tools (Directive 2014/24/EU, Recital 68)[41] might be fully exploited when used by CPBs because of their highly professional and specialized workforce (Directive 2014/24/EU, Recital 72). The new Directive provides for extensive use of electronic means by CPBs' contractual activity before other procuring entities (Directive 2014/24/EU, Article 37(3)). In order to implement electronic procurement fully, Member States may extend the period of time of 24 months to bring into force the laws, to 30 months. This extension of time is not applicable in the case of the mandatory use of IT-tools by CPBs (Directive 2014/24/EU, Article 90(2)).

The new Directive highlights that there is a strong trend emerging in the European Union towards the aggregation of demand by public purchasers, as the fragmentation of public demand in 250,000 procuring entities seems largely inefficient. Aggregation of public demand is a strategic instrument to obtain economies of scale, including lower prices and transaction costs, and to improve and professionalize procurement management. These objectives can be pursued by concentrating purchases, either by the number of contracting authorities involved or by volume and value over time. Possible problems of procurement aggregation may be an excessive concentration of purchasing power. Therefore, such aggregation should be carefully monitored in order to preserve transparency and competition, as well as market access opportunities for SMEs (Directive 2014/24/EU, Recital 59). Joint Procurement changes the perspective of public procurement since it requires different skills, wider

41. E-Procurement can play a strategic role as it can increase transparency and stimulate innovation and the development of e-marketplaces and participation of SMEs. Concerning the use of IT tools in public procurement see: G. M. Racca, 'The Electronic Award and Execution of Public Procurement', in Ius Publicum Network Review, 2012, available at http://www.ius-publicum.com/repository/uploads/ 17_05_2013_-19_31-Racca_IT_IUS-PUBLICUM-_EN.pdf.

market analysis, wider procurement strategies and the implementation of innovative IT solutions.

At present, centralized purchasing activities are used in some EU Member States, consisting of making acquisitions, managing dynamic purchasing systems or awarding public contracts or framework agreements for other contracting authorities by CPBs (Directive 2014/24/EU, Recital 69).

The activities of CPBs can follow two different models defined as "centralised purchasing activities" (Directive 2014/24/EU, Article 2(15)). The first model implies that CPBs operate as wholesalers, i.e., they buy, stock and resell supplies or services to the interested public entities. The second model entails that CPBs act as intermediaries by awarding contracts, concluding framework agreements or operating dynamic purchasing systems to be used by contracting authorities. The new Directive specifies that this intermediary role may in some cases be carried out by conducting the award procedures autonomously, i.e. without detailed instructions from the contracting authorities concerned, while in other cases, CPBs may conduct the award procedures under the instructions of the contracting authorities concerned, on their behalf and for their account (Directive 2014/24/EU, Recital 69).

Moreover, the new Directive highlights the importance of allocating responsibilities for the observance of obligations deriving from the Directive itself (Directive 2014/24/EU, Article 37(2)). Such responsibilities have to be allocated between the individual contracting authorities making recourse to a CPB and the CPB itself, following the principle that an entity is responsible only for the parts of the procedure directly carried on. The allocation of responsibility for the observance of the obligations pursuant to the EU Directives is considerable in case of multi-supplier framework agreements and framework agreements that require two different phases. The multi-supplier framework agreement normally is more complex, both in the award of the agreement and in the design of the call-off system. The award of a multi-supplier agreement is completed only upon conclusion of the call-off procedure, whether this procedure is carried out by ranking or mini-competition. This means that the responsibility for completing a multi-supplier framework agreement in general is shared between the CPB and the procuring entities, affecting the distribution of risk between the two parties for the final completion of the framework agreement.[42] In this perspective the new Directive establishes the responsibility of the contracting authority when the award of a contract under a framework agreement (operated by a CPB), is conducted by

42. OECD, Centralised Purchasing Systems in the EU, above fn. 1, 50.

the re-opening of competition (concluded by a CPB), and determines “which of the economic operators, party to the framework agreement, should perform a given task” (Directive 2014/24/EU, Recital 61). A multi-supplier framework agreement that establishes all the terms (concluded by a central purchasing body) can also be re-opened in order to set a mini-competition (Directive 2014/24/EU, Article 37(2c)). In the latter case, the contracting authority’ responsibility is also extended in case of a “closed” framework agreement provides a partial reopening of the competition (Directive 2014/24/EU, Article 33(4b)). The new Directive provide the mandatory use of electronic means of communication (Directive 2014/24/EU, Article 33(4b))

Further to providing the contractual activity carried out by CPBs, as legal entities established specifically for such purpose, the new Directive also recognizes the several forms of joint procurement that have been realized in the Member States (and therefore also on a local basis) and defined as “occasional joint procurement” (Directive 2014/24/EU, Article 38). According to the new Directive, the strengthened provisions concerning CPBs should not affect the current practices of occasional joint procurement. On the contrary, certain features of these practices should be clarified as joint procurement can play an important role, not least for innovative projects (Directive 2014/24/EU, Recital 71). Moreover, joint procurement may be carried out through many different forms, ranging from coordinated but separate award procedures to more centralized systems of management. Namely, these latter can be arranged by contracting authorities either by acting together or by delegating one contracting authority to manage the procurement procedure on behalf of all contracting authorities.

At a regional level, a procurement policy can be more flexible and meet local needs and circumstances. A deliberate strategy to improve collaborative procurement, however, can also be pursued with sub-regional or municipal consortia.[43] The aggregation of local procurement teams, should have the aim of improving the relevant skills. Many procurement officials might be freed up from the repetitive individual award procedures and deal with the contract management. The recourse to the contractual activity of CPBs gives rise to a

43. The Italian D.L. 24 April 2014, Article 9, above fn 16, states that municipalities purchase works, goods and services within the unions of municipalities (referred to in Article 32 of the Italian Legislative Decree 15 August 2000, n. 267), where they exist, or constituting a separate consortium agreement between the municipalities and availing themselves of the competent office, or by resorting to a “soggetto aggregatore” or to the provinces.

public service contract in the meaning of the new Directive (Directive 2014/24/EU, Article 2(9)), but such contract is not subject to the obligation of conducting an award procedure (Directive 2014/24/EU, Article 37(4)) and moreover exempts the individual contracting authorities using CPBs' activities from the award procedure obligations deriving from European Union law (Directive 2014/24/EU, Article 37(2)). Yet, in case of purchase through a framework agreement or a dynamic purchasing system (DPS), the new Directive specifies that responsibility remains with the individual contracting authorities for what concerns the award of specific contracts within a DPS, the reopening of competition under a framework agreement and, in case of a framework agreement concluded with more than one operator, the determining of the economic operator to whom a specific public contract should be awarded.

The new Directive allows Member States to identify categories of public contracts that can be awarded solely by CPBs or even by specific CPBs (Directive 2014/24/EU, Article 37(1)).

The recourse to organisational models for aggregation of public demand implies the need to identify the most appropriate level of aggregation depending on the goods and services required and characteristics of the supply market. The most innovative level of aggregation would be, of course, the European one. Indeed, geographic regroupings can be identified with the purpose to federate public entities active on the same territory, as well as regroupings set by the nature of the organization in order to set different forms of joint procurement (Directive 2014/24/EU, Article 38). This organisational model does not exclude forms of centralization based on the creation of specialized networks to purchase certain categories of goods and services, and possibly of innovative products. In both cases, the new Directive clarifies the distribution of responsibilities deriving from respect of EU public procurement law among the participating contracting authorities. Specifically, a distinction is made between activities carried out jointly by all the involved contracting authorities (where all such authorities are jointly responsible) and activities that are carried out individually by each contracting authority, like in case of a DPS or a framework agreement (Directive 2014/24/EU, Article 38(2)).

3.1. The ancillary purchasing activities

One of the novelties of the new EU Directive is the introduction of "ancillary purchasing activities" consisting in supporting purchasing activities through the provision of technical infrastructure, of advice on the conduct or design of award procedures, or of preparation and management of procurement procedures on behalf of a contracting authority (Directive 2014/24/EU, Article

2(15)). Contracts for the provision of ancillary purchasing activities should be concluded without applying the procedures provided in the Directive, when such activities are carried out by CPBs in the exercise of their central purchasing activities. Similarly, the Directive's rules do not apply in the instance where ancillary purchasing activities are not provided through a contract for pecuniary interest.

On the contrary, in all the other cases, that is whenever ancillary purchasing activities are not conducted by a CPB in connection with the provision of central purchasing activities, and/or they are conducted through a contract for pecuniary interest, the public service contract, including such ancillary purchasing activities, should be awarded in accordance with the rules provided in the Directive (Directive 2014/24/EU, Recital 70).

The ancillary purchasing activities might be conducted either by CPBs (Directive 2014/24/EU, Article 2(16)) or through the award of a contract to private entities specialized in such activities (Directive 2014/24/EU, Article 2(17)). In this latter case, it seems that the "procurement service provider" should be identified through a procedure for the award of a public service contract (Directive 2014/24/EU, Article 37(4). Indeed, the initial proposal of the European Commission expressly subjected the identification of such provider to an obligation to conduct an award procedure, yet without identifying whether such provision also concerns ancillary purchasing activities conducted by a CPB.[44]

4. The strategic tool of cross-border Joint Procurement

The express acknowledgment of the possibility for contracting authorities established in different Member States to act jointly in the award of public contracts can be considered as one of the main innovations of the new Directive (Directive 2014/24/EU, Article 39).

At present, joint cross-border procurement encounters specific practical obstacles and legal difficulties concerning conflicts of national laws, although the previous procurement directive implicitly allowed for such practice. In

44. European Commission, Proposal for a Directive of the European Parliament and of the Council on public procurement, 20 December 2011, COM(2011) 896 final, Article 36, "Ancillary purchasing activities": "The providers of ancillary purchasing activities shall be chosen in accordance with the procurement procedures set out in this Directive".

particular, contracting authorities are now experiencing considerable difficulties in purchasing from central purchasing bodies in other Member States.

One of the main objectives of the new Directive on public procurement is to remedy such difficulties, allowing contracting authorities to derive maximum benefit from the potential of the internal market in terms of economies of scale and risk-benefit sharing, especially for innovative projects where the risks cannot ordinarily be borne by a single contracting authority. Moreover, fostering cross-border joint procurement may help to create cross-border opportunities for economic operators (Directive 2014/24/EU, Recital 73).

The new Directive provides different models for adopting joint cross-border procurement.

The first model is referring to a CPB located in another Member State. In this regard, the Directive states that Member States "shall not prohibit their contracting authorities from making recourse to centralised purchasing activities offered by central purchasing bodies located in another Member State" (Directive 2014/24/EU, Article 39(2)). Member States may only specify which kinds of centralised purchasing activities their contracting authorities may use and particularly wholesaler or intermediary activities as defined in the Directive itself.

With regards to the determination of the applicable law, the Directive states that the national provisions of the Member State where the CPB is located should be applied (Directive 2014/24/EU, Article 39(3)). Such national provisions should apply also to the award of a contract under a dynamic purchasing system operated by a CPB, and, in case of a multiple framework agreement – i.e. a framework agreement with more than one economic operator – concluded by a CPB, to the reopening of competition and to the determination of which of the economic operators, party to the framework agreement, shall perform a given task. With regards to framework agreements, national provisions of the Member State where the CPB is located apply to the definition of the roles of the selected economic operators, specifically where the framework agreement is both multiple and with all the terms defined in the "master contract", without reopening the competition (closed framework agreement) or partly reopening the competition. This latter possibility, concerning the conclusion of a "partly closed framework agreement", has been provided by the new Directive[45] in order to pursue one of the objectives of the public procurement European law reform, which is flexibility. Moreover, the possibility of partly reopening competition should also apply to any lot of

45. See also the chapter by Lichère in this book.

a framework agreement which has all the terms defined in the master contract (Directive 2014/24/EU, Article 33(4b)).

The new Directive determines the conditions for cross-border utilisation of CPBs framework agreements and provides guidance for the choice of the applicable public procurement legislation, complementing the European rules governing conflict of laws.[46]

5. Cross-border Joint Procurement through a public-public cooperation, mainly among CPBs

Cross-border public-public cooperation is the second model provided to carry out joint cross-border procurement. The new EU Directive states that "Several contracting authorities from different Member States may jointly award a public contract, conclude a framework agreement or operate a dynamic purchasing system. They may also, to the extent set out in Article 33(2) second subparagraph, award contracts based on the framework agreement or on the dynamic purchasing system" (Directive 2014/24/EU, Article 39(4)).

These activities may be realized through the inclusion of a provision concerning cooperation in an international agreement concluded by Member States. Where there is no international agreement, the participating contracting authorities shall conclude an agreement that determines to identify the allocation of responsibilities among them, as well as the applicable national legal system and the forms of internal organization. When determining responsibilities and the applicable national law, "the participating contracting authorities may allocate specific responsibilities among them and determine the applicable provisions of the national laws of any of their respective Member States" (Directive 2014/24/EU, Article 39(4)). These choices shall also be mentioned in the procurement documents for the joint award procedure.

This organizational model appears to be an efficient way to achieve cooperation among contracting authorities of different Member States and mainly among Central Purchasing Bodies, that have the skills and the structure to implement such kind of cooperation also for the benefit of other Member States, setting a kind of European Central Purchasing body.

Such model has been tested by the "Healthy Ageing Public Procurement of Innovations – HAPPI Project) founded by the EU Commission with the

46. Regulation (EC) No 593/2008 of the European Parliament and the Council of 17 June 2008 on the law applicable to contractual obligations (Rome I).

aims to realize a first, concrete experience for a strategic collaboration among central purchasing bodies operating in the healthcare sectors of France, Italy, United Kingdom, Belgium, Luxembourg, Spain and Austria, opening also to the adhesion of other Member States. The objective is to perform the first European-level aggregated purchase of innovative solutions for the active and healthy ageing, also through market analysis and the split into lots in order to favor a broad participation.[47]

5. Cross-border Joint Procurement through the European Grouping of Territorial Cooperation or other entities established under Union Law

A third model to perform a joint cross-border procurement is to establish a joint legal entity. This may take the form of a European grouping of territorial cooperation (EGTC)[48] or another entity established under Union law. In such a renewed legal context, contracting authorities established in different Member States should be able to set up joint legal bodies established under national or Union law. Such joint legal entity may also act as a central purchasing body and might be established as a European association.[49]

The only major limit that procurement entities shall respect is, obviously, that they cannot exploit the possibilities for cross-border joint procurement for the purpose of circumventing mandatory public law rules in conformity with EU law, that may be for example provisions on transparency and access

47. See http://www.happi-project.eu/ and footnote No. 25.
48. Such instrument is regulated by Regulation No. 1082/2006 of the European Parliament and of the Council of 5 July 2006 on a European grouping of territorial cooperation (EGTC), as amended by Regulation (EU) No 1302/2013 of the European Parliament and of the Council of 17 December 2013 amending Regulation (EC) No 1082/2006 on a European grouping of territorial cooperation (EGTC) as regards the clarification, simplification and improvement of the establishment and functioning of such groupings.
49. One relevant experience in this sense is the constitution of the European Health Public Procurement Alliance (EHPPA), a European association established under French law (Association Loi 1901; see Loi du 1er juillet 1901 relative au contrat d'association) and made up by contracting authorities from different Member States. According to its recently updated statutes, EHPPA may act as a European CPB, the first to be expressly allowed to act this way (European Health Public Procurement Alliance (EHPPA), Statuts de l'association, art.Article 5).

to documents, as well as specific requirements for the traceability of sensitive supplies.[50]

The objective of an EGTC is to facilitate and promote cross-border, transnational and/or interregional cooperation (overall, territorial cooperation) between its members, which may be Member States, regional authorities, local authorities, and especially, bodies governed by public law, or associations made up of bodies belonging to one or more of these categories,[51] with the exclusive aim of strengthening economic and social cohesion.[52]

At first, the tasks of EGTC have been limited to the implementation of territorial cooperation programmes or projects co-financed by the Community through the European Regional Development Fund, the European Social Fund and/or the Cohesion Fund.[53] European territorial cooperation is particularly influential in thematic areas like energy efficiency, innovation, seeking solutions for better functioning of the single market and addressing territorial challenges in the fields of environment and risk prevention, transport and communication links, demographic change and maritime issues.[54] From a general viewpoint, moreover, an EGTC is a legal instrument capable of providing a strong legal basis for cross-border cooperation. This instrument aims to simplify administration, cooperation and financial control of territorial cooperation in Europe, which is therefore provided with a structure, stability and certainty.[55]

The EGTC is considered the first European cooperation structure with the above mentioned characteristics and provides a legal basis to apply to external activities of local and regional authorities. Nonetheless, as it is a relatively

50. Directive 2014/24/EU, cit., Wh. 73.
51. Regulation 1082/2006, cit., Article 3 (1).
52. Regulation 1082/2006, cit., Article 1 (2).
53. Regulation 1082/2006, cit., Article 7 (3). Nevertheless, an EGTC may carry out other specific actions of territorial cooperation also without a financial contribution from the Community, with the possibility however for Member States to limit the tasks that an EGTC may carry out without the EU financing. INTERACT, 'European Territorial Cooperation post 2013 – Position Paper', available at http://www.interact-eu.net/downloads/2152/INTERACT_Position_Paper_ETC_beyond_2013_07_2010.pdf.
54. INTERACT, 'European Territorial Cooperation post 2013 – Position Paper', cit.
55. Through Regulation No. 1082/2006, cit. See also METIS GmbH, 'The European Grouping of Territorial Cooperation (EGTC): state of play and prospects', 2009, available at http://cor.europa.eu/en/documentation/studies/Documents/c971da76-082c-4357-9b2c-10a176f1ddd8.pdf. An EGTC may be established on Community territory under the conditions and subject to the arrangements provided for by the EGTC Regulation, see Regulation 1082/2006, cit., Article 1, § 1.

recent instrument, it still needs to find its place in national legal systems of each Member State. This process is neither quick nor easy, yet its potential benefits should compensate the investment in time and efforts, especially in the procurement sector.[56] In late 2012, national provisions had been adopted in almost all Member States with the exception of Austria, Germany and Belgium, where the process is in a deadlock due to their federal administrative structures.[57]

The EGTC is probably one of the most innovative instruments in order to foster cooperation among Member States, also for setting a joint cross-border public procurement. Its potential in the procurement sector has not yet been highlighted, but is undoubtedly significant.

The EU Regulation on the EGTC explicitly provides the possibility for a contracting authority to participate in an EGTC. With the only limits of respecting competences under national law and of the composition of the EGTC by members located on the territory of at least two Member States,[58] an EGTC may be made up of "bodies governed by public law" in the meaning of the public procurement EU directive.[59]

According to the new public procurement directive, contracting authorities established in different Member States may establish an EGTC and agree on the applicable national procurement rules, choosing between the national provisions of the Member State where the joint legal entity has its registered office, and national provisions of the Member State where the entity carries out its activities.[60] This agreement formalized in a decision of the competent

56. Mission Opérationnelle Transfrontalière, 'The European grouping of territorial cooperation', 2008, available at http://www.espaces-transfrontaliers.org/document/Cahier_MOT7_GB_web.pdf.
57. See Metis GmbH, 'EGTC Monitoring Report 2013. Towards the New Cohesion Policy', February 2014, available at https://portal.cor.europa.eu/egtc/en-US/Events/Documents/EGTC_MonitoringReport_2013_Paper_pdf.pdf; Metis GmbH, 'EGTC Monitoring Report 2012' (2013) 3, available at https://portal.cor.europa.eu/egtc/en-US/discovertheegtc/Documents/Monitoring%20Report%202012/EGTC_Monitoring Report_2012.pdf. In the case of Belgium, one of the reasons why the adoption is still pending is the recent three-year long government crisis. Effectively, in these three countries, strong federalist structures have led to a situation where national provisions have been adopted by the regional bodies but federal law is still pending. Therefore, all Austrian and German Länder have adopted a legal framework for the EGTC while the federal authorities are expected to approve these provisions.
58. Regulation No. 1082/2006, cit. Article 3, § (1) and (2).
59. Regulation No. 1082/2006, cit. Article 3, § 1(d).
60. Directive 2014/24/EU, Article 39, § (5), This agreement "may either apply for an undetermined period, when fixed in the constitutive act of the joint entity, or may be

body of the joint legal entity may be established either for an undetermined period of time or for a determined period, as well as for certain types of contracts or for individual contracts (Directive 2014/24/EU, Article 39(5)).

For some countries, such as the UK, this solution would be particularly innovative, as it has never been used. Additionally, in different Member States, offices were settled in the context of the European programme aimed at providing assistance for European Territorial Cooperation, and therefore also for the constitution of EGTCs.[61]

The EGTC Regulation has recently undergone reform. The new Regulation on the EGTC, amending the former, provides an extension of the maximum period for approval of the EGTC – by the competent national authorities of prospective members – from three to six months. This extension is motivated by the fact that the present three-months period has been rarely respected and represents an obstacle to the establishment of new EGTCs.[62] The other novelty of the amended Regulation is that any EGTCs will be approved tacitly after 6 months in absence of objection (which has to be duly motivated) by the national authorities, provided that at least the Member State where

limited to a certain period of time, certain types of contracts or to one or more individual contract awards". Regulation No. 1082/2006, cit., Article 1 (3) and (4). The EGTC could act as a CPB and "the participating contracting authorities shall, by a decision of the competent body of the joint entity, agree on the applicable national procurement rules of one of the following Member States: (a) the national provisions of the Member State where the joint entity has its registered office; (b) the national provisions of the Member State where the joint entity is carrying out its activities".

61. Reference is made to the INTERACT Programme: http://www.interact-eu.net/.
62. Regulation (EU) No 1302/2013 of the European Parliament and of the Council of 17 December 2013 amending Regulation (EC) No 1082/2006 on a European grouping of territorial cooperation (EGTC) as regards the clarification, simplification and improvement of the establishment and functioning of such groupings, whereas 13: "Experience gained from establishing EGTCs shows that the three-month period for the Member States' approval procedure has rarely been respected. That period should therefore be extended to six months. On the other hand, in order to ensure legal certainty after that period, the convention should be deemed to be approved by tacit agreement, where applicable, in accordance with the national law of the Member States concerned, including their respective constitutional requirements. However, the Member State where the proposed registered office of the EGTC is to be located should have to formally approve the convention. While Member States should be able to apply national rules on the procedure for approval of a prospective member's participation in the EGTC or to create specific rules in the framework of the national rules implementing Regulation (EC) No 1082/2006, derogations to the provision concerning tacit agreement after the six-month period should be precluded, except as provided for in this Regulation."

the proposed EGTC's registered office would be located approves formally the convention.[63] Indeed, difficulties in getting the approval of the competent authorities in the Member States represent one of the main present obstacles to the establishment of new EGTCs.[64]

63. Regulation No. 1082/2006, Article 4 (3), 2nd-3rd sub-para.: "In the event of non-approval, the Member State shall state its reasons for withholding approval and shall, where appropriate, suggest the necessary amendments to the convention. The Member State shall reach its decision, with regard to approval, within a period of six months from the date of receipt of a notification in accordance with paragraph 2. If the Member State which has received the notification, does not raise an objection within that period, the participation of the prospective member and the convention shall be deemed to be approved. However, the Member State where the proposed registered office of the EGTC is to be located shall formally approve the convention in order to allow the EGTC to be established".
64. Metis GmbH, 'EGTC Monitoring Report 2012', cit., 102. Another present challenge concerns hiring staff to work in EGTCs. Effectively, almost all the established EGTCs faced procedural problems in this regard, and the main difficulty was overcoming the local bureaucratic obstacles to hiring staff from the EGTC's members to work in the structure. The legal situation of the staff of the EGTCs is clarified in the new regulation on the EGTC, where it is provided that the convention for the EGTC – and not the statute – will include provisions concerning the staff. Therefore, the members of an EGTC will be able to choose the applicable law to the recruitment and management of personnel. Regulation (EU) No 1302/2013, Recital 24: "The convention should, in addition to including a reference to the applicable law in general as laid down in Article 2 of Regulation (EC) No 1082/2006, also list the Union and national law applicable to the EGTC. In addition, it should be possible for that national law to be the law of the Member State where the organs of the EGTC exercise their powers, in particular in the case of staff that work under the responsibility of the director and are located in a Member State other than the Member State where the EGTCs has its registered office. The convention should also list the applicable Union and national law directly relevant to the EGTC's activities carried out under the tasks specified in the convention, including where the EGTC is managing public services of general interest or infrastructure."; Recital 26: "Given the importance of the rules applicable to staff of EGTCs and of the principles governing the arrangements concerning personnel management and recruitment procedures, the convention, not the statutes, should specify those rules and principles. It should be possible for different options as to the choice of rules applicable to staff of EGTCs to be laid down in the convention. The specific arrangements concerning personnel management and recruitment procedures should be addressed in the statutes"; Regulation No. 1082/2006, cit., Article Article 8 2 (k): "The convention shall specify the rules applicable to the EGTC's staff, as well as the principles governing the arrangements concerning personnel management and recruitment procedures".

The Regulation on the EGTC, even after its reform, does not deal with problems specifically related to joint cross-border procurement.[65] However, the new regulation on the EGTC states that such instrument may be used in the future for the "joint management of public services", with particular regard to services of general economic interest.[66] Overall, the EGTC might be the easiest and most innovative instrument in order to favour cooperation among Member States and central purchasing bodies in order to foster joint cross-border public procurement in the EU internal market.

6. Conclusions

The new Directive considers procurement as an instrument of economic policy and aims at enforcing public purchasing power. It does not only generally provide the possibility to perform joint procurement, but it offers specific models to be applied at national and European level. The introduction of new models of European joint procurement could foster cross-border participation and require to find the way to tackle the problem of the persisting differences among Member States' national procurement systems, as well as solutions to overcome legal, language barriers for the participation of economic operators and the subsequent correct performance all over Europe. New joint procurement strategies, through the use of electronic tools, especially by central purchasing bodies (CPBs), might change significantly the perspective of public procurement, overcoming the traditional individual award procedure. The dif-

65. Regulation (EU) No 1302/2013, Recital 25: "This Regulation should not cover problems linked to cross-border procurement encountered by EGTCs.".
66. Council of EU, 'Proposal for a Regulation of the European Parliament and of the Council amending Regulation (EC) No 1082/2006', Recital 8: "While Regulation (EC) No 1082/2006 allows for bodies established under private law to become members of an EGTC provided that they are considered as being bodies governed by public law as defined in Directive 2004/18/EC of the European Parliament and of the Council, it should be possible to use EGTCs in the future to jointly manage public services with a particular focus on services of general economic interest or on infrastructure. Other private or public law actors should also be able, therefore, to become members of an EGTC. Consequently, 'public undertakings' as defined in Directive 2004/17/EC of the European Parliament and of the Council, and undertakings entrusted with the operation of services of general economic interest, in fields such as education and training, medical care, social needs in relation to health care and long-term care, childcare, access to, and reintegration into, the labour market, social housing and the care and social inclusion of vulnerable groups, should be covered as well".

ferent models of framework agreements together with the possibility to define sets of different lots and of different conditions or to leave them to the second phase of competition permit the kinds of strategic sourcing which have otherwise been unknown in a single traditional award procedure. The analysis of the relevant market and of the different stakeholders' strategies could make efficiency become the primary goal and permit also to pursue innovation and sustainable procurement.

Overall, the abolition of barriers, especially on a cross-border basis, to co-operation between contracting authorities and to participation of economic operators in award procedures, would favour the adoption of common standards and requirements for formats as well as processes and messaging in procurement procedures conducted using electronic means of communication and evaluation . This policy can be carried out effectively by CPBs, considering the high amount of the value of the contracts that can involve a considerable number of undertakings. They could use the most innovative e-procurement platforms and assure translations, whenever the language can be a significant barrier to cross-border procurement. Equally, joint procurement presents an opportunity to introduce greater scrutiny within procurement systems, providing ways to apply more objectivity in selecting suppliers, supporting better governance and assuring the quality of the performance required.[67]

A professional complex organization, such as a CPB, might better resist the pressures of powerful lobbies on procuring entities and even on governments to act in their narrow interest. The high professionalism of such organizations, linked with transparency connected with the use of electronic tools and electronic archives, that allow comparison of prices, performances, quality, and customer satisfaction, might better counteract such pressures. Collaborative procurement has the potential to foster competition by crushing car-

67. Commission (EC) 'Evaluation of the 2004 Action Plan for Electronic Public Procurement Accompanying document to the Green Paper on expanding the use of e-Procurement in the EU' SEC(2010) 1214 final October 10, 2010, 7. G.M. Racca, 'Collaborative procurement and contract performance in the Italian healthcare sector': Illustration of a common problem in European procurement', above fn. 10.

tels and preventing abuse of dominant market positions[68] and foster efficiency and integrity in the procurement sector.[69]

Bibliography

G. L. Albano – L. Carpineti – F. Dini, L. Giamboni, F. Russo, G. Spagnolo, 'Riflessioni sull'impatto economico degli istituti innovativi del codice dei contratti pubblici relativi a lavori, servizi e forniture', in Quaderni CONSIP, 2007, IV, 13 et seq.;

S. Arrowsmith, 'Framework Purchasing and Qualification Lists under the European Procurement Directives' in P.P.L.R., 1999, 115-146 and 168-186;M. Burgi, 'In-house providing in Germany', in M. Comba and S. Treumer (eds.), The In-House Providing in European Law (Copenhagen, DJØF Publishing, 2010) 71-93;

J. Chard, G. Duhs, J. Houlden, (2008) 'Body beautiful or vile bodies? Central purchasing in the UK', in P.P.L.R., 2008, NA26;

J. Edler – L. Georghiou, 'Public procurement and innovation – resurrecting the demand side', in Research Policy, 2007, 36(7): 949-963;

G. I. Gordon – G. M. Racca, 'Integrity Challenges in the EU and U.S. Procurement Systems', Bruylant, in G. M. Racca – C. Yukins, Integrity and Efficiency in Sustainable Public Contracts, Bruylant, 2014, 117-145;

G. M. Racca, 'Professional Buying Organisations, Sustainability and Competition in Public Procurement Performance' proceeding at 4th International Public Procurement Conference, Seoul, August 26-28, 2010;

G. M. Racca, 'The role of IT solutions in the award and execution of public procurement below threshold and list B services: overcoming e-barriers' in D. Dragos – R. Caranta (eds.) Outside the EU Procurement Directives – inside the Treaty? (Copenhagen, DJØF, 2012) 373 et seq.;

G. M. Racca, 'Le modalità organizzative delle aziende sanitarie in relazione all'attività contrattuale e le prospettive di razionalizzazione degli acquisti connessi alla prestazione dei servizi sanitari pubblici', in A. Pioggia – M. Dugato – G. M. Racca – S. Civitarese Matteucci (eds.) Oltre l'aziendalizzazione del servizio sanitario (Milano, Franco Angeli, 2008) 264-297;

68. Commission EU, 'European code of best practices faciliting access by SMEs to public procurement contracts' SEC(2008) 2193, June 25, 2008.
69. G. M. Racca – C. R. Yukins (eds.) Integrity and Efficiency in Sustainable Public Contracts, (Bruylant, Bruxelles, 2014).

G. M. Racca, 'Collaborative procurement and contract performance in the Italian healthcare sector: Illustration of a common problem in European procurement', in P.P.L.R., 2010, 119 f.;

G. M. Racca, 'Aggregate Models of Public Procurement and Secondary Consideration: An Italian Perspective', in R. Caranta and M. Trybus (eds.), The law of green and social procurement in Europe (Copenhagen, DJØF, 2010) 165 f.;

G. M. Racca – R. Cavallo Perin, 'Organizzazioni sanitarie e contratti pubblici in Europa: modelli organizzativi per la qualità in un sistema di concorrenza', in A. Pioggia – S. Civitarese Matteucci – G. M. Racca – M. Dugato (eds.) I servizi sanitari: organizzazione, riforme e sostenibilità. Una prospettiva comparata, Santarcangelo di Romagna, 2011, 193;

G. M. Racca, 'The electronic award and execution of public procurement', in Ius Publicum Network Review, available at http://www.ius-publicum.com/repository/uploads/17_05_2013_19_31-Racca_IT_IUS-PUBLICUM-_EN.pdf;

S. Williams, T. Chambers, S. Hills, F. Dowson, 'Buying a better word: sustainable public procurement', 2008, available at http://www.forumforthefuture.org/projects/buying-a-better-world;

C. R. Yukins, 'Use and Regulation of Electronic Reverse Auctions in the United States', in S. Arrowsmith (ed.), Reform of the UNCITRAL model law on procurement: Procurement regulation for the 21st century, Danvers: Thomson Reuters/West;

C. R. Yukins, 'Are IDIQs Inefficient? Sharing Lessons with European Framework Contracting', in P.C.L.J., 2008, 545.

G. L. Albano – L. Carpineti – F. Dini, L. Giamboni, F. Russo, G. Spagnolo, 'Riflessioni sull'impatto economico degli istituti innovativi del codice dei contratti pubblici relativi a lavori, servizi e forniture', in Quaderni CONSIP, 2007, IV, 13 et seq.;

S. Arrowsmith, 'Framework Purchasing and Qualification Lists under the European Procurement Directives' in P.P.L.R., 1999, 115-146 and 168-186;M. Burgi, 'In-house providing in Germany', in M. Comba and S. Treumer (eds.), The In-House Providing in European Law (Copenhagen, DJØF Publishing, 2010) 71-93;

J. Chard, G. Duhs, J. Houlden, (2008) 'Body beautiful or vile bodies? Central purchasing in the UK', in P.P.L.R., 2008, NA26;

J. Edler – L. Georghiou, 'Public procurement and innovation – resurrecting the demand side', in Research Policy, 2007, 36(7): 949-963;

G. I. Gordon – G. M. Racca, 'Integrity Challenges in the EU and U.S. Procurement Systems', Bruylant, in G. M. Racca – C. Yukins, Integrity and Efficiency in Sustainable Public Contracts, Bruylant, 2014, forthcoming;

G. M. Racca, 'Professional Buying Organisations, Sustainability and Competition in Public Procurement Performance' proceeding at 4th International Public Procurement Conference, Seoul, August 26-28, 2010;

G. M. Racca, 'The role of IT solutions in the award and execution of public procurement below threshold and list B services: overcoming e-barriers' in D. Dragos – R. Caranta (eds.) Outside the EU Procurement Directives – inside the Treaty? (Copenhagen, DJØF, 2012) 373 et seq.;

G. M. Racca, 'Le modalità organizzative delle aziende sanitarie in relazione all'attività contrattuale e le prospettive di razionalizzazione degli acquisti connessi alla prestazione dei servizi sanitari pubblici', in A. Pioggia – M. Dugato – G. M. Racca – S. Civitarese Matteucci (eds.) Oltre l'aziendalizzazione del servizio sanitario (Milano, Franco Angeli, 2008) 264-297;

G. M. Racca, 'Collaborative procurement and contract performance in the Italian healthcare sector: Illustration of a common problem in European procurement', in P.P.L.R., 2010, 119 f.;

G. M. Racca, 'Aggregate Models of Public Procurement and Secondary Consideration: An Italian Perspective', in R. Caranta and M. Trybus (eds.), The law of green and social procurement in Europe (Copenhagen, DJØF, 2010) 165 f.;

G. M. Racca – R. Cavallo Perin, 'Organizzazioni sanitarie e contratti pubblici in Europa: modelli organizzativi per la qualità in un sistema di concorrenza', in A. Pioggia – S. Civitarese Matteucci – G. M. Racca – M. Dugato (eds.) I servizi sanitari: organizzazione, riforme e sostenibilità. Una prospettiva comparata, Santarcangelo di Romagna, 2011, 193;

G. M. Racca, 'The electronic award and execution of public procurement', in Ius Publicum Network Review, available at http://www.ius-publicum.com/repository/uploads/17_05_2013_19_31-Racca_IT_IUS-PUBLICUM-_EN.pdf;

S. Williams, T. Chambers, S. Hills, F. Dowson, 'Buying a better word: sustainable public procurement', 2008, available at http://www.forumforthefuture.org/projects/buying-a-better-world;

C. R. Yukins, 'Use and Regulation of Electronic Reverse Auctions in the United States', in S. Arrowsmith (ed.), Reform of the UNCITRAL model law on procurement: Procurement regulation for the 21st century, Danvers: Thomson Reuters/West;

C. R. Yukins, 'Are IDIQs Inefficient? Sharing Lessons with European Framework Contracting', in P.C.L.J., 2008, 545.

G. L. Albano – L. Carpineti – F. Dini, L. Giamboni, F. Russo, G. Spagnolo, 'Riflessioni sull'impatto economico degli istituti innovativi del codice dei contratti pubblici relativi a lavori, servizi e forniture', in Quaderni CONSIP, 2007, IV, 13 et seq.;

S. Arrowsmith, 'Framework Purchasing and Qualification Lists under the European Procurement Directives' in P.P.L.R., 1999, 115-146 and 168-186;M. Burgi, 'In-house providing in Germany', in M. Comba and S. Treumer (eds.), The In-House Providing in European Law (Copenhagen, DJØF Publishing, 2010) 71-93;

J. Chard, G. Duhs, J. Houlden, (2008) 'Body beautiful or vile bodies? Central purchasing in the UK', in P.P.L.R., 2008, NA26;

J. Edler – L. Georghiou, 'Public procurement and innovation – resurrecting the demand side', in Research Policy, 2007, 36(7): 949-963;

G. I. Gordon – G. M. Racca, 'Integrity Challenges in the EU and U.S. Procurement Systems', Bruylant, in G. M. Racca – C. Yukins, Integrity and Efficiency in Sustainable Public Contracts, Bruylant, 2014, forthcoming;

G. M. Racca, 'Professional Buying Organisations, Sustainability and Competition in Public Procurement Performance' proceeding at 4th International Public Procurement Conference, Seoul, August 26-28, 2010;

G. M. Racca, 'The role of IT solutions in the award and execution of public procurement below threshold and list B services: overcoming e-barriers' in D. Dragos – R. Caranta (eds.) Outside the EU Procurement Directives – inside the Treaty? (Copenhagen, DJØF, 2012) 373 et seq.;

G. M. Racca, 'Le modalità organizzative delle aziende sanitarie in relazione all'attività contrattuale e le prospettive di razionalizzazione degli acquisti connessi alla prestazione dei servizi sanitari pubblici', in A. Pioggia – M. Dugato – G. M. Racca – S. Civitarese Matteucci (eds.) Oltre l'aziendalizzazione del servizio sanitario (Milano, Franco Angeli, 2008) 264-297;

G. M. Racca, 'Collaborative procurement and contract performance in the Italian healthcare sector: Illustration of a common problem in European procurement', in P.P.L.R., 2010, 119 f.;

G. M. Racca, 'Aggregate Models of Public Procurement and Secondary Consideration: An Italian Perspective', in R. Caranta and M. Trybus (eds.), The law of green and social procurement in Europe (Copenhagen, DJØF, 2010) 165 f.;

G. M. Racca – R. Cavallo Perin, 'Organizzazioni sanitarie e contratti pubblici in Europa: modelli organizzativi per la qualità in un sistema di concorrenza', in A. Pioggia – S. Civitarese Matteucci – G. M. Racca – M. Dugato (eds.) I servizi sanitari: organizzazione, riforme e sostenibilità. Una prospettiva comparata, Santarcangelo di Romagna, 2011, 193;

G. M. Racca, 'The electronic award and execution of public procurement', in Ius Publicum Network Review, available at http://www.ius-publicum.com/repository/uploads/17_05_2013_19_31-Racca_IT_IUS-PUBLICUM-_EN.pdf;

S. Williams, T. Chambers, S. Hills, F. Dowson, 'Buying a better word: sustainable public procurement', 2008, available at http://www.forumforthefuture.org/projects/buying-a-better-world;

C. R. Yukins, 'Use and Regulation of Electronic Reverse Auctions in the United States', in S. Arrowsmith (ed.), Reform of the UNCITRAL model law on procurement: Procurement regulation for the 21st century, Danvers: Thomson Reuters/West;

C. R. Yukins, 'Are IDIQs Inefficient? Sharing Lessons with European Framework Contracting', in P.C.L.J., 2008, 545.

The Promotion of Small and Medium Sized Enterprises in Pulic Procucrement: A Strategic Objective of the New Public Sector Directive?

Martin Trybus

1. Introduction

The February 2014 Council Press Release,[1] issued when the eventual new Public Sector Directive 2014/24//EU was passed, highlights the promotion of Small and Medium-Sized Enterprises (SMEs)[2] as one of the five main points

* Thanks to Luke Butler (Bristol) for comments on an earlier draft of this chapter and François Lichère (Aix-en-Provence) for comments on a later draft, and to the participants of the EPPL meeting in Aix-en-Provence in July 2013 when the first version of this chapter was discussed, especially Pedro Telles (Bangor), Martin Burgi (Munich), and Mario Comba (Turin). Any mistakes, however, would be mine.

1. http://www.consilium.europa.eu/uedocs/cms_data/docs/pressdata/en/intm/140975.pdf [accessed March 2014]
2. The precise definition of an SME is not universally accepted and therefore varies in the Member States. The Commission defined SMEs as enterprises with up to 250 employees and an annual turnover of up to €50 million: Commission Recommendation 2003/361/EC of 6 May 2003 concerning the definition of micro, small and medium-sized enterprises [2003] OJ L-124/36. Annex 1, Article 2: "Staff headcount and financial ceilings determining enterprise categories
   1. The category of micro, small and medium-sized enterprises (SMEs) is made up of enterprises which employ fewer than 250 persons and which have an annual turnover not exceeding EUR 50 million, and/or an annual balance sheet total not exceeding EUR 43 million.

of the reform.[3] Thus SMEs are a separate issue in addition to 'strategic procurement' discussed in the previous Chapter by Dacian Dragos. Recital 124 of the new Directive emphasises the importance of SMEs for the Internal Market as well as the necessity to regulate any procurement measures in their favour at EU level.[4] Thus, while Directive 2004/18/EC provided very little to increase SME participation in procurement, the new Public Sector Directive 2014/24/EU allegedly contains four main 'innovations' directed at the promotion of SMEs: the division of contracts into lots, the European Single Procurement Document, the limitations of requirements for participation, and direct payments to subcontractors.[5] These new "appropriate provisions"[6] are contained in Articles 44, 58, 56, and 71 of Directive 2014/24/EU respectively.

There are aspects of SME promotion that explain why it is often classified as a secondary, horizontal or strategic objective. First, promoting SMEs

2. Within the SME category, a small enterprise is defined as an enterprise which employs fewer than 50 persons and whose annual turnover and/or annual balance sheet total does not exceed EUR 10 million.
3. Within the SME category, a microenterprise is defined as an enterprise which employs fewer than 10 persons and whose annual turnover and/or annual balance sheet total does not exceed EUR 2 million."

Article 83(3) Public Sector Directive 2014/24/EU now expressly provides: "For the purposes of this paragraph and paragraph 4 of this Article, 'SME' shall be understood as defined in Commission Recommendation 2003/361/EC, at 39."

3. Supra note 1: "Better access to the market for small companies – The package provides for concrete measures to remove barriers for market access by small and medium-sized enterprises (SMEs), such as simplification of documentation obligations in procurement procedures, the creation of a standardised document for selection purposes, an incitation for contracting authorities to consider the division of contracts into smaller lots that are more accessible for SMEs, and a reduction on requirements for participation."
4. Recital (124) to Directive 2014/24/EU: "Given the potential of SMEs for job creation, growth and innovation it is important to encourage their participation in public procurement, both through appropriate provisions in this Directive as well as through initiatives at the national level. The new provisions provided for in this Directive should contribute towards an improvement of the level of success, by which is understood the share of SMEs in the total value of contracts awarded. It is not appropriate to impose obligatory shares of success, however, the national initiatives to enhance SME participation should be closely monitored given its importance."
5. The 2011 Draft Directive identified four innovations in relation to SMEs: simplification of information obligations, division into lots, limitation of requirements for participation, and direct payments to subcontractors: COM (2011) 896 final (20th December 2011), Explanatory Memorandum, at 11.
6. Recital 124 Directive 2014/24/EU.

means promoting employment since SMEs create considerably more employment than large companies.[7] The promotion of employment clearly is a secondary or strategic objective in public procurement. Second, behind the promotion of SMEs there is often the intention to promote the local economy; smaller companies will often be local companies. Since 'local' normally means national, this implies a protectionist objective which cannot be reconciled with the objectives of the Internal Market and its procurement Directives. It is not least for this reason that the old Public Sector Directive 2004/18/EC did not contain many adjustments to favour SMEs and the Commission, while recognising the importance of SMEs for the European economy, initially followed a soft law rather than hard law approach when addressing the issue in its 2008 European Code of Best Practices Facilitating Access by SMEs to Public Procurement Contracts.[8] However, the protectionist aspect of the objective has to be put into perspective: not all SMEs can be seen as only local and therefore national operators. The division into lots discussed in section 2 below, for example, may well lead to, for example, Bavarian SMEs bidding for then smaller contracts in England's Midlands or in Provence.

This Chapter builds on, and continues, the previous Chapter by Dacian Dragos on secondary or horizontal objectives, now often called "strategic procurement", in the new Public Sector Directive 2014/24/EU. Social and environmental considerations are clearly to be classified as secondary and horizontal objectives and Dragos identified and discussed the relevant changes introduced by the new Directive. This Chapter will add to the discussion on secondary or horizontal objectives with an analysis of an objective and its accommodation in the new instrument which, for several reasons, is not universally accepted as a secondary or horizontal objective. The fact that, as mentioned above, the SME provisions are highlighted as a separate main point of the reform in addition to strategic procurement and the controversy of whether SME promotion in public procurement actually qualifies as a secondary objective at all justifies its discussion in a separate chapter. This Chapter on SMEs will be followed by a Chapter by Luke Butler on another 'controversial' secondary, horizontal, or strategic objective in the new Public Sector Directive: innovation. Thus this book provides a set of three chapters

7. According to Financing SMEs and Entrepreneurs 2012: An OECD Scoreboard (OECD Publishing: Paris, 2012), at 76, 91, and 119 respectively, 60.5% of the workforce in France, 80% of the workforce in Italy, and 72% of the workforce in Portugal are employed by SMEs.
8. SEC (2008) 2191, at 8.

on "secondary" or "horizontal" or "strategic" objectives in the new Directive in a broad sense.

This Chapter will discuss the four main 'new' regimes for the promotion of SMEs in the new Public Sector Directive 2014/24/EU: the division of contracts into lots (section 3. below), the European Single Procurement Document (section 4. below), the limitation of participation requirements (section 5. below), and direct payments to subcontractors (section 6. below). It will be argued that these 'regimes' are limited since they do not deviate significantly from what was possible under the previous Directives 2004/18/EC and 2004/17/EC. The new Directive 2014/24/EU also introduced a number of additional measures for SMEs which cannot be discussed here. These refer to large scale dynamic purchasing systems (Recital 66), time limits (Recital 80), design contests (Recital 120) and thresholds (Recital 134). Moreover, SME are mentioned for example in Recital 59 where the Commission calls for the monitoring of the aggregation of demand as a practice that has the potential to disadvantage SMEs. However, it is argued that the four regime discussed are the most important changes in relation to SMEs.

The Chapter will start with a section (2.) on the relevance of SMEs in the Internal Market, how their promotion interacts with other objectives of public procurement regulation and how this has been addressed in the old Directives. This will facilitate the understanding of the 'changes' introduced in the new Directive. The discussion will focus on the Public Sector Directive 2014/24/EU, although many of the issues raised will equally apply in the context of the new Utilities Directive 2014/25/EU.

2. SMEs in the Internal Market and the old Directives

There are differences in the economic importance and consequently the attitudes towards SMEs in the Member States. However, these differences only vary from 'important' to 'extremely important'. While the French economy, for example could be seen as dominated by large companies, the country also boasts 2.5 million SMEs.[9] Similarly, in Germany the likes of Volkswagen, Siemens, and Bosch are complemented by hundreds of thousands of compa-

9. That is 99.8% of all companies according to Financing SMEs and Entrepreneurs 2012: An OECD Scoreboard, supra note 7, at 76. According to François Lichère, when commenting on an earlier draft of this chapter, there has had a significant change of the number of public procurement contracts awarded to SMEs in France since a duty to divide contracts into lots has been introduced in 2006.

nies of the Mittelstand. In Italy 99.9 per cent of all enterprises are SME, with a particularly large proportion of very small or 'micro' companies.[10] The United Kingdom believes in an industrial revival through SMEs[11] and the small and medium-sized EU Member States have SME-based economies to match. For example, almost all of the 547,440 Hungarian companies and 99.7 per cent of all Portuguese enterprises are SMEs.[12] This economic importance has an impact on the discussion whether the promotion of SMEs is seen as a secondary or horizontal or strategic objective of public procurement regulation mentioned above. The Germans, for example, generally more reserved about secondary objectives, see SME promotion as a separate issue.[13] More SME participation in public contracts could increase competition through a wider supplier and provider base and thus have an effect on the objective of value for money. Moreover, since in contrast to large companies SMEs exist in all and especially also the smaller Member States, the participation of these companies has also an Internal Market dimension, furthering the free movement of goods and services in all Member States. Last but not least, SMEs create proportionately more employment than large companies (see above), provide economic stability even during an economic crisis, and are loyal to the regions in which they are situated.[14] For all these reasons, SMEs are not only close to the heart of politicians in many Member States but also to those of the EU, as shown inter alia by the references to SMEs in Articles 158(2)(b), 173(1) and 179(2) TFEU.

The main problems SMEs are facing most frequently in public and utilities procurement are the high financial and staff costs for participating in large contracts and connected to this challenge the administrative burden involved in producing the required documentation to prove financial and technical capability, demanding participation requirements for public contracts, and the

10. According to Financing SMEs and Entrepreneurs 2012: An OECD Scoreboard, ibid., at 91.
11. According to Financing SMEs and Entrepreneurs 2012: An OECD Scoreboard, ibid., at 153, 99.6% of all United Kingdom enterprises are SMEs.
12. According to Financing SMEs and Entrepreneurs 2012: An OECD Scoreboard, ibid., at 86 (Hungary) and 119 (Portugal).
13. See M. Burgi, "Secondary Considerations in Public Procurement in Germany", in Roberto Caranta and Martin Trybus (eds.), The Law of Green and Social Procurement in Europe (Djøf Publishing: Copenhagen, 2010) 105-142, at 136-138.
14. M. Burgi, "Small and medium-sized enterprises and procurement law – European legal framework and German experiences" (2007) 16 Public Procurement Law Review 284-294, at 285.

late payment of bills.[15] These are the conditions that would have to be addressed to increase SME participation in public procurement. These challenges also affect large companies. However, large companies have more staff to deal with the administrative burden of public procurement, can more easily meet financial participation conditions such as a minimum turnover requirement due to their size, and can wait longer for payments due to their larger resources and better access to private finance. A problem caused by any measures promoting SME participation in addition to the danger of protectionism highlighted above is that such measures will make the applicable procurement law more complicated and therefore less user-friendly and prone to violations and litigation.

Due to the positive effect of an increase in SME participation on competition and the Internal Market objectives discussed above, it is submitted that a provision introduced into the procurement Directives for the promotion of SMEs in public procurement constituted a regime favouring SMEs when the procurement rules were adjusted for that purpose to an extent that actually or potentially compromises the primary objectives of competition and value for money, of the contracting authority procuring what it needs to operate at the best possible terms.[16] More specifically with regards to the EU procurement Directives, a provision favouring SMEs would compromise their primary objectives which are non-discrimination (on grounds of nationality) and equal treatment.[17] A provision clearly favouring SMEs to an extent that the primary objectives are compromised would be, for example, provisions comparable to those of the US Small Businesses Act requiring a minimum number of SMEs to be selected in competitive procedures,[18] or procurement procedures limited

15. Ibid. Although a directive fighting late payment in general exists: Directive 2000/35/EC on combating late payment in commercial transactions [2000] OJ L-200/35 replaced by Directive 2011/7/EU on combating late payment in commercial transactions [2011] OJ L-48/1 (concerning late payment in general, not only for public procurement). Thanks to François Lichère for pointing this out to me when commenting on an earlier draft of this chapter.
16. See the differentiation between "SME-fair" and "SME-favouring" in Burgi, "Small and medium-sized enterprises and procurement law", supra note 14, at 287-288.
17. Thanks to Luke Butler for discussing this with me on the basis of an earlier version of this Chapter.
18. See also the judgment of the French Conseil d'Etat of 9 July 2007, n° 297711, ruling against a provision of the 2006 Code de Marchés Publics (public procurement code) allowing contracting authorities to select minimum number of SMEs at the bid stage: "Considérant qu'en autorisant les pouvoirs adjudicateurs, dans le cadre des procédures d'appel d'offres restreint, de marché négocié et de dialogue compétitif, à fixer un nombre minimal de petites et moyennes entreprises admises à présenter une offre, les

to SMEs comparable to the reserved contracts for sheltered workshops now regulated in Article 20 Directive 2014/24/EU.[19] Another example would be a margin of preference for SMEs at the contract award stage comparable to the "targeted procurement" in favour of previously disadvantaged businesses in post-Apartheid South Africa.[20] Competition would be limited by either excluding or disadvantaging large companies in favour of SMEs. Whether the new SME provisions of Public Sector Directive 2014/24/EU compromise the primary objectives to an extent that justifies their classification as regimes favouring SMEs is the issue to be discussed in this Chapter. If this was the case then the SME provisions of the new Directive would entail a seismic change from the previous competition and non-discrimination objectives of the 'old' Directives 2004/17/EC and 2004/18/EC and their predecessors.

The consultation conducted before the 2011 Draft Proposal had identified that, according to many stakeholders, better access of SMEs to public contracts was one of the issues of concern.[21] This should not only be achieved through the targeting of administrative burdens and costs of participation but also through changes to the EU legislative framework. This was supported by most stakeholders. The splitting of contracts into lots and caps on turnover were more controversial. Public authorities were generally sceptical whereas the private sector was divided over these issues.[22] The remainder of the Chapter will discuss the four regimes introduced in the new Directive to promote SME participation in public procurement to determine whether they constitute regimes favouring SMEs in the way explained above.

dispositions des articles 60, 65 et 67 du code des marchés publics, applicables respectivement aux trois procédures précitées, conduisent nécessairement à faire de la taille des entreprises un critère de sélection des candidatures ; qu'un tel critère qui n'est pas toujours lié à l'objet du marché revêt un caractère discriminatoire et méconnaît le principe d'égal accès à la commande publique […] ." Thanks to François Lichère for pointing this out to me when commenting on an earlier draft of this chapter.

19. And Article 38 Directive 2014/25/EU.
20. See Green Paper on Public Sector Procurement Reform in South Africa (Ministry of Finance and Ministry of Public Works: Pretoria, April 1997) and the Small Enterprises Development Agency SEDA http://www.seda.org.za/MYBUSINESS/ SEDA-BUILD/Pages/TargetedProcurement.aspx [accessed 23 June 2014].
21. European Commission "Working Paper, Green Paper on the Modernisation of EU Public Procurement Policy: Towards a More Efficient European Procurement Market, Synthesis of Replies http://ec.europa.eu/internal_market/consultations/docs/2011/public_procurement/synthesis_document_en.pdf [accessed in March 2014], at 14.
22. Ibid.

3. The division of larger contracts into lots

Public contracts can be very complex and of substantial size and value, requiring considerable financial capacity and technical expertise. Thus SMEs will often be excluded from public contracts simply because they lack the capacity to manage such a large contract in its entirety. A division of such large public contracts into smaller lots would extend the supplier and provider base to SMEs and at the same time increase competition. Article 9(5) Public Sector Directive 2004/18/EC and Article 17(6)(a) Utilities Directive 2004/17/EC already allowed the division of contracts into lots. However, the main concern of these provisions appears to have been the use of the division into lots with the intention to artificially push the contract value below the thresholds to avoid the application of the old procurement Directives. No other useful detail on lots was provided in either instrument. However, it is submitted that the provisions of the old Directives also allowed national laws to require the division into lots in addition to just allowing it, which is clearly backed by the wording of these provisions. The transposing laws in some Member States confirm this interpretation. For example, under French law, the division into lots has been mandatory under the Code des Marchés Publics 2006 (transposing Directives 2004/17/EC and 2004/18/EC) and German procurement law also provided for the division into lots.[23] Division into lots was also suggested by the 2008 Commission Staff Working Document European Code of Best Practices Facilitating Access by SMEs to Public Procurement Contracts which, however, also warned that this had to be "appropriate and feasible in the light of the respective works, supplies and services concerned."[24] This addresses an issue that needs to be balanced with the objective of facilitating SME access to public contracts: the effect of a division into lots on the costs, complexity and management of a public contract. These potential disadvantages are also reasons why, as already mentioned above, stakeholders were divided on the issue of division into lots during the consultation process for the new procurement Directives. Public authorities were in general quite sceptical about "coercive measures" whereas business' opinions were divided.[25]

Article 46(1) of the new Directive 2014/24/EU provides that contracting authorities may award contracts divided into separate lots while they are free

23. See Burgi, "Small and medium-sized enterprises and procurement law", supra note 14, at 288-289.
24. SEC (2008) 2191, at 8.
25. Green Paper, supra note 21, at 14.

to determine the size and subject-matter of such lots. In this case the division into lots would be optional. The division into lots is clearly intended as a technique to promote SME participation in public procurement as highlighted by Recital 78 of the new Directive:

> "[…] Such division could be done on a quantitative basis, making the size of the individual contracts better correspond to the capacity of SMEs, or on a qualitative basis, in accordance with the different trades and specialisations involved, to adapt the content of the individual contracts more closely to the specialised sectors of SMEs or in accordance with different subsequent project phases […]"

According to Article 46(4) Public Sector Directive 2014/24/EU, Member States may also require the division into separate lots in their national laws transposing the Directive. In this case division into lots would be mandatory. However, in cases in which division into lots has not been made obligatory by the implementing national law, contracting authorities shall indicate the main reasons for their decision not to subdivide into lots. This means that, while the default approach suggested by the Directive is the division into lots and Member States have the option to make this obligatory for all or parts of the contracts subject to the Directive and their transposing national laws, the new Directive does not require the division into lots, as the decision not to divide a contract into lots merely requires a communication of the reasons.

According to Article 46(2) Public Sector Directive 2014/24/EU, the contracting authorities may decide to allow the submission of "one, for several or for all of the lots" by the same tenderer. Article 46(3) of the new Directive allows combining bids from the same tenderer for multiple lots of the contract. To prohibit such multiple bids for the divided lots might not be in line with the very purpose of the division into lots, which is to increase SME participation by creating smaller and more manageable contract opportunities. In other words, what is the purpose of dividing a contract into lots when the bidder puts them back together again by bidding for more or all of the lots? However, this criticism does not take account of the fact that some bidders might still bid for only one lot and others only for a few rather than all lots. Moreover, preventing bidders from competing for more than one lot effectively restricts access to public contracts which is legally and economically problematic and contradicts the objective of the rules on the division into lots which is of promoting access for SMEs. However, in France, for example, contracting authorities are allowed to limit the number of lots awarded to a single contractor to foster competition.[26] The relevant French case law allows this limitation for both geographical divisions (if the lots have the same object) and material divisions (if the lots do not have the same object). If the different lots concern materially distinct supplies or services a limitation to the number of lots that a company can bid for appears more appropriate than in cases where the lots have the same object. In the interest of competition the French case law does not make this distinction.[27]

A related issue that is not clear from the text of the first subparagraph of the new Article 46(2) is whether in cases where multiple bids are allowed for contracts divided into lots, a tenderer may follow two parallel strategies: to bid for each or several of the lots with one price on the one hand and to bid for all the lots (or a combination of some but not all of the lots) with another price which is lower than the combined prices for the individual lots on the other hand. In other words, what is not clear is whether in the latter case Article 46(2) allows a bidder to offer a lower price for all or a combination of the lots in comparison to its combined price on the individual lots. For example, the possibility of such a rebate would contradict the current Article 10 of the French Code des Marchés Publics 2006 (based on Directive 2004/18/EC) which prohibits a rebate when multiple lots are awarded to the same bidder.[28] The reason for this prohibition is that such a rebate would favour large companies. That is quite a strong argument for the interpretation of a provision introduced to favour SMEs rather than large companies. Allowing the rebate could undermine the SME friendly objectives of the provision. However, this detail also illustrates the conflict between the primary objectives of notably value for money and the SME friendly approach of the new Article 46.[29] After all, a rebate is a lower price and not allowing it compromises value for money.

Article 46 of the 2014 Directive differs from Article 44 of the 2011 Draft Proposal which set a threshold of €500,000 for the division into lots. By

26. The French Conseil d-Etat in CE, 20 jan. 2013, Société laboratoires Biomnis, n° 363656. Thanks to François Lichère for pointing this out to me when commenting on an earlier draft of this chapter.
27. See the case note by François Lichère in e-competition of 20th January 2013 (on file).
28. Thanks to François Lichère for pointing this out to me when commenting on an earlier draft of this chapter.
29. There is Case law from the French Conseil d-Etat considering that division of a contract into lots would increase the costs of the contract: CE, Oct 27th 2011, Dépt des Bouches-du-Rhône, n° 350935.

abandoning that higher threshold of the 2011 Draft, the final text of Article 46 Directive 2014/24/EC extended the rules to its entire scope.

It is submitted that the only innovation introduced by Article 46 of the new Directive in contrast to the old regime under Article 9(5) Public Sector Directive 2004/18/EC[30] is the voluntary division of larger contracts into lots as the default approach. The default nature of the division into lots is introduced by the obligation to communicate the reasons for not doing so. As under the old Directive 2004/18/EC,[31] Member States may legally require the division into lots but the new Directive 2014/24/EU does not impose this as the only approach. It is submitted that as the new Directive does not require the division into lots, it would be difficult to challenge the decision of a contracting authority not to do so on the basis that the communicated reasons do not really justify to award the contract as a whole. However, Member States may legally require the division into lots as the default approach in their transposing legislation according to Article 46(4) Public Sector Directive 2014/24/EU. Moreover, it is submitted that they may then allow the award as a single contract in exceptional circumstances, require the communication of the reasons for doing so and allow challenging the decision not to divide into lots in national review bodies. The new Directive neither requires nor prohibits this. Considerable room for manoeuvre is therefore left to the national legislators and they should be aware of their legislative discretion. The new Directive allows for both a relatively light touch on the one hand and also rather strict regimes on the division into lots on the other hand. If a strict regime is chosen for the national transposition, possibly only continuing an already existing national tradition as for example in France, then litigation challenging deviations from a division into lots can be expected.[32] The regime on the division into lots is therefore an important instrument to promote SMEs. At least in theory this could lead to different regimes on the division into lots and, provided this instrument is as useful for its purpose as the Commission claims, to different levels of SME participation in public procurement.

While, as explained above, the only change introduced by the new Directive is the default nature of the division into lots, this could still be a significant innovation. The obligation to provide reasons for awarding a single

30. And Article 17 (6) (a) Utilities Directive 2004/17/EC.
31. And Directive 2004/18/EC.
32. See the tight judicial control of the decision not to divide into lots in French law: CE, Aug. 11th 2009, Cté urbaine de Nantes Métropole, n° 319949. In contrast judicial review of the number and composition of the lots is only limited: CE, May 21st 2010, Cne d'Ajaccio, n° 333737. See case note by Lichère, supra note 27.

contract forces contracting officers to pause to consider the possibility of a division into lots. They either have to divide the contract into lots or communicate reasons for not doing so. The number of single contract awards and the communicated reasons for not dividing them into lots will be in the public domain. This will make is possible for the Commission and national legislators to review the approach of Article 46 of the new Directive, to see whether the division in lots is seriously considered or whether the use of 'cut and paste' standard reasons to explain the award of a single contract suggests that there is an almost automated avoidance of the approach. The use in practice will determine whether Directive 2014/24/EU did really introduce the division into lots as a default approach. Thus the impact of the 'new' regime on the division of larger contracts into lots will not only depend on the precise transposition of Article 46 Public Sector Directive 2014/24/EU in the Member States on the background of considerable flexibility allowed in the new Directive, but also on how the potentially differing national regimes will be used by contracting authorities in practice. This will have to be evaluated after full transposition in all Member States and a couple of years of procurement practice based on the new national procurement laws. At time of writing in June 2014, a bit more than two months after the entering into force of Directive 2014/24/EU, it is clearly too early to make that assessment.

It is submitted that the division into lots regime in Article 46 of the new Directive is not a provision favouring SMEs in a way that compromises the primary objectives of procurement and the Internal Market. While the division into lots is the default approach and can cause additional costs and the complication of a procurement procedure, it is relatively easy to derogate from the obligation.

4. The European Single Procurement Document

Specific obstacles for SME participation repeatedly highlighted are the administrative burdens and costs of participation, particularly with regards to documentation for the qualification of candidates (evidence for selection criteria). Hence, during the consultation process, a vast majority of stakeholders argued that SMEs would benefit from the reduction of administrative burden related to the choice of bidders.[33] Stakeholders advocated in particular the use of self-declarations and the introduction of a rule according to which original

33. Green Paper, supra note 21, at 6, 14 and 15.

certificates may only be required from the winning bidder.[34] The basic problem with the reduction of administrative burden in this context is of course that this can be taken too far. After all, this documentation for the qualification of tenderers is collected for a good reason: to protect the contracting authority and ultimately the taxpayer from unreliable, incompetent and incapable economic operators and the negative consequences for the procurement procedures and the completion of the eventual contract that the selection of such companies can have. A certain level of administrative burden is justified to avoid additional costs, the waste of time and effort in dealing with unqualified bidders, and the delay or worse of the completion of the contract. Thus there needs to be a balance between the administrative burden involved in proving qualification on the one hand and the protection of contracting authorities from unqualified bidders on the other hand. The results of the consultation process suggest that, in the opinion of the participating stakeholders, this balance had not been achieved in Directive 2004/18/EC – that the administrative burden is too heavy and needs to be reduced.

To reduce the administrative burden with regards to qualification, Article 59 of the new Public Sector Directive 2014/24/EU provides for a "European Single Procurement Document (ESPD)". The ESPD is an "updated self-declaration" consisting of a formal statement to be accepted by contracting authorities as "preliminary evidence" for the fulfilment of a number of conditions in lieu of official or third party certificates at the time of the submission of tenders or requests to participate.[35] In this regard, the document evidences that the economic operator fulfils conditions relating to the exclusion grounds (Article 57 Directive 2014/24/EU), the selection criteria (Article 58 Directive 2014/24/EU); objective rules, and criteria (Article 65 Directive 2014/24/EU) including information relating to the capacity of other entities (Article 63 Directive 2014/24/EU). The Commission will establish the exclusively electronic standard form which will be the basis of the ESPD.[36]

Recital 84 of the new Public Sector Directive 2014/24/EU explains that the objective of the ESPD is not to remove but to "limit[…] a major obstacle to […] participation in public procurement" consisting "in administrative burdens deriving from the need to produce a substantial number of certificates or other documents related to exclusion and selection criteria." The ESPD "could result in considerable simplification for the benefit of both contracting authorities and economic operators." The reference to "economic op-

34. Ibid., at 14.
35. Article 59(1) Public Sector Directive 2014/24/EU.
36. Article 59(2) Public Sector Directive 2014/24/EU.

erators, and not least SMEs" in this Recital shows that the ESPD is not strictly an instrument promoting SME participation in public procurement, but also achieving simplification for larger companies as well. Nevertheless, as outlined above in section 2, the administrative burden created by the documentation addressed by the introduction of the ESPD requirements is heavier for SMEs who have fewer staff and other resources to meet these requirements. It should be pointed out that the ESPD goes beyond what existed before in some Member States. In France, for example, self-declaration was allowed since the Code de Marchés Publics 2006 but only with regard to exclusion grounds, not with regard to capacity requirements.[37] The new Directive therefore constitutes a step forward for the procurement laws of many Member States.

However, deviating from the use of the ESPD as the default approach, contracting authorities may ask tenderers to submit all or part of the supporting documents if this is considered necessary. According to Recital 84 of Directive 2014/24/EU "[t]his might in particular be the case in two-stage procedures", which are the restricted procedure,[38] the competitive procedure with negotiation (formerly negotiated procedure with prior publication of a contract notice),[39] the competitive dialogue[40] and the new innovation partnership,[41] the latter discussed in more detail in the Chapter by Butler and Telles. In all these procedures, the contracting authority may limit the number of candidates invited to submit a tender. Thus the submission of documentation when candidates are selected to be invited can be necessary to avoid the selection of candidates unable to submit the supporting documents before the award. This would deprive other qualified candidates of participation. It should be highlighted that the list of Recital 84 does not feature the open procedure. However, the words "in particular" suggest that even in open procedures contracting authorities may resort to requiring parts or all of the supporting documents.

Moreover, subject to certain exceptions, the successful tenderer has "to submit up-to-date supporting documents" and "to supplement or clarify the certificates received pursuant to Articles 60 and 62" before the contract is

37. Thanks to François Lichère for pointing this out to me when commenting on an earlier draft of this chapter.
38. Article 28 Public Sector Directive 2014/24/EU.
39. Article 29 Public Sector Directive 2014/24/EU.
40. Article 30 Public Sector Directive 2014/24/EU.
41. Article 31 Public Sector Directive 2014/24/EU.

awarded.[42] Thus the ESPD does not remove the requirement for full documentation for the successful tenderer. Full documentation needs to be provided before the contract is concluded or made. This is also clarified in Recital 84.[43] The provision of full documentation will not be required if it can be obtained "directly by accessing a national database in any Member State that is available free of charge, such as a national procurement register, a virtual company dossier, an electronic document storage system or a prequalification system" or if the contracting authority "already possesses these documents." In this context, Member States have an obligation to ensure that such databases may also be consulted by contracting authorities of other Member States. Member States have to "make available and up-to-date in e-Certis a complete list of these databases and "communicate to other Member States any information related" to such databases upon request. The Commission's e-Certis is an "on-line source of information to help companies and contracting authorities to cope with the different forms of documentary evidence required for cross-border tenders for public contracts."[44] It is free of charge.[45]

Finally, the new ESPD coexists in the new Directive with the 'traditional' means of proof in Article 60 Public Sector Directive 2014/24/EU, the "Online repository of certificates (e-Certis)" in Article 61 Public Sector Directive 2014/24/EU, "Quality assurance standards and environmental management standards" in Article 62 Public Sector Directive 2014/24/EU, and "Reliance on the capacities of other entities" in Article 63 Public Sector Directive 2014/24/EU. These "traditional means" are more in line with the rules of the previous Directives 2004/17/EC and 2004/18/EC.

42. Article 59(4) Public Sector Directive 2014/24/EU.
43. Recital 84: "The tenderer to which it has been decided to award the contract should, however, be required to provide the relevant evidence and contracting authorities should not conclude contracts with tenderers unable to do so."
44. European Commission, e-Certis End-user Guide, 29th June 2010, Version V1.0, at: http://ec.europa.eu/internal_market/publicprocurement/docs/eprocurement/e-certis/userguide_en.pdf [accessed 9 May 2014], at 3.
45. Ibid.: "e-CERTIS presents the different certificates frequently requested in procurement procedures across the EU. Currently, the documents required differ from one country to another. e-CERTIS help tenderers and contracting authorities to find their way through this maze. In particular, e-CERTIS can help: companies to find out which certificates issued in their country they need to include in tender files submitted to an authority in any partner country; contracting authorities to establish which documents issued by a partner country are equivalent to the certificates which they require to confirm the eligibility of the tender."

It appears that the ESPD is a rather late addition to the new Directive, which did not feature in previous drafts of the instrument. Recital 32 and Article 57 of the initial 2011 Draft[46] referred to "self-declarations and other means of proof" which were to be accepted by contracting authorities as preliminary evidence. All the other details of what is Article 59 in the final Directive are comparable. However, Article 59 of the 2011 Draft did provide for a "European Procurement Passport" which shares similarities with the ESPD as a single simplifying document designed to alleviate administrative burden. However, according to Article 59 of the 2011 Draft, the 'Passport' was to be "recognised by all contracting authorities as proofs of fulfilment of the conditions for participation covered by it" and, most importantly, "shall not be questioned without justification". This suggests that the European Procurement Passport, which was regulated in a separate article in addition to Article 57 of the 2011 Draft on self-declarations, was made of stronger paper than the ESPD. It is a crucial feature of the 'documentation regime' of the new Public Sector Directive 2014/24/EU that, while it introduces the ESPD as a default approach, it also allows contracting authorities to resort to requiring full documentation with relative ease. While the ESPD rescued some of the simplifying characteristics of the earlier 'Passport', the former is mainly a replacement for self-declarations and is consequently not called a 'passport'. The expression 'passport' suggests a document that normally has to be accepted. While the 'Passport' and self-declarations are closely connected, a fact highlighted by their introduction in the Explanatory Memorandum to the 2011 Draft,[47] the characterisation of the earlier as an instrument of "further clarification" in Recital 32 of the 2011 Draft suggests an additional and therefore separate instrument. This is also supported by the fact that the European Procurement Passport disappeared from the 2012 and 2013 drafts of the new Directive.

It was highlighted above that there needs to be a balance between the administrative burden involved in proving qualification on the one hand and the protection of contracting authorities from unqualified bidders on the other hand. Stakeholders argued that this balance had not been achieved in Directive 2004/18/EC, that the administrative burden was too heavy and needed to be reduced. It is argued here that the precise calibration of this balance under the new Public Sector Directive 2014/24/EU will depend on procurement practice after full transposition in all Member States. This is because, alt-

46. COM (2011) 896 final, supra note 5.
47. Ibid., at 11.

hough the use of the new ESPD is the default approach suggested by the new Directive, it does not require the use of the 'Document'. In other words, the use of the ESPD is normally required as Article 59 states that "contracting authorities shall accept the [ESPD]" – but contracting authorities may easily resort to requiring full documentation, as provided in Article 59(4).[48] Member States have discretion to make 'deviation' from the ESPD more difficult. Thus differences in transposition and practice will lead to differences in the precise calibration of the balance, which is therefore quite unpredictable at time of writing in June 2014, a little less than two months after Directive 2014/24/EU entered into force. To the best knowledge of the author no drafts of procurement laws transposing Directive 2014/24/EU are available yet. However, what can already be said on the basis of the text of the new Directive is that on the one hand with the ESPD the legislator has introduced an instrument intended and potentially capable to relieve some of the administrative burden, while on the other hand it has not tipped the balance dramatically away from the weight on the protection of contracting authorities from unreliable or incompetent tenderers. After all, it is not too difficult to resort to requiring full documentation, the ESPD is lighter than the European Procurement Passport, and most of the traditional documentation regime coexists alongside the ESPD in the Directive. While the very existence of the ESPD in the legislation will put pressure on contracting authorities to use it, it might be difficult to enforce this in review procedures when a contracting authority resorted to ask for parts or all of the documentation. Many but not all SMEs in many but not all Member States might be disappointed at the effect of the new 'ESPD regime' on the administrative burden they have to bear in procurement procedures. It is very early to talk about the next Public Sector Directive, but both the abandoned European Procurement Passport and making it more difficult to resort to full documentation might be back on the agenda soon.

48. Article 59(4) Directive 20014/24/EU reads: "4. A contracting authority may ask tenderers and candidates at any moment during the procedure to submit all or part of the supporting documents where this is necessary to ensure the proper conduct of the procedure".

5. Limitations on requirements for participation: especially minimum turnover

Limitations on requirements for participation have been introduced in the new Public Sector Directive to avoid "unjustified barriers" to the participation of SMEs in public contracts.[49] Article 58 Directive 2014/24/EU contains an exhaustive list of possible conditions for participation in procurement procedures, which are largely the same as in the old Directive 2004/18/EC: suitability to pursue the professional activity, economic and financial standing, and technical and professional ability. Moreover, the provision states explicitly that any such conditions must be restricted:

> "[…] to those that are appropriate to ensure that a candidate or tenderer has the [...] capacities and [...] abilities to perform the contract to be awarded."

According to the Commission, turnover requirements, a crucial element of economic and financial standing, are often "a formidable obstacle to access by SME[s]."[50] Therefore Article 58(3) of the new Public Sector Directive 2014/24/EU limits turnover requirements to now two times the estimated contract value.[51] There was no such limit in Article 47 of the old Public Sector Directive 2004/18/EC. Moreover, even the 2011 Draft for the new Directive had a higher limit at "three times the estimated contract value."[52] A minimum turnover requirement serves the interest of contracting authorities in ensuring the financial standing of bidders. In the understanding of the legislator turnover requirements are often set too high putting too much weight on the interests of the contracting authorities to the disadvantage of SME participation. The very introduction of a limit on turnover requirements shifts the balance away from the perfectly viable interest of the contracting authorities and puts more weight on the interests of SMEs in participating in public pro-

49. See Recital 83 Directive 2014/24/EU: "Overly demanding requirements concerning economic and financial capacity frequently constitute an unjustified obstacle to the involvement of SMEs in public procurement. Any such requirements should be related and proportionate to the subject-matter of the contract."
50. COM (2011) 896 final, supra note 5, at 11.
51. Article 58 (3) subparagraph 3 Directive 2014/24/EU: "Where a contract is divided into lots this Article shall apply in relation to each individual lot. However, the contracting authority may set the minimum yearly turnover that economic operators are required to have by reference to groups of lots in the event that the successful tenderer is awarded several lots to be executed at the same time."
52. COM (2011) 896 final, supra note 5, at 11.

curement. Based on the consultation process, the input of their advisory committees and their general expertise the Commission proposed a turnover limit and set it at three times the estimated contract value. The legislative process led to this limit to be lowered to twice the estimated contract value in the Council and the European Parliament. Thus the legislative process shifted the balance a bit more from the interests of the contracting authorities to the interests of SMEs. Under Directive 2004/18/EC Member States could introduce such turnover limits to facilitate the participation of SMEs in much the same way as the new Directive. However, after the transposition of Directive 2014/24/EU SMEs can be sure that a default turnover requirement of twice the estimated contract value is in place across the EU.

There are contracts for which the relatively low turnover limit of twice the estimated contract value is too low. Therefore, the limit on turnover requirements is subject to an exception "in duly justified cases" according to Article 58(3) subparagraph 2 Directive 2014/24/EU. The notion "duly justified cases" is clarified to an extent as "such as relating to the special risks attached to the nature of the works, services or supplies." However, no further explanation is provided, which might prove problematic since at least some contracting authorities might be aiming for more security than twice the turnover and the "duly justified cases" are an exception which like all exceptions has the potential to develop into a loophole if not clearly and narrowly defined and controlled. There are control mechanisms in place since "[t]he contracting authority shall indicate the main reasons for such a requirement in the procurement documents or the individual report referred to in Article 84." This requires contracting authorities who wish to go beyond the default rate of twice the annual turnover to pause and consider a higher turnover requirement and document the decision and the reasons for it, to justify the decision to an extent. This control mechanism could also facilitate the review of the decision to go beyond the twice the turnover limit in the context of procurement review proceedings. It is submitted that the exception of "duly justified cases" is to be interpreted narrowly. Firstly, because all exceptions are to be interpreted narrowly since if they become the norm rather than the exception in practice they defy the SME-friendly purpose of the provision. In the interest of protecting contracting authorities from financially unreliable bidders, higher turnover requirements were possible under the old Directive 2004/18/EC and even envisaged in the 2011 Draft for the new Directive. Again, the legislator has shifted the balance (slightly) away from this perfectly viable interest of the contracting authorities and put more weight on the interests of SMEs in participating in public procurement. This shift is the clear intention of the legislator. A wide interpretation of the exception would contradict that intention.

Secondly, the addition of the word "duly" to "justified cases" emphasises the exceptional character of the exception in its wording, "duly justified cases" implies a narrower concept than just "justified cases". Finally, the control mechanism with its documentation requirement facilitating the review of the decision to deviate from the maximum turnover requirement implies a threat not to abuse the exception.

The twice the estimated contract value limit on annual turnover, however, flexible, represents a change from Article 47 of the old Public Sector Directive 2004/18/EC on economic and financial standing which did not provide for such a limit and the 2011 Draft in which this was limited to three times the estimated contract value. During the consultation stakeholders were divided. Public authorities were sceptical whereas bidders were divided.[53] It is submitted that the turnover limit in in Article 58 of the new Directive is not a provision favouring SMEs in a way that compromises the primary objectives of procurement and the Internal Market. Large companies also benefit from the limit, it represents only a small shift away from the current approach, exceptions are possible, and the provision does not lead to additional costs or complication of procurement procedures.

6. Subcontracting: direct payments

There are many SME which are perfectly capable to act as prime contractors and have been awarded and successfully performed public works, supplies, and services contracts. However, due to their limited size and technical and financial capacity many SMEs will be subcontractors in, at times, very long supply chains of large companies acting as prime contractors. Thus there is a close connection between procurement rules favouring SMEs and procurement rules regulating subcontracting and the supply chain. Article 25 Directive 2004/18/EC was very short on this matter by only requiring:

> "In the contract documents, the contracting authority may ask or may be required by a Member State to ask the tenderer to indicate in his tender any share of the contract he may intend to subcontract to third parties and any proposed subcontractors."

53. Green Paper, supra note 21, at 14.

This information requirement is only complemented by a reference to prime contractor liability.[54] These rules are also included in Article 71(2) and (4) of the new Public Sector Directive.[55] However, the 2011 Draft Proposal had added the following provision which is now contained in Article 71(3) of the Directive 2014/24/EU:[56]

> "Member States may provide that at the request of the subcontractor and where the nature of the contract so allows, the contracting authority shall transfer due payments directly to the subcontractor for services, supplies or works provided to the economic operator to whom the public contract has been awarded (the main contractor). Such measures may include appropriate mechanisms permitting the main contractor to object to undue payments. The arrangements concerning that mode of payment shall be set out in the procurement documents [emphasis added]."

Thus Member States can provide in their transposing laws that subcontractors are paid directly by the contracting authority rather than having to wait for payments from the prime contractor. This offers subcontractors, which are often SMEs, an efficient way of protecting their interest in being paid. However, not all subcontractors are SMEs and therefore this provision might equally benefit large companies when acting as subcontractors. Nevertheless, inter alia the Explanatory Memorandum to the 2011 Draft of the new Directive clearly identifies this as one of four main measures to promote SME participation in public procurement.[57] It is submitted that this classification is appropriate because of the strong presence of SMEs in supply chains.

The July 2013 Draft and final text changed the wording of the 2011 Draft slightly as procedures permitting prime contractors to object to undue payments now only may be included, whereas in the 2011 Draft they had to be put in place. According to Article 71(7) of the new Directive 2014/24/EU Member States may "go further under national law on direct payments to subcontractors"; this can include a requirement for direct payments to subcontractors without them having to request them. Moreover, according to Article 71(8) of the new Public Sector Directive Member States having chosen to provide for measures pursuant to inter alia Article 71(3) must specify the implementing conditions for those measures. Member States may limit the applicability of these implementing measures, "for instance in respect of cer-

54. Article 25 subparagraph 2 Directive 2004/18/EC reads: "This indication shall be without prejudice to the question of the principal economic operator's liability."
55. Article 71(1) and (3) of the Draft Proposal 2011, COM (2011) 896 final, supra note 5.
56. Article 71(2) of the Draft Proposal 2011, COM (2011) 896 final, ibid.
57. COM (2011) 896 final, supra note 5, at 11.

tain types of contracts, certain categories of contacting authorities or economic operators or as of certain amounts." However, the general direct payment rule in Article 71(3) Directive 2014/24/EU, the possibility to go further in Article 71(7) Directive 2014/24/EU on the one hand, and the possibility to limit the applicability of the rule on the other hand are options – Member States do not have to implement the direct payment regime of the Directive at all, they can limit it and extend it. Thus the national legislators have a considerable margin of manoeuvre when transposing the direct payments to subcontractors-regime of the new Directive. Consequently, as with some of the other regimes discussed above, the impact of this regime will first of all depend on the transposition in the Member States. Of course there are a number of Member States such as Italy or France, were a requirement of direct payments to subcontractors has been in place for some time, in the case of the latter since 1975.[58] However, there is a potential that many of the other Member States will not transpose paragraph 3, many will make use of paragraph 8 and even more will ignore paragraph 7. This alone may lead to at least three main different types of direct payment regime: no paragraph 3, only paragraph 3 and paragraph 7, let alone variations due to the use of paragraph 8. Moreover, according to Article 71(3) Directive 2014/24/EU, direct payments should only be provided "where the nature of the contract so allows." It appears that this is subject to the judgment of the contracting authority and the impact of this reservation will depend on factors such as the extent to which this discretion is regulated or generally the criteria that should guide this assessment. There is no guidance for this assessment provided in Directive 2014/24/EU. Moreover, this will depend on whether the judgment of the contracting authority can be challenged, especially in review proceedings. Overall, depending on national transposition, there is potential for many different 'direct payment to subcontractor regimes' and the end result may well be a lack or only limited harmonisation of this issue.

The direct payment rule had been the only innovation to the subcontracting regime in the 2011 Draft Proposal. In the July 2013 Draft and the final 2014 Directive, Article 71 was significantly extended. However, it needs to be emphasised that the remainder of this subcontracting regime of the new Directive in its Article 71 (1)-(2), (4)-(6) and most of (8) does not promote the access of SMEs to public contracts as such. These paragraphs regulate issues such as ensuring that the social and environmental requirements applica-

58. Thanks to François Lichère for pointing this out to me when commenting on an earlier draft of this chapter.

ble to prime contractors are also fulfilled by subcontractors, information requirements for prime contractors on their subcontractors, liability rules, and the qualification and exclusion of subcontractors. Therefore the SME friendly direct payment rule is simply part of a more detailed subcontracting regime in the new Directive. Only the optional information requirement on subcontractors in Article 71(2) and the related liability rule in Article 71(4) Directive 2014/24/EU had already been contained in Article 25 Directive 2004/18/EC.

With regards to the promotion of SMEs through their access to public contracts by regulating subcontracting, the regime of Article 71 of the new Directive cannot be compared to that of Article 21 and Title III of the Defence and Security Procurement Directive 2009/81/EC, the latest procurement instrument before the current reform package. Directive 2009/81/EC contains four different options for subcontracting, including options involving the award of subcontracts through notice in the OJ. However, the subcontracting regime in Directive 2009/81/EC is intended as a substitute for the now almost banned defence-specific practice of offsets,[59] a context not applicable to 'civil' public sector procurement. Moreover, the extensive subcontracting regime of the Defence and Security Directive 2009/81/EC might be of limited benefit in the context of Directives 2014/24/EU and 2014/25/EU and even Directive 2009/81/EC itself, an issue that cannot be explored further in this chapter. Nevertheless, the extensive subcontracting regime of Directive 2009/81/EC shows how far the EU legislator is prepared to go. In comparison they did not go very far in the new Public Sector Directive.

During the consultation process, a majority of public authorities and civil society organisations favoured allowing public procurers to have more influence on subcontracting by the successful tenderer, while the other stakeholder groups rejected such a possibility.[60] "Other stakeholders" will mainly refer to prime contractors and their opposition is understandable since a more detailed regulation of their subcontracting interferes with their freedom of contract. However, as concrete instruments, those respondents in favour of more regulation proposed, for instance, a right to exclude individual subcontractors or the possibility to limit subcontracting to a certain share of the contract or to require that the contractor executes essential parts of the contract himself. In particular, civil society organisations placed great importance on the issue of

59. See Martin Trybus, Buying Defence and Security in Europe: The EU Defence and Security Procurement Directive in Context (CUP, 2014) forthcoming, Chapter 9.
60. Green Paper, supra note 21, at 13. According to a figure at 5 39% or stakeholders wanted more control of subcontracting and this is also mentioned under "other issues" at 18.

subcontracting. They insisted that contracting authorities must be able to enforce compliance with social requirements and labour laws not only at the level of the main contractor but also against subcontractors.[61]

However, a subcontracting regime and even a direct payment regime are also problematic. First, the enforcement of social requirements and labour laws against prime contractors – let alone subcontractors – might be more than contracting authorities can realistically deliver. The civil society organisations in favour of more regulation somewhat disregard the limited time and funds available to effectively enforce these standards. Other parts of the government might be better placed to ensure compliance with regards to both prime contractors and subcontractors, not least because they have the required resources, expertise and experience. Secondly, a subcontracting regime and even direct payments represent interference in what in many Member States such as Germany or the United Kingdom is a private law contract without a legal base for such interference. On the other hand it could also be argued that the approach of a direct payment requirement is too soft – how is this requirement to be enforced if it is disregarded by prime contractors? In Italy, for example, prime contractors have to show that they have paid their subcontractors before being paid by the contracting authority themselves,[62] a regime with teeth. Overall, however, the margin of manoeuver left to the Member when transposing the direct payment rule and the limited subcontracting regime of Directive 2014/24/EU and the flexibility given to contracting authorities discussed above, make this rule and regime merely an option which might not lead to much more harmonisation of the issue in the EU. Overall it is argued that the direct payment rule does not represent a measure compromising the primary objectives of inter alia value for money to favour SMEs.

7. Conclusions

It is submitted that the above innovations of the new Directive, based on the division into lots, the European Single Procurement Document, the limitation of participation requirements, and direct payments to subcontractors are adequate approaches to promote SMEs without significantly compromising the primary objectives of the Directive. It is argued that these measures cannot be

61. Green Paper, ibid., at 13.
62. Thanks to Mario Comba for pointing this out to me during the EPPL network meeting in Aix-en-Provence in July 2013 when a paper leading to this chapter was discussed.

considered as favouring SMEs in a manner that can be classified as promoting secondary or horizontal or strategic objectives. The provisions provide tools to balance the disadvantages of and create equal chances for SMEs. This promotes competition and equal treatment and creates an Internal Market for SMEs. The 'new' SME-friendly provisions of Directive 2014/24/EU are therefore not promoting secondary objectives but the primary objectives of EU procurement law and policy.

Moreover, the discussed measures are limited and with exception of Article 71(2) Directive 2014/24/EU directed at SMEs as prime contractors. SMEs do want to be prime contractors and subcontracting is seen as only the second best option since SMEs in supply chains often feel squeezed by the larger companies who act as prime contractors. However, to significantly promote SMEs as prime contractors, the new Directive would have to have provided a regime for public contracts below the thresholds. Such a regime regulated in the Directive rather than being based on the principles of the TFEU or, alternatively, lower thresholds would be more effective measures to improve the opportunities of SMEs as prime contractors rather than subcontractors. However, especially the introduction of a regulated regime for contracts below the thresholds is a controversial issue,[63] with the strongest opposition from Germany and the United Kingdom. This opposition is not only but to a large extent due to the fact that such a regulated regime would have to be subject to procurement review and remedies. With regards to improving the opportunities of SMEs as subcontractors, Title III of Directive 2009/81/EC shows that more could be done when the supply chain, where SME play a bigger role, is addressed extensively in the legislation. However, such a regime for the entire public sector would be burdensome and of doubtful benefit for most contracts.[64] More importantly, the four SME-friendly provisions are limited since the precise extent and impact of these provisions will depend on the transposition of the relevant provisions of the new Directive in the Member States, which have a wide discretion on many aspects of these provisions. Finally, their precise extent will depend on their use by contracting authorities in practice, since they are also given a relative wide margin of manoeuvre. We will

63. Some stakeholders criticised the lack of clarity of the rules for procurement below the thresholds, see Green Paper, supra note 21, at 12. However they were "evenly divided on the issue".

64. A possible exception here could be works concession since they are long term contracts. Thanks to François Lichère for pointing this out to me during the EPPL network meeting in Aix-en-Provence in July 2013 when the first version of this chapter was discussed.

have to wait a few years for their complete transposition in all Member States and their use by contracting authorities.

Regulation of Contract Changes in the New Public Procurement Directive

Steen Treumer

1. Introduction

Recent case law from the Court of Justice of the European Union (hereafter the Court of Justice) has made it painfully clear that substantial changes of contracts covered by the EU public procurement rules can imply that a contracting authority must retender the contract[1] even though it is frequently uncertain whether such a duty has materialized. This far-reaching consequence of the EU public procurement rules has previously been overlooked or denied by many in theory and practice.

The issue has been easy to overlook because the EU Public Procurement Directives so far have been focused on the actions of the contracting authority until the conclusion of the contract even though an exception to this principle can be found in Article 31(4) of the Public Sector Directive.[2] Contracting authorities and competitors could also easily overlook the issue because they focus their attention on contracts tendered out for competition. Competitors will typically not know of a breach of the duty to retender as it is difficult or perhaps impossible to obtain exact insight into the details of the original contract and the subsequent changes.

1. See in particular pressetext Nachrichtenagentur GmbH v Republik Österreich (C-454/06) E.C.R. I-4401. For an analysis of the development in the case law of the Court of Justice see J.M. Hebly and P. Heijnsbroek, "When Amending Leads to Ending; A Theoretical and Practical Insight into the Retendering of Contracts after a Material Change" in G. Piga and S. Treumer (eds.), The Applied Law and Economics of Public Procurement, Oxford, Routledge 2013.
2. Compare with Article 40(3)(f) of the Utilities Directive.

Many would also be tempted to deny the existence of a duty to retender in general or in a concrete case. It will typically be very inconvenient and controversial to handle a duty to retender a contract before its expiry as the contractual partner of the contracting authority normally has no interest in renewed competition before the expiry of the contract. Objections might be followed up by a claim for damages if the contracting authority eventually decides to retender before the anticipated time.

A possible duty to retender a concluded contract due to subsequent changes also tend to conflict with the state of law following from other legal and classical disciplines and with common practice in many Member States as such changes would be allowed if EU public procurement law was disregarded. As an example a change of the contractual partner is unproblematic from a classical contract law approach as long as you have the consent of the contracting authority whereas such a change frequently could be ruled out by EU public procurement law.[3] Substitution of the contractual partner might also be compliant with national laws on insolvency but ruled out according to the doctrine on substantial changes of the contract in EU public procurement law. A duty to retender might also conflict with the classical understanding and interpretation of the right to changes of public and administrative contracts in a given country[4] and on the scope for changes of works contracts.[5]

It is therefore extremely complex and controversial to regulate contract changes that lead to a duty to retender. However, the above-mentioned development in the case law of the Court of Justice has received considerable attention and the European legislator decided to regulate the issue in more detail in order to decrease legal uncertainty. The result is a new and elaborate provision on the issue in Article 72 of the new Public Procurement Directive (hereafter the Directive).[6] The purpose of this chapter is to analyse and comment on the regulation of contract changes that lead to a duty to retender in continuation of my previous articles on the subject.[7] It should be added that

3. See section 2 of this article.
4. France is likely to be such a country.
5. There is such a conflict in a Danish context.
6. Directive 2014/24/EU.
7. See S. Treumer, "Regulation of contract changes leading to a duty to retender the contract: The European Commission's proposals of December 2011" (2012) 21 Public Procurement Law Review (hereafter P.P.L.R.) 159; S. Treumer, "Transfer of Contracts Covered by the EU Public Procurement Rules After Insolvency" 23 (2014) P.P.L.R. 21 and S. Treumer, "Contract Changes and the Duty to Retender under the New EU Public Procurement Directive", (2014) 23 P.P.L.R. 143.

the same principles apply to other public contracts covered only by the Treaty as clarified in C-91/08, Wall.[8]

The structure of Article 72 is atypical and fundamentally deviates from the Commission's Draft.[9] It starts with outlining a number of very important exceptions in Article 72(1) and (2). The exceptions are essentially similar to those originally suggested in the Commission's Draft. However, some modifications of the Draft ensure an even more flexible state of law in the future. The approach is in general flexible and will allow many changes in procurement practice. It follows from Article 72(5) that (substantial)[10] modifications lead to a duty to retender if they are not covered by the exceptions in Article 72(1) and 72(2). This provision must be interpreted as a statement of principle and therefore not as a rule without exception in spite of the wording.

The key criteria for the concrete assessment of whether a change should be considered as substantial are listed in Article 72(4) in accordance with the ruling in the pressetext case.[11] However, it should be noted that it is stated in Article 72(4)(a) that changes are substantial when they introduce conditions that "would have attracted additional participants in the procurement procedure". This was not stated by the Court of Justice in the pressetext case but is a relevant and uncontroversial clarification of the criteria. It is relevant to consider a broader range of criteria and elements in the concrete assessment of whether a contract should be retendered.[12]

Change of the contractual partner and related changes (changes in the composition of a consortia, replacement of key personnel) is considered in section 2. The other exceptions regulated in Article 72 are addressed as fol-

8. *Wall AG v Stadt Frankfurt am Main* (C-91/08) [2010] E.C.R. I-2815.
9. Proposal for a Directive on public procurement COM(2011) 896 final. The Draft outlined the essential features of the doctrine on changes that lead to a duty to retender in subparagraphs (1) and (2). For a general analysis and comment to the modernisation process see G.S. Ølykke, C.R. Hansen and C.D. Tvarnø (eds.), *EU Public Procurement; Modernisation, Growth and Innovation*, Jurist- og Økonomforbundets Forlag, Copenhagen, 2012 and S. Arrowsmith, "Modernising the European Union's public procurement regime: A blueprint for real simplicity and flexibility" (2012) 21 P.P.L.R 71.
10. There is no explicit reference to this fundamental requirement that follows from the case law of the Court of Justice and implicitly from Article 72(4).
11. See fn. 1.
12. See for instance S.T. Poulsen, "The possibilities for amending a public contract without a new competitive tendering procedure under EU law" (2012) 21 P.P.L.R. 167 and K. Hartlev and M.W. Liljenbøl, "Changes to Existing Contracts Under the EU Public Procurement Rules and the Drafting of Review Clauses to Avoid the Need for a New Tender" (2013) 22 P.P.L.R. 51.

lows: Necessary additional works, services and supplies in section 3, changes due to unforeseen circumstances in section 4, small-scale modifications in section 5 and review clauses including options in section 6. Changes with the aim of remedying a breach of contract that eventually was not directly regulated is considered in section 7 and the conclusions are presented in section 8.

2. Change of the contractual partner and related changes

As a rule the replacement of the contractual partner shall be considered as a substantial change leading to duty to retender the contract as established in para 40 of the pressetext case. As follows from the ruling in the pressetext case there are certain modifications to the rule and Article 72(1)(d) list a number of exceptions that will be analysed below together with replacement of key personnel. The latter is addressed in the Directive but not in Article 72.

Restructuring[13] was addressed by the Court of Justice in the pressetext case and Article 72(1)(d)(ii) specifies that the duty to retender shall not apply in the event of universal or partial succession, following corporate restructuring operations, including takeover, merger, acquisition or insolvency,[14] into the position of the initial contractor of another economic operator that fulfils the initial selection criteria.

It is a condition that the other contract terms are not substantially amended and that the change is not aimed at circumventing the application of the Directive. The approach is straightforward and makes good sense and should not be interpreted as a general opening for transfer of public contracts to other companies than the one[15] that won the competition for the contract.

2.1. Change of the contractual partner following insolvency

It is currently unclear whether the insolvency of the contractual partner leads to a duty to retender in spite of its obvious relevance in public procurement practice. The issue has only been considered to a limited extent in legal literature and has not been considered in case law from the Court of Justice.[16]

13. See s. 5.4.3. of S.T. Poulsen, fn. 12.
14. The notion of corporate restructuring was not exemplified in the Commission's Draft. Instead it followed from recital 47 to the Draft that the notion included takeover, merger and acquisition.
15. Or those that won the contract in case that a group of companies submitted a tender.
16. See S. Treumer, "Transfer of Contracts Covered by the EU Public Procurement Rules After Insolvency", (2014) 23 P.P.L.R. 21 with references.

However, the German Complaints Board at federal level has established that it is not possible to transfer public contracts to a new contractual partner without retender after insolvency.[17] The same has been assumed in Italy where Consiglio di Stato has considered the issue.[18] It should be stressed that the Italian public procurement legislation allows the trustee to transfer the contract to a new contractor provided that the contract firstly is offered on the original contract terms to the second lowest bidder. If this declines the trustee is entitled to offer the contract to number three in the evaluation of the original tender procedure and so forth.[19] In France a closely related issue has been considered in a single case. An administrative appeal court considered that a transfer without the involvement of a trustee was ruled out stating that such a transfer would breach the principle of transparency in the public procurement rules and would imply differential treatment of the tenderers.[20] It appears that there is not case law on the issue in United Kingdom which is not surprising as the number of public procurement case in this country is relatively limited.

It is therefore important to be aware that the provision in Article 72(1)(d)(ii) clarifies or introduces an important change of law as it allows change of the contractual partner following insolvency. This presupposes according to the provision that 1) this does not entail other substantial modifications to the contract 2) that the new contractual partner fulfils the selection criteria established in the original tender procedure and 3) that the transfer is not aimed at circumvention of the Directive. Article 72(1)(d)(ii) implies that an insolvent estate has a legal right to take on the rights and obligations following from the contract as it has also been commonly assumed in legal literature.[21] More importantly, it appears to allow the trustee of an insolvent com-

17. Bundeskartelamt, 3. Vergabekammer des Bundes, decision of 29 June 2005 in the case *VK Bund*, VK 3-52/05.
18. Consiglio di Stato, advice of 22 January 2008 in case no. 4574/07. The advice was given after a request from the Italian Senate that had award a software contract to a company that became insolvent. Consiglio di Stato acts both as a court (Supreme Court) and as an advisory body for the Italian State.
19. Article 140 of the Italian Procurement Act (Codice dei contratti pubblici), Act no. 163 of 12 April 2006.
20. Judgment of 27 February 2007 from Cour Administrative d'Appel de Bordeaux in case no. 05BX00344. It appears that the contract was concluded with a municipality after the insolvency of the private contractual partner.
21. See for instance S. T. Poulsen, fn. 12 (p. 186), M. Comba, "Retendering or sale of contract in case of bankruptcy of the contractor? Different solutions in an EU and comparative perspective" in G. Piga and S. Treumer (eds.), *The Applied Law and Economics of Public Procurement*, Oxford, Routledge 2013 and K. Hartlev og M.W. Liljenbøl, fn. 12 (at p. 65).

pany to sell contracts[22] that the company won in EU tender procedures without this being a violation of a duty to retender the contract. Furthermore, it appears that the transfer can be made from a contracting authority directly to a new contractual partner upon the conditions outlined above. The latter situation is clearly the most controversial from a legal point of view.

At first sight the approach in Article 72 on the issue appears surprisingly flexible. However, the reader should be aware that the issue has been considered in the administrative practice of the European Commission on a number of occasions. The Commission does not have a settled practice but its civil servants have accepted a sale in several cases where emphasis has been put on the fact that bankruptcy is an extraordinary event that follows from circumstances that can be objectively established and where a change of the contractual partner is natural in the context. It has in all cases - that the undersigned have knowledge of - been a condition that the terms of the contract in principle was unchanged and that renegotiation of the terms of the contract in reality did not take place. Furthermore, it was a condition that a reel assessment of the qualifications of the potential buyer took place and that this third party had the necessary qualifications. Finally, there was also an assessment of whether the circumstances indicated circumvention either when the original contract was concluded or at the time of the subsequent sale of the contract. The new regulation of the issue is therefore essentially a codification of the administrative practice of the European Commission.[23]

The new provision removes the fundamental legal uncertainty linked to transfer of contracts after insolvency by allowing contracting entities a very broad margin of discretion in practice. Nevertheless, the above-mentioned condition that the transfer must not entail *other* substantial modifications to the contract than the change of the identity of the contractual partner can be problematic in practice. The background for this is that it in principle rules out a renegotiation as such, including negotiation of price between the trustee and potential new contractual partners.

The question of the margin of changes of the contract terms, including the works and the price has recently been highly relevant in a Danish case following the insolvency of a major Danish contractor.[24] Other contractors were generally unwilling to take over the contracts on the original terms, including

22. It is presumed that the trustee would have such a right in the national system in question.
23. See S. Treumer, fn. 16 above.
24. See S. Treumer, fn. 16 above and in particular section 4 on the margin for changes of the other contract terms.

price. A part of the problem seemed to be that the now insolvent contractor in recent years had submitted low tenders that apparently did not cover the risks associated with the concrete projects.

The question is whether and in the affirmative to which extent there might be access to accept some substantial changes due to extraordinary difficulties triggered by the insolvency in a concrete case. The answers are linked with fundamental uncertainty and it is remarkable that the issue of such concrete substantial changes apparently was *not* debated as such in the negotiations leading to Article 72 in the new Directive. The attention was instead focused on Article 72(2) on small-scale changes and to some extent on Article 72(4) on the notion "substantial".[25] The safe answer is to deny that substantial changes are allowed also bearing in mind the explicit wording of Article 72 on this point.

However, if it assumed that there is at least some scope for substantial changes of the time of delivery, time schedule and terms on liability are of particular interest to consider. The insolvency will certainly imply a delay of the implementation of the contract. The trustee shall decide to enter into the contract, subsequently identity a new contractual partner and the contracting authority then has to accept the transfer, including possible changes of the contract terms. Alternatively, the contracting authority has to identify a new contractual partner and might have to change some of the contract terms. The time of delivery or time schedule is normally to be considered as substantial in a public procurement context, but it cannot be excluded that complaints boards and national courts will allow adjustment of the time of delivery or time plan if it is directly linked to the insolvency, that is to say the delay from the insolvency decree until the transfer of the contract. It is far more uncertain whether it is possible to disregard substantial delay in deliveries from the now insolvent company *before* the insolvency. That would place the new contractual partner in a more favourable position than the original contractual partner and therefore appear to be ruled out.

Another important issue in practice is the liability for breach of contract. A new contractor will normally be unwilling to assume responsibility for the deliveries of the now insolvent company, at least if this risk is not followed by a clear increase of the price. It is therefore to be expected that the potential new contractual partner will be keen on adjustments of the contract terms on

25. See S. Treumer, fn. 16 above with reference to information from Peter Kring, the Danish Competition and Consumer Authority on the negotiations leading to Article 72.

liability. This is problematic as such terms normally cannot be modified as they are substantial. It is doubtful whether there is access to changes of these terms or an increase of the price instead.

It will be very difficult for the trustees, contracting authorities and potential new contractual partners to make an assessment of the range of "necessary" changes in order to allow for a meaningful transfer of the contract and at the same time uncertain whether there is any margin for substantial changes at all. Complaints boards and national courts will equally be challenged if they have to consider the legality of contract changes linked to insolvency. They will presumably assess the legality of such changes with a sound scepticism as it is obvious that substantial changes in principle are ruled out.

2.2. Changes in the composition of a consortia

Tenders may be submitted by a group of contractors and this is frequently seen in European procurement practice. Experience shows that changes in the composition of a group of contractors take place in numerous instances both before[26] and after the conclusion of the public contract. The background could for instance be financial problems, deficiencies in the performance of the contract or problems with co-operation between the members of the group of contractors. The exit of a member in a consortium that has been awarded the contract can lead to a duty to retender the public contract. The issue is at least partially regulated in Article 72.

The exception in Article 72(1)(d)(ii) for the insolvency situation applies also where a member of a consortium becomes insolvent. Furthermore, it appears to follow from this provision that it is possible for the contracting entity to accept that the remaining members of the consortium fulfil the contract if a member of the consortium drops out for *other* reasons than insolvency. This must be considered as a partial succession into the position of the former member of the consortia. The remaining members of the consortia might have considerable difficulties fulfilling the contract. However, it will be feasible in many instances and the consortium can engage subcontractors with the relevant competences. This approach is noteworthy as changes of the composition of a consortium after the conclusion of the contract typically does not lead to a retender of the contract in public procurement practice even

26. See S. Treumer,"The Discretionary Powers of Contracting Entities – Towards a Flexible Approach in the Recent Case Law of the Court of Justice" (2006) 15. P.P.L.R. 71 (77) and S. Arrowsmith, *The Law of Public and Utilities Procurement* (2nd ed., Sweet & Maxwell, London, 2005) p. 776. Compare with Ch. 4 and 19 of C. Berg, *Udbudsret i byggeriet*, Jurist og Økonomforbundets Forlag, København, 2012.

though several of those changes probably should be retendered based on the current state of law.

Another important question is whether Article 72(1)(d)(ii) covers the situation where you want to *substitute* a member of a consortium for other reasons than insolvency. It is submitted, that this is not the case and that the provision in Article 72(1)(d)(ii) should be understood as covering only situations relating to mergers, acquisitions and situations where a purely internal reorganisation takes place within a company that was not established to carry out the public contract.[27] Recital 110 supports this interpretation as it refers to "purely internal reorganisations". Furthermore, the alternative interpretation would allow entirely new companies to become part of the consortia without having any prior relationship to the consortia or contract that was tendered out and this would distort competition.

The scenario where you want to substitute a member of a consortium resembles changes in the composition of a consortium *prior* to the award of the contract. It has been assumed in legal literature that changes in a consortium at this stage cannot take place if the change was material because it would have altered the contracting entity's decision to qualify the consortia or to allow it to the next stage in public procurement procedures where participants are eliminated in stages.[28] This is also consistent with the main criteria established in para 35 of the pressetext ruling according to which it must be considered whether the change would have allowed admission of other tenderers or would have implied award of the contract to another tenderer than the one that eventually won the competition for the contract.

2.3. Replacement of key personnel

In this context should also be mentioned an issue that is likely to be overlooked in practice. Formally, the identity of the contractual partner remains unaltered when key personnel are replaced. However, replacement of key personnel can be problematic because the identity of the personnel can have been decisive for the qualification of the winning tenderer and for the award of the contract. It is therefore logical that the change of key personnel at least in some circumstances can lead to a duty to retender the contract. The Court of Justice has not addressed the issue and the author is not aware of national case law on the matter. Nevertheless, the Court of Justice has established that

27. Successful consortia frequently from a new legal entity where it members acts as subcontractors to the new entity.
28. See S. Treumer, fn. 26 at p. 77 and S. Arrowsmith, fn. 26.

replacement of subcontractors – that also does not entail a change of the contractual partner - for similar reasons can lead to a duty to retender.[29]

The range of the potential problems linked to the change of key personnel has increased considerably due to a substantial change of the rules on award criteria in the Directive. Many will surely be familiar with the legal uncertainty that until now have surrounded consideration of matters such as experience and CV's at the award stage. The issue has been considered in recent case law from the Court and the General Court, and namely in the Lianakis case,[30] and in legal theory.[31] The European legislator has implicitly overruled the restrictive approach of the Court of Justice as the provision in Article 67(2)(b) essentially removes the fundamental legal uncertainty linked to the consideration of organisation, qualification and experience of staff assigned to performing the contract. The provision allows this where the quality of the staff assigned can have a significant impact on the level of performance of the contract.

It should be noted that the European legislator have specified in recital 94 that contracting authorities that makes use of this possibility should ensure, by appropriate contractual means, that such staff can only be replaced with the consent of the contracting authority which verifies that the replacement staff affords an equivalent level of quality.[32] The lack of substitution in this situation can imply that the contracting is under an obligation to retender the contract. Nevertheless, to impose a duty to retender due to the replacement of key personnel is a very far-reaching consequence. It is submitted, that the duty to retender due to change of key personnel will materialize only as an exception and contracting authorities will normally be able to avoid the problem by hiring new key personnel with the same level of expertise and qualification.

29. See section 2.5.
30. *Lianakis* (C-532/06) [2008] E.C.R. I-251.
31. See in particular the Special Issue of the P.P.L.R. on the application and implications of the Lianakis case (2009) 18 P.P.L.R pp. 103-164 edited by S. Treumer. See also various articles on the theme in G. Piga and S. Treumer (eds.), *The Applied Law and Economics of Public Procurement*, Oxford, Routledge 2013 and P. Lee, "Implications of the Lianakis Decision" (2010) 19 P.P.L.R. 47.
32. The regulation of the issue was moved from the material provisions to the considerations. Compare with Article 66(2)(b) of the Commission's Draft.

2.4. The Contracting authority assumes the main contractor's obligations towards its subcontractors

This exception is considered in Article 72(1)(d)(iii) and was not included in the Draft. It is applicable where this possibility is provided for under national legislation pursuant to Article 71. The provision is merely a clarification based on the principle that the EU public procurement rules does not dictate that a contract is tendered out. Instead the rules are applicable once the contracting entity covered by the rules anticipates to contract ex-house.

2.5. Unequivocal review clause or option

Article 72(1)(d)(i) outlines that the contractor can be replaced as a consequence of an unequivocal review clause or option.[33] This provision was not a part of the Draft provision and supplements the general regulation of changes and review clauses in Article 72(1)(a) that is considered in section 6 below.

The Court of Justice indicated in the pressetext case that contract clauses could justify an exception from the duty to retender.[34] The ruling was to some extent misleading on this point as it comments on review clauses opening up for change of *subcontractors* even though the change of a subcontractor is not an example of change of a contractual partner.[35] Obviously a change of subcontractors can also be problematic as subcontractors might have been decisive for the selection and award of the contract even though this typically is not the case. The issue was subsequently considered explicitly by the Court of Justice in C-91/08, Wall[36] where the Court clarified that a change of subcontractor in *exceptional* cases may be substantial *even if the possibility of a change is provided for in the contract.* It follows from the Wall case that the fact that a review clause opens up for a change of subcontractor (and thereby also of a contractual partner by analogy) by no means necessarily imply that you can escape the duty to retender. This limitation following from the case law of the Court of Justice is reflected in the condition in Article 72(1)(d)(i) that the review clause or option shall be unequivocal.

33. See K. Hartlev and M.W. Liljenbøl, fn. 12 on drafting of review clauses.
34. Cf. "unless that substitution was provided for in the terms of the initial contract, such as, by way of example, provision for sub-contracting" as outlined in the very end of para 40 of the pressetext case.
35. It changes the contractual relationship between other parties – to be more specific between the (typical private) contractual partner and its subcontractors. The subcontractors have not concluded a contract with the public contracting entity but instead with the contractual partner of the contracting entity.
36. See fn. 8.

The regulation of changes in the composition of consortia in Article 72(1)(d)(ii) is unclear on certain points as outlined in further detail in section 2.2. It is to be expected that at least some contracting authorities will regulate this issue in unequivocal clauses as allowed in the current provision.

3. Necessary additional works, services and supplies by the original contractor

It follows from Article 72(1)(b) that a new tender is not required for necessary additional works, services or supplies by the original contractor. The provision was not included in the Draft. It is a condition that a change of contractor cannot be made for economic or technical reasons such as requirements of interchangeability or interoperability with existing equipment, services or installations procured under the initial procurement and would cause significant inconvenience or substantial duplication of costs for the contracting authority. It is also a condition that any increase in price may not be higher than 50% of the value of the original contract and contracting authorities shall publish a notice in the Official Journal of the European Union on such changes. If several successive modifications are made the limitation applies only to the value of each modification. It shall therefore not be assessed on the basis of the net cumulative value of the successive modifications as changes covered by Article 72(2).

This provision is heavily inspired by in Article 31(2)(b) on additional supplies and Article 31(4)(b) on repetitive works and services of the Public Sector Directive. Nevertheless, the scope of the exception has been widened on several points as some of the current conditions are deleted and others made more flexible. The conditions for the application of this exception is more flexible compared to the current regulation as the conditions now explicitly include *economic* considerations.[37] The current limitations on time in Article 31 is not part of the conditions outlined in Article 72(1)(b).[38] The condition in Article 31(4)(b) that limits the current exception to projects for which the original contract was awarded according to the open or restricted procedure is

37. Cf. Article 72(1)(b)(i) "cannot be made for economic .... reasons" and Article72(1)(b)(ii) "substantial duplication of costs for the contracting authority".
38. It follows from Article 31 on supplies that the length of such contracts as well as that of the recurrent contract may not, as a general rule, exceed three years. Article 31(4)(b) on works and services can only be applied during the three years following the conclusion of the original contract.

also deleted. Recital 108 clarifies that the application of the provision may be justified in particular where the additional deliveries are intended either as partial replacements or as the extension of existing services, supplies or installations.

4. Unforeseen circumstances

Several cumulative conditions are outlined in Article 72(1)(c) on unforeseen circumstances. The need for change must have been brought about by circumstances which a diligent[39] contracting authority could not foresee, the change must not alter the overall nature of the contract and finally a possible increase in price must not be higher than 50% of the original value of the contract or framework agreement. Finally, contracting authorities shall publish a notice in the Official Journal of the European Union on such changes.

The provision in Article 72(1)(c) on unforeseen circumstances is heavily inspired by Article 31(4)(a) of the Public Sector Directive. However, in contrast to the current provision any kind of change is covered and not only "additional works or services". Furthermore, the current condition that additional works and services must be inseparable from the original contract or strictly necessary has been replaced by the less demanding condition of "not altering the overall nature of the contract". The approach to changes based on unforeseen circumstances is therefore clearly more flexible than in the current Directive.

Recital 109 specifies that an alteration of the overall nature of the contract for instance would occur where the works, supplies or services to be procured are replaced by something different or where the type of procurement is fundamentally changed since in such a situation a hypothetical influence of the outcome may be assumed. Such a change could for instance be the introduction of a requirement for halal butchering concerning supplies of meat or a special requirement for labelling or colouring of a given product.

The condition "unforeseen circumstances" has only rarely been put to the test in the case law of the Court of Justice. National case law interpreting this condition also seems to be limited. Nevertheless, the number of cases is likely to increase with the new focus on changes that lead to a duty to retender the

39. It is not emphasized in the wording of Article 31(4)(a) of the Public Sector Directive that the circumstances must be unforeseen to a *diligent* contracting authority. However, this addition does not appear to imply a stricter approach but merely to be a clarification of something that was already apparent based on the current state of law.

contract in practice and theory. As the case law is limited it is important to be aware of the lengthy considerations on the notion in the preamble.

It follows from Recital 109 of the Directive that "Contracting authorities can be faced with external circumstances that they could not foresee when they awarded the contract, in particular when the performance of the contract covers a long period. In this case, a certain degree of flexibility is needed to adapt the contract to those circumstances without a new procurement procedure. The notion of unforeseeable circumstances refers to circumstances that could not have been predicted despite reasonably diligent preparation of the initial award by the contracting authority, taking into account its available means, the nature and characteristics of the specified project, good practice in the field in question and the need to ensure an appropriate relationship between the resources spent in preparing the award and its foreseeable future." The considerations in Recital 109 appear balanced and flexible as they take into account the need of a test with consideration of subjective elements and the characteristics of the specific project in question.

5. Small-scale modifications – the "de minimis" rule in Article 72(2)

It is specified in Recital 107 that modifications of the contract resulting in a minor change of the contract value up to a certain value should always be possible without the need to carry out a new procurement procedure. Article 72(2) establishes the exception for these small-scale modifications including conditions for the application of this provision. Those conditions were heavily debated during the negotiations and the final provision was more flexible than originally envisaged in the Draft of the Commission.[40]

The application of the exception presupposes that the value of the change can be expressed in monetary terms.[41] The value in itself cannot be higher than the thresholds of the Directive and the value shall be below 10% of the initial contract value for service and supply contracts and below 15% of the initial contract value for works contracts.[42] In addition, the changes must not

40. It followed from the Draft that the value should be below 5% of the value of the initial contract. As follows this value has now been increased to 10% for supplies and services and 15% for works.
41. This was explicitly stated in Article 72(4) of the Commission's Draft.
42. See Article 72(2)(i) and (ii).

alter "the overall nature of the contract or framework agreement" as commented upon in section 4.

The latter condition is important because a small-scale change that is immaterial measured in monetary terms still could have significant impact on competition. If the overall nature of the contract is changed other economic operators than those that participated in the original tender procedure would normally be interested in tendering.

6. Review clauses including options

Article 72(1)(a) establishes that contracts and framework agreements can be modified without a new procurement procedure where this has been provided for in the initial procurement documents in clear, precise and unequivocal review clauses. Such clauses may include price revision clauses and options and shall state the scope and nature of possible modifications, changes or options as well as the conditions under which they may be used.

Recital 111 informs us that such clauses for instance could ensure that communications equipment to be delivered over a given period continues to be suitable, also in case of changing communications protocols or other technological changes. Likewise it should be possible to provide for adaptations of the contract which are rendered necessary by technical difficulties which have appeared during operation or maintenance.

The background for this exception is specified in Recital 111 according to which "Contracting authorities should, in the individual contracts themselves, have the possibility to provide for modifications to a contract by way of review clauses, but such clauses should not give them unlimited discretion. This Directive should therefore set out to what extent modifications may be provided for in the initial contract."

Unlike several of the other exceptions outlined in Article 72, the provision does not specify any limitations measured in value. However, it is a condition that the modification does "not alter the overall nature of the contract or the framework agreement". The same limitation applies to the exceptions in Article 72(1)(c) on unforeseen circumstances and Article 72(2) on small-scale modifications commented upon above in sections 4 and 5.

The legislator has granted contracting authorities a *considerable* margin of discretion as the provision by far provides clear-cut boundaries for use of review clauses. The boundaries will be settled by the case law of national courts and review boards and ultimately by the Court of Justice. It is to be expected that competitors will challenge the impact of such review clauses and options and that national courts and review board will scrutinize such clauses and options carefully in order that they do not undermine the duty to retender the contract in practice.[43]

This provision is supplemented by Article 72(1)(d)(i) that specifies that the contractor can be replaced as a consequence of an unequivocal review clause or option. The latter provision is commented in section 2.5. above.

9. Changes with the aim of remedying a breach of contract

The Commission's Draft contained an important provision in Article 72(7)(b) that has now been deleted. The provision was based on a remarkable restrictive approach to changes with the aim of remedying a breach of contract. The Draft ruled out changes aiming at remedying deficiencies in the performance of the contractor, which can be remedied through the enforcement of the contractual obligations. The Draft provision in Article 72(7)(b) did not specify that the changes that are ruled out should be substantial[44] but this is likely to have been considered superfluous as access to contractual remedies that can be enforced typically presupposes a material breach of the contract.[45]

Such a general limitation would have been far-reaching as it would cut off the use of some of the tools available under contract law. The Draft was criticized by the undersigned that questioned whether the Draft was in accordance with the current state of law and predicted that the Draft was likely to be challenged in the negotiations on this point.[46] However, it should be noted that Recital 110 states that the successful tenderer should not be replaced without retendering where a contract is terminated because of deficiencies in the performance.

The parties to a contract would normally be able to change a contract to settle a disagreement on whether the performance has failed and to accept changes of the terms of the contract to your own disadvantage. The back-

43. See the references to Scandinavian case law with a rather restrictive approach in section 3 of the article of S. Treumer, fn. 16.
44. Nevertheless, this is done consistently in the other subsections of Article 72.
45. However, the assessment relates to different concepts based on different reasoning. The concept is based on equal treatment and transparency considerations in the procurement context whereas focus is on the reasonable expectations of the contractual partner in the contract law context.
46. See section 3 of S. Treumer, "Regulation of contract changes leading to a duty to retender the contract: The European Commission's proposals of December 2011" (2012) 21 Public Procurement Law Review.

ground for the likely limitation in the access to changes of contracts covered by the EU public procurement rules is consideration of the interests of the potential competitors. The needed changes to settle disagreements on a possible breach or deficiencies in the performance will frequently be substantial because other tenderers would have been selected or awarded the contract had the terms of initial contract been different from the start. This is obvious for instance with regard to a delay in deliveries but will equally so for many other changes of the contract terms.

The restrictive approach that was suggested in the Draft is not in accordance with the approach in practice be it in contracts covered or not covered by the EU public procurement rules. A contracting authority will typically be flexible and open to modifications of the contract on the condition that it considers that there is likelihood of (reasonable) contract performance. This tendency is outspoken when the public contract is complex and where the contract has partly been implemented. The background for this is that the ultimate consequence of a breach of the contract is a change of the contractual partner that can be very costly, cause great difficulties in practice and typically will be very time-consuming.

Contracting authorities will therefore tend to accept – perhaps implicitly – a delay in deliveries or other possible deficiencies in performance and to find a pragmatic solution after negotiations with the contractual partner. A contracting authority might also abstain from invoking pecuniary sanctions stipulated by the contract for deficiencies in the performance of the contract for various reasons. The deficiency of performance could for instance be disputed by the contractual partner and the authority do not want to run the risk linked to legal proceedings or it might be customary not to enforce your (possible) right to pecuniary sanctions in the field.[47]

The current state of law on the issue is linked with considerable legal uncertainty after the deletion of the Draft provision on the issue. It is submitted, that there is a larger margin for changes in case of deficiencies in the performance of the contract than in the standard scenario where this problem is not present.[48] The Court of Justice has not considered the margin for changes

47. It could also be that the pecuniary sanctions following from the contract are so burdensome that they will undermine the economy of the contractual partner and the authority therefore chooses not rely on the clauses ensuring a right to pecuniary sanctions.

48. See section 3.7 of M. Goller and K. S. Kreyberg, "Vesentlige endringer i kontrakter inngått etter regelverket om offentlige anskaffelser", Tidsskrift for Forretningsjus 2012 p. 37. See also S.T. Poulsen, section 4.1 of the article mentioned in fn. 12. For a

linked to deficiencies in the performance of the contract in its case law and the issue appears only to have been addressed in a few public procurement cases at national level.[49] It had been preferable that the Directive had clarified that the contracting authority can allow some changes in case of deficiencies of performance and outlined criteria for when such changes are allowed taking due account of the public interest in a more flexible approach to the issue.

However, a contracting authority must expect that courts or review bodies will scrutinize such settlement agreements and implicit acceptance of changes of the contract i.e. on the time of delivery to ensure that they do not constitute abuse and circumvention and that they are in fact needed and in the public interest. Some will claim that they introduced changes because of deficiencies in the performance of the contract where the reality was that there was no disagreement on the performance. The aim of such a transaction would instead be to introduce entirely new elements into the contracts or renegotiate the terms of the contract in general.

If services or deliverables of the initial contract is reduced the contractual partner of the contracting entity is likely to push for introduction of new elements into the contract or to introduce changes that alter the economic balance of the contract in favour of the contractual partner. Such changes would remedy the loss of profits following from the reduction of the initial contract. A settlement should not open up for a general negotiation of the contract but aim at maintaining the initial contract to the highest extent possible while at the same time ensuring a satisfactory contract performance. The same rationale underlies the regulation of the substitution of the contractual partner in the case of corporate restructuring operations and insolvency in Article 72(1)(d)(ii) where it is a condition that the succession does not entail other substantial modifications.[50]

10. Conclusions

The consequences of a breach of the duty to retender can be fundamental and far-reaching with ineffectiveness as the ultimate consequence. The elaborate provision on the duty to retender due to contract changes should therefore be welcomed. It was highly relevant to clarify the state of law and remove the

more restrictive interpretation see chapter 19 of C. Berg, *Udbudsret i byggeriet*, Jurist og Økonomforbundets Forlag, Copenhagen, 2012.

49. The lack of case law is also stressed by M. Goller and K. S. Kreyberg, fn. 48 above.
50. See section 2 of this article.

fundamental legal uncertainty linked to the Court of Justice's development of this traditionally neglected consequence of the EU Public Procurement rules.[51]

Article 72 ensures that contracting authorities can adopt a flexible approach to a broad range of contract changes. Article 72(1)(d) on corporate restructuring operations and insolvency is a noteworthy example of this with a very flexible approach to changes after insolvency. Article 72(1)(a) also allows diligent contract authorities a broad margin for changes through careful drafting of the contract terms. The regulation of changes caused by unforeseen circumstances is relatively flexible and clearly allow more scope for changes that the current regime. The provision on small-scale-modifications in Article 72(2) is also important and flexible in its approach.

However, some important issues were left open-ended. The Commission's draft provision on changes with the aim of remedying deficiencies in the performance of the contract in Article 72(7)(a) was deleted. That should be welcomed as it appeared out of tune with the need of a more pragmatic and flexible approach to this issue[52] but the lack of regulation creates legal uncertainty. The same applies for some of the issues linked to changes of the composition of a consortia that is frequently occurring in public procurement practice.

Bibliography

S. Arrowsmith, *The Law of Public and Utilities Procurement* (2nd ed., Sweet & Maxwell, London, 2005).

S. Arrowsmith, "Modernising the European Union's public procurement regime: A blueprint for real simplicity and flexibility" (2012) 21 P.P.L.R. 71.

C. Berg, *Udbudsret i byggeriet*, Jurist og Økonomforbundets Forlag, Copenhagen, 2012.

51. Compare with S. Arrowsmith, "Modernising the European Union's public procurement regime: A blueprint for real simplicity and flexibility" (2012) 21 P,P.L.R. 71, at p. 72 that instead generally favours that procurement would be regulated in lesser detail. Some Danish practitioners also have a clear preference for development of the issue in the national case law instead of legislation. They refer for instance to the regulation of competitive dialogue as an example of regulation that led to anything but the desired simplification and flexibility in the previous modernisation process back in 2004.
52. See the criticism of the Draft on this point in S. Treumer, fn. 46 at p. 166.

M. Comba, "Retendering or sale of contract in case of bankruptcy of the contractor? Different solutions in an EU and comparative perspective" in G. Piga and S. Treumer (eds.) *The Applied Law and Economics of Public Procurement*, Oxford, Routledge 2013.

M. Goller and K. S. Kreyberg, "Vesentlige endringer i kontrakter inngått etter regelverket om offentlige anskaffelser", Tidsskrift for Forretningsjus 2012.

K. Hartlev and M.W. Liljenbøl, "Changes to Existing Contracts Under the EU Public Procurement Rules and the Drafting of Review Clauses to Avoid the Need for a New Tender" (2013) 22 P.P.L.R. 51.

J.M. Hebly and P. Heijnsbroek, "When Amending Leads to Ending; A Theoretical and Practical Insight into the Retendering of Contracts after a Material Change" in G. Piga and S. Treumer (eds.), *The Applied Law and Economics of Public Procurement*, Oxford, Routledge 2013.

S.T. Poulsen, "The possibilities for amending a public contract without a new competitive tendering procedure under EU law" (2012) 21 P.P.L.R. 167.

S. Treumer, "Regulation of contract changes leading to a duty to retender the contract: The European Commission's proposals of December 2011" 21 (2012) P.P.L.R. 159.

S. Treumer, "Transfer of Contracts Covered by the EU Public Procurement Rules After Insolvency" (2014) 23 P.P.L.R. 21.

S. Treumer, "Contract Changes and the Duty to Retender under the New EU Public Procurement Directive", (2014) 23 P.P.L.R. 143.

G.S. Ølykke, C.R. Hansen and C.D. Tvarnø (eds.), *EU Public Procurement; Modernisation, Growth and Innovation*, Copenhagen, Jurist- og Økonomforbundets Forlag, 2012.

Sustainable public procurement in the EU: experiences and prospects

D. C. Dragos, B. Neamtu

1. Introduction

This chapter dwells on sustainable public procurement as promoted by the new 2014 Directives on public procurement, having as background the experience of implementing the 2004 Directives in several Member States.

Traditionally, public procurement had only to be economically efficient, with little regard for other objectives than the purely economic ones. In recent times, however, due to a more general ascension of the sustainable development concept, governments have been put in the position to "lead by example" and use their purchasing power in order to advance the goals of sustainable development; as a specific development, sustainable public procurement has been slowly creeping in. From "secondary considerations" in the 2004 Directives,[1] the need to include social and environmental considerations in public tendering procedures has led to the coining of new terms, much more

1. See generally on the theme of environmental and social considerations S. Arrowsmith and P. Kunzlik (eds.) Social and Environmental Policies in EC Procurement Law (Cambridge, Cambridge University Press, 2009); C. McCrudden Buying Social Justice. Equality, Government Procurement, & Legal Change (Oxford, Oxford University Press, 2007); J. Arnould 'Secondary Policies in Public Procurement: The Innovations of the New Directive' PPLR, 2004; R. Caranta and M. Trybus (eds.) The Law of Green and Social Procurement in Europe (Copenhagen, DJOF, 2010); R. Caranta 'Sustainable Procurement' in M. Trybus, R. Caranta and G. Edelstam (eds.) European Union Law of Public Contracts: Public Procurement and Beyond (Brussels, Bruylant 2014) 165 ff.

powerful and all-encompassing, such as "horizontal policies",[2] "sustainable procurement" or even "strategic procurement". We can state that with the new 2014 Directives, the sustainability paradigm is almost taking over the realm of public procurement, and it is marketed as a major "selling point" of the new legislation.

Sustainability has been for the last three decades a 'buzz' word in the environmental literature (but also beyond), conveying a multitude of meanings that are often divergent to a variety of individuals, professions, interest groups, governmental agencies, political leaders, NGOs and grassroots organizations,[3] The concept of 'sustainability' in its modern sense emerged in the early 1970s in response to a dramatic growth in understanding that modern development practices in all fields were leading to wor!dwide environmental and social crises.[4] The term is nonetheless very broad and abstract[5] thus creating confusion and cynicism as well as positive environmental change.[6] While sustainability is more directly related to biology and ecology,[7] the concept of sustainable development or sustainable economic development brings elements of economic activity more explicitly into the equation.[8] It is a catchword for alternative development approaches that could be envisioned as continuing far into the future.[9] Perhaps the most well-known definition is

2. S. Arrowsmith and P. Kunzlik 'Public Procurement and Horizontal Policies in EC Law: General Principles' in S. Arrowsmith and P. Kunzlik (eds.) Social and Environmental Policies in EC Procurement Law above fn 1, 35 ff; M. Comba 'Green and Social Considerations in Public Procurement Contracts: A Comparative Approach' in R. Caranta and M. Trybus (eds.) The Law of Green and Social Procurements in Europe above fn 1, 307 ff.
3. K. Portney Taking Sustainable Cities Seriously (Cambridge, Massachusetts: MIT Press, 2003); J. Zachary Sustainable Community Indicators: Guideposts for Local Planning (California, Community Environmental Council, Inc, 1995); P. Selman Local Sustainability: Managing and Planning Ecologically Sound Places (New York, St. Martin's Press, 1996).
4. S.M. Wheeler Planning for Sustainability. Creating Liveable, Equitable, and Ecological Communities (New York, Routledge, 2004) 19.
5. For a discussion about the existing branches of sustainability see B.J. Brown et al. 'Global Sustainability: Toward Definition' Environmental Management, 11(6)/1987, 713-719; C. Kidd 'The Evolution of Sustainability' Journal of Agricultural and Environmental Ethics, 5(1)/1992, 1-26.
6. K. Portney Taking Sustainable Cities Seriously above fn 3, 3.
7. R.W.G Carter, Coastal Environments: An Introduction to the Physical, Ecological and Cultural Systems of Coastlines (London, Academic Press, 1989).
8. K. Portney Taking Sustainable Cities Seriously above fn 3, 7.
9. S.M. Wheeler Planning for Sustainability above fn 4, 19.

the one from the Brundtland report, which defines sustainable development as development which meets the needs of the present without compromising the ability of future generations to meet their own needs.[10] It usually comprises three dimensions – economic, social/equity, and environmental.

In public procurement, it means that the government is embarking on socially and environmentally responsible practices through the use of public contracts. It has to be noted that sustainable public procurement encompasses not only social and environmental matters but also, in a wide interpretation, the participation of SMEs in public tendering processes. However, in this Chapter we will cover only the social and environmental aspects, SMEs being dwelt upon in other chapters.[11]

The chapter begins with an incursion into the development of sustainable considerations in EU legislation, in soft law and the jurisprudence of the Court of Justice. Then it will analyze the experience of several Member States in implementing the provisions of the 2004 Directives, in order to have a perspective on the background against which the new provisions of 2014 will be implemented. In the end, we will discuss sustainable procurement as envisaged in these new 2014 Directives.

2. From secondary considerations to strategic procurement: The journey of sustainable procurement in the EU law

The natural order of things – regulation, then case law – has been inversed in the case of sustainable procurement at EU level: case law led the way towards the use of social and environmental considerations in public procurement, and legislation followed suit.

2.1. The case law

In its decisions, the CJEU has constantly stressed as a matter of principle that the main objective of the EU law on public procurement is the opening up to competition of the public markets in the Member States and ensuring the free movement of goods and services throughout the territory of the EU.[12] However, in a series of decisions, the Court has stated that other objectives than

10. WCED (World Commission on Environment and Development) From One Earth to One World: An Overview (Oxford, Oxford University Press, 1987).
11. The next Chapter by M. Trybus and innovation in a third chapter by L. Butler.
12. See for instance C-454/06 Pressetext Nachrichtenagentur GmbH [2008] ECR I-4401, paragraph 31, and Case C-513/99 Concordia Bus [2002] ECR I-7213, paragraph 81.

the pure economical or Internal Market ones may be pursued by contracting authorities. These are either social objectives – employing persons that meet certain conditions or environmental ones – for instance eco-labels.

2.1.1. Bentjees

In Bentees, the plaintiff claimed that the decision of the awarding authority rejecting its tender (although it was the lowest) in favour of the next-lowest bidder had been taken in breach of the provisions of Directive 71/305/EEC,[13] then in force, because, inter alia, the contracting authority requested tenderers to prove that they will be able to employ long-term unemployed persons. The Court found that the condition relating to the employment of long-term unemployed persons was compatible with the directive under the condition that it had no direct or indirect discriminatory effect on tenderers from other Member States, and provided that such specific conditions had been mentioned in the contract notice.[14]

This case is considered to be the leading case in sustainable public procurement, although the main concern of the Court was still focused on giving full effect to the principles of non-discrimination and the free movement of services.[15]

The controversy stemming from Bentjees is whether social criteria may be used for the award of the contract or just as a contract performance condition. In later case law the Court clarified this conundrum.

2.1.2. Commission v French Republic (Nord-Pas de Calais)[16]

Bentjees was referred to later on in another key decision: Commission v. France, where a contracting authority had published award notices listing the promotion of employment among criteria for the award of the contracts. The case was about the award of public works contracts for the construction and maintenance of school buildings conducted by the Nord-Pas-de-Calais Region and the Département du Nord over a period of three years. The European Commission interpreted Bentjees in the sense that promotion of employment may be used only as a contract performance condition, and stated that the award criteria are restricted to two – the lowest price and MEAT. France, on the other hand, sustained that the social criterion may be added to the two

13. Case 31/87 Gebroeders Beentjes BV v State of the Netherlands [1988] ECR 4635.
14. Case 31/87 Bentjees paragraph 37. (iii).
15. R. Caranta 'Sustainable Public Procurement in the EU' in R. Caranta and M. Trybus (eds.) The Law of Green and Social Procurement in Europe above fn 1, 19.
16. Case C-225/98 Commission v. France [2000] ECR I-7445.

classical criteria based on Bentjees. Although generally admitting France's failure to fulfill the requirements to properly advertise the contract notices, the Court agreed with France on the issue of the admissibility of social conditions as award criteria. It concluded that provided that the criterion referring to an unemployment campaign is set and applied in a non-discriminatory manner, such considerations are admissible as award criteria. Due to the fact that the Commission had only criticized the reference to such a criterion as an award criterion, leaving untouched the lack of proper advertising of the contract notice, this complaint was rejected.

All in all, the decision has given the Court the opportunity to clarify that social considerations may be used either as award criteria or as performance conditions.

2.1.3. Concordia (Helsinki) Bus Finland[17]

The case brought to the public debate issues regarding the use of environmental considerations in public procurement. The municipality of Helsinki decided to award bus transport services to a company that would offer the most advantageous tender. When assessing the economic advantages of the tenders, the contracting authority relied on three sub-criteria: price, quality of the bus fleet, and the quality and environmental management of the operator. Under the second sub-criterion, buses with lower emissions and noise were preferred, while under the third criterion extra points were given to operators who met certified quality criteria and had a certified environment protection program. Concordia Bus came in second place, being penalized under the second and last criteria, although it had the lowest price. The company then claimed in court that the second criterion was discriminatory, as there was only one operator having the possibility to fully meet the criterion.

The decision of the court is important because, after recalling Bentjees in that award criteria must be applied in a non-discriminatory way and moving forward to state that it is admissible to have environmental considerations as award criteria, it introduces a third condition for admissibility of such criteria, namely that environmental criteria must be linked to the subject matter of the contract:

> Article 36(1)(a) of Directive 92/50 relating to the coordination of procedures for the award of public service contracts must be interpreted as meaning that where, in the context of a public contract for the provision of urban bus transport services, the contracting authority decides to award a contract to the tenderer who submits the economically most advanta-

17. C-513/99 Concordia Bus [2002] ECR I-7213.

geous tender, it may take into consideration ecological criteria such as the level of nitrogen oxide emissions or the noise level of the buses, provided that they are linked to the subject-matter of the contract, do not confer an unrestricted freedom of choice on the authority, are expressly mentioned in the contract documents or the tender notice, and comply with all the fundamental principles of Community law, in particular the principle of non-discrimination.

As to the claim that the contracting entity's own transport undertaking is one of the few undertakings able to offer a bus fleet satisfying the set criteria, the Court stated that the principle of equal treatment was not infringed by this fact.[18]

In conclusion, the judgment was a step forward for the use of secondary considerations, despite the continuous preoccupation for ensuring that no preference is given to national suppliers to the detriment of suppliers from other Member States.[19]

2.1.4. Wienstrom[20]

In this case, the tender documentation required bidders to supply electricity from renewable energy sources. In order to qualify, bidders had to prove that they are able to provide a minimum amount of electricity per year from renewable energy sources equivalent to the estimated annual consumption of the Austrian Federal Republic's offices. In addition to that, an award criterion which amounted to 45% of the weighting, awarded points for the amount of electricity from renewable sources which the bidder could supply in excess of the Austrian Federal Republic's estimated requirements.

The Court held first that it is acceptable to make use of ecological award criteria, even if the criterion in question doesn't provide an immediate economic benefit for the contracting authority, and such criteria may be given an important weighting in the overall assessment of the tenders. Furthermore, it is clearly admissible to establish an award criterion which is related to the production method of the purchased product, if relevant for the contract; however, in order for such criterion to be acceptable, it should be expressly linked to the subject-matter of the contract and should be capable of verification, which would imply that the contracting authority requires – through the

18. See paragraphs 69, 86, 88-93, operative part 1-3 .
19. P. Charro 'Case Note to Concordia Bus Finland' CMLR, 40 (1)/2003, 179
20. Case C-448/01 EVN and Wienstrom [2003] ECR I-14527; for a comment, see M. Dischendorfer 'The Rules on Award Criteria Under the EC Procurement Directives and the Effect of Using Unlawful Criteria: the EVN Case' PPLR 13/2004, NA83.

submission of certificates for example – elements enabling it to verify the information submitted by the bidders in relation to the criterion.

In this context, the requirement to provide in excess electricity from renewable sources is not linked to the object-matter of the contract and thus it cannot be used as an award criterion. The argument is that this would lead to unjustified discrimination against bidders who are fully able to meet the contract requirements, because such condition is related to the general capacity of the economic operator and not directly to the subject matter of the contract. However, it is important to note that the Court has left room for approaching later on the issue whether examining such capacity at the selection stage and not as an award criterion would be admissible.

2.1.5. Evropaïki Dynamiki v European Environment Agency[21]

The case tackled the issue whether general policies of the tenderers may be considered in the award phase.

Upon awarding a contract for the provision of IT consultancy services by the European Environment Agency (EEA), the award procedure was challenged because 10% of the marks at the award stage were based on the 'general environmental policy of the company'. The unsuccessful tenderer argued that the assessment of this criterion was flawed, as the EEA awarded the highest marks to a company which had a third-party certified environmental management scheme.

In its findings, the then First Instance Court held that the EEA was entitled to apply its discretion in the way it assessed the evidence submitted by tenderers in response to this criterion. The fact that tenderers without a certificate did not all receive the same score was taken by the Court to indicate that the EEA had made a comparative assessment of the tenders, evaluating whether the environmental policies submitted by the tenderers were genuine; and it found out that only one of them had already put such a policy in place, whilst the others merely indicated good intentions in that respect.[22] The Court has concluded that the EEA was entitled to award differential marks on this basis, and the applicant's complaint in this regard was rejected.

This case provides guidance on a tricky aspect of assessing environmental criteria, which is how much leeway contracting authorities have in assessing what is 'equivalent' evidence. Although third-party certification cannot gener-

21. Case T-331/06 Evropaïki Dynamiki – Proigmena Systimata Tilepikoinonion Pliroforikis kai Tilematikis AE v European Environment Agency (AEE) [2010] ECR II-136.
22. Paragraph 76 of judgment.

ally be required, the contracting authorities may nevertheless consider this certification as a strong evidence of a company's environmental standards.

The case is interesting for public procurement under the Directives even if it was decided on the basis of the Financial Regulation, which governs the award of contracts by the EEA and other EU agencies. The Financial Regulation and the Directives have similar wording on this matter.

2.1.6. Max Havellaar

A recent judgment, Commission v. Netherlands,[23] touched upon fair trade labels and alternative specifications. In 2008 the Dutch province of North Holland announced in a tendering procedure that it wished to procure coffee machines and the products necessary to make them function (coffee, tea, sugar, milk, cups), making it mandatory that those products bear the Max Havelaar label, a private label that observes the rules of the Fairtrade Labelling Organization. The case raised the question whether public authorities can purchase fair trade products, or are they debarred from specifically referring to the fair trade qualities of those products under the public procurement directive? Although the reference to a single label is against EU law, the Court held in this case that award criteria may concern aspects of the production process which do not materially alter the final product, so fair trade requirements can be considered as elements of the performance of the contract and consequently can be used as award criteria for public supply contracts.

2.2. The 'codified' law

The lead of the case law was followed by the adoption of the 2004 Directives, which mentioned secondary considerations from the very beginning, in Recital 1. Once recalling that the Directives were based on the established case law of the Court, the Recital specified that the Directive was codifying the case-law on award criteria, which clarifies the possibilities for contracting authorities to meet the needs of the public concerned, including in the environmental and/or social area, provided that such criteria are linked to the subject-matter of the contract, do not confer an unrestricted freedom of choice on the contracting authority, are expressly mentioned, and comply with the fundamental principles.

A number of pieces of EU legislation create substantive obligations for contracting authorities in different fields. For instance, the Clean Vehicles Di-

23. Case C-368/10 Commission v Netherlands delivered on 12 May 2012.

rective (2009/33/EC)[24] directs contracting authorities to take energy consumption and emissions into account in their purchases of road transport vehicles.[25] That Directive specifies the energy content of different fuel types and the lifetime mileage of different categories of vehicles. It also enables pricing emissions in order to be included in the evaluation and comparison of tenders. By way of Regulation (106/2008 – the Energy Star Regulation), central government authorities are required to purchase only office IT equipment meeting certain minimum energy-efficiency levels,[26] while another Directive requires that all new buildings owned and occupied by public authorities from 31st December 2018 must be "nearly zero-energy" as defined nationally according to a common framework methodology.[27] Other pieces of legislation, such as Directive 2006/32/EC[28] and Directive 2010/30/EU,[29] set targets for public procurement but do not impose obligations for contracting authorities.[30] The Eco-design Directive established a framework for eco-design requirements for energy-using products[31] and required that only appliances manufactured according to its prescriptions may be sold in the EU; consequently, contracting authorities are obliged to buy goods that are in compliance with the Directive.

2.3. The soft law

The 2004 Directives failed to fully clarify how sustainability may be integrated into the scope of public procurement,[32] thus justifying the need felt by the

24. Directive 2009/33/EC of the European Parliament and of the Council of 23 April 2009 on the promotion of clean and energy-efficient road transport vehicles.
25. For a critical view on this, see P. Kunzlik 'The Procurement of "Green Energy"' in S. Arrowsmith and P. Kunzlik (eds.) Social and Environmental Policies in EC Procurement Law above fn 1, 382.
26. Regulation (EC) No. 106/2008 on a community energy-efficiency labeling programme for office equipment (recast version).
27. Directive 2010/31/EU on the energy performance of buildings.
28. Directive 2006/32/EC on energy end-use efficiency and energy services.
29. Directive 2010/30/EU on the indication by labelling and standard product information of the consumption of energy and other resources by energy-related products.
30. A. Semple 'Reform of the EU Procurement Directives And WTO GPA: Forward Steps For Sustainability?' available at SSRN: http://ssrn.com/abstract=2089357 or http://dx.doi.org/10.2139/ssrn.2089357 at p. 9.
31. Directive 2009/125/EC of the European Parliament and of the Council of 21 October 2009 establishing a framework for the setting of ecodesign requirements for energy-related products (recast) .
32. R. Caranta 'Sustainable Public Procurement in the EU' above fn 15, 27.

Commission to intervene further. Through soft law mechanisms, the Commission has tried to guide procurers on the path of sustainability.

2.3.1. 'Buying Green' (2011)

Adopted in 2004 and revised in 2011, Buying Green! – A Handbook on green public procurement is a concrete tool to help contracting authorities choose goods and services with a lower environmental impact. It is also helpful for tenderers in procedures that use environmental considerations. The handbook explains how environmental considerations can be included at each stage of the procurement process, offers examples from the practice of contracting authorities in different EU Member States, and goes even further by including sector-specific green procurement approaches (buildings, food and catering services, electricity and timber).[33]

Another helpful piece of soft law is the Communication from 2008 (Public Procurement for a Better Environment, 16 July 2008), which set targets for Member States to achieve different levels of green public procurement (GPP) by 2010. While some Members States committed to even 100% green procurement for some products, others have settled with 20%. Based on these estimates and on the level of green procurement existent at the time, the Commission proposed that, by the year 2010, 50% of all tendering procedures should be green, where "green" means "compliant with endorsed common "core" GPP criteria as set in the Communication".[34]

2.3.2. 'Buying Social' (2012)

Buying Social – A Guide to Taking Account of Social Considerations in Public Procurement[35] tries to give more confidence to contracting authorities to be socially responsible when buying goods and services. It draws upon a previous Communication from 2001,[36] and touches upon the potential of public procurement to be used in order to stimulate greater social inclusion and thus

33. The handbook is available at http://ec.europa.eu/environment/gpp/pdf/handbook.pdf
34. Communication from the Commission to the European Parliament, the Council, the European Economic and Social Committee and the Committee of the Regions Public procurement for a better environment {SEC(2008) 2124} {SEC(2008) 2125} {SEC(2008) 2126}, available at http://eur-lex.europa.eu/legal-content/EN/TXT/?qid=1398255660927&uri=CELEX:52008DC0400 last accessed 29.04.2014
35. The handbook is available at ec.europa.eu/social/BlobServlet?docId=6457&-langId=en, last accessed 29.04.2014
36. Interpretative Communication of the Commission on the Community law applicable to public procurement and the possibilities for integrating social considerations into public procurement (2001/C 333/08) (COM(2001) 566 final).

to contribute to a sustainable development. The guide can be looked at as being part of the Europe 2020 Strategy and the EU goals for smart, sustainable and inclusive growth. It offers a number of practical examples covering a broad range of social issues, such as promoting equal chances and employment opportunities, improving labor conditions, social inclusion of vulnerable persons (for instance disabled persons), compliance in substance with the provisions of the fundamental International Labour Organization conventions, and so on.

2.4. An overview of national experiences

The responsiveness of Member States to the push for sustainability in public procurement is difficult to assess. Several studies were conducted on this issue, and the research group producing this book has also published a book on the subject in 2010, with reports from different Member States.[37] There can be identified two extreme positions regarding sustainable procurement versus value for money and competition.[38] The first one, embraced by the UK, sustains that there is no conflict between social considerations and value for money,[39] the latter being still the driving force of procurement, while the Spanish Sustainable Economic Bill seems to put the emphasis on sustainability.[40] Other systems (German, French, Italian, and Romanian) are trying to justify the coexistence of the two principles.[41]

In the group of "Green 7"- Sweden, Finland, Denmark, the Netherlands, United Kingdom, Germany and Austria, a study conducted in 2009 found that about 55% percent of procurement procedures (accounting for 45% of total contract value) included green criteria in the years 2006-2007. The impact of these criteria on life-cycle cost and CO_2 emissions has shown slightly lower costs overall for the sectors covered and significant reductions in emissions.

37. See R. Caranta and M. Trybus (eds.) The Law of Green and Social Procurement in Europe above fn 1.
38. M.E. Comba 'Green and Social Considerations in Public Procurement Contracts: A Comparative Approach' in R. Caranta and M. Trybus (eds.) The Law of Green and Social Procurement in Europe above fn 1, 299 ff.
39. M. Trybus 'Sustainability and Value for Money: Social and Environmental Considerations in the United Kingdom Public Procurement law' in R. Caranta and M. Trybus (eds.) The Law of Green and Social Procurement in Europe above fn 1, 259 ff.
40. J. Gonzales Garcia 'Sustainability and Public Procurement in the Spanish Legal System' in R. Caranta and M. Trybus (eds.) The Law of Green and Social Procurement in Europe above fn 1, 235 ff.
41. M.E. Comba 'Green and Social Considerations in Public Procurement Contracts: A Comparative Approach' above fn 38, 299 ff.

The study was based on data collected from Official Journal notices (this makes it incomplete) and on a questionnaire sent to a sample of contracting authorities.[42] Needless to say that authorities answering such questionnaires have something to report – thus being involved in green procurement, so the relevance of the data is questionable,[43] as there is no indication as to the number of authorities that do not resort to GPP or the reasons why they do not employ such considerations.

A second study looked at sustainable public procurement implementation in 9 Member States (Austria, Belgium, Denmark, Finland, France, Germany, the Netherlands, Sweden, and the United Kingdom) plus Norway.[44] The study has found that there are a great number of similarities and parallels between the national sustainable procurement schemes and that most national schemes focus on very similar product groups; furthermore, there is much commonality over which products are considered within these groups.[45]

A third study (published in 2011) concerned the strategic use of public procurement to achieve horizontal objectives.[46] Upon analyzing the national policies as well as a survey of about 2300 contracting authorities across the EU-27 and EEA Member States, the authors show that 64% of the respondent contracting authorities included environmental requirements in their tenders "regularly, sometimes or as much as possible", while 49% included social requirements with this frequency.[47]

42. PricewaterhouseCoopers, Significant and Ecofys, Collection of Statistical Information on Green Public Procurement in the EU, Brussels: European Commission, Directorate-General for the Environment, 2009, pp. 5-7.
43. A. Semple 'Reform of the EU Procurement Directives And WTO GPA: Forward Steps For Sustainability?' above fn 30.
44. L. Evans, D. Ewing, C. Nuttall and A. Mouat, Assessment and Comparison of National Green and Sustainable Public Procurement Criteria and Underlying Schemes: Final Report, Brussels: European Commission, Directorate-General for the Environment, 2010, available at http://ec.europa.eu/environment/gpp/pdf/Criteria-%20and%20Underlying%20Schemes.pdf, last accessed 28.04.2014
45. Ibidem, p. 116
46. M. Essig, J. Frijdal, W. Kahlenborn and C. Moser, Strategic Use of Public Procurement in Europe: Final Report to the European Commission, Brussels, Belgium: European Commission, Directorate-General Internal Market and Services, 2011, available at http://ec.europa.eu/internal_market/publicprocurement/docs/modernising_rules/strategic-use-public-procurement-europe_en.pdf, last accessed 28.04.2014
47. Ibidem, pp. 64-65 and pp. 74-75

A fourth study conducted in 2012 on 856 public authorities across 27 Member States concluded that more than 50% of the contracts signed included at least one 'green' criterion.[48]

The above studies seem to suggest an extensive use of both environmental and social considerations in procurement procedures. Environmental considerations are to be found mainly in the technical specifications, while social considerations are inserted among the conditions for contract performance.[49] However, the actual impact of such measures in terms of achieving the intended environmental or social objectives cannot be ascertained easily. The only way to tackle the causality gap is by analyzing case-by-case the contracts in which such considerations have been used and based on that assessment to draw some conclusions regarding outcomes, best practices and further policy recommendations.

3. The new Public Sector Directive (2014/24/EU)

3.1. The overall approach

The new directives had to be adopted since the previous ones were a bit outdated, especially considering the new economic, social, and political developments and current budgetary constraints, and the European Commission felt the need to give a new impetus to public procurement as an instrument of innovation. At least those are the main arguments put forward by the European Commission when proposing the new legislation. The declared goal of the new legal framework is to make rules simpler and more efficient for public purchasers and companies while still looking for best value for money, transparency and competition.

A particular motivation for reforming the rules is the belief that public procurement is becoming a policy strategy instrument: the new rules should encourage public purchasers to implement environmental policies and policies directed towards social integration and innovation. Thus, public authorities will be able to base their decision on the best life cycle cost of the goods offered, while more is done to encourage social integration.

48. Centre for European Policy Studies and College of Europe, The Uptake of Green Public Procurement in the EU27, Brussels, Belgium: European Commission, Directorate-General for the Environment, 2012, available at http://ec.europa.eu/environment/gpp/pdf/CEPS-CoE-GPP%20MAIN%20REPORT.pdf, p. 39.
49. M. Essig et al. above fn 46, p. 8; CEPS/CoE above previous fn. p. 46

Recital 91 reminds us that Article 11 TFEU calls for environmental protection requirements to be integrated into the definition and implementation of all Union policies and activities, in particular with a view to promoting sustainable development. In this context, the aim of the new directive is to clarify how the contracting authorities can contribute to the protection of the environment and the promotion of sustainable development, whilst ensuring that they can obtain the best value for money for their contracts.

It must be stated also that during the preparatory works, regarding the issue of strategic use of public procurement to achieve the societal goals of the Europe 2020 strategy, the stakeholders' opinions were mixed. Many stakeholders, especially businesses, showed a general reluctance to the idea of using public procurement in support of other policy objectives. Other stakeholders, notably civil society organizations, were strongly in favor of such strategic use and advocated far-reaching changes to the very principles of the European Union public procurement policy.[50]

3.2. The international background

The main international legal instrument for public procurement is the WTO Plurilateral Agreement on Government Procurement (GPA).[51] The European Union is bound by its provisions as party to the agreement, and this fact has been taken into consideration when drafting both the 2004 and the 2014 directives. An updated GPA was agreed upon in 2012.[52]

The GPA makes reference to the general principles of non-discrimination and transparency and provides for specific rules regarding technical specifications, selection of tenderers and evaluation of tenders. As to sustainable procurement, the GPA states the possibility to include environmental considerations in technical specifications and award criteria. According to Article X (6) technical specifications may "promote the conservation of natural resources or protect the environment", and environmental characteristics are listed among the (indicative) evaluation criteria in Article X (9).

50. European Commission, Proposal for a Directive of the European Parliament and of the Council on Public Procurement COM (2011) 896 final, p. 5.
51. European Commission, Internal Market and Services, EU public procurement legislation: Delivering results. Summary of evaluation report, p. 38, available at http://ec.europa.eu/internal_market/publicprocurement/modernising_rules/evaluation/index_en.htm.
52. See for details http://www.wto.org/english/tratop_e/gproc_e/thresh_e.htm, last accessed 29.10.2013.

There is no reference though to social considerations. However, this does not make them inadmissible, as long as they fulfil the requirements stemming from the general principles.

The Parties to the GPA left some unresolved issues. To address those issues, they committed to undertake an ambitious set of work programs as soon as they implement the revised GPA.[53] One of the work programmes concerns sustainable public procurement: upon acknowledging that several Parties have sustainable procurement policies, the document maintains that the GPA Parties have yet to address such policies in relation to the GPA. As a consequence, under the sustainable procurement work program, the Committee will examine topics that include the objectives of sustainable procurement and how to integrate the concept of sustainable procurement into procurement policies and apply it consistent with the principle of "best value for money," as well as with international trade obligations. The Committee will report on the best practices of such measures and policies.[54]

3.3. Scope for sustainability in the new directives

The first question to be raised here is where to include sustainable considerations? Based on the previous practices and on the reading of the new Directive, environmental and social considerations may be included in the technical specifications, in the award criteria, or in the performance conditions. The table below shows how this was actually done in the practice of EU Member States.

53. WTO Committee on Government Procurement, Annex E Decision of the Committee on Government Procurement on a Work Programme on Sustainable Procurement, 2012, available at http://docsonline.wto.org/imrd/directdoc.asp?DDFDocuments/t/PLURI/GPA/113.DOC, last accessed 28.04.2014.
54. WTO Committee on Government Procurement, Decision on the Outcomes of the Negotiations under Article XXIV:7 of the Agreement on Government Procurement, 2012, available at http://docsonline.wto.org/imrd/directdoc.asp?DDFDocuments/t/PLURI/GPA/113.DOC, last accessed 28.04.2014.

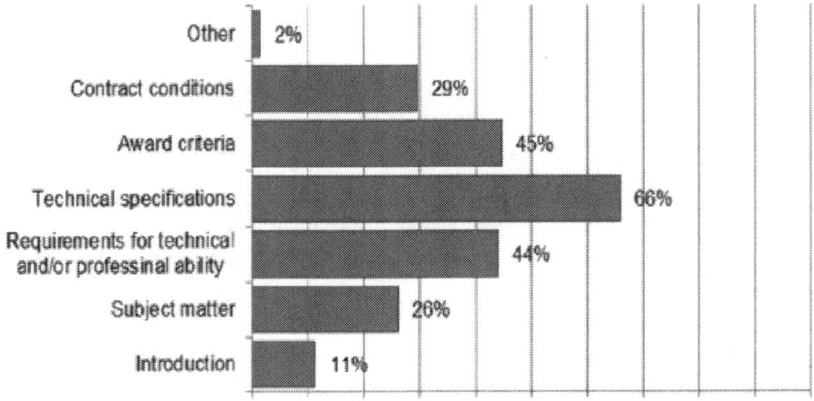

Figure 1: Stages in the PP process where sustainability considerations are included

Source: Essig et al., 2011, p. 8

Recital 40 of the directive states that

> Control of the observance of the environmental, social and labor law provisions should be performed at the relevant stages of the procurement procedure, when applying the general principles governing the choice of participants and the award of contracts, when applying the exclusion criteria and when applying the provisions concerning abnormally low tenders. The necessary verification for that purpose should be carried out in accordance with the relevant provisions of this Directive, in particular those governing means of proof and self-declarations.

3.3.1. Technical specifications

Technical specifications are the preferred stage where sustainability considerations are usually included. Thus, 66% of the contracts integrate sustainability conditions in technical specifications; only 45% go in award criteria and 29% in contract conditions (see the table above).[55]

Technical specifications may refer to the end work, service or good, but also to the production process or method. Explicit recognition that technical specifications may include reference to the production process or any other stage of the life-cycle for all types of contract is to be found in Article 42 of the new Public Sector Directive:

55. M. Essig et al. above fn 46, p. 8; CEPS/CoE above fn 48, p. 46

1. The technical specifications as defined in point 1 of Annex VII shall be set out in the procurement documents. The technical specification shall lay down the characteristics required of a works, service or supply.

Those characteristics may also refer to the specific process or method of production or provision of the requested works, supplies or services or to a specific process for another stage of its life cycle even where such factors do not form part of their material substance provided that they are linked to the subject-matter of the contract and proportionate to its value and its objectives. […]

3. Without prejudice to mandatory national technical rules, to the extent that they are compatible with Union law, the technical specifications shall be formulated in one of the following ways: (a) in terms of performance or functional requirements, including environmental characteristics, provided that the parameters are sufficiently precise to allow tenderers to determine the subject-matter of the contract and to allow contracting authorities to award the contract; […]

We shall recollect here that based on similar wording of the 2004 Directive, the Commission in its Buying Green Handbook gave a rather restrictive interpretation of the concept of "production process and methods" when it comes to their relevance for technical specifications. Based on this interpretation, technical specifications may only include those requirements which are related to the production of the good, service or work being purchased, without necessarily being visible.[56] In other words, the general policies of the company cannot be referred to – for instance, the use of recycled paper in tenderer's office. This may be a problem, as for many goods, services and works the bulk of environmental and social impacts will be incurred during the production process, and cannot be adequately addressed by specifying requirements for the end product.[57]

It is allowed to require methods of production that are widely available to economic operators across the EU: for instance, that electricity should be produced from renewable sources or that food is produced using organic methods. It would be inadmissible though to refer to a production process which is specific to one supplier – or to suppliers in one country or region – unless such reference is justified by the exceptional circumstances of the contract and accompanied by the words 'or equivalent.'[58]

56. European Commission, Buying Green, section 3.3; See for critical considerations P. Kunzlik 'The Procurement of "Green Energy"' above fn 25, 392.
57. A. Semple 'Reform of the EU Procurement Directives And WTO GPA: Forward Steps For Sustainability?' above fn 30, 9.
58. Buying Green, section 3.3.

3.3.2. Award criteria

The award criterion that accommodates sustainability considerations is the most advantageous economic tender (MEAT). According to Article 67 of the Directive, the most economically advantageous tender shall be identified on the basis of the price or cost, using a cost-effectiveness approach, such as life-cycle costing, and may include the best price-quality ratio, which shall be assessed on the basis of criteria, including qualitative, environmental and/or social aspects, linked to the subject-matter of the public contract in question. Such criteria may comprise, for instance: quality, including technical merit, aesthetic and functional characteristics, accessibility, design for all users, social, environmental and innovative characteristics and trading and its conditions.

The central test introduced by case-law (the linkage with the subject matter of the contract referred to by Concordia Bus Finland case) was incorporated in the Directives, with an additional reference to the life cycle of the works, supplies or services. Under Article 67(3) of Directive 2014/24/EU

> Award criteria shall be considered to be linked to the subject-matter of the public contract where they relate to the works, supplies or services to be provided under that contract in any respect and at any stage of their life cycle, including factors involved in: (a) the specific process of production, provision or trading of those works, supplies or services; or (b) a specific process for another stage of their life cycle, even where such factors do not form part of their material substance.

An example of award criterion that is not linked to the subject-matter of the contract was offered by EVN Wienstrom, where a criterion based upon tenderers' ability to supply electricity from renewable sources in excess of the amount required by the contracting authority was considered as unlawful. Generally, this means that criteria should not extend beyond goods/-services/works procured, so the general policy of a company cannot be subjected to the assessment.[59] Following EVN Wienstrom, other unrelated considerations are also inadmissible – for instance extra points given to tenderers that contribute to local infrastructure projects.

Environmental criteria may include: externalities linked to consumption (e.g. bus pollution); externalities linked to production (e.g. renewable electricity); life-cycle costing (acquisition, use, maintenance, and disposal; it can again include externalities).

59. A. Semple 'Reform of the EU Procurement Directives And WTO GPA: Forward Steps For Sustainability?' above fn 30, 12.

The issue to be discussed here, left unsolved by the Court of Justice in Concordia Bus Finland case, regards whether the award criterion must confer some advantage (economic or otherwise) directly to the contracting authority, or advantages may be accounted by the general public. The judgment makes reference to the link between the reduction of pollution and unburdening the city of Helsinki as regards health care, but this is still not conclusive. Does the contracting authority act in its own interest or in the interest of the public? In our opinion, the latter interpretation is the right one. By default, contracting authorities must bear in mind the public interest when resorting to sustainable considerations. Limiting their ability to resort to such strategic considerations is not in line with the public procurement philosophy.

As regards social criteria, although previously there were doubts about the legality of referring to them due to their being mainly linked to the behavior of the tenderer rather than to the subject-matter of the contract, Commission v Netherlands (Max Havelaar case) clarified that social criteria like Fair Trade production are admissible under certain conditions. The Court argued that "there is no requirement that an award criterion relates to an intrinsic characteristic of a product, that is to say something which forms part of the material substance thereof."[60] The conditions are laid down in Article 43 (1) of the Directive 2014/24/EU.[61]

The Directive gives further guidance as to the social considerations that may be included in award criteria or performance conditions in Recital 99:

> Measures aiming at the protection of health of the staff involved in the production process, the favouring of social integration of disadvantaged persons or members of vulnerable groups amongst the persons assigned to performing the contract or training in the skills needed for the contract in question can also be the subject of award criteria or contract performance conditions provided that they relate to the works, supplies or services to be provided under the contract. For instance, such criteria or conditions might refer, amongst other things, to the employment of long-term job-seekers, the implementation of training measures for the unemployed or young persons in the course of the performance of the contract to be awarded. In technical specifications contracting authorities can provide such social requirements which directly characterize the product or service in question, such as accessibility for persons with disabilities or design for all users.

This recital brings about an (unwelcomed) distinction between social considerations involving health protection and social integration of disadvantaged

60. Case C-368/10 European Commission v Kingdom of the Netherlands, judgment of 10 May 2012, not yet reported, paragraph 91.
61. See the section on the use of labels, below

persons and the rest of the social considerations – for instance, working hours or rates of pay[62] – suggesting that the latter are not admissible under EU law.

3.3.3. Selection criteria

Is there room for sustainability considerations in the selection criteria? The answer is definitely positive. Thus, although the principle of non-discrimination is in general excluding any form of protectionism for particular undertakings, the new Public Sector Directive contains exceptions to the rule. Some contracts may be put aside for special categories of operators. There is now increased scope for contracts to be reserved for enterprises employing disabled or disadvantaged workers (Article 20). The threshold of employees that fall within the category of disabled workers has been lowered from 50% in the 2004 directive to 30% in the new one:

> Member States may reserve the right to participate in public procurement procedures to sheltered workshops and economic operators whose main aim is the social and professional integration of disabled or disadvantaged persons or may provide for such contracts to be performed in the context of sheltered employment programmes, provided that at least 30 % of the employees of those workshops, economic operators or programmes are disabled or disadvantaged workers.

Under Article 57 exclusion criteria may be also used for advancing social considerations. An economic operator may be excluded from the procedure for not paying taxes or social security contributions, regardless of the fact that this was established by judicial or administrative decision or it is proved on the spot by the contracting authority.

Interestingly, under Article 57(3) the protection of the environment may be used as an escape door for cases where the operator has failed to comply with social security regulations. This possibility is at the disposal of Member States, which may or may not decide to use it.

The economic operators may be excluded if the contracting authority can demonstrate that they are in violation of applicable obligations in the fields of environmental, social and labour law established by Union law, national law, and collective agreements or by the international environmental, social and

62. A. Semple 'Reform of the EU Procurement Directives And WTO GPA: Forward Steps For Sustainability?' above fn 30, 14.

labor law provisions listed in Annex X.[63] This is an important tool for contracting authorities, as it follows also from the Recital 40.

> Control of the observance of the environmental, social and labour law provisions should be performed at the relevant stages of the procurement procedure, when applying the general principles governing the choice of participants and the award of contracts, when applying the exclusion criteria and when applying the provisions concerning abnormally low tenders. The necessary verification for that purpose should be carried out in accordance with the relevant provisions of this Directive, in particular those governing means of proof and self-declarations.

Another exclusion ground that may relate to social considerations is the one about "grave professional misconduct, which renders its integrity questionable".[64]

The professional misconduct may refer for instance to the prohibition of clandestine employment, non-compliance with provisions on equality of treatment, or on health and safety, or with provisions in favor of certain categories of persons.[65] However, defining grave professional misconduct is left at the discretion of the Member States.

Qualitative criteria aim at verifying the suitability to pursue the professional activity, the economic and financial standing and the technical and/or professional ability. When assessing these factors, past performance regarding environmental or social obligations may be considered. Thus, if a contract requires specific know-how in the 'social' field, specific experience may be used as a criterion as regards technical capability and knowledge in proving the suitability of candidates. Moreover, CSR[66] may be referred to only if it demonstrates the technical capability, within the meaning set out above, of the undertaking to perform a given contract.[67]

3.3.4. Performance clauses

First and foremost, Article 70 of Directive 2014/24/EU acknowledges that contract conditions may include social and environmental requirements.

63. Article 57(4)(a) corroborated with Article 18(2) of Directive 24/2014/EU.
64. Article 57(4)(c) of Directive 2014/24/EU.
65. COM (2001) 566 final, p. 10.
66. European Commission, Green Paper Promoting a European Framework for Corporate Social Responsibility, COM(2001) 366 of 18.7.2001.
67. COM (2001) 566 final, p. 10.

Contracting authorities may lay down special conditions relating to the performance of a contract, provided that they are linked to the subject-matter of the contract within the meaning of Article 67(3) and indicated in the call for competition or in the procurement documents. Those conditions may include economic, innovation-related, environmental, social or employment-related considerations.

Performance conditions may for instance include: purchasing products from small-scale producers in developing countries at favourable trading conditions (Fair Trade); Obligation to comply with ILO / human rights conventions during contract execution; delivering the product in an environmentally-friendly way (bulk delivery, outside peak traffic…); recuperating used products/packaging.

The main difference between including sustainability considerations in the technical specifications versus performance conditions is that unlike technical specifications, performance conditions do not allow for exclusion of tenderers on the basis of anticipated non-compliance.

The issue was differently assessed by the Advocate General and the Court of Justice in the Max Havelaar case. While the Advocate General considered the requirement according to which the tenderers had to comply with the 'criteria of sustainability of purchases and socially responsible business', inter alia by contributing to improving the sustainability of the coffee market and to environmentally, socially and economically responsible coffee production as a contract performance condition,[68] the Court of Justice disagreed and held that the requirements are part of the minimum level of professional capacity required from tenderers.

While for environmental considerations the preferred stage to take them into account is the technical specifications, social considerations are more easily fitted in contract performance clauses.[69]

As observed in the literature,[70] contract conditions are playing an important role in stressing the environmental or social commitments made by tenderers and providing for appropriate remedies in case of breach. In a practical way, they can be linked to bonus payments in order to offer incentives for high performance.

68. Case C-368/10 Commission v. Netherlands, paragraphs 128 ff.
69. European Commission, Buying Social: A Guide to Taking Account of Social Considerations in Public Procurement, Brussels, Belgium: Directorate-General for Employment, Social Affairs and Inclusion, 2010, pp. 43-44.
70. A. Semple 'Reform of the EU Procurement Directives And WTO GPA: Forward Steps For Sustainability?' above fn 30, 15.

Choosing the contract performance conditions as the place to include sustainability conditions has its deficiencies, because the tenderers promise to perform certain tasks by way of a simple declaratory statement, so there is no effective way of insuring that the actual implications are assessed properly. This may lead to situations where the delivery of the contract can be compromised, because the "cost of compliance outweighs the margin of profit achieved by the successful tenderer".[71]

3.4. Life cycle costing

3.4.1. Scope

The absolute novelty of the 2014 Directives regards the reference to the concept of life cycle costing (LCC). Article 68 is dedicated entirely to this new concept. The life cycle costing covers parts or all of the costs borne by the contracting authority or other users, such as: (i) costs relating to acquisition, (ii) costs of use, such as consumption of energy and other resources, (iii) maintenance costs, (iv) end of life costs, such as collection and recycling costs. It also covers costs imputed to environmental externalities linked to the product, service or works during its life cycle, provided their monetary value can be determined and verified; such costs may include the cost of emissions of greenhouse gases and of other pollutant emissions and other climate change mitigation costs.

The method used for the assessment of costs imputed to environmental externalities should be based based on objectively verifiable and non-discriminatory criteria. Where such methodology has not been established for repeated or continuous application, it shall not unduly favour or disadvantage certain economic operators. The method should be accessible to all interested parties, and data required should be provided with reasonable effort by normally diligent economic operators, including economic operators from third countries party to the GPA or other international agreements by which the Union is bound.

Under the new Public Sector Directive, LCC is no longer to be restricted to MEAT, as it was in the 2004 Directive; consequently, the lowest price/cost criteria will enable contracting authorities to resort to LCC as well. Article 67(2) provides that "The most economically advantageous tender from the point of view of the contracting authority shall be identified on the basis of the price or cost, using a cost-effectiveness approach, such as life-cycle costing in accordance with Article 68 [...]".

71. Ibidem.

The new Public Sector Directive makes LCC the centerpiece of sustainable public procurement, detailing its features and encouraging contracting authorities to make use of it. Life-cycle costing is still optional, but under Article 68(3) if there is a common EU methodology the life-cycle costing becomes mandatory.

Furthermore, the boundaries between lowest price and MEAT are not as clear as before. Resorting to LCC makes the award procedure using the lowest price criterion a complex one. The difference from MEAT will be that in case of an award based on the lowest price which in its turn is based on LCC, the price remains the only criterion for the award, so all the externalities have to be incorporated and monetized as elements of the price. MEAT, on the other hand, may be based on LCC that includes non-monetized externalities (externalities that don't necessarily have a financial value).

3.4.2. The concept of LCC

Based on the assumption that the purchase price alone does not reflect the financial and non-financial gains that are offered by environmentally and socially preferable assets as they accumulate during their operations and use stages, LCC is a tool which evaluates the costs of an asset throughout its life-cycle.[72] In the context of sustainable public procurement (SPP), the use of LCC is a very important element in the effort to shift the paradigm of public procurement beyond the confinement of using solely the purchase price of a good or service.[73]

Though many procuring entities in the EU are using life cycle-costing as a decision-making tool, its use is still far from being systematic and the calculation methodologies are often adapted to the circumstances of the bid.[74]

In the realm of public procurement, the calculation of LCC has to be different for products/works and for services. The life cycle of a product or work covers all stages from raw material acquisition until the final disposal: production, transport and maintenance. The life cycle of a service includes all

72. See for more details D. Dragons and B. Neamtu 'Sustainable Public Procurement: Life Cycle Costing (LCC) in the New EU Directive Proposal' EPPPL, 1/2013, 19-30.
73. O. Perera, B. Morton, T. Perfrement Life Cycle Costing in Sustainable Public Procurement: A Question of Value (International Institute for Sustainable Development, Winnipeg, 2009) 1.
74. See for instance this case study: E. Hochschorner and M. Noring 'Practitioners' Use of Life Cycle Costing with Environmental Costs – a Swedish Study' International Journal of Life Cycle Assessment, 16/2011, 897–902.

stages from its preparation to the end of its provision.[75] The costs to be taken into account include direct monetary expenses as well as external environmental costs, if the latter can be somehow valued in monetary terms.

The most common LCC methodologies used by governments are based on a purely financial valuation, and they consider four main cost categories: investment, operation, maintenance and end-of-life disposal expenses. In order to become an environmentally-relevant methodology, the LCC needs to include external costs associated with the work/service/product. In this way, the "externalities" are internalized and are given a financial value.

The methodology best adapted to sustainable public procurement is the environmental life cycle costing (ELCC). As stated above, on top of financial assessments it takes the external impact on the environment into consideration, which may be based on LCA (Life-cycle Assessment) analyses on environmental impacts. LCAs evaluate the effects that a product has on the environment over the entire period of its lifetime ('cradle-to-grave' analysis) with a view toward increasing resource-use efficiency. They measure for example the external costs of global warming contribution associated with emissions of different greenhouse gases.[76] Environmental costs can be calculated also with respect to acidification (grams of SO2, NOX and NH3), eutrophication (grams of NOX and NH3), land use (m^2*year) or other measurable impacts.[77]

Until now, the LCC has been scarcely used in public procurement. Studies show that it is not yet considered to be a critical component of sustainable public procurement worldwide.[78]

International experiences are nevertheless useful in order to put things in perspective. The U.S.A.,[79] Japan, Switzerland and Norway[80] may be alone in

75. C. Jobse and N. Dimitri ‚LCC-Calculations and the Principles of Public Procurement' available at https://underpinn.portals.mbs.ac.uk/Portals/70/docs/2.1%20-%20Jobse%20&%20Dimitri%20-%20LCC%20calculations%20v1%200.pdf, last accesed 15.01.2013.
76. See for details http://ec.europa.eu/environment/gpp/lcc.htm.
77. The SMART-SPP project developed and tested a tool for public authorities to assess LCC and CO2 emissions and to compare bids. It is available to download in four languages: http://www.smart-spp.eu/guidance.
78. O. Perera, B. Morton and T. Perfrement Life Cycle Costing in Sustainable Public Procurement: A Question of Value above fn 73, 1 .
79. C. McCrudden ‚Using Public Procurement to Achieve Social Outcomes' Natural Resources Forum, 28(4)/2004, 257-67.
80. B.E. Tysseland 'Life Cycle Cost Based Procurement Decisions – A Case Study of Norwegian Defense Procurement Projects' International Journal of Project Management, 26/2008, 366–375.

consistently applying LCC methodologies as a part of green and sustainable procurement policies. Sweden,[81] UK, Denmark, Germany, The Netherlands, France, Austria report to be conducting "some form of LCC analyses" or "derivatives of it" in the procurement/commissioning of new energy-efficient buildings; the refurbishment of existing buildings, especially heat, light and ventilation systems/units and building management systems; indoor and outdoor lighting, when budgets are over €50,000; solar thermal and PV applications; office equipment: computers, printers and photocopies when budgets are over €60,000. Some other nations, including Canada, Argentina, Spain, Italy, and Portugal report to "have experimented" with the use of LCC methodologies in the commissioning of energy-efficient buildings.[82] Some new EU Member States are embracing the idea at (yet) programmatic level.[83]

3.4.3. Environmental LCC

The methodology referred to in Article 68(2) of the new Public Sector Directive concerns only environmental externalities. Environmental externalities refer to an economic concept of uncompensated environmental effects of production and consumption that affect consumer utility and enterprise cost outside the market mechanism. As a consequence of negative externalities, the private costs of production tend to be lower than costs borne by the society at large. It is the aim of the 'polluter/user-pays' principle to prompt households and enterprises to internalise externalities in their plans and budgets.[84] Among the examples we can list inputs of natural resources / pollution generated during production, use and disposal of goods; impact on fauna and flora.

3.4.4. Social LCC

One question that arises in the context of LCC is whether there are other types of externalities that can be factored in, leaving aside environmental costs. Among these are the social costs, which are harder to assess but still important. Social LCC would entail taking into consideration for instance la-

81. E. Hochschorner and M. Noring 'Practitioners' Use of Life Cycle Costing with Environmental Costs – a Swedish Study' above fn 74, 897–902 argue that the use of LCC is custom-made and varies among different public authorities.
82. O. Perera, B. Morton and T. Perfrement Life Cycle Costing in Sustainable Public Procurement: A Question of Value above fn 73, 1.
83. J. Kulczycka 'Life Cycle Thinking in Polish Official Documents and Research. The Determination of Discount Rate for Green Public Procurement' International Journal of Life Cycle Assessment, 14/2009, 375–378.
84. Glossary of Environment Statistics, Studies in Methods, Series F, No. 67, (United Nations, New York, 1997).

bour conditions; equal opportunities; accessibility criteria and so on. The 'socially sustainable production process' is the production process linked to the subject matter of the contract that ensures respect for the health and safety of workers and for social standards.

The new Public Sector Directive does not go far enough on this. From Article 68 it can be inferred that social and employment criteria are excluded from LCC, which definitely represents a weakening of the full potential of LCC. Contracting authorities will be tempted thus to restrict LCC exclusively to ELCC (environmental life cycle costing).

Clearly, costs such as unemployment benefits, the payment of which would have been necessary without the procurement of a given asset, or health care costs that would have been necessary if environmentally preferable alternatives would not have been procured, are particularly challenging to forecast.[85] However, there are grounds for the widening of the scope of the LCC as to include such criteria as the social impact of the public procurement. The feasibility of societal LCC is still debated in the literature on organizations,[86] but it definitely finds its place within the rather broad context of sustainable public procurement. For instance, the life cycle of a product can be broken down into labor units (hours) and calculate the income per unit; that income can then be used to approximate the well-being of people in different regions, considered to be including such basic needs as food and housing.[87]

3.4.5. Methodologies

In the initial proposal table by the Commission, economic operators were allowed to submit their own LCC methodology, when such methodology was not provided for by the contracting authority. The final text of the new Public Sector Directive removed such possibility, but Article 68 does require that

85. O. Perera, B. Morton and T. Perfrement 'Life Cycle Costing in Sustainable Public Procurement: A Question of Value above fn 73, 3.
86. T.E. Swarr 'Societal Life Cycle Assessment – Could You Repeat The Question?' International Journal Life Cycle Assessment, 14/2009, 285-289; R. Grießhammer, C. Benoît, L.C. Dreyer, A. Flysjö et al. 'Feasibility Study: Integration of Social Aspects into LCA' 2006, available at http://www.saiplatform.org/uploads/Library/UNEP-SETACLifeCycleInitiativeTFonSocialIssues-FeasibilityStudy.pdf, last accessed 15.01.2014; A. Jørgensen, A. Le Bocq, L. Nazarkina and M. Hauschild 'Methodologies for Social Life Cycle Assessment' International Journal of Life Cycle Assessment, 13(2)/2008, 96–103.
87. D. Hunkeler 'Societal LCA Methodology and a Case Study' International Journal of Life Cycle Assessment, 11(6)/2006, pp. 371-382.

data requested for LCC "can be provided with reasonable effort by normally diligent economic operators, including operators from third countries party to the Agreement or other international agreements by which the Union is bound".

This enables the adoption of national requirements for the formats or types of data that can be provided in such circumstances. In the event such requirements are not in compliance with the standards set by the directive, the courts can then control the decisions of the contracting authorities, by resorting to the principle of proportionality. The yardstick against which the ELLC requirements will be measured is the 'diligent economic operator' concept. This will involve a high degree of expertise. In cases where national legislation does not complement the directives with the adequate methodologies or characteristics of data to be provided by bidders, the courts will again have the difficult task of assessing whether the data requested by the contracting authorities was available for a 'diligent economic operator'. Interesting case law may lie ahead in this field.

Article 68 of the new Public Sector Directive has not maintained the position from the Commission's draft that LCC methodologies must be 'established for repeated or continuous application' – meaning that tailor-made methodologies developed for the purpose of an individual contract would not be allowed. The adopted text only forbids methodologies which would favour a particular undertaking in the context of a specific contract.

While safeguards are undoubtedly needed to ensure that the integrity of LCC processes is maintained, this could arguably be met in the same way as for other award criteria – i.e. through the requirements of transparency and equal treatment as set out in the directives and case law. The publicity of the LCC methodology in the tender documents alongside with the weightings to be applied to different criteria should be sufficient to achieve this aim.

For certain contracts, an off-the-shelf LCC methodology which adequately captures all internal and external costs may not be available (either at EU or another level). Under the existing provisions, it seems that contracting authorities can modify an existing methodology, and must strictly apply a pre-existing methodology only when it was adopted at EU level. Given that the additional transparency benefits of using a pre-existing methodology over publishing the specific methodology in the tender documents are negligible, the second approach seems preferable and less likely to impede upon the adoption of LCC by contracting authorities.[88]

While the provision that enables EU-wide methodologies to be adopted may assist in preventing fragmentation and offer greater legal certainty to contracting authorities to carry out LCC in those sectors, its success depends very much on the quality and comprehensiveness of the methodologies developed at EU level.[89]

Semple argued that the inability of contracting authorities to insist on a particular methodology will have as an effect a weak application of the LCC, which is bound to interfere with the comparability of tenders and introduces further uncertainties into what is already often a complicated process. She proposes to go back to the initial proposal, where there was no requirement that LCC methodologies be established for repeated or continuous application, and alternative methodologies presented by suppliers were acceptable.[90] In our opinion, the current solution is in line with the principle of equal treatment, so it is hard to imagine a complete opposite one being accepted by the Court of Justice, but as any other provision of such kind, it may indeed complicate the life of contracting authorities and discourage them from using LCC. On the other hand, with a surge in methodologies for LCC in different fields complemented by 'nudging' Member States into providing quotas of procedures using LCC, this shortcoming may be compensated.

3.5. The use of labels

The Directive, building on the recent case law (Max Havelaar in particular), provides also the possibility to refer to specific environmental or social labels in technical specifications (Article 43). Eco labels may refer to environmental performance, and functional requirements can be laid down by reference to the specifications of an eco-label. Products bearing the eco-label are presumed to comply, but other means of proof must be accepted. Using as a reference point the Max Havelaar case, the provisions regarding the use of labels are quite detailed. The label must fulfil some conditions [art.43 (1)]: (a) the label requirements only concern criteria which are linked to the subject-matter of the contract and are appropriate to define characteristics of the works, supplies or services that are the subject-matter of the contract; (b) the

88. C. Jobse and N. Dimitri ‚LCC-Calculations and the Principles of Public Procurement' above fn 75, 5.
89. A. Semple 'Reform of the EU Procurement Directives And WTO GPA: Forward Steps For Sustainability?' above fn 30, 17.
90. Ibidem, p. 16.

label requirements are based on objectively verifiable and non-discriminatory criteria; (c) the labels are established in an open and transparent procedure in which all relevant stakeholders, including government bodies, consumers, social partners, manufacturers, distributors and non-governmental organisations, may participate; (d) the labels are accessible to all interested parties; (e) the label requirements are set by a third party over which the economic operator applying for the label cannot exercise a decisive influence.

Alternative ways of demonstrating the requirements are also possible: where tenderers were in the impossibility of obtaining the specific label indicated by the contracting authority or an equivalent label within the relevant time limits, for reasons that are not their fault, a technical dossier from the manufacturer can be presented.

It is pretty obvious that non-acceptance of equivalent labels would have been against the principles assumed by the EU under the GPA. However, as Semple observed, "the additional requirement to accept a manufacturer's own dossier completely removes the ability of the contracting authority to insist upon third-party certification regarding the environmental or social characteristics of the product they are buying. Not only does it lack any progression from the current position, it confuses the matter with seemingly contradictory wording".[91]

The eco-label is currently regulated by Regulation 2010/66/EC.[92] It is a voluntary scheme, intended to promote those products which have a high level of environmental performance. The regulation extends the use of eco-label in order to avoid the proliferation of environmental labeling schemes and to encourage higher environmental performance in all sectors for which environmental impact is a factor in consumer choice. However, procuring entities may refer to other equivalent labels, as the imposition of a mandatory use of the eco-label would be discriminatory towards potential bidders.[93]

4. Evaluation of the reform: challenges and opportunities

The new Public Sector Directive provides for many opportunities to include sustainability considerations in procurement processes, but areas of legal un-

91. A. Semple 'Reform of the EU Procurement Directives And WTO GPA: Forward Steps For Sustainability?' above fn 30, 11.
92. Regulation (EC) No 66/2010 of the European Parliament and of the Council of 25 November 2009 on the EU Ecolabel.
93. COM (2001) 274 final, II.1.2

certainty remain. The setting is better for environmental considerations than for social considerations. However, there will be reluctance at contracting authority level, as long as the Commission does not engage on the path of recommending quotas of sustainable public procurement.

LCC will be the pivotal element of the reform, and it may be regarded as the major novelty from the perspective of sustainable public procurement.

It is quite evident that buying green can save money, particularly when an LCC approach is taken during the procurement process. In a quote attributed to Einstein, we are warned that "not everything that can be counted counts and not everything that counts can be counted". In advocating the use of LCC, it is however important to acknowledge that the science of LCC is far from perfect. The success of LCC is dependent of its scope (meaning the inclusion of environmental externalities or/and other externalities) and the methodology used (which in many cases is incomplete[94] and based on experts' perceptions, not on hard scientific evidence[95]). Its results will be skewed further by the method based on which future costs are perceived and forecasted, by the reliability of the data used, by what discounting rates are applied and what stages of asset life cycle are included in the analysis. Additional uncertainties arise when quantifying the lowered risks, avoided environmental damage, avoided clean-up costs, and non-financial benefits such as the contributions to social cohesion through the creation of jobs, livelihoods and new industries. Forecasting such costs and benefits with an acceptable degree of certainty is very challenging,[96] although there are solutions envisaged by the doctrine.[97]

One problem that is arising when considering sustainable public procurement is that procuring goods, services or works on the basis of life cycle costing may mean paying more in the beginning. It has been argued[98] that in developing countries, the production of sustainable and LCC-efficient goods

94. E. Hochschorner and M. Noring E. Hochschorner and M. Noring 'Practitioners' Use of Life Cycle Costing with Environmental Costs – a Swedish Study' above fn 74, 897–902.
95. E. Korpi and T. Ala-Risku 'Life Cycle Costing: A Review of Published Case Studies' Managerial Auditing Journal, 23(3)/2008, 240–261.
96. C. Jobse and N. Dimitri, LCC-Calculations and the Principles of Public Procurement' above fn 75, 3.
97. A. Bala, M. Raugei, G. Benveniste, C. Gazulla et al. 'Simplified Tools for Global Warming Potential Evaluation: When 'Good Enough' Is Best' International Journal of Life Cycle Assessment, 15/2010, pp. 489–498.
98. O. Perera, B. Morton and T. Perfrement 'Life Cycle Costing in Sustainable Public Procurement: A Question of Value above fn 73, 3.

and services is still emergent, which means that the only way to acquire sustainable alternatives will be through expensive imports or paying a very high cost premium to stimulate infant local industries. In lower income economies, this difference can be higher, as much as 10 to 50 percent. The same authors believe that over time, however, the large volumes demanded by public procurement contracts can make economies of scale more feasible, and the prices of these products can be expected to decrease as more producers enter the market. Also, public procurers can begin to use their strong market positioning to negotiate bulk discounts as the market begins to mature.

One of the recurring deterrents to the application of LCC in public procurement is the fact that data in the public domain is often aggregated and incomplete, presented in different formats, thus making comparison and extrapolation difficult.[99] In addition to the lack of readily-available and representative data, the difficulty lays in how to effectively link the award criteria with the outcomes of the procurement process.[100]

Other impediments to the success of LCC are, for instance, the reluctance of the public sector accounting to embrace the multi-year accounting and budget frameworks that allow temporal flexibility to carryover or borrow-against-the-future, but also the fact that in many instances the procuring agency is not the same with the agency that will operate/use the product/service (end user).[101]

LCC has proved to be feasible in the case of selected goods and services. It is considered highly applicable to supplies such as office and server ICT equipment, vehicles, indoor and outdoor lighting, fuel and furniture, to services such as electricity, transport, waste handling, catering beverages, and to works such as construction of new buildings or refurbishment of existing buildings, railways, roads. Moderate applicability has been experienced for

99. Ibidem.
100. A. Semple'Reform of the EU Procurement Directives And WTO GPA: Forward Steps For Sustainability?' above fn 30, 4.
101. O. Perera, B. Morton and T. Perfrement'Life Cycle Costing in Sustainable Public Procurement: A Question of Value above fn 73, 1.

paper and food catering,[102] couriers and postal services, as well as landscaping. It is considered not applicable to office supplies and software.[103]

In times of economic crisis, LCC may prove hard to be implemented effectively due to the existence of 'buy national' policies, given the fact that 'regular' public procurement gives preference to local companies over foreign suppliers.[104] Not to mention that in the case of US 'buy American' policies, these tendencies are even enshrined in law.[105]

For contracting authorities it will be a challenge to assess the costing of the whole life cycle of products, services and supplies – especially due to fluctuations in commodity and electricity prices. A short-term consequence will be to favor undertakings that are providing full-serviced products over their entire life, and thus combine supply awards with service ones. In this context, we can also foresee a surge in central body purchasing or coordinated purchasing, due to its convenience when it comes to assessing environmental or other sustainable aspects of a bid.

It has been argued that cost concerns are the most serious obstacle for taking environmental factors into account in the purchasing process,[106] and that public authorities are more inclined to pursue sustainable procurement in contexts where they perceive win-win situations.[107] It will be much harder when the outcomes are not very clear or documented properly and then competition rules are taken into consideration.

Sustainability is itself a contested and complex concept, and procurement professionals may lack the skills and knowledge necessary to successfully implement sustainable procurement. A survey found that 83% of the purchasing professionals considered themselves ill equipped to deliver sustainability

102. Although there are studies that maintain that the LCA for food and drinks is possible and advisable, for both private and public purchasers – see for details N. Peacock, C. De Camillis, D. Pennington, H. Aichinger et al. 'Towards a Harmonised Framework Methodology for the Environmental Assessment of Food and Drink Products' International Journal of Life Cycle Assessment, 16/2011, 189–197.
103. O. Perera, B. Morton and T. Perfrement'Life Cycle Costing in Sustainable Public Procurement: A Question of Value above fn 73, 3.
104. M. Brulhart and F. Trionfetti 'Public Expenditure, International Specialisation and Agglomeration' European Economic Review, 48(4)/2004, 851-81.
105. S. Vagstad 'Promoting Fair Competition in Public Procurement, Journal of Public Economics' 58(2)/1995, 283-307.
106. H. Min and W. Galle 'Green Purchasing Practices of US Firms' International Journal of Operations & Production Management, 21(9)/2001, 1222-38.
107. P. Rao and D. Holt 'Do Green Supply Chains Lead to Competitiveness and Economic Performance?' International Journal of Operations & Production Management, 25(9/10)/2005, 898-916.

through procurement.[108] Other studies, although not that recent, have shown that purchasing managers are unsure of how to incorporate ethical and social issues in their procurement.[109]

Government procurement can play an important role as a stimulus for innovative activity among companies within a certain region. It is no wonder that public procurement has been at the center of recent discussions on innovation policy at both the European and national levels.[110] In the context of the public sector, research in this area has shown that government procurement is a key part of a demand-oriented innovation policy.[111] Sustainable public procurement can have a role in indirectly stimulating social and environmental benefits through exerting pressure on suppliers to reduce their own impact on the environment. This was showcased, for instance, in the relation between hospitals and suppliers of medical products, although LCC was considered to be a difficult task.[112] [113]

Selected references

S. Arrowsmith and P. Kunzlik (eds.), Social and Environmental Policies in EC Procurement Law, Cambridge, Cambridge University Press, 2009.

108. P. Snell ‚Struggle with Sustainability' Supply Management, News section, No. 16 November 2006.
109. R. Cooper, G. Frank and R. Kemp 'A Multinational Comparison of Key Ethical Issues, Helps and Challenges in the Purchasing & Supply Management Profession: The Key Implications for Business and the Professions' Journal of Business Ethics, 23(1)/2000, 83-100.
110. L. Aho, E. Cornu, J. Georghiou and A. Subira Creating an Innovative Europe: report of the independent expert group on R&D and innovation (European Commission Publication, Brussels, 2006).
111. J. Edler and L. Georghiou ‚Public Procurement and Innovation – Resurrecting The Demand Side' Research Policy, 36(7)/2007, 949-963; B. Aschhoff and W. Sofka ‚Innovation on demand – can public procurement drive market success of innovations?' Research Policy, 38(3)/2008, 1235-47; See also the chapter on innovation by R. Butler, in this book.
112. G. Gwenaëlle and J.-C. Rico ‚The Impact of Sustainable Public Procurement on Supplier Management – The Case of French Public Hospitals' Industrial Marketing Management, 41/2012, 573–580.
113. Acknowledgement: The research for this chapter undertaken by Bogdana Neamtu was financed by Babes Bolyai University through a post-doctoral research grant, contract no. GTC_ 34058/2013.

R. Caranta and M. Trybus (eds.), The Law of Green and Social Procurement in Europe, DJOF, 2010.

R. Caranta, Sustainable Procurement, in M. Trybus, R. Caranta and G. Edelstam (eds.), European Union Law of Public Contracts: Public Procurement and Beyond, Bruylant, 2014.

Centre for european policy studies and college of Europe, The Uptake of Green Public Procurement in the EU27, Brussels, Belgium: European Commission, Directorate-General for the Environment, 2012, available at .http://ec.europa.eu/environment/gpp/pdf/CEPS-CoE-GPP%20MAIN%-20REPORT.pdf, last accessed 29.04.2014.

D. Dragos and B. Neamtu, Sustainable Public Procurement: Life Cycle Costing (LCC) in the New EU Directive Proposal, EPPPL, 1/2013, pp. 19-30.

M. Essig, J. Frijdal, W. Kahlenborn and C. Moser, Strategic Use of Public Procurement in Europe: Final Report to the European Commission. Brussels, Belgium: European Commission, 2011, Directorate-General Internal Market and Services, available at http://ec.europa.eu/internal_market/-publicprocurement/docs/modernising_rules/strategic-use-public-procurement-europe_en.pdf, last accessed 28.04.2014.

Jobse and N. Dimitri, LCC-Calculations and the Principles of Public Procurement, available at https://underpinn.portals.mbs.ac.uk/Portals/ 70/-docs/2.1%20-%20Jobse%20&%20Dimitri%20-%20LCC%20calculations%20v1%200.pdf, last accesed 15.01.2014.

Mccrudden, Buying Social Justice. Equality, Government Procurement, & Legal Change, Oxford, Oxford University Press, 2007.

O. Perera, B. Morton and T. Perfrement, Life Cycle Costing in Sustainable Public Procurement: A Question of Value, International Institute for Sustainable Development, Winnipeg 2009.

Semple, Reform of the EU Procurement Directives And WTO GPA: Forward Steps For Sustainability?, Available at SSRN: http://ssrn.com/abstract=-2089357 or http://dx.doi.org/10.2139/ ssrn.2089357.

Innovation in Public Procurement: Towards the "Innovation Union"

Luke Butler

1. Introduction

Innovation is scarcely mentioned in the Treaty on the Functioning of the European Union ("TFEU").[1] Yet, since 2000, the EU has identified innovation as a cornerstone of EU policy, including promotion of the use of public procurement to this end.[2] For the first time, Directive 2014/24/EU specifically incorporates reference to innovation as part of the language of the Directive.[3] Against the backdrop of an emerging EU policy and academic discourse, this Chapter first examines the Directive's approach to defining innovation and its designation as a strategic objective before examining certain select provisions.[4] The latter concern the provisions relating to research and development ("R&D"),[5] preliminary market consultations, technical standards and specifications, variants, innovation as an aspect of choice of procedure, award and contract performance and occasional and joint procurement. A detailed dis-

1. See Articles 173(1), 148 and 153(2)(a) TFEU.
2. For an overview, see Section 2 below.
3. The only references to innovation in Directive 2004/18/EC are those contained in the Annexes and which refer to the names of relevant national bodies which have "innovation" in their title. Of course, this did not necessarily preclude the use of certain of the Directive's provisions to achieve innovation.
4. The focus on certain select provisions corresponds to those aspects identified by the Commission Public Procurement Reform Fact Sheet No. 9: Innovation (2014) with a few additions.
5. The Commission Fact Sheet only identifies the "exemption of research and development projects", although this Chapter also discusses the Directive's provisions on R&D.

cussion of the new innovation partnership has been consciously omitted on the basis that its designation as a "procedure" legitimates its proper treatment alongside the other established procedures in the Chapter on procedures featured in this book. Further, this Chapter does not consider the range of other potential contributions of Directive 2014/24/EU to innovation.[6]

This Chapter argues that Directive 2014/24/EU demonstrates uncertainty and/or ambivalence as to the legitimate scope of the procurement function in achieving innovation. This argument is borne out, in particular, by the Directive's approach to the provisions on R&D. It is fundamentally questioned whether Directive 2014/24/EU is adequately calibrated to act as an effective instrument to facilitate the achievement of innovation. Further, the difficulties of qualifying, quantifying and empirically validating innovation render it difficult to determine whether and to what extent certain additional features of Directive 2014/24/EU are likely to translate into tangible innovation outcomes for users. Notwithstanding, Directive 2014/24/EU takes the important first step of raising the consciousness of otherwise price and risk averse contracting authorities to the possibility of using the public procurement machinery to facilitate innovation. A process of observation and institutional learning is inevitable.

2. Spurring Innovation through Procurement: Towards an Innovation Union

Whilst for many years the EU had promoted innovation in pursuit of broader economic and social goals, it was only after the launch of the Lisbon strategy by the European Council in 2000 that innovation gained traction as a policy

6. For instance, the Commission Fact Sheet on innovation (n 4) also identifies the use of total life cycle costing (an aspect discussed by Dragos in this book), simplification of the competitive dialogue (discussed by Telles and Butler in this book and innovation in social and health services (discussed by Caranta). This Chapter also does not discuss aspects not otherwise identified by the Fact Sheet but which may also correspond to innovation objectives. On example concerns the Directive's provisions on SMEs (discussed by Trybus in this book). This Chapter also omits from its discussion consideration of the ways in which the Directive could be said to provide a more "innovative" set of procurement processes. For instance, this Chapter does not examine use of dynamic purchasing systems (Article 34), electronic auctions (Article 35) and electronic catalogues (Article 36) or other adjustments to facilitate communication. These aspects are discussed by Lichere and Richetto in this book.

priority.[7] Europe's weakness in innovation had been attributed, inter alia, to the EU's comparatively low R&D expenditure when compared, for example, to the US and Japan and which resulted in a commitment to increase R&D spend towards 3% of GDP by 2010.[8] In the same year, the Commission published a Communication, 'Innovation in a knowledge-driven economy',[9] which identified five priorities to steer Member State and EU-level actions to promote innovation,[10] one of which was a "regulatory framework conducive to innovation".[11] In 2003, the Commission published a Communication, 'Innovation policy: updating the Union's approach in the context of the Lisbon strategy'.[12] In order to reorient the design and implementation of innovation policy, the Communication sought to conceptualise innovation in broader

7. The aspiration of the Libson Strategy was to make the EU the most competitive and dynamic knowledge-based economy in the world by 2010. See Presidency Conclusions, Lisbon European Council, 23 and 24 March 2000.
8. Commission, 'More Research For Europe, Towards 3% of GDP' (Communication) COM(2002) 499 final.
9. Commission, 'Innovation in a knowledge-driven economy' (Communication) COM(2000) 567 final.
10. These were as follows: (1) coherence of innovation policies, (2) a regulatory framework conducive to innovation, (3) encourage the creation and growth of innovative enterprises, (4) improve key interfaces in the innovation system, and (5) a society open to innovation. See Commission, 'Innovation in a knowledge-driven economy' (n 9) 17-24. This was followed up with the report Innovation policy in Europe, 2002, Innovation papers No 29, European Commission, 2003.
11. Ibid, although, the Communication makes no reference to Directive 2004/18/EC or other forms of regulating public procurement. Rather, the Communication identifies areas such as intellectual and industrial property rights, obstacles in the form of rules and statutes to the diffusion and exploitation of research results obtained with the support of public funding, unnecessary over-regulation slowing the introduction of new products and services on the market (not specified), state aids and the reporting and documenting of companies' intangible assets. See Commission, 'Innovation in a knowledge-driven economy' (n 9) 18-19. In fact, the role of public procurement law as an aspect of EU economic law has generally been neglected in commissioned studies and working papers. See for example, Directorate-General for Enterprise (commissioned), 'Innovation tomorrow: innovation policy and the regulatory framework: Making innovation an integral part of the broader structural agenda, Innovation papers No 28; L Battaglia, P Larouche and M Negrinotti, 'Does Europe Have an Innovation Policy? The case of EU economic law' GRASP Working Paper 11, January 2011, 1 which only identifies EU economic law as comprising competition law, intellectual property law, sector-specific regulation (especially electronic communications regulation) and standardization.
12. Commission, 'Innovation policy: updating the Union's approach in the context of the Lisbon strategy' (Communication) COM(2003) 112 final, 2.

terms than focusing exclusively on R&D and technological innovation to include other forms.[13]

EU Policy on Innovation and Public Procurement

Following the Report of an appointed expert group,[14] procurement (in particular, public technology procurement in sectors such as health and public security) was identified as a "direct measure" in stimulating private investment in research as part of a Research Investment Action Plan to promote inter alia the implementation of measures in support of the 3% of GDP R&D spend objective.[15]

In 2004, the Kok Report on the Lisbon Strategy recognized that procurement could be used to provide pioneer markets for new research and innovation-intensive products.[16] In 2005, the Commission published the findings of an expert group Report which identified 25 recommendations to develop procurement practices favourable to R&D and innovation.[17] The EU also published the findings of a Study which conducted case studies of innovative procurement and which found that the EU framework was neither conducive nor prohibitive to innovation; rather the need is to stimulate and disseminate its application at the EU and national policy levels.[18] Further, the Commission also published a Communication, 'Research and Innovation – Investing for Growth and Employment: A Common Approach' which also reinforced the use of public procurement to foster research and innovation.[19]

13. The Communication identified various forms such as "incremental innovation", "value innovation", "organisational innovation", "business model innovation" and "presentational innovation". See Commission, 'Innovation policy: updating the Union's approach in the context of the Lisbon strategy' (n 12) 6.
14. Report to the European Commission from an Independent Expert Group, Raising EU R&D Intensity: Improving the Effectiveness of Public Support Mechanisms for Private Sector Research and Development: Direct Measures, 2003, 4-5, 39-45.
15. Commission, 'Investing in research: an action plan for Europe' (Communication) COM(2003) 226 final/2.
16. Facing the Challenge, The Lisbon strategy for growth and employment, Report from the High Level Group chaired by Wim Kok November 2004.
17. Expert Group Report presented to the European Commission, Public Procurement for Research and Innovation, Developing procurement practices favourable to R&D and innovation, September 2005.
18. Study for the European Commission, Innovation and Public Procurement. Review of Issues at Stake, Final Report, December 2005, Executive Summary conclusions, XI.
19. The Communication makes repeat references to "the possibilities offered by the new public procurement legislative framework" but does not specifically identify precisely what those possibilities are. See Commission, 'Implementing the Community Lisbon

2. *Spurring Innovation through Procurement: Towards an Innovation Union*

Having formally integrated procurement within broader EU innovation policy, since 2006, the EU has attempted to implement procurement policy in practice. For instance, the EU has adopted a Council Decision establishing a Competitiveness and Innovation Framework Programme ("CIP") aimed primarily at assistance with regard to financing and investment of certain projects.[20] The CIP comprises the Entrepreneurship and Innovation programme, the ICT Policy Support Programme and the Intelligent Energy – Europe programme.[21] There have been calls under such programmes to support so-called PPI (public procurement of innovative solutions) Pilots, specifically, for public procurement bodies to submit proposals for collaborative, cross-border projects.[22] Also, in 2006, the Commission published a Communication presenting a "broad-based innovation strategy for Europe" [23] which specifically identified the potential for the procurement Directives to offer scope for "innovation-oriented tendering".[24] Whilst not explicit, the Communication makes reference to describing needs in a broad, performance based way,[25] use of life cycle costing (as opposed to focusing on costs at the time of pur-

Programme: More Research and Innovation – Investing for Growth and Employment: A Common Approach (Communication) COM(2005) 488 final, 8.

20. Decision No 1639/2006/EC of the European Parliament and of the Council of 24 October 2006 establishing a Competitiveness and Innovation Framework Programme (2007 to 2013) OJ L 310, 09/11/2006, 15–40.
21. More information on these programmes is available at: <http://europa.eu/legislation_summaries/information_society/strategies/n26104_en.htm> accessed 15 April 2014
22. At the time of writing, there is currently a call for proposals open for PPI pilot actions (deadline for submission of proposals 14 May 2013) that provides EC co-financing to consortia of procurers for deploying innovative ICT solutions in the areas of ICT for health and ageing well under Call 7 of the ICT part of the 2013 CIP: CIP-PSP-2013-7. The same call also supports networking of procurers that wish to prepare future PPIs in the areas of smart sustainability mobility and resource efficient data servers for smart cities. The Commission's proposal for the 2014-2020 EC research and innovation support programme, Horizon 2020, foresees the continuation of similar EC grants that co-finance the costs for consortia of public procurers from a minimum of three different Member States and/or Associated Countries to undertake together a from of pre-commercial procurement or PPI. For more details see, <http://cordis.europa.eu/fp7/ict/pcp/links_en.html> accessed 15 April 2014.
23. Commission, 'Putting knowledge into practice: a broad-based innovation strategy for the EU' (Communication) COM(2006) 502 final.
24. Ibid, 11-12.
25. This appears to refer to the possibility of formulating technical specifications in such terms under the Directive. Technical specifications are discussed in Section 6 below.

chase),[26] the use of technical dialogue,[27] as well as provisions relating to SMEs.[28] The Commission also published a Communication on 'An innovation-friendly, modern Europe' which recommended smart use of the large procurement budgets of governments by requesting innovative solutions.[29]

In 2007, the Commission published a Communication launching a 'Lead Market Initiative for Europe',[30] which identified a set of markets with potential to become lead markets, as well as action plans to improve these markets.[31] The Communication specifically identified a lack of knowledge within the construction market as to the possibilities under the existing legal framework for public procurement that could facilitate demand for innovation-oriented solutions.[32] The Communication also identified the need for changes within national, regional and local procurement offices to identify and award the economically most advantageous tender on the basis of life cycle cost assessments, as well as the possibility for requirements of interoperability and the replacement of small scale purchases by grouped orders as useful in the development of competitive and innovative solutions.[33]

Continuing in the vein of practical implementation, the Commission also published a Guide on 'Dealing with Innovative Solutions in Public Procurement: 10 Elements of Good Practice', certain aspects of which will be considered in this Chapter.[34] In conjunction, the Commission also published a

26. Discussed by Dragos in this book.
27. For a discussion in this regard, see Section 5 below.
28. Commission, 'Putting knowledge into practice: a broad-based innovation strategy for the EU' (n 23) 12. For a discussion of SME's in this context, see Trybus' Chapter in this book.
29. Commission, An innovation-friendly, modern Europe (Communication (Informal meeting in Lahti – Finland, October 2006) COM(2006) 589 final, Brussels, 12/10/2006, 7.
30. Commission, 'A lead market initiative for Europe' (Communication) COM(2007) 860 final.
31. These markets currently include: eHealth, sustainable construction, protective textiles, bio-based products, recycling and renewable energies. Details on the progress of the action plans in each sector can be found at: <http://ec.europa.eu/enterprise/policies/innovation/policy/lead-market-initiative/index_en.htm> accessed 15 April 2014.
32. Commission, 'A lead market initiative for Europe' (Communication) (n 30) 5.
33. Ibid 7.
34. Commission, Guide on Dealing with Innovative Solutions in Public Procurement, 10 Elements of Good Practice, Commission staff working document SEC(2007) 280 <http://ec.europa.eu/research/era/docs/en/ec-era-instruments-3.pdf > accessed 15 April 2014. Earlier Communications had prospectively identified the publication of a

Communication on pre-commercial procurement ("PCP").[35] PCP is said to cover activities such as solution exploration, design and prototyping up to original development of a limited volume of first products.[36] However, PCP does not cover the purchase of the products resulting from this process, procurement of which requires a separate procedure conducted in accordance with the Directive. The Communication also provides a model for conducting this form of procurement in line with the legal framework existing under Directive 2004/18/EC and EU law generally.[37] In this regard, the PCP Communication only applies to R&D service contracts under Article 16(f) which are excluded from Directive 2004/18/EC.[38]

In 2010, the European Council launched the 2020 strategy.[39] The new strategy announced seven flagships, one of which is the "Innovation Union" specifying aims which include making full use of demand side policies e.g. through public procurement and "smart regulation".[40] The Commission published a Communication outlining the Innovation Union's objectives.[41] In particular, the Communication identified a failure to use public procurement strategically.[42] Specifically, the Communication referred to "an enormous and overlooked opportunity to spur innovation using procurement" and identified that whilst public procurement of innovative products and services is vital for improving the quality and efficiency of public services at a time of budget constraints, little public procurement in Europe is aimed at innovation,[43] "despite the opportunities under the EU procurement directives."[44]

"Handbook" suggesting something much more substantial than the "Guide" that was eventually published.

35. Commission, 'Pre-commercial Procurement: Driving innovation to ensure sustainable high quality public services in Europe' (Communication) COM(2007) 799. Earlier Communications had also emphasized the potential for pre-commercial procurement to facilitate innovation. See Commission, 'Putting knowledge into practice: a broad-based innovation strategy for the EU' (n 23) 12 which identified pre-commercial procurement as "a yet untapped opportunity for public authorities in Europe."
36. Ibid, 2.
37. Ibid.
38. These R&D services are discussed in more detail in Section 4 below.
39. Commission, 'Europe 2020, A strategy for smart, sustainable and inclusive growth' (Communication) COM(2010) 2020 final.
40. Ibid 12.
41. Commission, 'Europe 2020 Flagship Initiative Innovation Union' (Communication) COM(2010) 546 final.
42. Ibid, 7.
43. Ibid, 16. The Communication attributes this state of affairs to a range of factors which include: incentives that favour low-risk solutions; a lack of knowledge and capabili-

In contrast, the Communication pointed to significant U.S. spend on procurement of R&D through pre-commercial procurement, in particular through its Small Business Innovation Research ("SBIR") programme, as well as its spend on procurement of innovation beyond R&D (e.g. new technologies, products and services).[45]The Communication identified that several Member States (such as the UK and Netherlands) have started using pre-commercial procurement and adaptations of the U.S. SBIR models to support innovation and encouraged the use of pre-commercial procurement more widely in combination with joint procurement between different contracting authorities.[46] The Communication called for Member States and regions to emulate the U.S. model by setting aside dedicated budgets for pre-commercial procurement and procurements of innovative products and services.[47]

The Communication also outlined the objectives of European Innovation Partnerships ("EIPs")[48] also launched as part of the Europe 2020 strategy. EIPs have been launched in certain areas (e.g. active and healthy ageing, agricultural sustainability and productivity, smart cities and communities, water and raw materials).[49] Among the listed objectives include the mobilization of demand, in particular, through better coordinated public procurement and to build upon existing instruments and initiatives e.g. pre-commercial and commercial procurement schemes.[50] As will be discussed below and in more

ties regarding successful procurement of new technologies and innovations; and a disconnection between public procurement and policy objectives. Further, because public procurement markets remain fragmented across Europe, procurements often fail to achieve the critical scale needed to trigger innovative investments.

44. Ibid. Again, however, the Communication does not specify precisely what those purported opportunities are although references are made later on in the document to the use of output-based specifications and the award of contracts based on qualitative criteria which favour innovative solutions such as life-cycle analysis rather than lowest price and, further, that opportunities for joint procurement are exploited. Ibid 35.
45. The Communication identified that based on 2004 figures, the U.S. spends at least 49 billion dollars per year on pre-commercial procurement (i.e. procurement of R&D), certain of which is spent via the SBIR programme.
46. Ibid 16.
47. Ibid 17.
48. Ibid 23.
49. For further details, see <http://ec.europa.eu/research/innovation-union/index_en.cfm?pg=eip> accessed 15 April 2014.
50. Ibid. An independent expert group was set up in 2013 by the European Commission to assess progress and evaluate the overall performance of the European Innovation Partnerships. See Report of the Independent Expert Group to the Commission, 'Out-

detail in the Chapter on procedures in this book, partnership models of this kind are now specifically promoted by the inclusion of an innovation partnership procedure.

Innovation as a Form of Strategic Procurement under Directive 2014/24/EU
Directive 2014/24/EU contains repeat references to the Europe 2020 strategy.[51] In this regard, Directive 2014/24/EU refers specifically to innovation as an aspect of "strategic procurement".[52] Innovation is identified alongside social and environmental procurement.[53] It could even be suggested that innovation is assigned a fundamentally more strategic role than other strategic objectives. As will be discussed in Section 3 below, Directive 2014/24/EU defines "innovation" unlike social and environmental considerations. Further, the Directive's references to "social innovation" and "eco innovation"[54] envisage innovation as an integral or overarching objective in relation to other objectives.[55]

riders for European Competitiveness, European Innovation Partnerships (EIPs) as a Tool for Systemic Change' 2014.

51. See Recitals 2, 47, 95, 96 and 123 and Article 2(1)(22).
52. Recital 123. The Impact Assessment identified problems and uncertainty affecting the ability of purchasers to legally and consistently utilise public procurement rules to achieve strategic policy goals, such as developing new, innovative products and technologies. It also identified inflexible procedures defined at EU level that do not allow contracting authorities and entities to make the best use of non-standard procurement solutions e.g. purchasing innovative goods and services, with a clear majority of respondents advocating further promoting and stimulating innovation through procurement. See Commission Staff Working Paper, Impact Assessment Accompanying the document Proposal for a Directive of the European Parliament and of the Council on Public Procurement and the Proposal for a Directive of the European Parliament and of the Council on procurement by entities operating in the water, energy, transport and postal sectors, SEC(2011) 1585 final, 24.
53. Recitals 95 and 123. On social and environmental considerations in EU public procurement generally, see S Arrowsmith and P Kunzlik (ed), Social and Environmental Policies in EC Procurement Law: New Directives and New Directions (CUP 2009) and R Caranta & M Trybus (ed), The Law of Green and Social Procurement in Europe (Djøf 2010).
54. Recital 47.
55. Certain of the Directive's provisions e.g. Article 70 concerning contract performance conditions also refer to innovation-related considerations alongside economic, environmental and social (or employment-related) considerations. For a discussion of these aspects, See Section 8, below.

Yet, the case for innovation qua strategic objective is not fully made out, at least not in the official EU policy documentation. Innovation has not gained recognition as one of the key desiderata in public procurement systems. [56] Further, the Impact Assessment to the Directive makes reference to innovation in conjunction with environmental and social considerations but perhaps unsurprisingly given the limited national experiences of "innovation-oriented tendering" on which to draw, focuses almost exclusively on social and environmental procurement.[57] The Impact Assessment also candidly states that the "jury is still out on whether strategic procurement can have a decisive impact in supporting the general dissemination of superior technologies or solutions."[58] In any event, Directive 2014/24/EU confirms that the EU remains opposed to the setting of general mandatory requirements or quotas in respect of environmental, social and innovation procurement. [59]

The reality is that stakeholders continue to express uncertainty with regard to the integration of strategic goals within their procurement. As the Impact Assessment has observed, contracting authorities are unsure as to how far they can integrate strategic goals in their procurement, an issue attributable, in part, to a lack of specialist knowledge and competence both in a given strategic area and in adapting procurement practices to incorporate strategic issues whilst remaining compliant with the Directive.[60] The Impact assessment observes that evaluations of stakeholder views indicate a lack of appropriate national guidance setting strategic objectives and linking them to public procurement, in particular.[61] Specifically, the Impact Assessment identifies that in certain areas, particularly in relation to innovative purchases, that the resultant uncertainty and risk/fear of non-compliance appears to be proving too great, in turn, deterring many contracting authorities from using public procurement to support and achieve such objectives.[62] As official EU publica-

56. Whilst there is no consensus, nine goals are frequently identified for government procurement systems: (1) competition; (2) integrity; (3) transparency; (4) efficiency; (5) customer satisfaction; (6) best value; (7) wealth distribution; (8) risk avoidance; and (9) uniformity. See generally S L Schooner, 'Desiderata: objectives for a system of government contract law' (2002) 2 PPLR 10, identifying that an improper obsession with risk avoidance can suffocate creativity and stifle innovation without identifying innovation as a desideratum per se.
57. Commission Staff Working Paper, Impact Assessment (n 52) 119-124.
58. Ibid 89-90.
59. Recital 95.
60. Commission Staff Working Paper, Impact Assessment (n 52) 122.
61. Ibid.
62. Ibid.

tions have themselves acknowledged, notwithstanding EU innovation policy initiatives, procurement policy alone is not sufficient to encourage a wider uptake of innovation and that other framework conditions are necessary for a systematic approach such as education, research, finance, knowledge transfer, support for small business, intellectual property management and a high quality regulatory environment.[63] Whilst it has been identified that Directive 2004/18/EC offered more opportunities to use "innovation-oriented" tendering than had previously been available, the key obstacles to innovation stimulating public procurement, such as risk aversion, flow not from the legal framework but rather from organisational issues and the lack of practical experience and expertise that need to be addressed directly.[64]

Whilst it appears that the EU legislator has a sufficiently informed view to incorporate and expand on strategic procurement within the Directive's provisions through the inclusion of innovation, the Directive acknowledges that it currently lacks a clear view of developments in the field of strategic procurement.[65] It may seem axiomatic but the reality is that the utility of any additions or revisions to the Directive in pursuit of innovation objectives will ultimately dependent on experiential factors as it becomes necessary to translate innovation policy into procurement practice through a process of institutional and mutual learning.

3. "Innovation" qua Legal Construct under Directive 2014/24/EU

Since at least the mid-1990's, EU policy had given serious consideration to conceptual meanings of "innovation".[66] However, as indicated in Section 2, whilst an intense EU policy drive emphasized the role of public procurement

63. Commission, Guide on Dealing with Innovative Solutions in Public Procurement, 10 Elements of Good Practice (n 34).
64. Ibid, 6.
65. Recital 123.
66. See Commission, Green Paper on Innovation COM(95) 688 final, 1 which defined "innovation" as follows: "innovation is the renewal and enlargement of the range of products and services and the associated markets; the establishment of new methods of production, supply and distribution; the introduction of changes in management, work organization, and the working conditions and skills of the workforce." Many definitions of innovation have also been posited within academic literature. One which is commonly found is the "capacity to valorize new R&D results into marketable products and services". This definition is found in an EU commissioned expert report: Pre-Commercial Procurement of Innovation, A Missing Link in the European Innovation Cycle, March 2006.

in facilitating innovation, Directive 2004/18/EC contained no specific reference to this concept. In fact, a definition of "innovation" was only added as late as the 2013 Draft of Directive 2014/24/EU.[67] Specific reasons necessitating a legal definition have not been clearly identified. Article 2(1)(22) Directive 2014/24/EU defines the term as follows:

> 'innovation' means the implementation of a new or significantly improved product, service or process, including but not limited to production, building or construction processes, a new marketing method, or a new organisational method in business practices, workplace organisation or external relations inter alia with the purpose of helping to solve societal challenges or to support the Europe 2020 strategy for smart, sustainable and inclusive growth[.]

This definition is not exhaustive and thus includes, but is not limited to, so-called "product innovation"[68] and "process innovation".[69] According to one innovation taxonomy,[70] innovation can be classified according to two dimen-

67. See Article 2(23a) Proposal for a Directive of the European Parliament and of the Council on public procurement (Classical Directive) (First reading), Brussels, 12 July 2013, 11745/13. The 2011 Draft did not contain a specific definition of innovation. See Proposal for a Directive of the European Parliament and of the Council on public procurement, COM(2011) 896 final, Brussels, 20.12.2011.
68. "Product innovations" are new or improved material goods as well as new intangible services and concern what is produced. See C Edquist and J M Zabala-Iturriagagoitia, 'Why Pre-Commercial Procurement is not Innovation Procurement', Paper no. 2012/11, Centre for Innovation, Research and Competence in the Learning Economy (CIRCLE), Lund University, 5.
69. "Process innovations" are new ways of producing goods and services; they may be technological or organizational and concern how things are produced. See C Edquist and J M Zabala-Iturriagagoitia, 'Why Pre-Commercial Procurement is not Innovation Procurement' (n 68) ibid.
70. The taxonomy appropriated for the purposes of this Chapter is provided by C Edquist and J M Zabala-Iturriagagoitia, 'Why Pre-Commercial Procurement is not Innovation Procurement' (n 68) 6, which is, in turn, based on taxonomies developed in other work in innovation theory, namely C Edquist, L Hommen, L Tsipouri (eds), Public Technology Procurement and Innovation (2000 Boston/Dordrecht/London, Kluwer Academic Publishers); L Hommen and M Rolfstam, 'Public Procurement and Innovation: towards a taxonomy' (2009) 9(1) Journal of Public Procurement, 17-56; J Edler, 'Demand Policies for Innovation in EU CEE Countries' (2009) Manchester Business School Working Paper No 579, The University of Manchester; E Uyarra and K Flanagan, 'Understanding the innovation impacts of public procurement' (2010) 18(1) European Planning Studies, 123- 143, all cited in Edquist and Zabala-Iturriagagoitia, 'Why Pre-Commercial Procurement is not Innovation Procurement' (n 68) 6, fn6.

sions, the first of which is the user of the resulting product (good, service or system).[71] This dimension can be further classified into the categories of "direct public procurement for innovation" ("PPI")[72] and "catalytic procurement for innovation".[73] Both categories appear to be covered by the Directive's definition. The second dimension refers to the character of the procurement process and the degree of innovation of the resulting product.[74] This dimension can be further classified into the categories of so-called "Pre-commercial procurement" ("PCP"),[75] "developmental PPI"[76] and "adaptive PPI".[77]

71. Edquist and Zabala-Iturriagagoitia, 'Why Pre-Commercial Procurement is not Innovation Procurement' (n 68) 6
72. Direct PPI occurs when the purchasing entity is also the end-user of the product resulting from the procurement. This is described as the "classic" case, namely when the purchasing entity undertakes the procurement to meet its needs. Here, the purchasing entity uses the resulting product itself and thus uses its own demand or need to influence or induce innovation. However, the resulting product of PPI is often diffused to other users e.g. other purchasing entities as well as for society more generally. See Edquist and Zabala-Iturriagagoitia (n 68) 6.
73. Catalytic PPI occurs when the purchasing entity is a catalyst, coordinator and technical resource for the benefit of the end-users. In contrast to direct PPI, the purchasing entity does not utilize its own needs as 'buyer' as the purchasing entity is not the end-user of the product; rather the purchasing entity aims to purchase new products on behalf of other actors (public or private). It acts to catalyse the development innovations for broader public use as opposed to supporting the purchasing entity's objectives. See Edquist and Zabala-Iturriagagoitia (n 68) 6. As indicated, Article 2(1)(22) contains a curious reference to the term "external relations". This might be said to capture this aspect of innovation.
74. C Edquist and J M Zabala –Iturriagagoitia (n 68) 6.
75. According to C Edquist and J M Zabala –Iturriagagoitia (n 68) 6: "Pre-commercial procurement (PCP) refers to the procurement of (expected) research results, i.e. it involves direct public R&D investments. However, it does not involve the purchase of a (non-existing) product, so no buyer is involved. This type of procurement may also be labeled 'contract' research." As indicated in Section 2, the EU has published a Communication on PCP (n 35). The Communication at 2 identifies PCP as concerning the R&D phase before commercialisation. The Communication states that PCP is intended to describe an approach to procuring R&D services other than those where "the benefits accrue exclusively to the contracting authority for its use in the conduct of its own affairs, on condition that the service provided is wholly remunerated by the contracting authority". As will be discussed in Section 4, below this refers to the wording of a specific exclusion of certain R&D services contained within Article 16(f) Directive 2004/18/EC.
76. Developmental PPI implies the creation of new-to-the-world products and/or systems as a result of the procurement process. It may be regarded as "creation oriented" PPI and involves radical innovation. See C Edquist and J M Zabala –Iturriagagoitia (n 68) 6.

This second dimension is less clearly defined under the Directive. A prime example in this regard concerns PCP. As indicated in Section 2, in 2007, the Commission published a Communication on PCP providing a model applicable to the procurement of certain R&D services, the subject of a specific exclusion contained in Directive 2004/18/EC. According to this model, PCP covers a number of discrete stages which constitute the R&D phase. The final stage of PCP is identified as "original development of a first product or service". This may include limited production or supply in order to incorporate the results of field-testing and to demonstrate that the product or service is suitable for production or supply in quantity to acceptable quality standards.[78] On this model, R&D does not include commercial development activities such as quantity production, supply to establish commercial viability or to recover R&D costs, integration, customization, incremental adaptations and improvements to existing products or processes.[79] It is said to follow from this separation between the "R&D phase" and "deployment of commercial volumes of end-products" that whilst the procurement of this category of R&D services does not have to comply with the Directive by virtue of their prima facie exclusion, the purchase of the results of the PCP procedure must be conducted in compliance with the Directive.[80]

It is immediately apparent that the Directive's definition does not incorporate an explicit distinction between the R&D and the so-called "uptake/commercialization phase" such as to differentiate PCP as an excluded field of activity and commercial purchases which are regulated by the Directive. References to "implementation"[81] of a "new or significantly improved"[82] "product, service or process"[83] could be intended to differentiate

77. Adaptive PPI occurs when the procured product or system is only new to the country (or region) of procurement. Innovation is thus required in order to adapt the product to specific (national, local) conditions. It may also be labeled "diffusion oriented" or "absorption oriented" PPI and implies incremental innovation. See C Edquist and J M Zabala –Iturriagagoitia (n 68) 6.
78. Commission, 'Pre-commercial Procurement' (n 35) 2 citing at fn 7 the corresponding WTO Government Procurement Agreement, article XV.
79. Commission, 'Pre-commercial Procurement' (n 35) 2-3.
80. Ibid, 4.
81. The Directive does not use the terms "valorization" or "commercialization". Implementation is not necessarily synonymous with either of the former.
82. It is not clear what might constitute a "significant" "improvement". The Innovation Partnership procedure does not expressly refer to the definition of innovation in Article 2(1)(22) but rather provides in Article 31(1) that: "[t]he contracting authority shall

the uptake / commercialization phase from the R&D phase. The Communication on PCP refers to "first test-products or services". It is unclear whether such products are excluded from the Directive's definition on the basis that such products cannot be said to be "new", "significantly improved" or "implemented" because they are not commercialised. According to the Communication on PCP, R&D does not include inter alia "improvements to existing products or processes". [84] On the Directive's definition, implemented products must not only constitute improvements but "significant" improvements. Further, as will be discussed in Section 4 below, public supply contracts for products manufactured purely for the purpose of research, experimentation, study or development fall within the Directive's scope.[85] It is not clear whether the exceptional award of such contracts (under the negotiated procedure without publication of a contract notice) is therefore conceptualized as facilitating innovation within the Directive's definition. In any event, the definition itself does not distinguish between products under research, experimentation, study or development phases and subsequent purchases of products subject to the other procedures of the Directive. Clarity is not aided by the reference in the Directive to "including but not limited to production."[86]

The definitional ambiguity surrounding the delimitation of excluded PCP and resultant purchases subject to the Directive is not simply a matter of academic excursion but rather strikes at the heart of precisely what EU policy and law determines to constitute innovation such as to prescribe the appropriate regulatory response. Whilst the Communication on PCP identifies PCP as a form of innovation,[87] recent research in innovation theory has suggested that PCP is conceptually distinct from procurement for innovation such that it

identify the need for an innovative product, service or works that cannot be met by purchasing products, services or works already available on the market [...]".

83. It is not clear whether the definition incorporates only the resulting "end" product, service or process or could also incorporate test-products, services or processes.
84. Commission, 'Pre-commercial Procurement' (n 35) 3.
85. According to Article 32(3)(a), such contracts are subject to the negotiated procedure without prior publication of a contract notice.
86. This could be read so that innovation is not limited to commercial production. Therefore, this could incorporate certain stages prior to commercial products such as original development of a limited volume of first products/services in the form of a test series, curiosity driven research, solution exploration and prototypes. Alternatively, "included but not limited to production" could refer to process innovation given the reference to building or construction processes.
87. As will be identified below, Recital 47 acknowledges pre-commercial procurement as contributing to innovation in its reference to the fact that the Directive should also contribute to facilitating public procurement of innovation (italics added).

should be identified as a form of "pre-competitive R&D program" rather than a procurement instrument so as to better correspond with its origins and use in practice.[88]

Yet, if PCP only concerns excluded R&D services and innovation theory suggests that such services do not constitute innovation because they are not commercialized, it is not clear what role Directive 2014/24/EU can be said to play in relation to those R&D services falling within the Directive's scope[89] and the forms of R&D permitted under the negotiated procedure without publication.

Recital 47 of Directive 2014/24/EU confirms this fundamental uncertainty. Recital 47 indicates that procurement models of the kind outlined in the Communication on PCP "deal with the procurement of those R&D services not falling within the scope of this Directive".[90] Recital 47 indicates that whilst such models would continue to be available, Directive 2014/24/EU should also contribute to facilitating public procurement of innovation and help Member States in achieving the Innovation Union targets.[91] Yet, as will be discussed below with regard to those excluded R&D services, it is not clear whether phases of the Innovation Partnership procedure which permits not only the procurement of services but the results of those services correspond to PCP phases which are said not to fall within the Directive's scope.[92]

The above discussion indicates the complexity of the task faced by the EU legislator. Innovation is not a static concept and is difficult to conceptualize let alone translate into a legal term or a quantifiable outcome for the user.[93]

88. C Edquist and J M Zabala –Iturriagagoitia (n 68) 19. For instance, it has been suggested that the language used in the Communication on PCP to describe the final PCP phase, namely original development (identified above) is confusing because testing a prototype under field conditions is not the same as developing a product innovation, product innovation necessitating commercialization by launching on the market. Although, this begs the question: what constitutes "commercialization"?
89. As will be discussed in Section 4 below, covered R&D services include a requirement that the benefits accrue exclusively to the contracting authority for its use in the conduct of its own affairs. It is not clear whether the accrual of benefits, those benefits themselves and their use by a contracting authority in its own affairs necessarily mean that those R&D services have been "implemented" and/or "commercialized".
90. Ibid.
91. Italics added.
92. Incidentally, Article 31 on the dedicated Innovation Partnership procedure does not incorporate, or specifically cross- reference to, the definition in Article 2(1)(22).
93. Early Communications were candid in their assessment. See for example, the apposite statement in Commission, 'Innovation policy: updating the Union's approach in the context of the Lisbon strategy' (Communication) COM(2003) 112 final at 12:

The pre-existence of the PCP model, which Directive 2014/24/EU continues to recognize, may have been one reason necessitating, or affecting approaches to, a broad-brush definition which does not set clear boundaries in relation to the fields of activity which it then purports to exclude and regulate.[94] To this extent, Directive 2014/24/EU simply reflects uncertainty at the level of EU policy as to the legitimate scope of the procurement function to achieve innovation.

4. Research and Development and Innovation

Section 3 adverted to the fact that although innovation theory indicates that R&D does not necessarily constitute innovation, EU law and policy recognizes a link between the two.[95] It should be observed that unlike "innovation", Directive 2014/24/EU does not define "research and development". This is so notwithstanding that the Directive makes several references to R&D in relation to both innovation and provisions which are said to implicate innovation considerations.[96] This should be contrasted with Directive 2009/81/EC on defence and security procurement ("Defence Directive") which does not contain any reference to "innovation" but does define "research and development"[97] and has even published a specific Guidance Note on R&D.[98]

"These multiple dimensions confirm the ubiquitous nature of innovation policy. This characteristic is the main obstacle to effective policy – because innovation is everywhere, it is nowhere."

94. This is quite apart from the latitude afforded to Member States to determine what they consider to constitute "innovation" requiring the use of the Directive's procurement machinery.
95. Directive 2014/24/EU makes reference to research alongside innovation (Recital 47). The Innovation Partnership procedure (Article 31) expressly envisages a symbiosis of research and innovation. The Communication on PCP applicable to excluded R&D services also identifies the procedure as part of EU innovation strategy. See Commission, 'Pre-commercial Procurement' (n 35) 2.
96. For instance, Article 2(1)(20) defining "life cycle" includes R&D as part of its definition. Further, Article 31(6) in relation to the innovation partnership procedure permits that in the selection of candidates, contracting authorities must, in particular, apply criteria concerning the candidate's capacity in the field of research and development and of developing and implementing innovative solutions.
97. Article 1(27) provides: "'Research and development' means all activities comprising fundamental research, applied research and experimental development, where the latter may include the realisation of technological demonstrators, i.e., devices that

Notwithstanding this difference, both Directives adopt a relatively similar regulatory approach in excluding or limiting the Directives' application to procurement involving R&D.[99] In the defence context, it has been suggested that maximum flexibility is necessary in the award of contracts for research supplies and services in order to strengthen the European Defence Technological Industrial Base ("EDTIB"),[100] although specific reasons for such flexibility have not been fully articulated. Similarly, in the civil context, certain R&D services have been excluded from the public sector Directive on the basis that the performance of R&D activities requires more flexibility than allowed by regulated procedures (a reason for their exclusion from the WTO GPA).[101] It has been observed that an historic rationale for excluding R&D services of the kind discussed below was to exclude R&D projects financed

demonstrate the performance of a new concept or a new technology in a relevant or representative environment [.]" See also Recital 13 which provides an extensive description of the types of research which should be covered by the concept of R&D under the Defence Directive (e.g. fundamental research, applied research and experimental development) as well as what is excluded by the concept of R&D (e.g. the making and qualification of pre-production prototypes, tools and industrial engineering, industrial design or manufacture.

98. Directorate General Internal Market and Services, Guidance Note, Research and development, Directive 2009/81/EC on the award of contracts in the fields of defence and security. A host of reasons may explicate a greater focus on R&D within the Defence Directive, not least the technological complexity of solutions necessitating R&D and fewer forms of available off-the-shelf solutions.
99. The Defence Directive contains slightly more extensive provision. Firstly, Article 13(j) is a specific exclusion of certain contracts for R&D services (which broadly corresponds to Article 16(f) Directive 2004/18/EC). Secondly, Article 28(2)(a) allows for the use of the negotiated procedure without prior publication for the award of R&D services other than those referred to in Article 13 and which, therefore, logically only applies to contracts wholly remunerated by the contracting authority and where the benefits accrue exclusively to the contracting authority (which broadly corresponds with Article 14 Directive 2014/24/EU, although, as will be discussed below, Article 14 does not confine the procurement of such services to the negotiated procedure without prior publication). Thirdly, Article 28(2)(b) allows contracting authorities to apply the negotiated procedure without prior publication of a contract notice for the award of contracts for products manufactured purely for the purpose of R&D with the exception of quantity production to establish commercial viability or recover research and development costs (which broadly corresponds to Article 32(3)(a) Directive 2014/24/EU).
100. See Recital 55 to the Defence Directive.
101. See Annex 4 of Appendix I, WTO GPA.

under public programs.[102] In this regard, the exclusion is intended, essentially, to exclude from the procurement procedures, R&D contracts of an "altruistic nature" which are for the benefit of society as a whole, for example, where the benefits of government funded R&D accrue to research institutes, universities or private companies.[103] Yet, as discussed in Section 3, the Directive's definition of innovation appears to expressly acknowledge the distinct role which the Directive should play in facilitating innovation in order to achieve altruistic objectives. To this extent, altruism does not fully explain a variegated approach to regulating certain forms of R&D whilst excluding others under the public procurement Directives.

The realities of R&D contracts may provide a clearer justification. R&D contracts may involve work that is speculative given that R&D contracts provide no, or little, early assurance of full success and which usually equates to no assurance of commercial success or even successful innovation.[104] Further, there is also a concern that the R&D contract could be used to predetermine the choice of tenderer for later phases thereby limiting competition.[105] For this reason, the Directives institute a prima facie separation between the R&D contract (which is either excluded or may be subject to a negotiated procedure without prior publication) and later phases requiring general application of the Directives. This position often seems somewhat counterintuitive for those operators that perceive a risk in investing in R&D which already runs the risk of not materializing into final solutions and who may not be awarded subsequent contracts relating to results of R&D.[106] However, even this risk is exaggerated. The reality is that contracting authorities recognize the benefits in many cases of awarding a subsequent contract to a tenderer awarded an R&D contract. Attempts by the Directives to separate R&D and

102. P Trepte, Public Procurement in the EU, A Practitioner's Guide (2nd ed OUP 2007), 4.145.
103. Ibid.
104. The U.S. Federal Acquisition Regulation ("FAR") 35.002 in its statement of general principles applicable to contracting for research and development identifies the difficulty of judging the probabilities of success or required effort for technical approaches, some of which offer little or no early assurance of full success.
105. Directorate General Internal Market and Services, Guidance Note, Research and development (n 98) 1.
106. As will be discussed below, it has been argued in relation to Directive 2004/18/EC and Directive 2014/24/EU that the Directive fails to translate the possibility to buy first products resulting from R&D, in turn, failing to stimulate innovation. For a useful discussion in this regard, see A R Apostol, 'Pre-commercial procurement in support of innovation: regulatory effectiveness?' (2012) 6 PPLR 213-225.

subsequent purchases are intended to limit the potential for such awards to limit access of other competitors rather than eliminate any possibility for contracting authorities to award R&D and subsequent contracts to the same contractor where there are legitimate grounds for doing so. Moreover, as will be discussed in Section 5 below, EU case law developments (now reflected in Directive 2014/24/EU) indicate that EU law is at least able to acknowledge that the award of an R&D contract to a tenderer does not necessarily prejudice the tenderer's position when seeking to tender for a subsequent commercial procurement simply because the tenderer has acquired certain advantages from any R&D undertaken.

Fundamentally, the EU legislator faces an issue confronting all developed public procurement systems, namely whether the award of R&D contracts constitutes a form of procurement,[107] which does or should fall within the proper province of public contract regulation.[108] It is perhaps this existential uncertainty which has resulted in a variable approach to the coverage of R&D under the Directive and, correspondingly, the Directive's somewhat ambivalent approach to defining and regulating activity said to concern "innovation". This preliminary discussion raises important questions about the overall coherence of the public procurement Directives in the field of R&D, especially when considering the purported contribution of R&D to innovation objectives.

107. This issue is exacerbated by the fact that Directive 2014/24/EU only provides a very brief definition of 'public contracts'. See Article 2(1)(5).
108. For instance, the leading treatise on U.S. Government contract law identifies R&D as a specialized form of service contracting which constitutes a separate category of procurement but procurement nonetheless. This question has also faced the U.S. courts. It has been observed that in a "very questionable decision", the Court of Federal Claims ruled that it did not have jurisdiction of a protest concerning an R&D contract because it was not a "procurement" contract but rather in the nature of a grant, a decision seemingly influenced by the fact that R&D appropriations are separate from "procurement" appropriations. See J Cibinic Jr, R C Nash Jr and C R Yukins, Formation of Government Contracts (4th edn, CCH 2011) 13-14 and citing R&D Dynamics Corp v. United States, 80 Fed. Cl. 715 (2007), aff'd, 309 Fed. Appx. 388 (Fed. Cir. 1009). Yet, as the same text observes, the U.S. Government Accountability Office has regularly taken jurisdiction of Small Business Innovative Research protests, understanding that they are procurements. See for example, Quimba Software, Comp. Gen. Dec. B-299000, 2007 CPD ¶ 14 and R&D Dynamics Corp., Comp. Gen. Dec. B-298776, 2006 CPD ¶ 195.

Research and Development Services

As indicated in Section 2 above, Article 16(f) Directive 2004/18/EC contained a "specific exclusion" in respect of certain so-called "shared" R&D services. The provision was "somewhat unwieldy"[109] in its wording. Article 16(f) provides that the Directive does not apply to public service contracts for R&D services with the exception of services where the benefits accrue exclusively to the contracting authority for its use in the conduct of its own affairs. In order to constitute an R&D service contract subject to the Directive, the provided service must satisfy the condition that it is wholly remunerated by the contracting authority.[110] It follows that a "shared" R&D service appears to be one in which "risks and benefits" are shared between the tenderer and contracting authority.[111] Therefore, although technically a "specific exclusion", because Article 16(f) does not specify any independent definition or conditions for the exclusion of shared services, such services are simply excluded by default in not meeting the definition of covered R&D services.[112] It is recalled that the procurement of shared R&D services is now said to be subject to models of the kind proposed in the Communication on PCP. There is no reported CJEU case law on the use of Article 16(f).[113]

109. This expression is used by DG Internal Market and Services to describe the almost identical provision in Article 13(j) of Directive 2009/81/EC and which is also designated as a "specific exclusion" (but which relies on a discrete definition of R&D). See Directorate General Internal Market and Services, Guidance Note, Research and development (n 98).
110. Ibid. Although, it has been identified that it is sufficient if the service provided is "mostly" remunerated by the contracting authority. See P Trepte, Public Procurement in the EU, A Practitioner's Guide (n 102) 4.145. No authority is specifically cited in this regard.
111. Commission, 'Pre-commercial Procurement' (n 35) 3. Whilst not explicitly clear in the Communication on PCP, "risk" appears to concern not only financial risk but also a range of other risks e.g. relating to IPRs (risks that would ordinarily be assumed by the public authority under exclusive development).
112. Of course, determining such excluded R&D services is rendered even more difficult by the fact that the definition of expressly covered services and the condition(s) to which they are subject (on which the determination of exclusion itself depends) are themselves undefined.
113. There has been some discussion on this provision as a matter of national law. In France, for example, see Tribunal Administratif Versailles ord. L22, 8 juillet 1999, Sté Fujitsu, Systems Europe Ldt, req. n° 994384 ; Tribunal Administratif Paris 14 décembre 1999, SA Dataid, n° 95-02912 cited by F. Lichere, III.222.2 in O. Guezou, F. Lichere (eds), Droit des marchés publics et contrats publics spéciaux, Editions du Moniteur, 2013.

Article 14 Directive 2014/24/EU has attempted to address certain issues of wording. For instance, Article 14 now falls under Section 4 entitled "specific situations".[114] Article 14 specifically identifies R&D services subject to the Directive as those with Common Procurement Vocabulary ("CPV") reference numbers 73000000-2 to 73120000-9, 73300000-5 and 73430000-5. Further, Article 14 now clarifies that in order to fall within the scope of the provision, two express conditions must be satisfied, namely that: (1) benefits must accrue exclusively to the contracting authority for its use in the conduct of its own affairs[115] and (2) the service must be wholly remunerated by the contracting authority.

However, a number of outstanding issues remain with regard to expressly covered R&D services. Terms such as "benefit"[116] accruing exclusively to the contracting authority,[117] for its "use" in the "conduct of its own affairs" and "remunerated" continue to remain uncertain. Further, unlike the equivalent provision in the Defence Directive which appears to confine such services to award under the negotiated procedure without publication of a contract notice, [118] Article 14 Directive 2014/24/EU does not contain a stipulation as to which procedure may be utilised.

With regard to formerly excluded shared services, given that the provision no longer constitutes a "specific exclusion" of shared R&D services, such services simply do not fall within the Directive's scope.[119] Recital 47 states that such services continue to be subject to the application of pre-commercial

114. This category comprises two subsections, one covering subsidised contracts and R&D services (Subsection 1 (Articles 13 and 14)), the other covering procurement involving defence and security aspects (Subsection 2 (Articles 15, 16 and 17)), respectively. It is not explicitly clear why these contracts are grouped collectively under this category. Of course, such R&D services contracts do not correspond to the other category of contracts subsidized by contracting authorities because the contracting authority wholly remunerates the service.
115. As indicated above, Article 16(f) did not identify this aspect as a condition but rather constituted an intrinsic part of the definition of the covered service.
116. EU policy documentation has generally identified "benefits" as including IPRs. However, this does not exclude the possibility of other benefits (howsoever determined). See e.g. Commission, 'Pre-commercial Procurement' (n 35) 7.
117. It is not clear whether this could incorporate more than one contracting authority.
118. Article 28(2)(a) of the Defence Directive. For guidance on the use of Article 28(2) Directive 2009/81/EC, see Directorate General Internal Market and Services, Guidance Note, Research and development (n 98), 4-6.
119. This should be contrasted with the Defence Directive which, it is recalled, contains a specific exclusion of R&D services (Article 13(j)). See (n 99) above.

procurement models.[120] As will be discussed in more detail in the Chapter on procedures in this book, the innovation partnership procedure applies to both the development of an innovative product, service or works and the subsequent purchase of the resulting supplies, services or works. EU guidance states that pre-commercial public procurement and innovation partnerships are two "alternative approaches that correspond to different needs and/or situations".[121] Further, the innovation partnership is a "genuine public procurement procedure with full legal guarantees, while pre-commercial procurement is an exemption and falls outside the scope of the Directive".[122] However, it has been observed that it is not made clear how the sequence of steps in the research and innovation process under the innovation partnership procedure correspond to the PCP R&D phases (solution exploration, prototyping, field tests).[123] It has also been argued that the innovation partnership can be implemented irrespective of the sharing of IPRs or costs between the contracting authority and the private partner and that no reference is made to the situation in which the risks and benefits of the R&D services are shared between the contracting authority and the service provider.[124] It is therefore open to question whether Directive 2014/24/EU adequately addresses the cor-

120. The equivalent exclusion in Article 13(j) Defence Directive does not identify any specific model for the award of such services. According to the Directorate General Internal Market and Services, Guidance Note, Research and development (n 98) 4: "[c]ontracting authorities/entities are not obliged to apply one of the procedures of the Directive for the award of contracts covered by Article 13(j). This gives them the opportunity to devise the award procedure in a way that offers sufficient flexibility, while providing the desired level of competition. They may, for instance, organise a limited competition, conduct negotiations with several potential service providers, or even decide to conclude the contract directly with a specific service provider. They may also award research contracts in parallel to competing providers for specific phases, in order to benefit from alternative approaches." The Guidance Note at 6, point 21 provides that: "If a contracting authority/entity that has awarded a research contract under Article 13 (j) or Article 28 (2) intends to conclude follow-on contracts for the pre- production phase and/or supply contracts for the production phase, it has to apply the normal procedures provided for by the Directive. This usually means that such contracts have to be awarded in European-wide competition through a restricted procedure or a negotiated procedure with the publication of a contract notice or, where applicable, a competitive dialogue.''
121. Public Procurement Reform, Fact Sheet No.9: Innovation (n 4). No illustration of these differing needs and situations is provided.
122. Ibid.
123. A R Apostol, 'Pre-commercial procurement in support of innovation: regulatory effectiveness?' (n 106) 221-1.
124. Ibid 222.

respondence between excluded fields of activity and those regulated fields purportedly providing such "full legal guarantees". Importantly, the Impact Assessment appeared to express some concern that guidance on excluded fields of activity cannot compensate for gaps or shortcomings in the legislation.[125]

Another technical point concerns the position of shared R&D services in relation to the WTO GPA. The fact that such services do not fall within the prima facie scope of the Directive means that shared R&D services do not have to be opened to competition from GPA Parties.[126] However, with regard to the former Article 16(f), the Communication on PCP identified that public purchasers can decide case by case on the "openness to worldwide offers and on the relevant conditions" but that ultimately, the final choice for opening part of the R&D market is left to the contracting authorities.[127]

A final observation concerns a somewhat overlooked aspect, namely the potential for abuse of the R&D services provision. The only indication in this regard is contained in Recital 35 which states that co-financing of R&D programmes by industry sources should be encouraged but clarifies that the Directive only applies where there is no such co-financing and where the outcome of the R&D activities go to the contracting authority concerned.[128] The Recital also states that "fictitious sharing of the results of the R&D or purely symbolic participation in the remuneration of the service provider" should not prevent the Directive's application.[129] This may be contrasted with the De-

125. Commission Staff Working Paper, Impact Assessment (n 52) 35.
126. A R Apostol, 'Pre-commercial procurement in support of innovation: regulatory effectiveness?' (n 106) 219.
127. Commission, 'Pre-commercial Procurement' (n 35) 10; A R Apostol, 'Pre-commercial procurement in support of innovation: regulatory effectiveness?' (n 106) 219 and citations at fn40 and 41 who appears to go further and suggests that the Communication on PCP specifically advocates such openness.
128. This appears to reiterate the Directive's provision on covered R&D services. However, the Recital further states that this should not exclude the possibility that the service provider (having carried out those activities) could publish an account thereof, providing the contracting authority retains the exclusive right to the use of the outcome of the R&D in the conduct of its own affairs. This issue is not further elaborated in the Directive's provisions.
129. This reference appears to derive from an interpretative declaration in relation to the former Services Directive 92/50/EEC (OJ 1992 L 209/1), as amended by Directive 97/52 (OJ 1997 L 328/1) stating that any fictitious sharing of the results of R&D or any symbolic participation in the remuneration of the service provided will not prevent the application of the Directive. See P Trepte, Public Procurement in the EU, A Practitioner's Guide (n 102) 4.146 citing at fn 252 G de Graaf, 'The political agree-

fence Directive which appears to recognize the risk of potential abuse. For instance, according to Article 13(c) Defence Directive which permits the exclusion of cooperative procurement based on R&D, such procurement must be based on a "genuine cooperative concept" and not simply constitute a means to circumvent the Directive's application.[130] Further, Article 11 Defence Directive provides what has been referred to as a "general safeguard clause" stipulating inter alia that the Directive's exclusions must not be utilised to circumvent the provisions of the Directive.[131] Importantly, Guidance issued in relation to R&D under the Defence Directive specifically emphasized that it was "crucial to delimit the research and development phase correctly" in order to safeguard against such a risk.[132]

R&D Supply Contracts under the Negotiated Procedure without Prior Publication

In addition to the category of R&D services falling within the scope of Article 14 Directive 2014/24/EU, Article 32(3)(a) Directive 2014/24/EU (formerly Article 31(2)(a) Directive 2004/18/EC)[133] provides for the use of the negotiated procedure without prior publication of a contract notice for public supply contracts where the products involved are manufactured purely for the purpose of research, experimentation, study or development. Importantly, however, such contracts "shall not include quantity production to establish commercial viability or to recover research and development costs". [134] It had been observed in relation to the predecessor Article 31(2)(a) Directive

ment on a common position concerning the utilities services Directive' (1992) PPLR 471 at 473.

130. See for example, Directorate General Internal Market and Services, Guidance Note, Defence- and security-specific exclusions, Directive 2009/81/EC on the award of contracts in the fields of defence and security, 7-8 which states at 7: "participation in a cooperative programme therefore means more than just the purchase of the equipment, but includes in particular the proportional sharing of technical and financial risks and opportunities, participation in the management of and the decision-making on the programme." Article 13(c) also includes specific requirements in this regard, namely reporting to the Commission on the share of R&D expenditure, the cost-sharing agreement and the intended share of purchases per Member State.
131. Directorate General Internal Market and Services, Guidance Note, Research and development (n 98) 4.
132. Ibid, 1.
133. The equivalent but not identical provision in the Defence Directive is contained in 28(2)(b).
134. Article 31(2)(a) stipulated that the provision did not "extend to" quantity production to establish commercial viability or to recover research and development costs.

2004/18/EC that this provision covers only products which are still at an R&D stage and does not extend to the purchase of "first" products, namely products which are commercially viable but are not yet available on the market.[135] On this view, this provision cannot, for example, justify the negotiated purchase of results of the PCP process directly from the finalist in a PCP procedure.[136] In this regard, Directive 2014/24/EU continues to preclude subsequent purchases of the results of any PCP procedure which must therefore be conducted in accordance with the procedures under the Directive unless another exclusion or exception under the Directive[137] or Treaties permit an alternative means.

Prior to the adoption of the final text, it had been argued that by not adequately translating into the Directive's provisions the possibility to purchase first products or services which result from the PCP processes through direct negotiations, the EU has failed to strike an appropriate balance between the need to stimulate innovation from the demand side whilst ensuring the pursuit of innovation under EU-wide competition.[138] The innovation partnership procedure now provides for a possible follow through from pre-commercial procurement to subsequent purchases of the results in a single procedure. However, as will be discussed in more detail in the Chapter on procedures, the innovation partnership is not without criticism.

It follows from the above that whilst Directive 2014/24/EU has sought to provide a clearer definition of covered R&D services and their distinction from formerly excluded shared R&D services through non-inclusion, there continues to exist areas of legal uncertainty in the definition of all R&D services, as well as the relative application of the PCP and innovation partner-

135. A R Apostol, 'Pre-commercial procurement in support of innovation: regulatory effectiveness?' (n 106) 220.
136. Ibid.
137. One possible alternative could be to rely on Article 32(2)(b) Directive 2014/24/EU which provides for the use of the negotiated procedure without prior publication with regard to public works, supply and service contracts where the works, supplies or services can only be supplied by a particular economic operator for reasons which include the protection of exclusive rights including intellectual property rights. For a discussion of the reasons militating against the possible recourse to this provision in order to directly purchase the the results from the PCP procedure see A R Apostol, 'Pre-commercial procurement in support of innovation: regulatory effectiveness?' (n 106) 221.
138. A R Apostol, 'Pre-commercial procurement in support of innovation: regulatory effectiveness?' (n 106) 225.

ship procedures. It will be necessary to monitor to what extent, if at all, these issues give rise to problems in practice.

5. Preliminary Market Consultations

Whilst contracting authorities may have considerable expertise at their disposal in identifying, accessing and assessing the kinds of technologies available on the market, on occasion it may be necessary to consult suppliers.[139] In its Guide on Dealing with Innovative Solutions in Public Procurement: 10 elements of good practice, the Commission identifies the importance of the use of a "technical dialogue" (as well as other means) to determine what is available on the market.[140] Partly in order to ensure compliance with the WTO GPA, Directive 2004/18/EC did not contain an express provision permitting contracting authorities to seek or accept advice which could be used to prepare specifications.[141] Rather, Recital 8 simply stated that contracting authorities could, before launching a procedure for the award of a contract, use a "technical dialogue"[142] to seek or accept advice which could be used to prepare specifications provided that such advice did not have the effect of precluding competition.

For the first time, Article 40 Directive 2014/24/EU now expressly provides that contracting authorities may conduct "market consultations" with a view to preparing the procurement and informing economic operators of their procurement plans and requirements. Article 40 also contains additional provision which appears to give effect to certain propositions identified by the ECJ in Fabricom,[143] a case providing clarification on the issue of exclusion of

139. As P Trepte, Public Procurement in the EU, A Practitioner's Guide (n 102), 5.46 observes: "this applies most clearly to complex, new or cutting edge technologies but the field of technical specifications and innovation is sometimes no less complex and difficult in the case of less sophisticated products (footnote omitted)."
140. Commission, Guide on Dealing with Innovative Solutions in Public Procurement, 10 Elements of Good Practice (n 35) 10.
141. Article VI:4 WTO GPA provided that "Entities shall not seek or accept, in a manner which would have the effect of precluding competition, advice which may be used in the preparation of specifications for a specific procurement from a firm that may have a commercial interest in the procurement."
142. As Directive 2004/18/EC contained no express provision in relation to the technical dialogue, this term was not defined.
143. Joined Cases C-21/03 and C-34/03 Fabricom SA v Belgian State [2005] ECR I-1559. For a useful discussion of this case, see S Treumer, 'Technical Dialogue and the prin-

tenderers from a procurement procedure where they had participated in a prior technical dialogue. Article 40 identifies acceptance of advice from independent experts, authorities or market participants as an example of one means of conducting a market consultation, thereby suggesting that other legitimate means are possible. Advice obtained by such means may be used in the planning and conduct of the procurement procedure.[144] This is subject to the important qualification that such advice does not have the effect of distorting[145] competition and must not result in a violation of the principles of non-discrimination and transparency.[146] In addition, Directive 2014/24/EU contains a further new provision in Article 41 which is intended to ensure that where a candidate, tenderer or related undertaking has provided such advice (whether in the context of Article 40 or not) or has been involved in the preparation of the procurement procedure, the contracting authority must take appropriate measures to ensure that competition is not distorted by the participation of the candidate or tenderer and which must include the communication to the other candidates and tenderers of relevant information[147] exchanged in the context of or resulting from the involvement of the candidate or tenderer in the preparation of the procurement procedure and the fixing of adequate time limits for the receipt of tenders.[148] Importantly, the candidate or tenderer concerned must only be excluded from the procedure where there are no other means to ensure compliance with the duty to observe the principle of equal treatment.[149] Article 41 further provides that prior to any such exclusion, candidates or tenderers must be given the opportunity to prove that their in-

ciple of equal treatment – dealing with conflicts of interest after Fabricom' (2007) 2 PPLR 99-115.

144. Ibid.
145. It has been observed that reference to "preclude" competition in Recital 8 was misleading as it had been clear for several years that a lesser degree of impact on competition would be a violation of the principle of equal treatment. See S Treumer, 'Technical Dialogue and the principle of equal treatment' (n 143) 102 and citation at fn15. Article 40 Directive 2014/24/EU now refers to the requirement that such advice must not have the effect of "distorting" competition in accordance with the ruling in Joined Cases C-21/03 and C-34/03 Fabricom.
146. Article 40.
147. What will constitute "relevant information" will continue to be fact and context dependent.
148. Ibid.
149. Ibid.

volvement in preparing the procurement procedure is not capable[150] of distorting competition.[151]

Whilst certain of the risks associated with technical dialogue continue to remain under preliminary market consultations in its new form, namely a concern that prior consultations with a particular operator will result in an award to that operator, the measures which contracting authorities must take to ensure the provision of "relevant information" and the fixing of adequate time limits provide important assurance. The provisions also counterbalance the candidate or tenderer's interests by confirming their ability to demonstrate that their prior involvement is not capable of distorting competition and that equal treatment requires that exclusion should not be permitted unless there are no other means to ensure compliance.

These provisions give important recognition to the possibility of engaging earlier and more openly with the supplier community representing the other half to the demand side of the innovation equation whilst respecting the integrity of the non-discrimination and equal treatment principles sustaining the Directive (not to mention competition). Whilst it is difficult to verify the use of preliminary market consultations in practice, such provision corresponds with other aspects of the Directive aimed at maximizing engagement with suppliers e.g. through performance/function specifications, the provision of variants, design contests and the possibility for economic operators to submit requests to participate in an innovation partnership.

150. Treumer has observed that the provision under Directive 2004/18/EC was also misleading because the wording in Recital 8 in reference to "does not have the effect of precluding competition" gives the impression that the technical dialogue must distort (sic) competition before exclusion becomes relevant when it is evident that there will also be an infringement where a technical dialogue is likely to distort (sic) competition such that it is not necessary to establish that the dialogue has actually distorted competition. See S Treumer, 'Technical Dialogue and the principle of equal treatment – dealing with conflicts of interest after Fabricom' (n 144) 102 and citations at fn17. Article 41 retains the reference to the fact that advice "does not have the effect of distorting competition" which could give the same impression. However, Article 41 also provides that candidates must be given the opportunity to prove that their involvement in preparing the procurement procedure is not "capable of distorting competition". These two references therefore appear inconsistent but may be reconcilable on Treumer's alternative interpretation.

151. Ibid.

6. Technical Standards and Specifications

It is recalled from Section 2 that EU policy documents made repeat references to the role which Directive 2004/18/EC could play in "innovation oriented tendering", with particular emphasis placed on the possible recourse to performance/function based specifications. Before examining the modifications introduced by Directive 2014/24/EU, it is useful to identify the discrete role which standards and specifications are said to play in facilitating innovation.

Facilitating Innovation through Standards and Specifications
There is no consensus of opinion in economic theory concerning the role of standards in the achievement of innovation.[152] Economic studies have indicated that standards stimulate innovation but are perceived as complex, costly, and lacking visibility and accessibility.[153] A number of characteristics of formal European standards have been said to influence innovation. For example, a formal standard can: constitute a consolidation of good practice; a method to ensure common understanding of relevant characteristics; offer a high level of quality in terms of accountability and transparency; and mitigate the potential for standards to serve so-called "winning technologies" through private or de facto standards.[154] Further, the adoption of standards in functional/performance terms in a way that defines public interest matters (e.g. interoperability, safety, health and security in terms of output) can enable economic operators to devise innovative solutions.[155] A number of general positive roles have also been identified. These include inter alia enabling interoperability and compatibility between old and novel products and services, guarantees of quality and safety of such products and services and the provi-

152. For a useful overview of economic theories on the impact of standards on innovation, see R Apostol, 'Formal European standards in public procurement: a strategic tool to support innovation' (2010) 2 PPLR, 57-72, 60-61 and citations at fns15-24.
153. Ibid 58 and citations at fns 5 and 6.
154. Ibid, 62.
155. Ibid. Apostol states that this is most clearly reflected in formal European standards created on the basis of a legislative mandate, according to the so-called "new approach" legislative technique. This technique demonstrates how certain objectives of public interest are defined by the government while finding the ways to achieve these objectives and thus define the content of the standards in terms of performance lying with all the interested parties. For details of the "new approach", see Commission, 'Methods of referencing standards in legislation with an emphasis on European legislation' Enterprise Guides, 2002.

sion of test methods and measurement of their quality.[156] In turn, it has been observed that these impact on the user communities in a number of ways.[157]

In concurrence with the EU's policy initiatives in the field of innovation discussed in Section 2, the Commission has similarly explored the potential to stimulate innovation through the use of standards generally, and in public procurement, in particular. One such example was the so-called Steppin (Standards in European Public Procurement Lead to Innovation) project.[158] The Steppin project had three principal objectives: first, to find proof that the use of standards in public procurement promotes innovation; second, to identify which standards have the most potential to stimulate innovation in public procurement and how they could be used within the current legal framework for public procurement; and third, to increase the visibility of standards and promote their use.[159] The findings of the Study are instructive. There was no conclusive proof that the use of standards in the procurement process lead to the purchase of innovative products.[160] One of the main general conclusions

156. R Apostol, 'Formal European standards in public procurement' (n 153) 60.
157. For example, these characteristics are said to give private/public consumers confidence in the quality, safety and the superior performance of innovations (R Apostol, 'Formal European standards in public procurement' (n 153) 60, citing at fn20 G M P Swann, "The Economics of Standardization" Final Report for Standards and Technical Regulations, Directorate Department of Trade and Industry, December 11, 2000, 18). More broadly, it had been suggested that by opening access to a large market (public, private or both), standards lead to lower costs of new products which could, in turn, lead to network effects (Apostol, ibid). In behavioural terms, it has been suggested that by acting as first customers of innovative solutions, public authorities can inspire the private market thereby encouraging investment in further R&D. It has also been suggested that the formalisation of European standards, in terms of the quality of technical content and standardisation processes, itself enables innovation and which is further reinforced when their visibility and accessibility leads to a broad acceptance and application by the user communities (ibid, 62).
158. The Steppin Project was one of six Standards Networks of the Europe Innova initiative. For a useful overview of the Steppin Project, see the Steppin Handbook available at: <http://www.steppin.eu/handbook/website.html> accessed 25 April 2015. For details of the Europe Innova initiative, see <http://ec.europa.eu/enterprise/policies/innovation/support/europe-innova/index_en.htm> accessed 25 April 2014.
159. For an overview of the Steppin Project's methodology, see R Apostol, 'Formal European standards in public procurement' (n 153) 59.
160. Out of the 500 tenders analysed, only a few were found to constitute proof that the use of standards in the procurement process lead to the purchase of innovative products. See Apostol, ibid 63 and 71. For a more detailed breakdown, see Steppin Project Handbook (n 159) Chapter 2: The Role of Standards in the Public Procurement Process to Promote Innovation, 10-11.

was that the use of open standards formulated in terms of performance or functionality (as opposed to detailed standards) has a positive impact on innovation.[161] However, the conclusion of workshops conducted with Member States as part of the project was that public procurers have limited knowledge of standards, rarely use them in public procurement and that even more rarely do they realize the potential of standards to stimulate innovation.[162] The legal risks indicated by public procurers related mostly to the application of the Procurement Directives and to their interaction with other European standardization rules or the principle of mutual recognition.[163]

Performance/Functional Specifications

One of the main changes instituted under Directive 2004/18/EC concerned the fact that it was no longer required to use formal European standards; equal emphasis was given to the use of performance/functional specifications.[164] Further, the Directive emphasized a requirement for public authorities to accept equivalent solutions to the ones prescribed by such formal standards.[165] In similar vein, Directive 2014/24/EU institutes a number of further specific changes. Firstly, Directive 2014/24/EU places further emphasis on characteristics. Article 42 now specifically provides that technical specifications must lay down the characteristics required of a works, service or supply contract. In this regard, a further subparagraph has been inserted which provides as follows:

161. R Apostol, 'Formal European standards in public procurement' (n 153) 63
162. Ibid 64 and 72, and who also states at 64: "This is due to the fact that most innovation policies of Member States do not mention standards as an innovation instrument and public procurers are not directly interested in promoting societal objectives such as enhancing innovation, unless mandated by legislation or central/internal policy. Budgetary restrictions as well as risks of legal proceedings or of corruption accusations constitute barriers to using procurement for other ends than procuring the best quality product for the lowest price. The procurers seemed more interested in standards for their potential to ease their work, but mentioned some practical difficulties, as well as the legal risks as important barriers to their use. Among the practical difficulties, the public procurers mentioned the cost of standards and the difficulty in identifying and applying the relevant standards on a case-by-case basis. The legal risks indicated by the public procurers related mostly to the application of the Procurement Directives and to their interaction with other European rules, such as the "new approach" directives or the principle of mutual recognition."
163. Ibid.
164. Directive 2004/18/EC, Article 23(3)(b).
165. Directive 2004/18/EC, Articles 23(4) and (8).

Those characteristics may also refer to the specific process or method of production or provision of the requested works, supplies or services or to a specific process for another stage of its life cycle even where such factors do not form part of their material substance[166] provided that they are linked to the subject-matter of the contract and proportionate to its value and objectives.[167]

Further, Directive 2014/24/EU has reaffirmed the importance of performance/function based specifications above formal standards. In contrast to Directive 20041/8/EC which identified the order of preference by reference to standards,[168] Directive 2014/24/EU has reversed this sequence to specify performance/functional requirements as a first option for formulating specifications.[169] Recital 74 specifically emphasizes functional and performance related requirements as an appropriate means to favour innovation in public procurement. The Impact Assessment also identified stakeholder views encouraging wider use of performance requirements to achieve innovation.[170] It is submitted that the institution of this change is largely symbolic and merely consolidates a growing policy consensus on the beneficial use of performance based contracting. Given the Directive's overall objective to facilitate flexibility and improve innovation, this emphasis is expected. Ultimately, however, there is little empirical evidence to substantiate a dramatic shift towards performance specifications or the merits of such an approach.[171] Contracting authorities continue to display a preoccupation towards formal adherence to standards by simple virtue of the fact of their existence. It is perhaps no surprise that the major criticisms of recent years have concerned the tendency to use unnecessary hierarchies of multiple and obsolete standards in many cases, reflecting a sense of obligation to comply over and above the interests of ensuring the best solution.

The ability of the contracting authority to adequately set out their performance or functional requirements will also continue to be imperative. For instance, Article 42(6) Directive 2014/24/EU retains the provision under which

166. "material substance" is not defined.
167. See also Article 42(4) which extends the list of references to which technical specifications must not refer to include not only references to a specific make or source but also a particular process "which characterises the products or services provided by a specific economic operator".
168. Directive 2004/18/EC, Article 23(3)(a).
169. Directive 2014/24/EU, Article 42(3)(a).
170. Commission Staff Working Paper, Impact Assessment (n 52) 65.
171. See generally, European Defence Agency (Commissioned) 'Study into the Role of European Industry in the Development and Application of Standards', July 2009, EDA ref. 08-ARM-003.

a contracting authority, when using the option to prescribe its requirements in performance or functional terms, cannot reject a tender which complies with a prescribed standard. It had been observed in relation to the equivalent provision contained in the former Directive 2004/18/EC that such a requirement could affect a contracting authority's ability to seek innovative and cutting edge solutions.[172] A contracting authority may have deliberately chosen not to refer to any specific standards or other technical specifications for a host of reasons e.g. standards may be out of date, or constitute the result of technical compromise between opposing national experts or institutions resulting in the lowest common denominator and which could stultify technological development.[173] Therefore, by providing that tenders may not be rejected if they comply with a listed standard if they address the performance or functional requirements, it could result in a position in which tenderers claim that compliance with a listed standard meets the purchaser's requirements even where the latter disagrees as a result of its search for innovative products.[174]

Management of Intellectual Property Rights

A further notable inclusion in Directive 2014/24/EU relates to intellectual property rights. Directive 2014/24/EU provides that technical specifications may also specify whether the transfer of intellectual property rights will be required.[175] This permissive provision is a rare reference to the difficult and circumstance dependent issue of IPR management. Whilst not expressly regulating the issue, the Directive at least takes an important first step in its recognition of the decisive role which IPR can play in the initial selection and application of technical standards and specifications. In practice, this is likely to be a key consideration in any event the Directive merely rendering this consideration explicit.

172. P Trepte, Public Procurement in the EU, A Practitioner's Guide (n 102) 5.35.
173. Ibid.
174. Ibid. Trepte identifies that Directives predating Directive 2004/18/EC provided the possibility of an exception to an obligation to refer to European standards applying, for example, in the case of technical developments which post-date the adoption of the European standard or in cases of a genuinely innovative nature. See Annex III of Council Directive 93/36/EEC OJ 1993 Ltl Q / 1 consolidating and amending the Original Supplies Directive, as amended by Directive 97/52 (OJ 1997 L328/1) ("Supplies Directive") and Council Directive 93/37/EEC (OJ 1993 L199/54), consolidating the Original Works Directive 71/305/EEC (OJ 1971 L 185/1) as amended by Directive 89/380/EEC (OJ 1989/L 210/1), Decision 90/380/EEC (OJ 1990 L210/1), Decision 90/380/EEC (OJ 1990 187/55) and Directive 97/52 (OJ 1997 L328/1).
175. Article 42(1).

Future Use of Standards and Specifications

The Steppin project had observed in relation to Directive 2004/18/EC that whilst the procurement Directives were designed to allow room for the use of standards to promote innovation, they do not spell out the specific way that standards should be used to this end.[176] In this regard, Directive 2014/24/EU does not directly address this issue. Rather, research appears to indicate that many of the issues concerning use of standards do not result from the Directive itself, but are, in fact, attributable to misconceptions on the part of contracting authorities regarding the choices available in the selection of standards and the assessment of equivalence,[177] in particular, in relation to standards formulated under the auspices of the so-called "new approach".[178] These criticisms simply reflect longstanding issues in relation to standards, namely the continuance of outdated standards, their timeous formulation and publication, proliferation of standards, and correspondence between standardization initiatives. It may, therefore, be more appropriate to issue specific policy guidance which could better guide contracting authorities on the selection and application of technical standards in public procurement, focusing on aspects such as the assessment of equivalence and the application of the Directive relative to standards referenced under other Directives. As indicated above, the extent to which the continued emphasis on functional/performance requirements will improve innovation, remains to be seen.

176. Steppin Handbook, Chapter 3, Legal Aspects (n 159) 7.
177. Consequently, the burden lies on the contracting authority to decide on the appropriate moment to select the standards, on the appropriate standards or parts of a standard to use, and on the appropriate manner to use the standards throughout the procurement procedure. It had also been observed that this generates a "capacity burden" on the contracting authority which needs to identify the standards which are capable to promote innovation, and whether it is necessary to use only parts of the standard, or even supplement the standard's requirements. See R Apostol, 'Formal European standards in public procurement' (n 153) 66. A further criticism of Directive 2004/18/EC had been that, in practice, the concept of equivalence shifts the burden of proof from the supplier to the contracting authority, as the contracting authority needs to justify when it rejects a proposal as non-equivalent to the referenced standard. Yet, the contracting authority may be inadequately equipped to evaluate whether a solution proposed by a supplier is equivalent to a referenced standard. Ibid 65-66.
178. See generally, Apostol, 'Formal European standards in public procurement' (n 153) 66-9.

7. Variants

It has been observed that increased emphasis on performance/function based specifications, the possibility to use a technical dialogue (or now preliminary market consultations) and specific procedures designed to elicit technically suitable specifications, reduce the need to rely on variants in most instances.[179] However, the Impact Assessment indicated that in addition to broader use of performance requirements in technical specifications and life-cycle costing, stakeholders advocated wider use of variants as a measure to promote and stimulate innovation.[180] Recital 48 to Directive 2014/24/EU also specifically encourages contracting authorities to allow variants as often as possible in light of the "importance of innovation".

Ultimately, Directive 2014/24/EU substantially replicates the provision in Directive 2004/18/EC with minor variations and which could signal a continued reduction in their status. For instance, whilst previous Directives provided that the contracting authorities should specify in the contract notice when a variation was not permitted,[181] Directive 2004/18/EC required contracting entities to state whether or not variants were authorized.[182] It had been argued that such a shift on the issue of permissibility indicated a possible reduction in the need to rely on variants.[183] Article 45 Directive 2014/24/EU provides that contracting authorities may authorize or require tenderers to submit variants and must indicate in the contract notice, or where a prior information notice is used, in the invitation to confirm interest, whether or not they authorize or require variants. Therefore, Directive 2014/24/EU continues to confirm the requirement to state whether or not variants are authorized but also adds that variants may be required. To this extent, the Directive provides an opportunity for contracting authorities to explicitly require variants with a clearer indication that variants will (rather than may) be considered. It is unclear to what extent this addition will be sufficient to reverse an emerging trend against the

179. P Trepte, Public Procurement in the EU, A Practitioner's Guide (n 102) 5.53 and 5.54.
180. Commission Staff Working Paper, Impact Assessment (n 52) 40, 65, 124 and 191. See also Expert Group Report presented to the European Commission, Public Procurement for Research and Innovation, Developing procurement practices favourable to R&D and innovation (n 17), Recommendation 19.
181. Council Directive 93/37/EEC OJ 1993 L199.54, Article 18; Council Directive 93/36/EEC OJ 1993 Lt1Q/1, Article 16; Directive 92/50/EEC OJ 1992 L 209/1, Article 24.
182. Article 24(1) and (2).
183. See P Trepte, Public Procurement in the EU, A Practitioner's Guide (n 102) 5.56.

use of variants in practice. Nevertheless, this addition provides another example of further procedural strengthening of provisions intended to facilitate innovation.

Article 45 also contains additional provisions to provide greater control over the use of variants. For instance, it is now expressly stipulated that variants must be linked to the subject-matter of the contract. The Directive also emphasizes that contracting authorities must also ensure that the chosen award criteria can be applied to variants meeting those minimum requirements as well as to conforming tenders which are not variants. Finally, contracting authorities that have authorized or required variants must[184] not reject a variant on the sole ground that it would, where successful, lead to either a service contract rather than a public supply contract or a supply contract rather than a public service contract.

EU policy documentation and commissioned studies have not specifically identified the role which variants could play in facilitating innovation other than their constituting a means to offer an alternative and thus more flexibility. The Impact Assessment identified a universal trend across the Member States of allowing variants in fewer cases confirming that the use of variants does not appear to be a widespread choice at present.[185] In this regard, the Impact Assessment states that measures or incentives may be needed if it were considered desirable to reverse this trend.[186]

8. Choice of Procedure, Selection, Award and Contract Performance

Whilst the previous Sections have focused on discrete provisions of the Directive, innovation is also specifically incorporated as a means to inform substantive decisions regarding choice of appropriate procedure, selection criteria the formulation and application of contract award criteria, conditions for performance of contracts and principles of award pertaining to certain types of contract.

With regard to choice of procedure, arguably the most symbolic inclusion from the perspective of innovation is the institution of an entirely new procedure called the innovation partnership under Article 31. The innovation part-

184. Directive 2004/18/EC, Article 24(4) used "may" instead of "shall".

185. Commission Staff Working Paper, Impact Assessment (n 52) 120. The Impact Assessment identifies Ireland as an exception at fn 133.

186. Ibid.

nership must aim at the development of an innovative product, service or works (which cannot be met by solutions already available on the market) as well as the subsequent purchase of the resulting supplies, services or works, provided that these correspond to the performance levels and maximum costs agreed between the contracting authorities and the participants.[187] Importantly, both aspects are conducted under a single procedure as opposed to requiring separate contracts for R&D and subsequent purchases of the results. According to this procedure, a contracting authority uses a negotiated procedure with prior call for competition to select one or more private partners for the purpose of conducting R&D activities.[188] On award of the contract, partners then execute the contract by undertaking sequential steps in a "research and innovation process", which may include the manufacturing of products, the provision of services or the completion of works. [189] This process is to be arranged in "successive phases".[190] Article 31 appears to require the setting of intermediate targets to be attained by the partners.[191] After conducting at least one phase (which appears to be mandatory), a contracting authority may decide to terminate the partnership or, where there is more than one partner, reduce the number of partners by terminating individual contracts.[192] On conclusion of the research and innovation phase, a contracting authority may decide to purchase the results. As indicated in the Introduction, this procedure is examined in more detail in the Chapter on procedures.

Whilst not widely commented on in the public procurement literature on Directive 2014/24, it should be observed that procedures already in existence under national law bear some correspondence to the innovation partnership in its current iteration. One illustration in this regard is the procedure challenged in Commission v France.[193] In this case, the Code des marchés publics provided for a single procedure for instances in which a contracting authority could not define the scope of a contract at the outset. Under a first stage, a contracting authority could, through the use of an open competition, award a contract for definition setting the scope of work or services to be carried

187. Recital 49 and Article 31(2).
188. It is understood that where there are multiple partners, R&D activities must be conducted separately.
189. Article 31(1) and (2).
190. Ibid.
191. Ibid.
192. Ibid.
193. Case C-299/08 Commission v France [2009] ECR I- 1 1587.

out.[194] Under a second stage, a contracting authority could, through use of a closed competition, award a contract for execution of the results of the definition contract to one of the operators which carried out the definition contract. In response to Commission infringement proceedings alleging incompatibility of the procedure with Directive 2004/18/EC, one argument proffered by France was that the definition and execution procedure represented an implementation of the competitive dialogue procedure. The ECJ rejected this argument on the basis that the competitive dialogue is a procedure for the award of a single contract,[195] whereas the definition-execution procedure constituted a means for awarding several contracts.[196]

This case is perhaps instructive in its indication of attempts at the national level to provide for a follow through from design to execution in a way that Member States at least perceived was not otherwise available under the existent procedures of Directive 2004/18/EC or which necessitated a variation thereof. There are certain comparisons which may be drawn with the innovation partnership procedure. For example, both forms are single procedures. Further, a contract awarded for initial R&D under the innovation partnership could be equated to the award of a contract for design under the design-execution procedure, although it is not clear to what extent the design phases under the design-execution procedure correspond to the research and innovation phases under the innovation partnership. Importantly, however, unlike the design-execution procedure which may result in two contracts (definition and execution), the innovation partnership need only concern the award of one contract after a competitive procedure with negotiation, contract execution comprising R&D development. A partnership may be terminated during this phase. In the instance that a partnership continues, orders may then subsequently be placed for the purchase of the results of the research and innovation phase but ultimately as an execution of the contract originally awarded. Perhaps more fundamentally, it is interesting to observe that both the design-execution procedure and innovation partnership procedure might be com-

194. This competition required a sufficient number of bidders and the award of at least three contracts. See Article 73(5) Code.

195. The ECJ's identification of competitive dialogue as a "procedure for the award of a single contract" is arguably technically incorrect. For instance, it has been observed that read in conjunction, Articles 28 and 35(2) Directive 2004/18/EC appear to permit use of competitive dialogue in the conclusion of framework agreements which may involve several contracts. See J Knibbe, 'Case Comment, Whether the award procedures laid down by Directive 2004/18 are exhaustive: Commission v France (C-299/08) (2010) 3 PPLR, 91, 93.

196. Case C-299/08, Commission v France at [37].

pared to the competitive dialogue procedure, as has been indicated in France. This raises a question regarding the extent to which the innovation partnership is a necessary or useful addition to existing procedures available under the public sector procurement Directives.

In addition to a specifically designated innovation partnership procedure, Directive 2014/24/EU has also incorporated innovation as a factor in the choice of other procedures under the Directive. Article 26 now requires that Member States must provide that contracting authorities may apply a competitive procedure with negotiation or a competitive dialogue with regard to works, supplies or services which include "design or innovative solutions". It has been observed in relation to this ground for use of the procedures that there appears to be no de minimis or majority value test so that it is presumed that any requirement for design or innovation qualifies, however peripheral.[197] In addition, Directive 2014/24/EU also continues to permit the use of design contests.[198] In its Guide on Dealing with Innovative Solutions in Public Procurement: 10 elements of good practice, the Commission identifies the use of design contests as a means of enabling the market to propose creative solutions.[199]

With regard to selection criteria, Article 31(6) concerning the innovation partnership procedure provides that in selecting candidates, contracting authorities must, in particular, apply criteria concerning the candidate's capacity in the field of R&D and of developing and implementing innovative solutions.[200]

In terms of award criteria, Article 67 identifies "innovative characteristics" as an example of a criterion under the assessment of the best price-quality ratio. It has been observed that a broader understanding of the requirement concerning "link to the subject-matter" in light of recent CJEU jurisprudence favours the admissibility of, innovative considerations as award criteria.[201] In addition, within the context of the Directive's provisions on particular pro-

197. J Davey, 'Procedures involving negotiation in the new Public Procurement Directive: key reforms to the grounds for use and the procedural rules' (2014) 3 PPLR, 103, 105.
198. Directive 2014/24/EU, Articles 78-82, formerly Articles 66-74 Directive 2004/18/EC.
199. Commission, Guide on Dealing with Innovative Solutions in Public Procurement, 10 Elements of Good Practice (n 34) 13.
200. For a detailed discussion of this aspect, see Section 4.3.3. of the Chapter on procedures by Telles and Butler in this edition.
201. P Bordalo Faustino, 'Award criteria in the new EU Directive on public procurement' (2014) 3 PPLR 124, 129 and 130 citing Case C-368/10 Commission v Netherlands, 10 May 2012 at [91].

curement regimes, Article 76 provides that in relation to the award of social and other specific services, Member States must ensure that contacting authorities may take into account the need to ensure innovation.[202]

Finally, concerning contract performance, Article 70 identifies "innovation-related" considerations as one of the special conditions which contracting authorities may lay down relating to the performance of a contract. Whilst it is possible to identify tangible contract performance conditions in relation to environmental, social or employment-related considerations, it is not clear what might constitute an "innovation-related" consideration. Much will depend on the extent to which contracting authorities' practices in relation to innovation are assimilated to those practices undertaken in relation to environmental and social considerations.[203]

In light of the above, it is clear that Directive 2014/24/EU has sought to integrate innovation into the substance of contracting authority decision making, although it is open to question whether innovation could have constituted a consideration under each of the above aspects under Directive 2004/18/EC. Whilst innovation as a choice is now rendered explicit, as indicated, there appears to be substantially no or limited threshold criteria enabling Member States to guide the exercise of their decision making in light of the additional freedom which they now appear to have been granted.

9. Occasional and Cross-Border Joint Procurement

A final important set of changes instituted by Directive 2014/24/EU in relation to innovation concerns joint procurement between contracting authorities. Joint procurement has, for some years, been identified as an important means of achieving innovation. For instance, the EU has issued specific guidance on joint procurement in the field of green procurement.[204] Joint procurement is also identified as a specific commitment identified in pursuit of the Innovation Union.[205] Directive 2004/18/EC was said to "implicitly" allow

202. This is reinforced in the Public Procurement Reform Fact Sheet No. 9: Innovation (n 4).
203. As indicated in Section 2, Directive 2014/24/EU appears to envisage a close correspondence between these and other strategic objectives.
204. See European Commission Green Public Procurement (GPP) Training Toolkit – Module 1: Managing GPP Implementation (2008).
205. Further information on these commitments is available at: <http://i3s.ec.europa.eu/commitment/22.html> accessed 25 April 2014.

cross-border joint public procurement.[206] However, Directive 2014/24/EU identifies that contracting authorities continue to face considerable legal and practical difficulties in purchasing from central purchasing bodies in other Member States or jointly awarding public contracts.[207] There are said to be a number of effects which result from the failure to exploit joint procurement. Aside from the fact of few cross-border projects, specific issues include: insufficient achievement of economies of scale, fractured buying power of contracting authorities, insufficient steering of the market by contracting authorities, insufficient pooling and sharing of know-how between contracting authorities and risk related to innovative procurement and high-scale projects.[208] Directive 2014/24/EU has placed specific emphasis on the need to remedy the legal and practical issues not least for innovative projects involving a greater amount of risk than that which is ordinarily assumed by a single contracting authority.[209]

To this extent, Directive 2014/24/EU introduces two provisions. Article 38 concerns "occasional" joint procurement. Recital 71 identifies such procurement as "less institutionalised and systematic common purchasing". [210] Recital 71 further states that certain features of joint procurement should be clarified because of the important role which joint procurement may play, not least in connection with innovative projects. However, this provision is sparse in content. Article 38 permits two or more contracting authorities to agree to perform certain procurements jointly. This provision simply iterates that when a procurement is carried out jointly in the name and on behalf of all the contracting authorities concerned, they will be jointly responsible for ful-

206. Directive 3014/24/EU, Recital 73.

207. The Innovation Union commitment identifies insufficient use of the possibilities to procure jointly by public procurers due to lack of awareness of the possibilities available and perception of legal insecurity (because of absence of practical guidance and, subject to verification, lack of specific rules to address particular issues for cross border joint procurement). For details, see <http://i3s.ec.europa.eu/commitment/22.html> (n 206).

208. ibid.

209. Recital 73.

210. According to Recital 71: "Joint procurement can take many different forms, ranging from coordinated procurement through the preparation of common technical specifications for works, supplies or services that will be procured by a number of contracting authorities, each conducting a separate procurement procedure, to situations where the contracting authorities concerned jointly conduct one procurement procedure either by acting together or by entrusting one contracting authority with the management of the procurement procedure on behalf of all contracting authorities."

filling their obligations.[211] Article 38 also provides that where the conduct of a procurement procedure is not in its entirety carried out in the name and on behalf of the contracting authorities concerned, they are jointly responsible only for those parts carried out jointly but each will have sole responsibility for fulfilling its obligations in respect of the parts it conducts in its own name and on its own behalf.

Article 39 is a more substantial provision in terms of content. Article 39 provides that contracting authorities from different Member States may act jointly in the award of public contracts. Specifically, contracting authorities may purchase works, supplies and/or services through the use of centralized purchasing activities[212] offered by central purchasing bodies[213] located in another Member State.[214] The provision of centralized purchasing activities must be conducted in accordance with the national provisions of the Member State where the central purchasing body is located.[215] Further, Article 39 provides that several contracting authorities from different Member States may jointly award a public contract.[216] In this regard, participating contracting authorities must conclude an agreement that determines two issues. The first concerns the responsibilities of the parties and the relevant applicable national provisions.[217] When doing so, the participating contracting authorities may allocate specific responsibilities among them and determine the applicable provisions of the national laws of any of their respective Member States.[218]

211. This also applies in cases where one contracting authority manages the procedure, acting on its own behalf and on behalf of the other contracting authorities concerned. See Article 38.
212. Article 2(14) defines 'centralised purchasing activities' as: "activities conducted on a permanent basis, in one of the following forms: (a) the acquisition of supplies and/or services intended for contracting authorities, (b) the award of public contracts or the conclusion of framework agreements for works, supplies or services intended for contracting authorities [.]"
213. Article 2(16) defines a 'central purchasing body' as: "a contracting authority providing centralised purchasing activities and, possibly, ancillary purchasing activities [.]"
214. Article 39(2) and (3). The provisions on centralized purchasing activities and central purchasing bodies are contained in Article 37.
215. Article 39(3).
216. This includes the joint conclusion of framework agreements and joint operation of dynamic purchasing systems (as well as the award of contracts based on the framework agreement or dynamic purchasing system, to the extent set out in the second subparagraph of Article 33(2)). See Article 39(4).
217. Article 39(4)(a).
218. The allocation of responsibilities and the applicable national law must be referred to in the procurement documents for jointly awarded public contracts.

This is said to complement EU conflict of law rules.[219] The second concerns the determination of the internal organization of the procurement procedure.[220]

The Directive also makes specific provision for contracting authorities from different Member States which have set up a joint entity under national or EU law, including European Groupings of territorial cooperation.[221] This includes a requirement to agree on the applicable national procurement rules of one of the Member States.[222]

It is difficult to discern to what extent additional provision in Directive 2014/24/EU aimed at facilitating cross-border cooperation between contracting authorities is likely to increase innovation. The provisions on joint procurement are intended to reverse an historical trend in which one authority is designated as lead with sole responsibility for a joint procurement. In doing so, all authorities will be incentivized to ensure compliance. In innovation terms, the aggregation of demand may provide for a clearer distribution of risk under innovative projects and which may, in turn, render such projects more attractive in terms of risk capital. It is clear that this approach reflects a discernable emphasis in the Directive on the realisation of innovation through partnerships in one form or another. Whilst aggregation, cost saving and efficiency (rather than innovation) could skeptically be posited as the main reason for the Directive's approach, the financial cost of achieving innovation may be substantial, particularly in high-tech projects requiring considerable public and private investment. Cooperating Member States will expect to receive corresponding returns on investment so as to justify their involvement. Such projects are only likely to be undertaken by large contracting authorities with the necessary capabilities, expertise and need. What is clear is that the public sector Directives cannot themselves address the complexity of the institutional, legal, financial and management issues that arise in such projects.

219. Regulation (EC) No 593/2008 of the European Parliament and the Council of 17 June 2008 on the law applicable to contractual obligations (Rome I) (OJ L 177, 4.7.2008, 6). See Recital 73.
220. This includes the management of the procedure, the distribution of the works, supplies or services to be procured, and the conclusion of the contracts. See Article 39(4)(b).
221. Under Regulation No 1082/2006. For more information on the European grouping of territorial cooperation (EGTC), see <http://europa.eu/legislation_summaries/agriculture/general_framework/g24235_en.htm> accessed 25 April 2014.
222. These rules may be either: (a) the national provisions of the Member State where the joint entity has its registered office or (b) the national provisions of the Member State where the joint entity is carrying out its activities. Article 39(5).

It remains to be seen to what extent such forms of procurement are used by contracting authorities in pursuit of innovation objectives.

10. Conclusions

Directive 2014/24/EU takes the important first step of bringing visibility to innovation, instrumentalising use of the Directive to achieve this objective. The Directive expressly permits close-to-source interaction through preliminary market consultations. Life-cycle costing and performance/function based specifications continue to provide the framework for a more holistic assessment and determination of need. Innovation can also feature as part of the selection and award criteria. A measure of further procedural flexibility is also introduced through the freer use of procedures, new procurement arrangements for complex innovation projects e.g. through innovation partnerships and joint procurement. Few would question attempts to use the public procurement machinery to achieve innovation, even if certain skepticism exists about the extent to which public procurement regulation will facilitate such objectives.

However, leading up to the Drafts and final adoption of Directive 2014/24/EU, it is perhaps striking that there was no real discussion in EU policy documents and stakeholder consultations of precisely what role EU public procurement Directives should play in facilitating innovation, aside from token requests to use performance/function based specifications and include innovation within award considerations. This Chapter has argued that there needs to be a more fundamental political and legal debate concerning the following (which is not exhaustive): the correspondence between R&D and innovation; how this translates into questions about which fields of activity the Directive should regulate as an instrument of "procurement"; fields of excluded activity[223] and how such fields should be regulated or governed; the differentiation between preliminary R&D phases and subsequent purchases; and the extent to which the EU public procurement Directives should adopt uniform or distinct approaches in this field.[224] At present, this sense of uncer-

223. This should not simply concern fields such as pre-commercial procurement. There is increasing momentum in support of the adoption of an EU Small Business Innovation Research Program modeled on certain national SBIR programmes.
224. This is quite apart from the contribution of public procurement to Title XIX, Article 179-190 TFEU concerning research and technological development and space. Article 179(2) TFEU provides that the Union shall enable: "[...] undertakings to exploit

tainty is arguably reflected in the strained attempts to present a coherent approach by emphasizing the complementarity of the Communication on PCP and Directive 2014/24/EU. Further, a discrete innovation partnership procedure has been added but there has been little attempt to explain (or legitimate) its existence independently of competitive dialogue and competitive negotiation. Ultimately, time will tell whether contracting authorities will use Directive 2014/24/EU as a tool to construct the Innovation Union. Any such attempt would have to be supported by policy initiatives that are able translate innovation ideology into procurement practice at the EU and national levels.

Bibliography

R Apostol, 'Formal European standards in public procurement: a strategic tool to support innovation' (2010) 2 PPLR, 57

A R Apostol, 'Pre-commercial procurement in support of innovation: regulatory effectiveness?' (2012) 6 PPLR 213

S Arrowsmith and P Kunzlik (ed), Social and Environmental Policies in EC Procurement Law: New Directives and New Directions (CUP 2009)

P Bordalo Faustino, 'Award criteria in the new EU Directive on public procurement' (2014) 3 PPLR 124

R Caranta & M Trybus (ed), The Law of Green and Social Procurement in Europe (Djøf 2010)

J Cibinic Jr, R C Nash Jr and C R Yukins, Formation of Government Contracts (4th edn, CCH 2011)

J Davey, 'Procedures involving negotiation in the new Public Procurement Directive: key reforms to the grounds for use and the procedural rules' (2014) 3 PPLR, 103

C Edquist, L Hommen, L Tsipouri (eds), Public Technology Procurement and Innovation (2000 Boston/Dordrecht/London, Kluwer Academic Publishers)

J Knibbe, 'Case Comment, Whether the award procedures laid down by Directive 2004/18 are exhaustive: Commission v France (C-299/08) (2010) 3 PPLR, 91

L Hommen and M Rolfstam, 'Public Procurement and Innovation: towards a taxonomy' (2009) 9(1) Journal of Public Procurement, 17

the internal market potential to the full, in particular through the opening-up of national public contracts, the definition of common standards and the removal of legal and fiscal obstacles to that cooperation."

S L Schooner, 'Desiderata: objectives for a system of government contract law' (2002) 2 PPLR 10

P Trepte, Public Procurement in the EU, A Practitioner's Guide (2nd ed OUP 2007)

S Treumer, 'Technical Dialogue and the principle of equal treatment – dealing with conflicts of interest after Fabricom' (2007) 2 PPLR 99

E Uyarra and K Flanagan, 'Understanding the innovation impacts of public procurement' (2010) 18(1) European Planning Studies, 123

List of cases

CASES
Number order
Court of Justice

C-31/87 Gebroeders Beentjes BV v. Kingdom of the Netherlands, [1988] ECR 4635 p. 304, 335
C-3/88 Commission v. Italy [1989] ECR 4035 p.76
C-215/88 Casa Fleischhandels-Gmbh v. Bundesanstalt [1989] E.C.R. I-2789 p. 22
C-331/92 Gestión Hotelera Internacional [1994] ECR I-1329 p.75, 76
C-70/95 Sodemare [1997] ECR I-3395 p. 93, 94
C-16/98 Commission v. France [2000] ECR I-8315 p. 79
C-107/98 Teckal [1999] ECR I-121 p. 18, 52, 54, 55, 57, 59
C-225/98 Commission v. France (Nord Pas de Calais) [2000] ECR I-7445 p. 35, 304, 335
C-324/98 Telaustria Verlags GmbH v. Telekom Austria AG [2000] ECR-I 10745 p. 226,
C-399/98 Ordine degli Architetti and Others [2001] ECR I5409 p. 71, 72
C-475/99 Ambulanz Glöckner [2001] ECR I8089 p. 85
C-513/99 Concordia Bus Finlans v. Helsingin Kaupunki (Concordia Bus Finland) [2000] ECR I-7213 p. 303, 305, 335
C-59/00 Vestergaard [2001] ECR I-9505 p. 36
C-411/00 Felix Swoboda [2002] ECR I10567 p. 76
C-448/01 EVN AG v. Austria (EVN-WIenstrom) [2003] ECR I-14527 p. 35, 306, 335
C-113/02 Commission v. Kingdom of the Netherlands, [2004] ECR I-9707 p. 235
C-21/03 and C-34/03 Fabricom SA v. Belgian State [2005] ECR I-1559 p. 363, 364
C-205/03P Federación Española de Empresas de Tecnología Sanitaria (FENIN) v. EC Commission [2006] ECR I-6295 p. 235, 385

General Court (formerly Court of first instance)

About the authors

Martin Burgi is Professor of Public and European Law at the Ludwig Maximilian University in Munich, the Director of the only research institute for Public Procurement Law and Administrative Cooperation in Germany and a Visiting Professor at the George Washington University Law School. He is the founder and scientific chairman of the "Düsseldorfer Vergaberechtstag". In 2013, he was elected as the chairman of the Association of German Constitutional Law Professors. He is the author and editor of various books and articles and works as a consultant for public bodies as well as for private entities.

Luke R. A. Butler is a Lecturer in Commercial Law and Trusts Law at the University of Bristol Law School (UK). Luke holds an LLB(Hons) (Class 1), an LLM in European Law (Distinction) and a Ph.D in public procurement law (University of Birmingham, UK), completed under the supervision of Professor Martin Trybus. Prior to his appointment, in 2009, Luke was called to the Bar of England and Wales. Luke's research interests primarily lie within the fields of EU and international trade law, comparative public and defence procurement law and aspects of English private law, in particular, commercial applications.

Roberto Caranta is full professor of Administrative law with the Law Department of the University of Turin (Italy). He is Director of two master programs on Public Procurement Management for Sustainable Development organized by his University and the ITCILO and frequently involved in formation and consultation projects. He was the General rapporteur to the 2014 FIDE Congress in Copenhagen. Together with Steen Treumer he is editing the *European Procurement Law Series* to which this book belong. He has written extensively on public contracts. Among his most recent contributions on the subject in this series 'The Borders of EU Public Procurement law in D. Dragos – R. Caranta (eds) *Outside the EU Procurement Directives – Inside* *the Treaty?* (DJØF, 2012); 'Award criteria under EU law (old and new)' in M. Comba – S. Treumer (eds) *Award of Contracts in EU Procurements* (DJØF, 2013). With M. Trybus and G. Edelstam he edited *EU Public Contract Law. Public Procurement and Beyond* (Bruxelles, Bruylant, 2014), also contributing a chapter on 'Sustainable Procurement'. Also he penned the 'General Report' in U. Neergaard, C. Jackson, G.S. Ølykke (eds) *Public Procurement Law: Limitations, Opportunities and Paradoxes. The XXVI FIDE Congress in Copenhagen, 2014 Congress Publications Vol. 3* (DJØF, 2014). He is a member of the Procurement Review Board of the European Space Agency (ESA).

Mario Comba is full professor of public comparative law with the Law Department of the University of Turin (Italy). He is President of the University Institute of European Studies and Director of the Master GOMAP (gouvernance et management des marches publics en appui au développement durable) jointly managed by the University of Turin, the Paris Science Politiques School and ITC-ILO Turin. He is member of both the research networks Public Contracts in Legal Globalization / Contrats Publics dans la Globalisation Juridique and PLAN – Procurement Law Academic Network. He is responsible for Turin unit of the national research project, funded by the Ministry of education, about Jurisdiction and Pluralisms. His more recent publications in the field of public procurement include a book on the execution of public procurement: "L'esecuzione dei lavori pubblici. Profili comparatistici", Torino, Giappichelli, 2011, and numerous articles. Among the most recent: "Retendering or sale of contract in case of bankruptcy of the contractor? Different solutions in an EU and comparative perspective", in G. Piga – S. Treumer (eds), "The Applied Law and Economics of Public Procurement", Routledge, London, 2012, pp. 201-211; "Contract Legal Models with a Common Core", in EPPPL, 4/2013, pp. 1-7.

Dacian C. Dragos is Jean Monnet Professor of Administrative and European Law at the Public Administration Department, Babes Bolyai University, Cluj Napoca, Romania, and Co-director of the Center for Good Governance Studies. Chair of the "Law and Administration' Panel of the European Group of Public Administration (since 2010). Member of the editorial board of European Public Procurement and PPP Law Review, International Journal for Court Administration, Transylvanian Review of Administrative Sciences. His research publications include 2 edited books, 7 chapters in international books, 4 books in Romanian as single author and 4 in collaboration, over 30 papers in scientific journals. *Recent publications*: Dragoș, Neamțu, Suciu,

The theory and practice of award criteria in the Romanian procurement law, in Comba & Treumer, *Award of contracts in EU procurements*, DJOF, 2013; Dragos and Caranta (eds), EU Public Procurement – Outside the Directives, inside the Treaty? DJØF, 2012; Dragos and Neamtu, *LCC in the new directive proposal*, in European Public Procurement and PPP Law Review, 2013; Dragos, D, Neamtu, B. Veliscu, R., "Remedies in Public Procurement in Romania", in S Treumer, F. Lichere (eds), Enforcement of EU Public Procurement Rules, DJØF Copenhagen, 2011.

François Lichère is Professor of public law at the University of Aix-Marseille, France. After graduating in law at the University of Montpellier (Licence) and at the Institut d'études politiques d'Aix-en-Provence in political sciences, he passed a Master degree (Diplome d'Etudes approfondies) in 1993 and then his PhD (doctorat) at the University of Montpellier in 1998 and was appointed lecturer in public law (Maître de conferences) in 1999 and Professor of public law in 2000 after he succeeded at the "Agregation". Since then, he has taught public contract law and administrative law in different Master degrees in France and in Europe.

Professor Lichère has published numerous books and articles, mainly in the field of public contracts law and administrative law dealing with business ("Droit public économique"), in French and English. He is co-editor with Steen Treumer of the book Enforcement of EU public procurement rules, Djof publishing, 2011, and co-editor with Duncan Fairgrieve of the book Public Procurement Law : Damages as an effective remedy, Hart Publishing, 2011. He is editor of the Droit des marchés publics et contrats publics spéciaux, the main reference in public procurement law in France. He is co-author of the Lamy Droit du numérique, in charge of the section on public procurement contracts dealing with IT.

Professor Lichère is also a consultant to law firms, advising clients in the public sector and the private sector in the field of administrative law, both in French law and comparative law.

Bogdana Neamtu is PhD, Associate Professor with the Public Administration Department at Babes Bolyai University, Cluj Napoca, Romania, and co-director of the Center for Good Governance Studies. Her academic background includes a BA in public administration (2002) and a M.A. in European law (2003) from Babes Bolyai, as well as a M.A. in urban planning from Michigan State University, US (2006). She obtained her PhD in sociology in 2008. Since 2009, she has been involved in several researches/projects addressing public procurement. Her recent publications on public procurement include: Dragoş, Neamţu, Suciu, The theory and practice of award criteria in the Romanian procurement law, in Comba & Treumer, *Award of contracts in EU procurements*, DJØF, 2013; Dragoş, Neamtu, LCC in the new directive proposal, in European Public Procurement and PPP Law Review, 2013; Dragoş, Neamţu, Velişcu, Public Procurement outside EU Directives in Romania: Is Voluntary Compliance Leading to Effectiveness?, in Dragoş & Caranta, *Outside the EU Procurement Directives – Inside the Treaty*, DJOF, 2012.

Gabriella M. Racca is Professor of Administrative Law and Deputy Director of the Department of Management of the University of Turin. She is in charge of the Italian Unit of the EU project on Healthy Ageing and Public Procurement of Innovation funded by the EU Commission (DG Enterprises) for a EU joint procurement in Healthcare (Call ENT/CIP/11/C/N02C011). She is in charge of the coordination of the Ius Publicum Network (www.ius-publicum.com) founded by the main European Review on Public Law. She is Member of the Scientific Board of the Master on Public Procurement Management for Sustainable Development jointly organized by the International Training Centre of International Labour Organization (ITC – ILO) and the University of Turin and of the Master en gouvernance et management des marches publics en appui au developpement durable jointly organized by the ITC – ILO, the University of Turin and SciencesPo. She is member of many research network in the field of public procurement including: ICON-S, ReNeual, European Law Institute, European Procurement Law group, Public Contracts in Legal Globalization comparative law network (www.contrats-publics.net). She is co-editor with C. R. Yukins (George Washington University Law School) of the forthcoming book on Integrity and Efficiency in Sustainable Public Contracts. Corruption, conflicts of interest, favoritism and inclusion of non-economic criteria in Public Contracts (Bruylant, 2014). Some of her most recent publications are available at http://ssrn.com/author=1571949.

Sara Richetto is a practicing lawyer having practiced at Turin Bar since 2011. Her professional activity focuses on litigation and advisory activity on public procurement, public-private partnership, utilities, state aid to private companies, zoning and building permission, and the environment. Her works include 'Tutela giurisdizionale e risarcimento del danno derivante dall'applicazione della direttiva 2003/87/CE' in *Responsabilità civile e previdenza* n. 11/2010; 'Risarcimento del danno ambientale' in *Commentario del Codice Civile – Dei fatti illeciti*, UTET, 2013 and, in collaboration with Mario E.

Comba, 'Horizontal Cross fertilization in EU administrative law' in *Review of European Administrative Law* n. 2/2012, and with Roberto Caranta 'Sustainable Procurements in Italy: Of Light and Some Shadows' in R. Caranta and M. Trybus (eds) *The Law of Green and Social Procurements in Europe* (DJØF, 2010).

Albert Sanchez Graells joined the Law School of the University of Leicester as a Senior Lecturer in Commercial Law in October 2013. Until September 2013 he was a Lecturer in Law at the University of Hull. Prior to this appointment and since October 2009, Albert was Lecturer in European and Commercial Law at the Law Faculty of the Comillas Pontifical University (Madrid, Spain. Albert has spent significant research time at the Library of Congress (Washington, USA), the Centre for Competition Law and Policy of the University of Oxford (UK) and the Law Department of the Copenhagen Business School (DK). His research interests are in law and economics, especially regarding competition and public procurement law. His working papers and some of his most recent publications are available at http://ssrn.com/ author=542893.

Steen Treumer is a Professor of Public Procurement Law and Privatization Law at the Faculty of Law, University of Copenhagen. He published his prize awarded Ph.D.-dissertation in 2000 on the principle of equal treatment of tenderers in the EU public procurement rules. His numerous international publications on public procurement law include many in the recognized international journal *Public Procurement Law Review* which he has coedited as from 2006. He is also editing the *European Procurement Law Series* together with Roberto Caranta. Among his most recent works on public procurement is *Award of Contracts in EU Procurements* (editor with M. Comba), *The Applied Law and Economics of Public Procurement* (editor with G. Piga), Routledge 2013; *Competitive Dialogue in the EU* (editor with S. Arrowsmith), Cambridge University Press 2012 and *Enforcement of the EU Public Procurement Rules* (editor with F. Lichère), DJØF Publishing 2011. He has organised more than 30 international conferences and seminars including two global public procurement conferences in 2010 in collaboration with Sue Arrowsmith, University of Nottingham. He is currently Deputy Chairman of the Danish Association for Public Procurement Law, member of the Danish Complaints Board for Public Procurement and has been a consultant in numerous public procurement cases.

Martin Trybus is Professor of European Law and Policy and Director of the Institute of European Law at the University of Birmingham, United Kingdom and Senior Research Fellow at RAND Europe. He is the author of European Defence Procurement Law (Kluwer, 1999) and Buying Defence and Security in Europe (CUP, 2014) and the co-editor (with S. Arrowsmith) of Public Procurement: The Continuing Revolution (Kluwer, 2002), (with Roberto Caranta) of The Law of Green and Social Procurement in Europe (DJØF, 2010), and (with R. Caranta and G. Edelstam) of EU Public Contract Law: Public Procurement and Beyond (Bruylant, 2014). Martin has published over 40 articles and book chapters on public procurement law and European defence and security law. He is a member of the Procurement Review Board of the European Space Agency (ESA) in Paris and has worked on numerous projects for the OECD, the ILO, the European Commission, and the EDA.

Index